THE ART OF THEATRE

THE ART OF THEATRE

A CONCISE INTRODUCTION

THIRD EDITION

William Missouri Downs
University of Wyoming

Lou Anne Wright
University of Wyoming

Erik Ramsey
Ohio University

WADSWORTH
CENGAGE Learning™

Australia • Brazil • Japan • Korea • Mexico • Singapore • Spain • United Kingdom • United States

The Art of Theatre: A Concise Introduction
Third Edition
William Missouri Downs, Lou Anne Wright, Erik Ramsey

Senior Publisher: Lyn Uhl

Publisher: Michael Rosenberg

Development Editor: Megan Garvey

Assistant Editor: Erin Bosco

Editorial Assistant: Rebecca Donahue

Media Editor: Jessica Badiner

Marketing Program Manager: Gurpreet Saran

Content Project Manager: Aimee Chevrette Bear

Art Director: Linda May

Manufacturing Planner: Doug Bertke

Rights Acquisition Specialist: Mandy Groszko

Production Service: MPS Limited, a Macmillan Company

Cover Designer: Rokusek Design

Cover Image: ©Broadway.com

Compositor: MPS Limited, a Macmillan Company

Library of Congress Control Number: 2011940410

Student Edition:

ISBN-13: 978-1-111-34831-1

ISBN-10: 1-111-34831-6

Wadsworth
20 Channel Center Street
Boston, MA 02210
USA

Cengage Learning is a leading provider of customized learning solutions with office locations around the globe, including Singapore, the United Kingdom, Australia, Mexico, Brazil and Japan. Locate your local office at **international.cengage.com/region**

Cengage Learning products are represented in Canada by Nelson Education, Ltd. For your course and learning solutions, visit **www.cengage.com**.

Purchase any of our products at your local college store or at our preferred online store **www.cengagebrain.com**.

Instructors: Please visit **login.cengage.com** and log in to access instructor-specific resources.

Printed in China
2 3 4 5 6 7 15 14 13 12

This book is dedicated to

David Hall,

Holly Allen,

Greer Lleuad,

Stephanie Pelkowski Carpenter,

Megan Garvey,

and

Michael and Barbara Rosenberg,

each a vital link in the long chain that brought this book to publication

Brief Table of Contents

Table of Contents

PART 3 Styles, Genres, and Isms

Preface

Tonight in the United States, over 80 million people will watch television, and another 10 million will take in a movie, but only about 200,000 will attend the theatre. Most students who take the introductory theatre course know little or nothing about theatre, but they're well versed in theatre's direct descendents: movies and television.

As professors who teach and regularly oversee the teaching of introduction to theatre, we craved a text that would meet students where they are—steeped in screens big and small, and therefore more knowledgeable than they might realize—and bridge them to the eternal basis for it all. After many years of searching and failing to find a text that truly spoke to our students, we decided to craft it ourselves. *The Art of Theatre: Then and Now* and *The Art of Theatre: A Concise Introduction* employ popular screen entertainments as a touchstone to begin exploring the unique art of theatre. *The Art of Theatre* challenges students to interpret, criticize, and appreciate the roles theatre plays in society through **positive** comparisons to television and film. From theatre's ritual origins to modern musicals, from controversies surrounding the NEA to the applicability of acting lessons to everyday life, this book provides a first step toward a deeper awareness of theatre's enduring significance as the still thriving roots and trunk from which all other branches of dramatic art spring.

Organized into three distinct sections, the text provides flexibility to organize the course in a variety of ways. Adding to the flexibility of this unique approach to the introductory course is the book's availability in two versions. *The Art of Theatre: Then and Now* contains seventeen chapters, including seven chapters covering theatre history in both Western and non-Western contexts. *The Art of Theatre: A Concise Introduction* contains twelve chapters, paring back historical coverage to one chapter on theatre's key movements (such as realism, absurdism, etc.) and another on musical theatre.

Each of *The Art of Theatre's* three sections covers a distinct aspect of the introductory theatre course:

Because most theatre departments stage their first play about four weeks into the term, **Part 1, "Theatre Literacy,"** contains four chapters of background information to prepare students to attend their first theatre production as knowledgeable theatregoers. In these chapters, we explore the differences between art and entertainment while defining the most common types of theatre: commercial, historical, political, experimental, and cultural. We explain how screen entertainment differs from theatre in purpose, mediums, and financing, and describe theatre's relationship to culture. We investigate how cultural diversity manifests itself in U.S. theatre today, and discuss how theatre can give a voice to groups who are ignored by historical and commercial theatre. In this first part of the book, we also outline audience etiquette, introduce play analysis, and discuss free speech.

By introducing students to these fundamental topics early on, we provide a bridge between what students already know about movies, television, and culture and what they need to know about theatre.

Part 2, "The Arts within the Art," gives students a firm background in the primary arts and techniques needed to create a theatre performance. We concentrate first on a day in the life of a typical theatre, and then move to playwriting, acting, directing, and design. This section concludes with an overview of creativity. Whenever possible, we provide a look at the nuts and bolts, the how-to's, of the art rather than concentrating solely on appreciation of the art. We show the readers how they can use acting techniques, character analysis, story structure, ensemble work, and creativity in their own lives. By the time they are finished with this part of the book, students should be ready to see their second production with a fuller understanding of the spectrum of skills and talents needed to stage a play.

Part 3, "Styles, Genres, and Isms," contains two chapters exploring the many types of theatre that exist today. Chapter 11 covers straight plays including comedy, tragedy, realism, expressionism, melodrama, Romanticism, and absurdism, as well as non-Western theatrical traditions of Africa, India, China, Japan, and the Islamic world. Chapter 12 deals with the evolution of the musical, a fun and popular theatrical form with which students are often the most familiar.

With strong coverage of the many diverse forms of drama and current events in theatre, a highly accessible writing style, and intriguing and meaningful features, *The Art of Theatre* makes a strong case for theatre's place in society and its relevance to students today.

Features of This Book

- **Thorough coverage of diversity in theatre.** Diversity is woven throughout the text narrative and in the examples, quotations, and photos. Additionally, Chapter 3, Theatre and Cultural Diversity, discusses diversity in modern U.S. theatre, including the theatre of identity, the theatre of protest, and cross-cultural theatre. And Chapter 11, The Many Types of Theatre, discusses African, Indian, Chinese, Japanese, and Islamic theatre traditions.
- **Entire chapter on creativity**. Chapter 10, "A Creative Life," compares technique and talent, describes the attributes of creative people, provides tips students can use to enhance their creativity, and outlines the steps of creative problem-solving.
- **Spotlight boxes**. These boxes look behind the scenes at the people, places, trends, and events that have shaped theatre. Examples of Spotlight boxes are "The Life of an Actor: Terri White" (in Chapter 7, The Art of Acting) and "Understanding Non-Western Theatre" (in Chapter 11, The Many Types of Theatre). To further highlight varied traditions and give students an understanding and appreciation of the many voices in theatre, some of these boxes focus on non-Western theatre and others on diversity in U.S. theatre. These boxes describe not only ethnic and cultural diversity in the theatre but also diversity of thought. Examples of these Spotlight boxes are "The Life and Death of Ken Saro-Wiwa" (in Chapter 1, Theatre, Art, and Entertainment), "Color-Blind Casting" (in Chapter 8, The Art of Directing), and "The Life of a Playwright: Sarah Ruhl" (in Chapter 6, The Playwright and the Script).

- **Interesting and relevant timelines**. Throughout the history chapters, timelines relate theatrical events to cultural and social events to illustrate theatre's place in world history.
- **Pronunciation guide**. The glossary includes pronunciation tips for theatre terms that may be unfamiliar to students.

New to this Edition

There are many new features in the 3rd edition including over fifty new photographs, new and revised spotlights, enhanced material, and new side bar quotes:

Part 1, "Theatre Literacy"

Chapter 1 (Theatre, Art, and Entertainment) contains several new examples that build on this chapter's discussions about the art of theatre and its place in the modern world. In addition, a new spotlight highlights how theatre and art help us find structure in life and therefore meaning. Chapter 2 has a new simplified title (Stage and Screen), and contains updated information on how digital entertainments relate to the theatre, even mega-musicals like *Spider-Man*. In addition, this chapter contains current data on the NEA and funding of the arts as compared to movies and television. Chapter 3 (Theatre and Cultural Diversity) continues to grow. In this edition there are revised examples and a new spotlight on how technology may be creating a cultural divide, and how theatre can help close that gap. Chapter 4 (Experiencing and Analyzing Plays) has been expanded with improved guidelines concerning audience etiquette, including rules on twittering, texting, and standing ovations. In addition, there are new resources that help students find many of the great regional theatres across the United States, especially those nearest them.

Part 2: "The Arts within the Art"

Chapter 5 (A Day in the Life of a Theatre) now includes detailed information about how difficult it is to make a living as a theatre artist. Chapter 6 (The Playwright and the Script) has a new spotlight on the life of playwright Sarah Ruhl, while Chapter 7 (The Art of Acting) has two new spotlights on the life and times of Terri White, the Broadway actress who was homeless for a while, and an interesting spotlight on the actor's nightmare: what happens when they forget their lines. The most extensively revised chapter in the book is Chapter 10, A Creative Life. Along with a new title, these pages have expanded sections on how creativity applies to the theatre and the student's everyday interactions with education and the world. This chapter also includes a new spotlight on how creativity relates to the imagination.

Part 3: "Styles, Genres, and Isms"

This section of the book has been lightly revised to help the student learn about all the many types of theatre and musical theatre that are available.

Resources for Students

- **Theatre CourseMate for *The Art of Theatre.*** Cengage Learning's Theatre CourseMate brings course concepts to life with interactive learning, study, and exam preparation tools that support the printed textbook including Theatre Workshop. **Theatre Workshop** is a series of activities that include clips and images from live theatre performances, accompanied by critical thinking questions. Make the most of your study time by accessing everything you need to succeed—online with Theatre CourseMate. You can access this tool and more at **http://www.cengagebrain.com**.
- **InfoTrac® College Edition™**. Four months of free anywhere, anytime access to InfoTrac College Edition, the online library, is available with this textbook's online resources. InfoTrac College Edition puts cutting-edge research and the latest headlines at your students' fingertips, giving them access to an entire online library for the cost of one book. This fully searchable database offers more than twenty years' worth of full-text articles (more than 10 million) from almost 4,000 diverse sources such as academic journals, newsletters, and up-to-the-minute periodicals, including *Time, Newsweek, American Theatre,* and *Criticism*.
- ***Theatregoer's Guide,* Third edition**. This brief introduction to attending and critiquing drama enhances the student's experience and appreciation of theatre as a living art. This essential guide can be packaged for free with this text.
- **WebTutor™ Toolbox**. WebTutor™ Toolbox offers basic online study tools including learning objectives, flashcards, and practice quizzes.

Resources for Instructors

- **Theatre CourseMate for *The Art of Theatre.*** Cengage Learning's Theatre CourseMate brings course concepts to life with interactive learning, study, and exam preparation tools that support the printed textbook. Watch student comprehension soar as your class works with the printed textbook and the textbook-specific website. Theatre CourseMate goes beyond the book to deliver what you need! Learn more at **http://www.cengage.com/coursemate**.
- **Sundance Choice Drama.** Create a customizable, printed anthology of plays for your course by choosing from a large selection of plays, including many discussed in this text, at **http://compose.cengage.com**. With your customized anthology, students only pay for the plays you assign!
- **Instructor's Website**. This protected companion website provides exclusively instructor materials, including PowerPoint® presentations for the entire text, as well as the Instructor's Manual written by all three authors.
- **Instructor's Resource Manual**. Save time, streamline your course preparation, and get the most from the text. This indispensable manual offers easy-to-use chapter-by-chapter outlines, as well as a listing of the key terms and

people mentioned in each chapter. It also provides a wealth of ideas for class discussions and papers, lecture notes that go beyond the text, exam questions, and easy-to-use quizzes for busy professors.

- **PowerLecture Featuring ExamView® Computerized and Online Testing**. Create, deliver, and customize tests and study guides (both print and online) in minutes with this easy-to-use assessment and tutorial system. PowerLecture featuring ExamView offers both a "Quick Test Wizard" and an "Online Test Wizard" that guide you step-by-step through the process of creating tests—you can even see the test you are creating on the screen exactly as it will print or display online. You can build tests of up to 250 questions using up to twelve question types. Using ExamView's complete word processing capabilities, you can enter an unlimited number of new questions or edit existing questions. This CD also contains an electronic version of the Instructor's Resource Manual, and predesigned Microsoft® PowerPoint® presentations. The PowerPoint presentations contain text and images that can be used as is or customized to suit your course needs.
- **WebTutor™ Toolbox**. Available for various platforms, including WebCT™ and Blackboard®, WebTutor™ Toolbox offers basic online study tools including learning objectives, flashcards, and practice quizzes.
- **Evans Shakespeare Editions.** Each volume of the new Evans Shakespeare Editions is edited by a Shakespearean scholar. The pedagogy is designed to help students contextualize Renaissance drama, while providing explanatory notes to the play. The plays included in this series are *The Tempest, A Midsummer Night's Dream, As You Like It, Hamlet, Macbeth, Richard III, Measure for Measure, The Winter's Tale*, and *King Lear*. These critical editions can be packaged with a Wadsworth Cengage Learning theatre title. Consult your local sales representative for packaging options.

Acknowledgments

A very special thank-you goes to Mike Earl, Lee Hodgson, Larry Hazlett, and Karl Brake for their help with the chapters on design, and to Sean Stone for his help with the chapter on musical theatre. All donated their time, their designs, and their thoughts, and we are very grateful.

We also send our gratitude to other colleagues who gave us valuable assistance, including the University of Wyoming's Oliver Walter, Tom Buchanan, Jack Chapman, Don Turner, Ron Steger, Adam Mendelson, Ted Brummond, Ellen Bredehoft, and Kathy Kirkaldie; and Ohio University's Charles Smith. Special thanks to Jakob Holder, Susan Marrash-Minnerly, David Podanis, Harry Woods, Wolf Sherill, Rich Burk, J. Kevin Doolen, David Lee-Painter, Michael Wright, Keith Hull, Lew Hunter, Dr. James Livingston, Linda deVries, Peter Grego, Robin Russin, William and Doris Streib, James and Billie Wright, Barbara Brunett Ramsey, Shozo Sato, and our amazing students, past and present, at the University of Illinois, Colorado State, University of Colorado, University of Nevada-Las Vegas, University of California-Los Angeles, University of Wyoming, and Ohio University.

Thanks also to the many reviewers of this book, especially those that helped us craft the third edition: Christopher R. Boltz, Fresno City College; Mary Guzzy, Corning Community College; Nadine Charlsen, Kean University; William Godsey, Calhoun Community College; and Joe Jacoby, North Idaho College.

We also want to thank all those reviewers who worked on earlier editions with us, including: John Bagby, State University of New York College at Oneonta; Paula Barrett, Gannon University; Robbin Black, Utah State University; Ro Willenbrink Blair, Edinboro University of Pennsylvania; Christopher Boltz, Fresno City College; John R. Burgess, University of Tennessee at Chattanooga; Suzanne Chambliss, Louisiana State University; Donald Correll, Lower Columbia College; Florence Dyer, Lambuth University; Oliver Gerland, University of Colorado; Rebecca Gorman, Metropolitan State College of Denver; Cleo House, The Pennsylvania State University; Dennis Maher, The University of Texas-Arlington; Leslie Martin, California State University-Fresno; Elena Martinez-Vidal, Midlands Technical College; Jason Pasqua, Laramie County Community College; Tony Penna, Clemson University; Sheilah Philip, Johnson County Community College; Pam Reid, Copiah-Lincoln Community College; Rick Rose, Piedmont College; Korey Rothman, University of Maryland; William G. Wallace, Hamlin University; Darby Winterhalter Lofstrand, Northern Arizona University; and Rhea Wynn, Alabama Christian Academy. We also want to thank reviewers of the first edition, whose influence can be seen on these pages as well: Stacy Alley, Arkansas State University; Blair Anderson, Wayne State University; Robin Armstrong, Collin County Community College; Dennis Beck, Bradley University; Robert H. Bradley, Southwestern Missouri State University; B. J. Bray, University of Arkansas-Little Rock; Mark Buckholz, New Mexico State University-Carlsbad; Lon Bumgarner, University of North Carolina-Charlotte; Carol Burbank, University of Maryland; Katherine Burke, Purdue University; Gregory J. Carlisle, Morehead State University; Dorothy Chansky, College of William and Mary; Leigh Clemons, Louisiana State University-Baton Rouge; Patricia S. Cohill, Burlington County College; Anita DuPratt, California State University-Bakersfield; Thomas H. Empey, Casper College; Jeff Entwistle, University of Wisconsin-Green Bay; Rebecca Fishel Bright, Southern Illinois University; Anne Fliotsos, Purdue University; Christine Frezza, Southern Utah State University; Keith Hale, State University of New York-Albany; Ann Haugo, Illinois State University; Charles Hayes, Radford University; Robert A. Hetherington, University of Memphis; Allison Hetzel, University of Louisiana-Lafayette; Helen M. Housley, University of Mary Washington; Jackson Kesler, Western Kentucky University; Yuko Kurahashi, Kent State University; Howard Lang Reynolds, Marshall University; Don LaPlant, California State University-Bakersfield; Jeanne Leep, Edgewood College; Nina LeNoir, Minnesota State University-Mankato; Sherry McFadden, Indiana State University; Ray Miller, Appalachian State University; Joel Murray, University of Texas-El Paso; Kevin Alexander Patrick, Columbus State University; Paula Pierson, San Diego State University; Ellis Pryce-Jones, University of Nevada-Las Vegas; David Z. Saltz, University of Georgia; Kindra Steenerson, University of North Carolina-Wilmington; Jennifer Stiles, Boston College; Shannon Sumpter, University of Nevada-Las Vegas; Stephen Taft, University of Northern Iowa; Vanita Vactor, Clemson University; Thomas

Woldt, Simpson College; Boyd H. Wolz, University of Louisiana-Monroe; and Samuel J. Zachary, Northern Kentucky University.

And thank you very much to the Cengage publishing team: Michael Rosenberg, publisher; Megan Garvey, development editor; Erin Bosco, assistant editor; Rebecca Donahue, editorial assistant; Jessica Badiner, media editor; Gurpreet Saran, marketing project manager; Aimee Bear, production project manager; Linda Helcher, art director.

About the Authors

William Missouri Downs has taught Introduction to Theatre courses for eighteen years. More than 14,000 students have taken his class and he has won eighteen university teaching and research awards, including seven Top Ten Professor honors. Bill is a full professor at the University of Wyoming, where he heads the playwriting program and teaches in the Department of Religious Studies. Also a playwright, Bill has authored twenty full-length plays, won numerous playwriting awards, and had over one hundred productions from New York to Singapore and from Austria to South Africa, including productions at the Kennedy Center and the Berkeley Rep. In addition, Samuel French and Playscripts have published several of his plays. In Hollywood he was a staff writer on the NBC sitcom *My Two Dads* (which starred Paul Reiser). He also wrote episodes of *Amen* (Sherman Helmsley), *Fresh Prince of Bel Air* (Will Smith), and sold/optioned screenplays to Imagine Pictures and Filmways. He is a member of both the Writers Guild of America and the Dramatists Guild of America. Bill holds an MFA in acting from the University of Illinois and an MFA in screenwriting from UCLA film school. He was trained in playwriting by Lanford Wilson and Milan Stitt at the Circle Rep in New York City and was a member of the Denver Center for the Performing Arts Playwrights unit. He has directed over thirty plays, including the musical *Good Morning Athens*, which was performed at the Kennedy Center during the American College Theatre Festival. He has authored several articles and three other books including: *Screenplay: Writing the Picture* and *Naked Playwriting*, both published by Silman/James.

Lou Anne Wright is an actor, dialect coach, professor, and writer; she holds an MFA in Voice, Speech, and Dialects from the National Theatre Conservatory and is a certified Fitzmaurice Voicework teacher. Lou Anne has served as voice/dialect coach for such companies as the Colorado Shakespeare Festival, Denver Center for the Performing Arts, and the Playmakers Repertory Theatre. Film roles include Judy Shepard in HBO's *The Laramie Project* and Nell in *Hearsay*. As a playwright, she authored the play *Kabuki Medea*, which won the Bay Area Critics Award for Best Production in San Francisco. It was also produced at the Kennedy Center. She is the coauthor of the book *Playwriting: From Formula to Form*, and her screenwriting credits include the film adaptation of Eudora Welty's *The Hitch-Hikers*, which featured Patty Duke and Richard Hatch (for which she was nominated for the Directors Guild of America's Lillian Gish Award). Lou Anne teaches acting, voice, speech, dialects, and theatre history at the University of Wyoming, where she has won several teaching awards.

Erik Ramsey is an Associate Professor of Playwriting at Ohio University; he is Head of BFA Playwriting and teaches in the MFA Playwriting Program. Several of his plays are available from Samuel French and Dramatic Publishing. His recent play *Lions Lost* has been developed at numerous regional theaters including Cleveland Public Theatre, American Stage, Victory Gardens, and Pittsburgh Irish and Classical Theatre. Currently, he is writing a trilogy of historical dramas about the surprising turn of events that boosted Joseph Smith from a rural crystal ball gazer to Prophet of the Mormon Church; the first in the series, titled *Smith Unearthed*, was workshopped at the International Society of Contemporary Literature and Theatre Conference in Estonia (July 2007), the Gwen Frostic National Reading Series at Western Michigan University (November 2008), Brick Monkey Theater Ensemble (December 2008), and Pittsburgh Irish and Classical Theatre (January 2011). After several years of new-play dramaturgy nationwide, working with both professional and emerging playwrights, Erik was named a Kennedy Center Faculty Fellow (2007) and has been appointed as Director of Innovation and Research Theory for WordBRIDGE Playwrights' Laboratory (2010). Most recently, he taught master classes in playwriting and new play development techniques at Lubimovka Playwrights Laboratory in Moscow, Russia.

THE ART OF
THEATRE

Actors take a curtain call after the musical Fiddler on the Roof *at the Fulton Opera House in Lancaster, Pennsylvania.*

Photos on this spread Michael Falco/The New York Times/Redux

CHAPTER 1

Theatre, Art, and Entertainment

OUTLINE

On a recent January morning in Washington, D.C., at the L'Enfant Plaza Metro Station, a street musician began to play beside a trash can. A thousand commuters rushed by over the next hour. Many failed to hear the recital—barely six people stopped to listen, and only one person realized that the musician was no ordinary violinist, but the internationally acclaimed virtuoso and heartthrob Joshua Bell. The violin he played was a one-of-a-kind Stradivarius made in 1713, worth over $3.5 million. Only three days before, Mr. Bell had played to a standing-room-only crowd at Boston's Symphony Hall. Cheap tickets for that performance cost

Internationally acclaimed violinist Joshua Bell during a concert.

one hundred dollars, meaning Bell's concert raked in approximately one thousand dollars per minute. But three days later, in the cold D.C. Metro station, Mr. Bell's open violin case pocketed $32.17 in donations. It would have been $12.17, except that the one person who did recognize him tossed in a twenty.

Two hundred years ago, a performance by a great artist like Joshua Bell would have been, for the majority of us, a once-in-a-lifetime experience. Today, if you want to hear Joshua Bell you can download his music to your MP3 player for 99 cents. Two hundred years ago, if you wanted to see a great painting like the *Mona Lisa* you would have had to travel hundreds, perhaps thousands, of miles. Today, you can carry the *Mona Lisa* in your pocket by making it the background image on your smart phone. And if you wanted to attend a play two hundred years ago, it meant making detailed plans, buying tickets, and doing a lot of waiting. Today you can push a button and see great actors in an instant. Our technological and societal advancements may make enjoying art an almost effortless activity, but has that same effortlessness also devalued art in some way? Have we cheapened the Mona Lisa by letting it appear on our various portable screens?

The *Washington Post* staged Bell's Metro station violin concert as an experiment to test people's perceptions and priorities. It led to many questions. Perhaps the most important question was, "If we do not have a moment to stop and listen to one of the best musicians in the world, playing some of the finest music ever written, on one of the most beautiful and expensive instruments ever made . . . how many other things are we missing?" The true value of art is not its price tag, but its ability to make us feel and think. Because of this, art can be a powerful force within our lives, but there is one obstacle art cannot overcome: an individual's *inability* to perceive and enjoy it. Before you read this first chapter, take a moment to watch Bell's Metro station concert on YouTube. Would you have been one of the walking masses who never heard him, or one of the rare few who knew how to appreciate fine art?

This chapter provides a discussion that will help you understand the nature and purpose of art, and describes why theatre is a unique form of art. It also defines the major categories of theatre and explores the distinction between art and entertainment and the roles that both play in our lives.

Art, or Not Art, That Is the Question

Art takes time and education. Yet in this hurried world it seems that fewer and fewer of us have a spare moment to contemplate, appreciate, or learn about it, even as technology makes great art more and more available to all. Thomas McEvilley, a professor of Art History at Rice University, wrote, "What's hard for people to accept is that issues of art are just as difficult as issues of molecular biology. . . ." The philosopher, mathematician, and social critic Bertrand Russell put it another way: "When the public cannot understand a picture or a poem, they conclude that it is a bad picture or a bad poem. When they cannot understand the theory of relativity they conclude (rightly) that their education has been insufficient." It takes years of schooling to comprehend the arts, but those who take the time soon find that art becomes an indispensable part of their lives, and that it opens up new avenues of understanding about our world and our place in it.

Think about how often the word *art* appears in everyday conversation. It is used in a wide array of contexts but generally conveys three main ideas: art as "skill," art as "beauty," and art as "meaning." When describing Hank Aaron's spectacular homerun swing, a sports reporter might call him an "artist." In this sense, the word *art* means "skill," and it derives from the Latin word *ars*, synonymous with the ancient Greek word *techne*, which means "skill" or "technique." The word *artist* also describes a person who has a great deal of skill or talent or whose work shows considerable technical proficiency or creativity. This is why we have phrases such as "the art of war" or the "mechanical arts."

> Art making is spiritual, long-lasting, and (compared to psychotherapy and drug rehab) relatively inexpensive; it contains and even expands many parameters of well-lived life that have to date mostly been attributed only to work, religion, family and community. In addition, an engagement with art permits us to indulge our drive toward success and self-realization without forcing us to buy into the nastiness of America's unhappy rat race.
>
> ***Bill Ivey,***
> Chairman of the National Endowment for the Arts, 1998–2001

We use *art* in the second sense when we make such comments as "The sunset at the beach was a work of art." When we use the word *art* to describe something of great beauty, whether it's a real and magnificent sunset or an exact watercolor replica of that same sunset, we are talking about aesthetics. **Aesthetics** is the branch of philosophy that deals with the nature and expression of beauty. Aestheticians ask questions such as: Does beauty have objective existence outside the human experience? What environmental factors or moral judgments affect our perception of beauty? What purpose does art serve other than to delight the eye, please the ear, and soothe the senses?

In the third sense, *art* can be defined as "meaning." When Martin Luther King, Jr., gave his "I have a dream" speech on the steps of the Lincoln Memorial in 1963, he did not set out to create art but rather to address America about civil rights: "I have a dream that one day this nation will rise up and live out the true meaning of its creed: 'We hold these truths to be self-evident: that all men are created equal.'"[1] This speech is now considered to be the single most important oration of the twentieth century because of its poetic and artful ideas. King's speech, his vision for America, is often referred to as a work of art because of its meaning and its message.

> Art is a selective re-creation of reality according to an artist's metaphysical value judgments. Man's profound need for art lies in the fact that his cognitive faculty is conceptual, i.e., that he acquires knowledge by means of abstractions, and needs the power to bring his widest metaphysical abstractions into his immediate perceptual awareness.
>
> ***Ayn Rand,***
> Author and philosopher

Similarly, artists such as playwrights frequently use the word *art* in terms of meaning. Artists commonly view their art as their own interpretation or judgment of existence, rather than simply as an act of skill or a work of beauty. When the word *art* is used in this way, the implicit meaning is "this is life as I, the artist, see it. This is my personal take on things." Certainly, when artists set out to create meanings, they may choose to do so in a socially acceptable manner. They may even choose to support their meanings with great skill and beauty. However, an artist may also choose to ignore, challenge, or utterly defy traditional social values and disregard common standards of technique and beauty. The idea that art can reflect no skill, contain little beauty, and be unpleasant is hard for some to comprehend.

Theatre, or any kind of art that confronts or violates the popular understanding of skill, aesthetics, and meaning, can be dangerous to create. What if the audience disagrees with the artist's interpretation, finds it offensive, or simply refuses to pay attention? For example, when playwright and filmmaker Neil LaBute was a student at Brigham Young University, he directed David Mamet's controversial play *Sexual Perversity in Chicago*. The strong reaction made him think that the purpose of drama is to confront the audience. He now often writes plays and movies about homophobes and misogynists. His play *Filthy Talk for Troubled Times* was so controversial that some audience members shouted, "Kill the playwright!" Later LaBute said that performance was one of the best theatre experiences he has ever had.

Clearly, there is much disagreement about what art is. This is nothing new. For millennia people have been debating whether art is simply a means to create

[1]From Dr. Martin Luther King, Jr., "I Have a Dream" Speech delivered August 28, 1963, at the Lincoln Memorial, Washington, D.C. Reprinted by arrangement with The Heirs to the Estate of Martin Luther King Jr., c/o Writers House as agent for the proprietor New York, NY. Copyright 1963 Dr. Martin Luther King Jr; copyright renewed 1991 Coretta Scott King

> When people are confronted with a real work of art, they discover that they don't believe what they thought they believed all along. In a way, the great art, the great subversive art, is art that makes you realize that you don't think what you thought you did.
>
> ***David Hare,***
> Playwright

objects of beauty and pleasure, a tool to educate, inform, influence, and incite—or all of these things. For example, in ancient Greece, comic playwright Aristophanes (ca. 450–ca. 388 BCE) said of the theatre arts, "The dramatist should not only offer pleasure but should also be a teacher of morality and a political adviser." Yet his near contemporary, Greek astronomer and mathematician

Warner Bros./The Kobal Collection/Picture Desk

Because the notion of art is so closely tied to the notion of beauty, art that is unconventional, unfamiliar, or unpleasant can provoke a hostile response. This has been true throughout history. For example, the paintings of French impressionist Claude Monet, which are now adored by the general public, were considered shocking and controversial when they were first exhibited in 1874. More recently, work that is considered art by some—such as Oliver Stone's movie Natural Born Killers *(shown here), Chris Ofili's painting* Holy Virgin Mary, *and Karen Finley's performance piece* We Keep Our Victims Ready*—has been condemned by others.*

Eratosthenes (276–194 BCE), said the function of the theatre arts was to "charm the spirits of the listeners, but never to instruct them." Similarly, Greek philosophers Plato (427–347 BCE) and his student Aristotle (384–322 BCE) disagreed about the nature of theatre. Aristotle believed theatre is a creation meant to interpret the world and awake the soul, but Plato maintained that art should be a tool of the state and promote the well-being of the body politic. (For more about Plato and Aristotle, see the Spotlight "Plato, Aristotle, and the Theatre Arts.")

The debate over what art is has been going on for centuries and will continue for centuries to come. Therefore, is it possible to define art? One way is to attempt to find the basic qualities of art.

> The purpose of art, like that of metaphysics, is to capture the essential form of things. It is an imitation or representation of life, but no mechanical copy; that which it imitates is the soul of the matter, not the body or matter itself; and through this intuition and mirroring of essence even the representation of an ugly object may be beautiful. Beauty is unity, the cooperation and symmetry of the parts in a whole.
>
> ***Will Durant,***
> Historian

The Qualities of Art

A few years ago, a janitor in a modern art gallery accidentally left his grimy mop and bucket on the gallery floor overnight. The next morning the gallery manager was shocked to find patrons gathered around the mess, admiring it as a work of art. This story illustrates how difficult it is to provide an exact definition of a word like *art*. In fact, defining any abstract word can be a challenge, as you've probably noticed when you've looked up certain words in the dictionary and found that they mean a number of different things. In his book *Philosophical Investigations*, British philosopher Ludwig Wittgenstein (1889–1951) points out that trying to find all-encompassing definitions is not only difficult, but also introduces boundaries that limit our imagination. Instead, he suggests we define words by pointing out their "family resemblances," or the ways in which the many different meanings of a word resemble one another. So rather than nailing down the exact definition of the word *art*, let's list the five basic qualities that all works of art share to a certain extent: human creation, subject and medium, structure, and reaction.

> I am suspicious of any theory of art which says that art is just one thing and that it can be defined in a single aim, function, or purpose.
>
> ***Harold Taylor,***
> Art philosopher

Art Is a Form of Human Expression Human beings and only human beings can make art. The *American Heritage Dictionary* says art is "a *human effort* to imitate, supplement, alter, or counteract the work of nature." *Webster's Deluxe Unabridged Dictionary* says that art is "the disposition or modification of things by *human skill* . . ." (emphasis added). From these definitions it is easy to see how the word *art* springs from the same root as the word *artificial*. It is not the real thing but rather a human creative endeavor that involves the perceptions and imagination of an artist who is trying to say something in his or her own particular way. And so every work of art has an individual style that reflects a person's talent, technique, historical period, and unique way of looking at the world. Therefore, the snow-capped Rocky Mountains, no matter how beautiful, meaningful, or inspiring, are not art because humans did not create them, and those same mountains cannot become art until a person interprets them through a medium such as oil paint on canvas.

> Art is the means we have of undoing the damage of haste. It's what everything else isn't.
>
> ***Theodore Roethke,***
> Poet

Art Consists of a Subject and a Medium Every work of art has a subject and a medium. The **subject** of the work is what that work is about, what it reflects or attempts to comprehend. The **medium** is the method, substance,

SPOTLIGHT ON Plato, Aristotle, and the Theatre Arts

The debate over the purpose of theatre has been going on for centuries. Over two thousand years ago great philosophers like Plato and Aristotle pondered the subject—their arguments sound a lot like those we hear today in the modern media.

Plato (427–347 BCE) was a teacher, a philosopher, and an amateur playwright. However, early in his career he was persuaded by the philosopher Socrates (ca. 469–399 BCE) that playwriting was a waste of time, so he burned all of his plays. Later he wrote a series of dialogues between Socrates and others. These dialogues, conversation-like plays meant to be read rather than performed, deal with art, metaphysics, immortality, religion, morals, and drama. Plato also founded "The Academy," which is often called the first university. His most famous student was Aristotle.

The philosopher Aristotle (384–322 BCE) wrote on such diverse topics as logic, natural philosophy (what we would call physics today), astronomy, zoology, geography, chemistry, politics, history, psychology, and playwriting. His treatise *Poetics* is the first known text on how to write a play. Aristotle founded a rival school to Plato's Academy called the "Lyceum." His most famous student was Alexander the Great (356–323 BCE).

Plato accused those involved with the theatre of promoting "vice and wickedness." In his book *The Republic* he says that people forget themselves and are highly manipulated—even irrational—when under the influence of the arts. He felt that the danger of the theatre is its power to instill values hostile to the community, so he banished the poets (by which he meant "playwrights," but the word did not yet exist) from the ideal state in order to protect citizens from being mindlessly spellbound. He worried that when people join together in an audience, particularly young people, their thoughts can be swept away by the power of the crowd and as a result they lose the ability to reason for themselves. He said, "The poet is a sophist, a maker of counterfeits that look like the truth."

If there had to be theatre, Plato felt that it must be subservient to the state and to society: playwrights should be of high moral character, appointed by official decree, and their writing should be closely supervised and their plays checked by a government-appointed panel of judges. He said, "The poet shall compose nothing contrary to the ideas of the lawful, or just, or beautiful, or good . . . nor shall he be permitted to show his composition to any private individual, until he shall have shown them to the appointed

William Missouri Downs

According to most dictionary definitions, only humans can make art. This untitled painting was created by "Add," a nine-year-old elephant in Thailand. Would you call it art?

censors and the guardians of the law, and they are satisfied with them." Plato justified this call for censorship by asserting that man is an imitative animal and tends to become what he imitates. He cautioned, therefore, that if we allow theatre we should ensure that it only contains characters that are suitable as role models.

Over the centuries, other philosophers have occasionally agreed with Plato. Blaise Pascal (1623–1662) disliked the theatre because he felt that the consciences of audience members stop functioning during performances. Jean-Jacques Rousseau (1712–1778) said that the arts "spread flowers over the chains that bind people, smothering their desire for liberty."

Aristotle disagreed with his mentor, Plato. He felt that art and theatre do not stir undesirable passions, but rather they awaken the soul. He argued that seeing a play in which a son marries his mother, as in the ancient Greek tragedy *Oedipus Rex,* doesn't cause the young men in the audience to run out and propose marriage to their mothers. (As modern independent film director John Waters once said, "No story is that good.") Instead, he believed that good theatre fortifies us because it allows us to release repressed emotions in a controlled, therapeutic way.

Nature, according to Aristotle, tends toward perfection but doesn't always attain it. We tend to be healthy but we become sick. We tend to be nonviolent but there is war. We tend toward love but there is hate. Therefore, we need art and theatre to correct the deficiencies of nature by clarifying, interpreting, and idealizing life.

Ted Spiegel/Corbis

Plato and Aristotle (l to r), detail from Raphael's The School of Athens *(1510–1511)*

style, and technique used to create the work. In other words, the medium is the vehicle for communication. For example, the subject of a painting may be a flower, but the medium is paint on canvas. The subject of a dance might be the beginning of spring, and its medium is choreographed physical movement. The subject of a song might be an "Achy Breaky Heart," but the medium is a combination of words, tone, pitch, and volume. Every genre of art has a different medium that defines it and makes it unique. The **spatial arts,** such as sculpture and architecture, are created by manipulating material in space. The **pictorial arts,** such as drawing and painting, are created by applying line and color to two-dimensional surfaces. The **literary arts** are created with written language. Theatre is classified as a performing art, as are music, opera, and dance. The medium of the **performing arts** is an act performed by a person. In this way the performing arts are unique because they exist only in the time it takes an actor, singer, musician, or dancer to complete a performance.

In one sense the aim of the scientist and the aim of the artist are the same since both are in pursuit of what they call truth; but the difference between them may be said to consist in this, that while for science there is only one truth, for the artist there are many.

Joseph Wood Krutch,
Author and philosopher

Therefore they also have a beginning, middle, and end. Once a performance ends, the work of art no longer exists, leaving behind no tangible object such as a painting or a statue.

Theatre is unique because it is the only art for which the medium and subject are exactly the same: the subjects of a play are human beings and human acts, and the mediums of a play are also human beings and human acts. The actors' bodies are like canvas and paint to the painter—they are the mediums of the art. But you might ask yourself: what about the musical *Cats?* That's not about humans and human acts; it's about felines, right? Actually, the emotions, thoughts, and actions staged for the musical are purely human—invented by humans to represent an idea of what cats might think and feel. Ultimately, people can only experience the world through their own senses and thoughts, and therefore any "animal," "monster," or even a child dressed up like a "tornado" in a school play is really a human idea of how an animal, monster, or tornado might think, feel, and behave.

Michal Daniel/Proofsheet

One of the reasons why the plays of William Shakespeare continue to be staged and filmed today is that they tell timeless stories and evoke universal feelings. Although these plays were written hundreds of years ago, their plots and characters still amuse us, sadden us, call us to arms, inspire us, and make us think. Their ability to affect us in meaningful ways is what makes them art. This production of Othello *featured Keith David as Othello and Kate Forbes as Desdemona; it was directed by Doug Hughes at The Public Theater, New York, 2001.*

Art Makes You Feel Something The power of art comes from its capacity to evoke a response. Art does not come to life until a spectator, a listener, or an audience breathes life into it by experiencing it. Art provokes in us a reaction that causes us to consider, judge, emote, or perceive meaning in some way. This reaction may be spiritual, intellectual, or emotional. Yet each person views a work of art through the lenses of his or her own experiences, education, preconceptions, assumptions, and interests. And because each of us is unique, what constitutes *art* for one person may not be *art* for another. This is at the root of the difficulty in finding a definition of art on which most can agree. But it also means that arts education is critical. According to the educator and art philosopher Harold Taylor (1914–1993), the spectator must know how to "respond to other people and other ideas, different from his own," rather than react against them. Spectators must "learn to accept difference as natural rather than as a threat to their whole style of life." In essence, Taylor is saying that art depends on the open minds of those who experience it. We need not approve of any given piece of art, yet we must attempt to understand the perspective of the artist who created it before we can dismiss it or judge it.

> Life is very nice, but it lacks form. It's the aim of art to give it some.
>
> ***Jean Anouilh,*** Playwright

Art Provides a Perception of Order It is often said that artists "select and arrange" their perceptions of the world and in doing so find or create a structure—a meaningful order or form. "It is the function of all art to give us some perception of an order in life, by imposing order upon it," said poet T. S. Eliot.

American philosopher and novelist Ayn Rand (1905–1982) interpreted the notion of structure in art quite elegantly with the following example. Imagine that a beautiful woman in a lovely evening gown enters a ballroom. She is perfect in every way except for the fact that she has a rather large, ugly cold sore on her lip. What do we make of it? What does it mean? Not much—many people are afflicted with cold sores, and they are perhaps unfortunate but have little meaning. However, if a painter paints a picture of a beautiful woman in a lovely evening gown and portrays her with the same ugly cold sore, the blemish suddenly takes on great importance.

> The world of the theatre is a world of sharper, clearer, swifter impressions than the world we live in.
>
> ***Robert Edmond Jones,*** Set designer

This minor imperfection, says Rand,

> acquires a monstrous significance by virtue of being included in the painting. It declares that a woman's beauty and her efforts to achieve glamour are futile and that all our values and efforts are impotent against the power, not even of some great cataclysm, but of a miserable little physical infection.

By including the cold sore—by emphasizing certain parts of life and de-emphasizing others—the artist finds order and imposes meaning. This editorial process troubles some who believe the artist's duty is, as Shakespeare's Hamlet says, to hold a "mirror up to nature." Some people believe art should merely imitate life, nothing more. Yet, if art simply imitates, then it would serve only to reflect what we already see and experience, not help us understand it. Additionally, the process of "holding up a mirror" is inherently editorial anyway—even if one does set out to simply hold up a mirror to nature, what one chooses to reflect in the mirror is, in itself, an editorial process or value judgment that focuses our eyes on one particular setting or idea instead of another.

Art is never a slavish copy. It always is a selective re-creation that is given form by the artist's individual view of existence. Perhaps the Polish sociologist Zygmunt Bauman said it best: "To be an artist means to give form and shape to what otherwise would be shapeless and formless. To manipulate probabilities. To impose an 'order' on what otherwise would be 'chaos'; to 'organize' an otherwise chaotic—random, haphazard and so unpredictable—collection of things and events by making certain events more likely to happen than all others." When artists find order they also cultivate insight and understanding about our world and ourselves. (For more on this subject, see the Spotlight "To Be an Artist Means Finding Form and Structure.") This means that inherent in any work of art are the artist's opinions, interpretations, philosophy, and beliefs. In short, art is inherently political and often has political consequences.

> In theatre, the immeasurable wealth and unfathomable complexity of Being are compressed into a concise code, which, while a simplification, attempts to extract what is most essential from the substance of the universe and to convey this to its audience. This, in fact, is what thinking creatures do every day when they speak, study, write, or meditate. Theatre is simply one of the many ways of expressing the basic human ability to generalize and comprehend the invisible order of things.
>
> ***Václav Havel,***
> Playwright and former president of the Czech Republic

The Politics of Art (The Good, the Bad, and the Ugly)

Every time artists make a choice about what aspect of existence to select and arrange, they express a value judgment and reveal their beliefs. In this way art is like politics in the broad sense: it reflects people's conflicting ideas about how we should live, how society should be organized, and how the world is. Artists select those aspects of existence they believe are significant, isolate them, and stress them to create meaning. The result is that artists' fundamental views of life are embodied within their art. Therefore, at the core of every artist is a political individual who states an opinion that may challenge an audience's values and shatter their preconceptions.

This is probably why many artists eventually become political leaders, join political causes, or simply stand up and publicly state their opinions. In countries where religion and government have recently lifted censorship on theatre, it has become common for actors, playwrights, and other artists to be politically active. In the United States most artists have particular political causes that they support—we see them standing on the platforms during national political conventions, testifying before Senate committees, doing public service announcements, and lending their names to political causes, organizations, and campaigns. Bands from Rage Against the Machine to the Dixie Chicks are well known for their political opinions. South African playwright Athol Fugard has spent his life writing plays that attack apartheid, or state-sponsored racial segregation.

SPOTLIGHT ON To Be an Artist Means Finding Form and Structure

French novelist Gustave Flaubert said that emotions are important in art, but that feelings are not everything: "Art is nothing without form."

Our need for form and structure is really the need to simplify. At nearly fifteen hundred pages, *War and Peace* is a condensed version of the French invasion of Russia, the play *Long Day's Journey into Night* is an edited version of Eugene O'Neill's family traumas, and $E = mc^2$ is an abbreviated version of Einstein's insights. Why do we need a simplified structure? The great Russian writer Dostoyevsky said humans "crave miracles, mystery, and authority." In other words, we crave a well-structured map through the confounding experiences of life.

Our need for structure shows itself in common phrases like "Everything happens for a reason," "What goes around comes around," or "God helps those who help themselves." Each statement takes the raw data of nature, edits it, and adds structure. The result is theme. Theme comes when one begins to see patterns in nature and life—whether those patterns are imagined or real. Anthropologist Pascal Boyer called this the "hypertrophy of social cognition," which is our tendency to see purpose, intention, and design where only randomness exists.

For example, the first day you walk to your new job, it is novel. Perhaps you pass a house with a red door, a tree shaped like a Y, and a park bench near a bus stop. At first the door, the tree, and the bench have no meaning. But as you walk to work the next day and the next, the walk develops a structure. The red door means you are at the beginning of your walk; the tree denotes the midway point, while the bench signifies the end. If you begin to dislike your employment, the door, tree, and bench can take on new significance. The red door symbolizes how you hate to leave your house, the tree the missed opportunity to take the "Y" in the road, and the park bench your desire to retire. Your walk now has structure, and, as a result, theme and meaning. Years later, long after you have left the job, when you see a similar door, tree, or bench you will read meaning into it even though no inherent meaning, theme, or structure exists.

Humans need structure and theme because the world in which we find ourselves appears to be disorganized or at least lacking in purposeful design. Nature, says Adam Phillips in his book *Darwin's Worms,* does not "have what we could call a mind of its own, something akin to human intelligence. Nor does nature have a project for us; it cannot tell us what to do; only we can. It doesn't bear us in mind because it doesn't have a mind. . . ." Some argue that there is a chaos to nature, others that nature has too much structure. Either way, we must simplify in order to find meaning or to create it.

Art, along with science and religion, helps us find structure; with structure comes meaning.

William Missouri Downs

On the right is a photo of Sawtooth Mountain in Colorado, on the left Sumi-E artist Shozo Sato's painting of the same mountain. An artist takes the raw data of life and edits it into order to find or impose order and meaning.

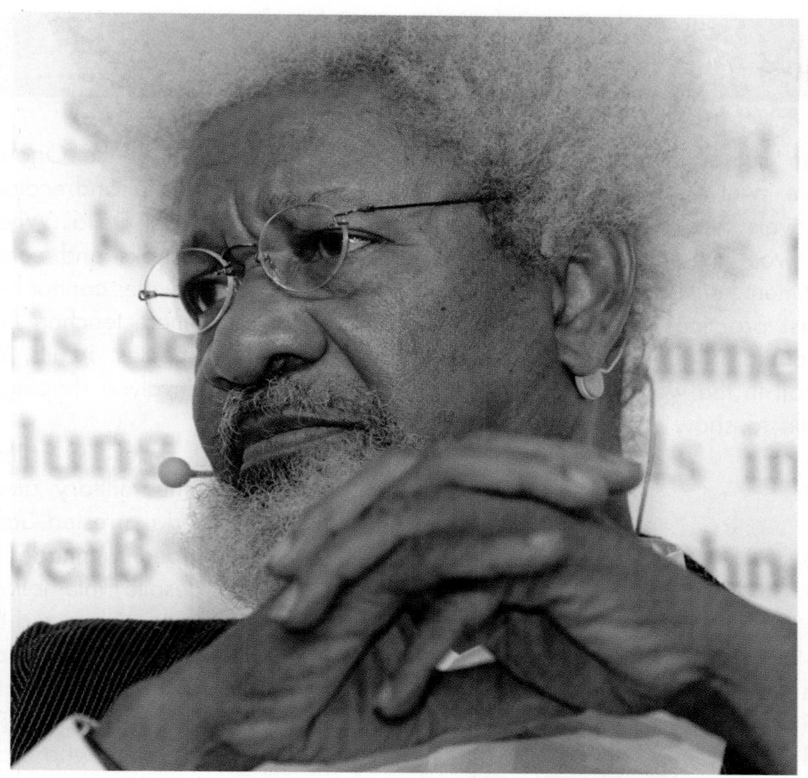

AP Photo/Keystone/Georgios Kefalas

Like many artists, playwright and Nobel Prize winner Wole Soyinka has played an active role in politics. His efforts to broker a peace agreement during the 1967 Nigerian Civil War resulted in his arrest and twenty-two months in solitary confinement. Today, Soyinka continues to be an outspoken critic of political tyranny.

Taking the connection a step further, Vigdís Finnbogadóttir, director of the Reykjavík Theatre Company, was elected president of Iceland, and movie stars N. T. Rama Rao of India and Joseph Estrada of the Philippines both became successful politicians in their respective countries. And, of course, we cannot overlook the former actor, movie star, and president of the Screen Actors Guild who became president of the United States, Ronald Reagan.

Yet the road for artists into politics has often been perilous. For example, before Czechoslovakian playwright Václav Havel became president of the new Czech Republic in 1993, he was arrested so often by the former communist regime that he carried his toothbrush with him—ready to go to jail at a moment's notice. Nigerian writer and playwright Wole Soyinka, the first African writer to win the Nobel Prize for Literature (1986), spent two years in solitary confinement—secretly writing on toilet paper and discarded cigarette wrappers—after he was arrested for his political views during Nigeria's civil war. In 2007, art students at Maharaja Sayajirao University in India were jailed for making art that "attacked Indian culture." In 2004, filmmaker Theo van Gogh was murdered in the streets of Amsterdam for making *Submission: Part 1,* an eleven-minute movie critical of the treatment of women by Islam. And in 1995, playwright and author Ken Saro-Wiwa was executed for his outspoken views about the military government of Nigeria and the environmental and economic practices of the Shell oil company. (For more information, see the Spotlight "The Life and Death of Ken Saro-Wiwa.") As Polish actor Zygmunt Hubner, former director of the Powszechny Theatre in Warsaw, said, "Beware of underestimating the theatre! The theatre is . . . a lens that focuses the rays of many suns. And a lens can start a fire." That lens is the artist's interpretation of how the world is or should be. Often it is the artists who get burned, but on occasion art can also stoke an inferno that reduces tyranny to ashes.

SPOTLIGHT ON The Life and Death of Ken Saro-Wiwa

During his lifetime, Nigerian author Ken Saro-Wiwa (1941–1995) wrote twelve children's books, eight plays, five novels, two memoirs, and many poems. But it was his outspoken criticism of the Nigerian government, environmental pollution, and the unfair business practices of Shell oil company that got him into trouble. Nigeria is the sixth-largest producer of crude oil in the world, but the people of Nigeria have little to show for their country's wealth. Most people still live in poverty; the infant mortality rate is one of the highest on the planet; and the average life expectancy is only fifty-four years.

Most of Nigeria's oil revenues lined the pockets of the military regime while Shell Oil was allowed to pump crude oil from the Niger Delta with few, if any, environmental regulations. Saro-Wiwa began campaigning to share the government's wealth with its people. He also called for clean air, land, and water. Then he organized peaceful protests, wrote pamphlets on minority and environmental rights, and launched the grass-roots, community-based political movement called the Survival of the Ogoni People (MOSOP), which called for social and ecological justice for the people of the Niger Delta. When asked why a writer of children's books and comic plays was doing this he said, "The writer cannot be a mere storyteller; he cannot be a mere teacher; he cannot merely X-ray society's weaknesses, its ills, its perils. He or she must be actively involved shaping its present and its future."

Reuters/Corbis

Ken Saro-Wiwa (1941–1995)

In order to silence his voice, the military government of Nigeria arrested Saro-Wiwa on trumped-up murder charges and, despite international protests, he was executed by hanging eight days later along with eight of his compatriots. Saro-Wiwa wrote before his execution, "The men who ordain and supervise this show of shame, this tragic charade, are frightened by the word, the power of ideas, the power of the pen; by the demands of social justice and the rights of man. Nor do they have a sense of history. They are so scared of the power of the word that they do not read. And that is their funeral."[2]

What Is Theatre? What Is Drama?

The word *theatre* comes from the ancient Greek word *theatron,* which means "seeing place." The word *drama* comes from the ancient Greek verb *dran,* which means "to take action, to do, to make, or to accomplish." These meanings still apply today—theatre is about an audience witnessing a production or a theatrical event, whereas drama is a form of theatre that tells a story in which characters set out to do, to accomplish, or to take some sort of action.

In his book *The Empty Space,* English director Peter Brook states that all that is needed for theatre to occur is an empty space and someone to walk across that space while someone else watches. In later chapters we'll discuss the various types of spaces, or stages, used throughout history and today. At this point, simply note that, at its most basic, theatre requires only a space, a performer,

[2]From Ken Saro-Wiwa, "Letter from Saro-Wiwa's jail cell."

and an audience. Story, characters, spectacle, costumes, lights, script, and sets are all unnecessary. They may improve the theatrical experience, but they are optional. As such, many events can qualify as a kind of theatre: weddings, award banquets, football games, political rallies, church services, or even a supermodel walking down a runway. Any time people get together with the common purpose of throwing the focus on a particular person, we have a theatrical event.

As mentioned previously, **drama** is a form of theatre that tells a story about people, their actions, and the conflicts that result. **Conflict** is the key to the movement of a story and is what qualifies a theatrical work as a play. Whether explicit or implicit, conflict is at the core of drama. As Professor David Ball, author of *Backwards & Forwards: A Technical Manual for Reading Plays,* puts it, "People who talk about, write about, or do theatre agree on little. But there is one thing: 'Drama is *conflict*!' we all cry in rare unanimity. Then we go back to squabbling over whether *Measure for Measure* is a comedy." Comedy is a subgenre of drama in which the conflicts work out to achieve a happy ending. The conflicts in comedy may be humorous or even ridiculous, but they are conflicts nonetheless, driving the story along. If there is no conflict, there is no power struggle, and if there is no power struggle, there is no story—whether lightly comedic or darkly dramatic. Without a story, there may be theatre but not drama.

Both theatre and drama have three qualities that make them unique art forms. First, theatre is always live. This means that theatre cannot be replayed, like a film. You can watch a movie again and again and it is always the same. This is not so in the theatre, because no two performances are ever exactly the same. No two Hamlets ever ask the question "To be, or not to be . . ." in precisely the same way. So, if you go to the theatre on Monday night and tell a friend that you loved the performance, and your friend goes to the same show on Tuesday night and says that he hated it, you both may be right because the two of you did not see the same exact performance or see it with the same audience.

> When you come into the theater, you have to be willing to say, "We're all here to undergo a communion, to find out what the hell is going on in this world." If you're not willing to say that, what you get is entertainment instead of art, and poor entertainment at that.
>
> ***Playwright David Mamet,***
> *Three Uses of the Knife*

The second quality that makes drama and theatre unique was introduced earlier in this chapter: they are always about human beings. A painting might be about a flower, a poem might be about the stars, but theatre and drama can only be about human beings and human emotions. At their most basic, theatre and drama always express something fundamental about the human condition with the intention to touch, arouse, inform, entertain, or even enrage the audience by portraying aspects of themselves.

The third quality that makes theatre and drama unique is that they are often collaborative forms of art, requiring more than one type of art and artist to produce. This is not true of most other forms of art, which are the product of a single individual. For example, art museums are often very quiet. They do not feature music, because it would interfere with the visual art. Similarly, we do not need music, dance, or a director to help us read a book. In contrast, plays often use lights, sound, movement, words, and actions. When you attend the theatre, more often than not you experience art made by an ensemble of artists. Often the final product is a result of how well all these artists coordinated their artistic visions. (In Chapters 5, 6, 7, 8, and 9 we will explore in greater detail the various artists involved in crafting theatre.)

Now that you've learned a bit about what makes theatre unique among the arts, let's explore the five most common categories of theatre: commercial, historical, political, experimental, and cultural.

William Missouri Downs

Commercial theatre offers audiences politically safe themes and entertainment designed to appeal to a majority of the general public. Examples of successful commercial plays include the blockbuster Broadway musicals Hairspray, Wicked, Jersey Boys, *and* The Wedding Singer.

The Common Categories of Theatre

There are many types of theatre, most of which are covered in greater detail in later chapters of this text. However, let's take some time here to survey the most common categories in order to understand the various roles theatre plays in society.

Perhaps the most familiar category of theatre is **commercial theatre,** which includes big musicals as well as comedies and dramas that are intended to be entertaining and profitable. Commercial plays offer safe themes, plenty of laughs, and spectacle designed to appeal to a majority of people, thereby filling lots of seats and ideally making lots of money. Big Broadway musicals like *Beauty and the Beast* or *Spider-Man: Turn Off the Dark* are perfect examples of commercial theatre, but it can also include familiar plays appealing to the widest possible demographic staged by small local theatres. The commercial theatre has been around for thousands of years. As we will see next, most other types of theatre are not designed to be purely entertaining or to turn a profit.

Historical theatre presents dramas that use the styles, themes, and staging of plays of a particular historical period. And there is plenty of history to be staged, for theatre has been around for thousands of years and has reflected hundreds of styles and themes. From the classical forms of theatre, such as Sophocles' *Oedipus Rex* and Shakespeare's *Hamlet,* to the dawn of modern drama with Henrik Ibsen's *A Doll's House,* historical theatre attempts to show how far humanity has come by presenting costumes, acting styles, language, and subject matter that express universal human concerns rather than ideas that are specific to the current generation. When you attend this type of theatre, you'll probably enjoy it more if you have some knowledge of history and do some research beforehand into the background of the particular playwright and theatrical style. When you attend historical theatre, you are not just being entertained; you are also getting a lesson in history. And one of those lessons may be that though a play is hundreds of years old, the themes are still very relevant.

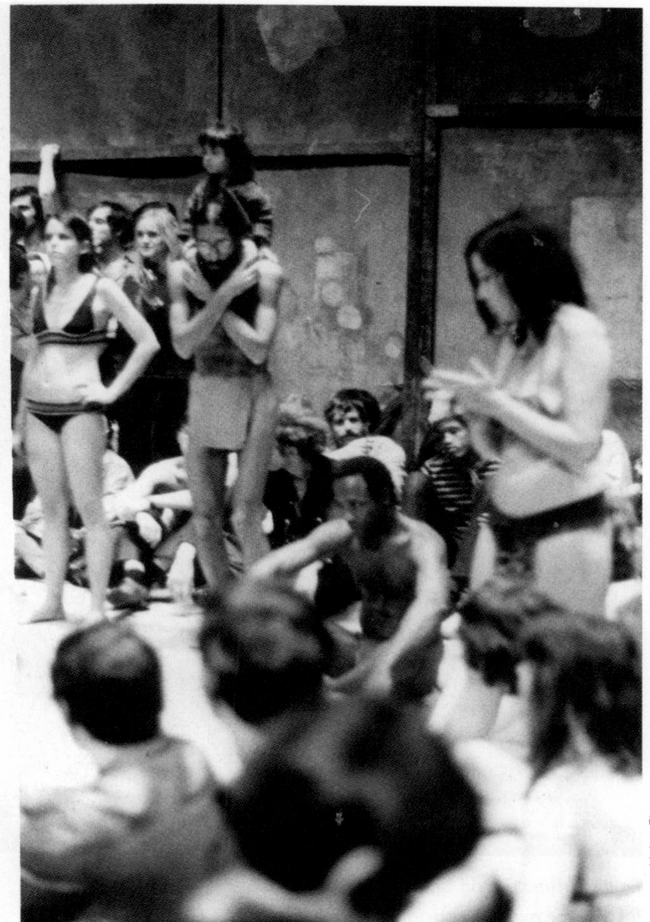

Courtesy, Living Theatre

Experimental plays test the bounds of theatre. One of the most famous experimental plays is Paradise Now (1968), which was staged by The Living Theatre during the Vietnam war. This play directly confronted the audience by staging an "aesthetic assault" on their culture and values.

Political theatre allows playwrights, directors, and actors to express their personal opinions about current issues, trends, and politics. This type of theatre is a bully pulpit, an open mic, and a bullhorn that allows the artist to express ideas that are seldom heard in the mainstream media or in commercial theatre. Political theatre allows artists to ask an audience to join them in a protest or in calling for social change. For example, the play *The Exonerated,* written by Erik Jensen and Jessica Blank, revolves around the stories of six former death row prisoners who were falsely accused, wrongly convicted, and eventually exonerated—several after being imprisoned for decades. Once the play is over, the cast and crew invite the audience to stay afterward to discuss the wisdom of imposing the death sentence and provide information about how they can personally take steps to end the practice of it. In addition to being a voice for the disenfranchised of society, political theatre can be designed by "the powers that be" in order to control the hearts and minds of the people. For example, during World War II, Nazi Germany's rulers produced propaganda plays and highly theatrical political rallies designed to win the people over to their way of thinking.

Plays can also be experimental in nature. Just as automakers display concept cars that try out new designs, theatre artists also experiment with styles and ideas in **experimental plays** that push the limits of theatre. These plays might break down barriers by eliminating the distance between actor and audience, trying out new staging techniques, or even questioning the nature of theatre

© P. Switzer

Political Theater can be a powerful tool for exposing social ills. For example, Steven Dietz's play God's Country is about the 1984 assassination of liberal radio talk show host Alan Berg after he spoke out against the white supremacist movement. This production was staged by National Theatre Conservatory at the Denver Center for the Performing Arts.

itself. For example, The Living Theatre of the 1960s dedicated itself to staging such works as *Paradise Now* (1968), in which actors asked the audience to join them in a protest calling for a social revolution. Experimental plays are an attempt to reinvent theatre, for all art forms must avoid stagnation by constantly searching for what the future of the art form might be.

Finally, there is **cultural theatre,** which is designed to support the heritage, customs, and point of view of a particular people, religion, class, country, or community. This theatre celebrates human diversity by providing the audience a window into a world that is different from their own or by preserving the unique traditions of a particular society. As later chapters of this book will discuss, when you attend Japanese Kabuki plays, African ritual plays, or Peking Opera, you reinforce your own culture or learn about other peoples' cultures by witnessing aspects of their religion, history, customs, folklore, or worldviews.

When attending the theatre, remember that any given performance doesn't necessarily fit neatly into just one of these categories. For example, a play can be both cultural and commercial, and another might be political and experimental. But knowing about these basic categories can increase your enjoyment of the theatre. For example, if you go to the theatre expecting a purely commercial production and find yourself watching an experimental play, you might not enjoy it. Or, you might be offended. But try to keep an open mind, determine what type of theatre you're witnessing, and enjoy or study it for what it is rather than what you thought it would be. And remember that theatre is not always designed simply to entertain us. Sometimes it teaches us, sometimes it insults us, and sometimes it makes us think.

Art versus Entertainment

The fundamental difference between art and entertainment is that artists create primarily to express themselves, making no compromise to appeal to public taste, whereas entertainers create to please an audience by reinforcing the audience's values and beliefs. Entertainment is meant to amuse us and make us feel good about who we are and what we believe, not necessarily to challenge us or make us think. Such entertainment, according to Dana Gioia, former head of the National Endowment for the Arts, "promises us a predictable pleasure—humor, thrills, emotional titillation, or even the odd delight of being vicariously terrified. It exploits and manipulates who we are rather than challenging us with a vision of who we might become. A child who spends a month mastering *Halo* or *NBA Live* on Xbox has not been awakened and transformed the way that child would be spending the time rehearsing a play or learning to draw."

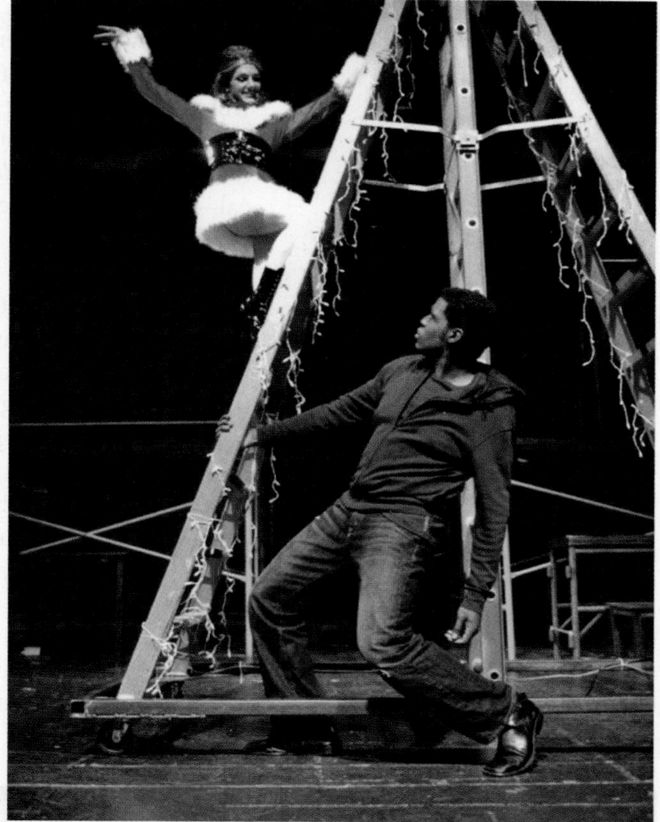

Photo courtesy of Karen Berman

Sometimes plays test the boundaries of cultural acceptance at first and later become mainstream. The musical Rent, *music and lyrics by Jonathan Larson, tells the story of penniless young artists and musicians who struggle to live and create art in New York in the shadow of HIV/AIDS. This is subject matter that, at one time, was deemed offensive to many, but the musical is now commonly staged in high schools, although in a slightly revised form. Dr. Karen Berman at the Georgia College & State University staged the production pictured here.*

Art may also confirm our values and beliefs, but artists do not necessarily *seek* to confirm them. True, artists often desperately want their audience to understand and appreciate their creation, which is why they may pay attention to criticism and audience reaction. But artists do not always take an audience's opinion into consideration when creating work, whereas entertainers always do. Many, if not most, major movie and television producers show works in progress to test with audiences before formally releasing the "product." These test audiences, usually recruited from a targeted age or social group, fill out questionnaires after the showing about what they liked and didn't like, what they thought about the story and the characters, after which the producers, writers and directors rewrite and edit to make it more audience friendly. In essence, a test audience is a tool for producers to match the values of the product to the consumer, thereby making the product more entertaining and marketable.

What are values? **Values** are the principles, standards, or qualities considered worthwhile or desirable within a given society. Entertainers want to confirm our values because they want to make us feel good about who we are and what we believe so that we buy their product. Otherwise, we may change the channel or spend our money on a different movie. When entertainment fails to reinforce the audience's values, it is often suppressed. For example, the producers of the raucous animated sitcom *Family Guy* made an episode in which the mother (Lois Griffin) has an unwanted pregnancy and contemplates abortion. The episode was full of frank discussions and outrageous comedy that Fox Network executives felt was a "fragile subject matter at a sensitive time," so they pulled it off the air. Other episodes of *Family Guy* have been rejected even before they made it into production, including one in which the father (Peter Griffin) pushes for his son to convert to Judaism so that he would be "smarter." At other times Fox has insisted that the writers edit individual jokes, including one that contained the phrase "World Trade Center." Fox censored these jokes and episodes because they consider *Family Guy* not a work of art, but pure entertainment, and good entertainment does not make the audience think too much, nor does it challenge the audience's values.

> Art is an individual experience. It forces us to examine ourselves. It broadens perspective. Entertainment masquerading as art, by contrast, herds viewers and audience into the collective. It limits perspective to that experience by the masses.
>
> ***Chris Hedges,***
> Journalist and author

In his book *Life: The Movie—How Entertainment Conquered Reality,* Neal Gabler describes entertainment as a "rearrangement of our problems into shapes which tame them, which disperse them to the margins of our attention." In other words, entertainment is the art of escape. Stephen Sondheim, one of America's leading writers of musical theatre, tells a story about a man walking out on the musical *West Side Story* when it was first produced: "He wanted a musical—meaning a place to relax before he has to go home and face his terrible dysfunctional family. Instead of which he got a lot of ballet dancers in color-coordinated sneakers snapping their fingers and pretending to be tough. His expectation had been defeated." Entertainment fulfills your expectations, it makes you believe that change is not needed, that your way of life is justified; it makes you *think* that you are thinking. Writer Don Marquis said, "If you make people think they're thinking, they'll love you; but if you really make them think, they'll hate you." In short, entertainment fulfills our expectations. Art, on the other hand, makes no compromise for public taste as it inspires us to consider life's complexities and ambiguities. Art is the opposition testing the strength of societal and cultural values—values that are thoughtlessly adopted by the mass of individuals living unexamined lives and all who cannot imagine a different way of seeing life.

All this is not to say there is anything wrong with entertainment—we all need and enjoy entertainment. From sitcoms and amusement parks to the Ice Capades, entertainment is a wonderful way to relax. It adds to the enjoyment

Art and entertainment are not mutually exclusive. Entertaining works can be considered art and art can be entertaining. The musical Miss Saigon *contains powerful political themes about American involvement in the Vietnam War and yet it can be called entertainment. The production pictured here was staged by the Arvada Center for the Arts and Humanities.*

of life and is often worth the price of admission. To most people, a life devoid of entertainment seems hardly worth living. Even in the harshest environments, people long to be entertained. For example, the USO (United Service Organizations) has been bringing entertainment to American soldiers on the front lines for more than sixty years, evidence of entertainment's ability to be therapeutic and increase morale.

Never in history have there been so many ways to entertain yourself as there are today, including movies, satellite radio, iTunes, iPods, iPads, video games, Xbox, Wii, YouTube, and billions of websites on the ever-evolving Internet. There are now over 100,000 titles that you can rent or download from Netflix, and YouTube has over ten billion hits per month. According to the Bureau of Labor Statistics, the average American family spends more money on entertainment than on gasoline, clothing, and household furnishings. In addition, Americans watch about two hundred billion hours of television every year. To get an idea of how much time that is, let's compare it to the amount of time it took to create the popular web encyclopedia Wikipedia. Clay Shirky, in his book *Cognitive Surplus,* estimates that it took about one hundred million hours for human beings to build Wikipedia into what is today the largest encyclopedia in the world. That means that if Americans turned off the TV for one year they would have enough time to create two thousand Wikipedia-sized projects.

With a flick of a remote or a mouse, we can usually find a TV program, movie, or song that makes us feel good about who we are and what we believe. But what happens when we indulge in a diet dominated by entertainment? What happens when we watch and listen only to what confirms our values? We may become apathetic and convinced of our own point of view, but more importantly, we can become intolerant of new ideas and alternative opinions of how the world is or should be. Seth MacFarlane, creator of *Family Guy,* said, "People in America, they're getting dumber, they're getting less and less able to analyze something and think critically, and pick apart the underlying elements. And more and more ready to make a snap judgment regarding something at face value, which is too bad." This same sentiment was paralleled by the great philosopher Ludwig Wittgenstein, who said that philosophical illnesses usually stem from dietary insufficiency. A diet of only one philosophy, religion, or way of looking at the world leads to philosophical illness and a limited view of the world. Art and theatre help balance our diet. They challenge us, teach us, and sometimes even insult us by calling our values into question. (For more on this subject, see the Spotlight "The Differences between Art and Entertainment.")

Curtain Call

Why does the ancient art of theatre still exist in a world dominated by movies and television? We need art and theatre because they help us *see life differently.* Entertainment allows us to see life as *we* see it, with our values and perceptions intact. Art, on the other hand, allows us to expand our experience, intensify our perceptions, challenge conventional wisdom, and introduce another frame of reference—that of the artist. Thus, art, as Harold Taylor said, allows us to "move

SPOTLIGHT ON The Differences between Art and Entertainment

A work can be *both* art and entertainment. For example, the popular 1970s sitcom *All in the Family* and the HBO drama *Deadwood* are often considered both art and entertainment. But it is important to understand that there are still differences, many of which are listed here.

Art

- Lets us see another's point of view
- Is directed toward the individual
- Makes us think
- Is about education
- Demands an intellectual effort to appreciate it
- Requires active viewing
- Is about self-examination
- Has great potential as an agent of social change
- Challenges the audience
- Is about edification, transcendence, contemplation
- Does not compromise for public taste

Entertainment

- Pulls us into ourselves, reaffirms our point of view
- Is directed toward the largest possible number
- Makes us think we're thinking
- Is about sameness
- Makes no intellectual or other demands on the viewer
- Can be done with passive viewing, is audience friendly
- May examine life but does not lead to criticism
- Is easily digested
- Has little potential as an agent of social change
- Flatters the audience
- Is about gratification, indulgence, escape

freely into areas of experience which were formerly unknown." The American set designer Robert Edmond Jones once said:

> Here is the secret of the flame that burns in the work of the great artists of the theatre. They seem so much more aware than we are, and so much more awake, and so much more alive that they make us feel that what we call living is not living at all, but a kind of sleep. Their knowledge, their wealth of emotions, their wonder, their elation, their swift, clear seeing surrounds every occasion with a crowd of values that enriches it beyond anything which we, in our happy satisfaction, had ever imagined. In their hands it becomes not only a thing of beauty but a thing of power. And we see it all—beauty and power alike—as a part of the life of the theatre.

Summary

Philosophers, artists, and critics have been debating the meaning of the word *art* for thousands of years. Few have been in agreement, and even today the debate continues. Often when we use the word *art,* we are referring to a skill or a talent, the aesthetics of a piece of art, or the meaning inherent in a piece of art. Generally, artists see art as a means of finding or conveying meaning. They create art to educate, inform, influence, and sometimes even offend and enrage an audience.

Rather than attempt an all-encompassing definition of art, we may find it more useful to describe art in terms of the qualities that all works of art have in common. These qualities include human creation, subject and medium, structure, and reaction. By describing art in this way, we can embrace all of the different forms art takes.

Art is important in our lives because it can bring order to what seems to be a chaotic universe. Religion and philosophy help us explain *why* events occur, science can explain *how* events occur, and art can fine-tune our understanding by expressing events in human terms. Artists isolate the aspects of nature they regard as essential and integrate them into a concrete, focused, and organized view of life. With this organization comes meaning and significance. In addition, every artist is a political individual who states an opinion that may challenge an audience's values, shatter their preconceptions, or help them see the world in a new way.

Theatre is a dynamic form of performing art that focuses on the human experience. All that is needed for theatre to occur is an empty space, someone to walk across that space, and someone to watch. We often refer to theatre as drama, but in fact there is a difference. Drama is a form of theatre that tells us stories about people, their actions, and the conflicts that result. Conflict is the key to the movement of a story and is what qualifies a theatrical work as a play. Conflict is at the core of drama.

Theatre is also a unique form of art because it is always live, it is always about the human experience, and it is a particularly collaborative form of art, requiring more than one type of art and artist to produce. There are many different categories of theatre, the most common being commercial theatre, historical theatre, political theatre, experimental theatre, and cultural theatre.

Theatre can be considered artistic, entertaining, or both. The fundamental difference between art and entertainment is that artists create primarily to express themselves and communicate their particular perspective, whereas entertainers create to please an audience. Entertainment is meant to amuse us and make us feel good, not necessarily to challenge our values and beliefs. Art may also confirm our values and beliefs, but artists do not necessarily seek to confirm them. This means that art is far more likely to have controversial themes that make us think.

The Art of Theatre ONLINE

To access this chapter's interactive theatre workshop activities, along with many other learning tools, log onto your Theatre CourseMate. Access is available at cengagebrain.com.

Key Terms

aesthetics / 5
commercial theatre / 16
conflict / 15
cultural theatre / 18
drama / 15
experimental plays / 17
historical theatre / 17
literary arts / 9
medium / 7
performing arts / 9
pictorial arts / 9
political theatre / 17
spatial arts / 9
subject / 7
theatre / 10
values / 19

The Blue Man Group performs during their debut show at the Venetian Resort Hotel in Las Vegas.

Photos on this spread Ethan Miller/Getty Images

CHAPTER 2

Stage versus Screen

OUTLINE

For thousands of years the theatre has had little competition, but in the modern world it must vie with movies, television, and other screen entertainments. Although theatre, film, and television have some obvious elements in common, there are key differences when it comes to acting, directing, funding, creative control, ownership, and audience participation that make the theatre unique. In this chapter, we'll look at each of these elements to understand why the ancient art of theatre remains vital and valuable in our modern world of diverse screen entertainments.

The invention of film and television had a major effect on the theatre. For a time, some critics were saying that screen entertainments

> Television's hypnotic power lies in the fact that it roasts us with its light like butterflies around a lamp: it produces continuous jets of flowing colors and impressions that we suck down with a never-ending thirst. Television is an animated piece of furniture and it speaks, it serves the function of making dullness bearable.
>
> ***Pascal Bruckner,***
> Writer

> We're so accustomed to the unchanging nature of film (and recording and computer effects) that we're less tolerant of theatre's human fallibility. Nothing in our responses can change a movie; it's invulnerable, as no actor or play, however great, can be.
>
> ***Margo Jefferson,***
> *New York Times* theatre critic

> Think of this moment. All that has ever been is in this moment; all that will be is in this moment. Both are meeting in one living flame, in this unique instant of time. This is drama; this is theatre—to be aware of the Now.
>
> ***Robert Edmond Jones,***
> Theatre designer

would lead to the theatre's demise. "The theatre is dying" was a common catchphrase. But today, over a hundred years after the invention of the movies, and fifty years after television became a dominant force, the stage is thriving. It has stood the test of time because film and television, as well as the Internet, Xbox 360s, apps, and avatars, have not improved upon or replaced the art of theatre.

Audience: No Cell Phones, Please!

Movies and television require only passive participation. You can leave the movie theatre if you don't like a movie, or hit Pause or Rewind on the DVD player, and it will not affect the actors. However, in the theatre the performers can hear you and often see you. If the audience doesn't laugh at a line that the cast believes is funny, that affects them. If an audience finds a performance amusing, the actors will "hold for laughs" to make sure the next funny line will be heard. And if a cell phone goes off or there is a disturbance in the audience, an actor might be distracted enough to forget lines. Even when the audience is perfectly silent, cast members often say they can feel an "energy" coming from them. One thing is certain: give stage actors your full attention and they will do a better job. *New York Times* theatre critic Margo Jefferson says there is something almost "primal" about the relationship between a theatre audience and the actors because of their physical proximity and the power the audience has to affect the actors' performances. Theatre is sometimes called "the living stage" or a "living art"—movies and television separate the actor and audience with lenses and screens, whereas the theatre is immediate. Theatre always takes place in your presence.

Communication flows in only one direction during screen entertainments: from the TV screen to your easy chair, or from the big screen to your sticky megaplex seat. You can throw tomatoes at screens big and small and it won't change a thing about the show. The audience has two choices: to watch or not to watch. This makes for a very different level of audience participation than at the theatre. For example, when was the last time you were at a movie where the audience applauded at the end? When you're watching TV, do you stand and applaud in your own living room? No matter how brilliant the acting, no matter how much the film or television show affected you, you don't usually applaud. Why? Because the performers can't hear you. There is no communication between you and them. In Yoruba, the western part of Nigeria, television is called *ero asoro maghese,* which means "the machine that speaks but accepts no reply." Theatre, on the other hand, accepts replies. Actor John Lithgow, who acts in films, television, and on the stage, says that performing in the theatre is "the purest form of acting," because it belongs to both the audience and the actors.

Theatre is a risky business. The unrepeatable nature of live theatre makes watching it like watching a high-wire act—something can always go wrong and you never know what you're going to get. Not only are no two performances exactly the same, but unless you read a review of a play before you see it, you probably know only the basics of the plot, not the specifics of the play's content. In contrast, movie studios and television networks advertise their products heavily before they're seen. Before you go see a movie or watch a

Jay Yamada/Courtesy California Shakespeare Theater

Peter Cade/Stone/Getty Images

Theatre is live and immediate. The actors can hear and see you, and your reaction to them changes the production from performance to performance. With screen entertainments, communication flows in only one direction, but in the theatre communication is a two-way street. This is why theatre is often called a "living art."

television show, you usually have a pretty good idea of what to expect. Movies and television in the United States also have a rating system that warns you when a show or movie includes sexual content, violence, or adult language, and movie theatres even limit who can attend particular movies. Most of the time you can avoid seeing material you think will insult you or challenge your values. All this information makes for a safety net not generally available in the theatre. In short, when you go to the theatre, you're taking a chance. But this element of chance is also what makes live theatre exciting and rewarding to watch.

Acting: I'm Ready for My Close-Up

Many people think that what stage actors and movie actors do is essentially the same. In many ways it is, but there are also some key differences. Actors who work primarily on stage are often called "legitimate" actors. The term *legitimate* is not a form of snobbery but rather comes from eighteenth-century England, where censorship laws required theatre companies to be licensed. A company of actors that had such a license was called "legitimate." Today, the term has come to mean a theatre that does only live plays, or an actor who acts only on stage in front of a live audience. Being a star of the legitimate stage requires years of training. Many movie actors also have considerable theatre training, although it's possible to become a movie star with a little charisma, a bit of talent, and a lot of luck. For example, models such as Cameron Diaz have become successful movie stars, as have athletes such as Shaquille O'Neal, but you seldom see people with little or no theatre training acting on the legitimate stage.

> We're tightrope walkers. When you walk the wire in a movie, the wire is painted on the floor, but when you walk it on the stage, it's a hundred feet high without a net.
>
> ***Al Pacino,***
> Actor

Even after some rehearsal, if the film actor can't perform what the script or director calls for, doubles can fill in and perform the dance, jump off the skyscraper, or sing the song. For example, in the movie *West Side Story,* Natalie Wood did not sing her own songs while playing the character of Maria. Rather

Photofest

Photofest

When you see movie stars singing in films, you're often hearing someone else's voice. This process, dubbing, *is common in movies. In the movie* West Side Story, *the singing voice of Natalie Wood (at left) was dubbed by professional singer Marni Nixon (at right), who also dubbed Audrey Hepburn's voice in* My Fair Lady. *But you can't dub in theatre, so actors in musical theatre must sing their own songs.*

than spending time and money training her to be a better singer, the film studio simply dubbed in another voice. A stage actress named Marni Nixon was the real singer in that movie—she also dubbed songs for Audrey Hepburn in the movie version of *My Fair Lady,* for Deborah Kerr in *The King and I,* and even sang the phrase "These rocks don't lose their shape" for Marilyn Monroe in *Gentlemen Prefer Blondes.* "Hollywood wanted recognizable stars," Nixon said. "And the fact that a lot of the stars couldn't sing was only a minor inconvenience to the big [Hollywood] producers." But if you see *West Side Story, My Fair Lady,* or *The King and I* on stage, there can be no substitution. The actress playing the part must be able to act, dance, and sing.

Actors in films and TV are sometimes called "talking heads" because there are so many close-up shots in which an actor expresses an emotion with the face or even part of the face. Stage actress Dame Judith Anderson learned about close-ups in her first movie acting experience. The director called her aside and said, "Watch your eyebrows." He explained that when she moved her eyebrows on stage, it was a matter of only a fraction of an inch, but when she raised them in a close-up shot, it was the same as moving them three feet on screen. In the theatre, there is no such thing as a close-up. Everything is a wide shot, so actors must learn to express themselves with their entire body. Also, theatre actors spend years training their voices to fill large theatres without microphones and amplification. Film actors don't have to project their voices because the boom mic is always right over their heads, just out of the frame. (In fact, if you watch closely enough, you can occasionally see the boom mic accidentally drop into the shot.)

Additionally, screen actors often don't have to remember as many lines as stage actors. Many movies and most television shows generally have fewer lines of dialogue than plays, and screen actors seldom have to remember more than just a few minutes' worth of dialogue at a time. Screen actors often learn their lines on the day of shooting; sometimes they don't have to remember lines at all because cue cards and teleprompters can be placed just off camera, allowing them to simply read their lines. This is especially true for television actors in many soap operas and live shows such as *Saturday Night Live.* Stage actors don't have it so easy. They must memorize thousands of lines of dialogue and long speeches before they dare to perform in front of a live audience—and if they forget their lines there is no one there to help. (See Spotlight in Chapter 7, "The Actor's Nightmare—Forgetting Lines.")

But the most important difference is that in movies and TV screen actors are allowed to fail. If they don't get it right on the first take, they can always try again. If they fail a hundred times in a row, they can still win an Oscar if they get it right on the hundred-and-first take. In contrast, stage actors must get it right the first time, night after night after night. For example, in the movie version of the stage musical *Chicago,* Richard Gere tap-dances, Catherine Zeta-Jones struts her stuff, and Renée Zellweger sings. They all look pretty good, yet the director had the luxury of cutting to a new shot or a different take every few seconds, thereby covering up all their missteps and wrong notes.

Not that acting for the camera is easy. Movies are often shot out of sequence, so in the morning a film actor might start shooting a tender love scene, die that afternoon on the battlefield, and in the evening go back to finishing the love scene. In general, though, actors who train for the stage need much more training, more hours of rehearsal, and perhaps even more talent, for there is no safety net in the theatre, no editor to make errors disappear, no cue cards or teleprompters, and no retakes or second chances. This is the very nature of the live theatre: anything can happen!

Photofest

Because many parts in plays require hoofers, from the competent to the accomplished, theatre actors are often trained in dance. Film stars are usually not as well trained. They may have to train hard for a few months before shooting difficult dance scenes. Or the director may have the film edited so that the best one- to five-second clips of an actor's dance moves are shown in quick succession, creating the illusion that the actor is a good dancer. The film rendition of Chicago *included all these possibilities. Catherine Zeta-Jones was a musical theatre pro in Europe before making it big in Hollywood; Renée Zellweger and Richard Gere required a lot of training prior to shooting; and skilled editing contributed to an entertaining musical full of splashy dance numbers.*

Directing: There Is No Director's Cut in the Theatre

Film is often called a director's medium, because the director has a great deal of creative control. The director is all-powerful and tells everyone what to do, except for the producers, who bankroll the production. Directors can change the script, rewrite a scene, and control exactly what the audience will see moment by moment and shot by shot. If they don't like one take, they can shoot a scene repeatedly until they get what they want. Interestingly, the opposite is true in most television sitcoms and dramas. In television the directors often go unnoticed and are sometimes even subservient to the writers. Television is so fast-paced, delivering new ideas, scripts, and episodes each week, that it makes sense for the person in charge to be the one who produces those scripts: the writer or the producer.

> . . . acting for film is like a musician playing in a recording studio and acting in the theatre is like playing live in concert . . . .
>
> **_Willem Dafoe,_**
> Actor

> It's much harder to write for the stage because it's got to be really tight; it's got to work—actors are dependent on their cues, they're live. . . . In film, they can garble it and mangle it and get it backwards, but if you shoot it and it comes out funny that way, you have it and it's great for all time.
>
> ***Woody Allen,***
> Director, screenwriter, and playwright

As we will discuss in later chapters, theatre directors can also be very powerful, but they never have absolute control over every moment of the production. Each performance is different, and no matter how skilled they are, no actor can exactly duplicate what he or she did the night before. In most instances the director chooses, or "casts," the actors, and during rehearsal the director will suggest, urge, and even demand certain things from them. Yet, once the curtain goes up, no director can bring it down to make adjustments. Nor does the theatre director have absolute control over the script—the playwright owns the copyright, except when the script is in public domain, which is the case for plays written long ago, such as Shakespeare's plays. (The ideas of copyright and public domain are covered in greater detail later in this chapter.) The special collaborative aspect of play production usually makes theatre a little more democratic than film or television. You hear the words *ensemble* and *team* used often in the theatre but not always in film and television, even though these mediums also require a collaborative effort. As a result, in a good theatre production—one where egos are not battling for control, and collaboration is based on mutual respect—more voices are heard and more creative individuals are working together, rather than a solitary authority telling everyone what to do. In the theatre, there is no "director's cut."

Funding: Follow the Money

Another major difference between most theatre and screen entertainments is funding and profit. With only a few notable exceptions, such as the big Broadway production companies, theatres are generally nonprofit companies. "Nonprofit" companies do not have stockholders and pay no dividends or federal taxes. The Internal Revenue Service created nonprofit status for companies and organizations that are not designed for private financial gain and that provide the general public with charitable, educational, and recreational services, such as the United Way, the Red Cross, and the American Cancer Society. Most theatres apply for and receive nonprofit status because the sad fact is that most plays—and the theatre companies that produce them—lose money. If it weren't for tax exemptions, donors, and patrons of the arts, most theatres would cease to exist. And even the best for-profit theatres don't fare much better.

In the 2009–10 season, 11.9 million people attended plays or musicals at one of the thirty-nine Broadway theatres in New York City. By comparison, during and after a typical season finale for the Fox show *American Idol,* viewers will cast well over 60 million votes for their favorite singers. Broadway's combined gross sales (not profits) that same year were just over $1 billion—one of Broadway's best years ever. That sounds good until you realize that *American Idol* by itself also brings in about $1 billion a year for Fox and the production companies that produce it. One billion is about the same amount of money the movie *Batman: The Dark Knight,* which was seen by over one hundred million people worldwide, earned at the box office. It's roughly equal to the amount of money the sitcom *Seinfeld* has generated from syndication revenues (reruns) in the last decade. The main point is this: Broadway—often booked as full of commercial entertainments as with truly artistic endeavors, and being the single

William Missouri Downs

Theatre audiences are tiny compared to those who watch movies and television. Even a play such as Agatha Christie's The Mousetrap, *which has run in London at the St. Martin's Theatre for more than fifty years, has been seen by fewer people than watch a popular sitcom like* Two and a Half Men *on a single night.*

most lucrative theatre venue of all time—at its financial best only equals the gross sales of a single hit television show or movie.

Funding the Screen

Each year people all over the world pay tens of billions of dollars to go to the movies, rent DVDs, and watch television. But that is only part of the big media companies' income. They also make money through advertising. When you go to the movies or watch television and see a star drinking a particular type of soda, driving a specific type of car, or wearing distinct apparel, it is more than likely that a soft drink, car, or clothing company paid millions to have their product featured. Product placement is becoming so big that in 2010 U.S. corporations paid more than $10 billion to have their products strategically located within a shot or weaved into a storyline. Some Hollywood movies have as much as twenty-five percent of their production costs funded by product placement. For example, a recent James Bond movie had product placement deals with Heineken, Avis, BMW, and Smirnoff vodka. Most product placement is simple, such as Adam Sandler enjoying Popeye's chicken in the movie *Little Nicky,* but sometimes it is not so subtle. For example, when Staples introduced a new paper

University of Wyoming Archives

Unlike Hollywood movies, which can employ dozens if not hundreds of actors, professional theatres often operate on such tight budgets that they can only afford to produce plays with small casts. While this is not the case with college and amateur productions where the actors are not paid, many professional theatres have an unwritten rule that if a play has more than seven roles the chances of it getting produced are small. One popular two character full-length play is Arlene Hutton's Last Train To Nibroc. *This production featured Katrina DeSpain and Nicholas Linn and was produced at the Snowy Range Summer Theatre.*

shredder, they paid the producers of the NBC show *The Office* to create two episodes where the plot revolved around their product.

Television makes money not only through product placement but also by selling commercial time. The more commercials a network can pack into an hour, the more money it can make. For example, on average MTV spends 18 minutes and 11 seconds per hour airing commercials; UPN, 17 minutes and 40 seconds; FOX, 16 minutes and 36 seconds. And the amount of commercial time continues to increase—Disney's ABC has augmented the amount of time given to commercials by 34 percent since 1989.

Funding Theatre and the Arts

When you divide the cost of a Hollywood blockbuster movie, which can cost upwards of $200 million to produce, by the tens of millions of people who will see it on the screen or on video, the production cost per audience member is tiny. The same is true of television. On the other hand, a play costs far less to produce—anywhere from a few thousand dollars for a community theatre production to several million for a big Broadway production. The Broadway musical *Spider-Man: Turn Off the Dark* (music and lyrics by U2's Bono and The Edge) cost over $65 million to produce, making it perhaps the most expensive production in the history of the theatre. However, when the expenses of producing live theatre are divided by the limited number of seats available, the cost per audience member is high in comparison to

Everett Collection

Product placement is common in Hollywood movies and television. Not only do companies pay billions to have their products placed within a scene, but they also send a representative to the set to make sure the actors prominently display products within the production. There are even public relations and marketing agencies that specialize in forging ties between products and celebrities. In this scene from the movie Syriana, *Matt Damon and Amanda Peet star with a box of Cheerios.*

screen entertainments. In fact, it can easily be twenty, fifty, or even one hundred times more expensive per person. In that sense, theatre is expensive. (For details about the costs of one production, see the Spotlight "Theatre Can Be Expensive.")

The problem in funding theatre stems from the nature of theatre: It is a live medium. Theatre is labor-intensive and comparatively low-tech, with few technological innovations to make it cheaper. Screen entertainments benefit from numerous technological advances that replace the expensive labor force once required to produce a movie or TV show. But in theatre, the cost of producing a play is continually on the rise precisely because it depends on human labor, much of which cannot be replaced by machinery. For example, the lighting changes for a play can be programmed into a computer, but no computer can predict what will happen during each live performance. On the screen, an actor can adjust for technology. In the theatre, technology must adjust to the performer. Put simply, inspired human minds are always required backstage to support the inspired human minds and bodies onstage, as they attempt to inspire a live audience.

Another obstacle in funding theatre is that ticket sales at most nonprofit theatres cover only 60 percent of the cost of producing a performance. If most theatres had to depend solely on ticket sales, they would have to raise their prices to the point where only the very rich could afford a seat. In that case, theatre would become so scarce that most people would never see a play. So, to satisfy demand and make theatre available to more people, nonprofit theatres cut ticket prices and try to make up the difference through alternative forms of funding. A recent poll by the Theatre Communications Group questioned 262 theatres on the sources of their funding. It found that 59 percent of their income came from tickets and concession sales, and 41 percent had to come from outside sources, including grants and contributions. Individual contributors, corporations, foundations, and federal, state, and local entities keep theatre alive.

> Arts groups are notoriously undercapitalized, living year to year (or even week to week). As a result, even mild economic downturns can be devastating. In this era of free market fetishization, it may be difficult for many people to grasp, but the arts don't come close to paying their own way. They need welfare—public or private.
>
> ***Christopher Shea,***
> Writer, in *The American Prospect* magazine

SPOTLIGHT ON Theatre Can Be Expensive[1]

A play costs more per audience member to produce than any Hollywood movie. Whether you are attending a local community playhouse or the professional theatre, be prepared to pay more for your tickets. For example, if you pay $9 to see a two-hour Hollywood movie, you are paying 7.5 cents a minute to be entertained, not counting popcorn. If you pay $80 a month for cable and watch as much as the average American does, you'll be paying a little over one cent a minute. But if you go see a two-hour play at a professional theatre, the cost can be anywhere from 35 cents to 85 cents a minute. According to the League of American Theaters and Producers, the average cost of a Broadway ticket today is $78. And premium seats can be as much as $200 or $300. Why is theatre so expensive?

Theatre is expensive because it is labor-intensive and it plays to very limited audiences. Costs include not only designing, building, and maintaining the costumes, sets, and lights, but also advertising, utilities, insurance, rental fees, maintenance fees, payroll taxes, union benefits, royalties, and salaries for actors, directors, stage crews, technicians, musicians, ushers, box office personnel, accountants, and security.

Recently, producer Emanuel Azenberg opened his account books to a *New York Times* reporter to show how expensive it was to produce a play on Broadway. The play was Eugene O'Neill's *The Iceman Cometh*, starring Kevin Spacey at the Brooks Atkinson Theatre. Before the curtain even went up on the opening night, $350,000 was spent to buy and rent the stage equipment and pay workers to set up the set, costumes, lights, and sound. Azenberg saved money by using the same set that was used when he produced the play in England, but it cost another $90,000 to adapt it to the Broadway house. The lighting and sound equipment budget was $75,000, which included $20,000 for special light bulbs that cost as much as $700 each. Other pre-opening night costs included a dialect coach, a fight director, an assistant director, and a production staff, as well as salaries for actors and other members of the creative team during rehearsals—totaling more than $300,000.

After opening night, weekly salaries, including payroll taxes and pensions, for everyone from actors to technical supervisors came to $79,489.56 a week or $1,033,364.20 for the run of the play. This was kept low because star Kevin Spacey, who earns millions to be in movies, agreed to do the play for only about $1,000 a week. The theatre itself cost $10,000 a week to rent plus a percentage of the show's gross income, plus thousands more to pay the theatre staff and box-office crews. To advertise the play before it opened cost $250,000, plus another $40,000 per week during the run. Miscellaneous expenses for everything from throat lozenges to coffee came to $2,500 a week. In the end, the play took an initial capital investment

Individual contributors to the arts, or **patrons**, come in all sizes. They range from billionaire philanthropists who give away millions, to average Americans who donate a few extra, hard-earned bucks. Most nonprofit theatres print a list of their donors in the program you're handed by the ushers. The people who contribute the least are listed as "donor" or "patron," whereas those who give greater amounts might be labeled "benefactor" or "producer" or given a creative name like "angel" or "protector." Most theatres are nonprofit, so donors' gifts are tax-deductible, or free from federal income taxes. Theatres also offer donors other benefits, such as special opening or closing-night parties, first choice of seats, thank-you gifts, membership in patron clubs, and the opportunity to serve on the theatre's board of directors.

Corporate funding for the arts, whether from the smallest mom-and-pop companies or mammoth corporations, is good for business. Small businesses, such as restaurants, will donate to a local theatre because a successful theatre in

[1]Based on data from "$100 a Ticket?! Here's Why" By Jesse McKinley, The New York Times, April 8, 1999 "The High Cost of Breaking Even" by Jesse McKinley, The New York Times, February 26, 2006.

of $1.5 million and cost $250,000 a week to run for a total cost of $4.75 million. Even with a movie star name attached, and performing one of the most famous American plays of all time, Azenberg only managed to break even. (For more information, see the *New York Times,* April 8, 1999.)

The *New York Times* also reported on the situation with smaller theatres. The play *Bug,* written by Tracy Letts, ran at Barrow Street, a 199-seat theatre in New York City, and barely made money. Here is an example of what was spent and what came in each week.

Weekly Costs and Income

Theatre rent	−$8,000
Marketing	−$9,560
Salaries (actors to accountants)	−$13,325
Miscellaneous	−$2,675
Credit card fees	−$2,189
Royalties	−$7,000
Total weekly cost	−$42,449
Average weekly ticket sales	+$43,780
Average weekly profits	**+$1,031**

Bug went on to become a major Hollywood movie starring Ashley Judd, Harry Connick, Jr., and Michael Shannon. The movie grossed millions.

© Joan Marcus

Kevin Spacey in The Iceman Cometh, *directed by Howard Davies at the Brooks Atkinson Theatre, 1999.*

Jed Bernstein, the former president of The Broadway League, estimated that only one in five Broadway shows recoups its investment. But if a show becomes a hit, like the musicals *The Producers* or *Spamalot,* they can pay back the producers' investment many times over. This seldom happens, however, prompting *New York Times* columnist Joseph Nocera to say ". . . we should stop talking about 'investing' in a play, and start calling it what it is; an act of philanthropy."

the neighborhood can increase dinner receipts. Studies show that for every dollar a theatre spends, it brings in five dollars in goods and services for related or neighboring enterprises. Private parking lots, restaurants, taverns, coffeehouses, and retail stores reap the benefits of increased traffic, which boosts the local economy. Large corporations often make donations to gain political clout, tax write-offs, or publicity.

Sometimes corporations make donations to theatres in an effort to suggest that they are "giving something back" to the community. For example, The Metropolitan Life Insurance Company underwrites the PBS television series *Live from Lincoln Center,* which often presents opera and theatre performances. Recently, however, corporate funding for the arts and theatre has been in decline. According to the Giving USA Foundation, an educational and research program of the American Association of Fundraising Counsel, corporate funding of the arts has dropped by nearly one-half in the last decade. And when corporations today do fund the theatre, the money often comes with strings attached. Some corporations will give money only if free tickets are given to their employees; others require that company promotional material be included in the play's programs, posters and other advertisements, and even printed on the tickets. Some corporations fund theatre because they have a vested interest in the subject matter. For example, Serono, a biotechnology company that makes fertility drugs, sponsored the musical *Infertility*. It appears as if today's corporations are less interested in philanthropy and more interested in targeting specific demographics with commercials for its products, as well as controlling the message of the entertainment produced. In some cases corporate sponsors attach restrictions on subject matter, forcing theatres to avoid plays about labor unions, factory pollution, socialism, communism, workers' rights, workers' safety, closing corporate tax loopholes, the need for greater government regulations, or any theme that corporations find objectionable. With more than 150 different corporate sponsors, PBS programming faces similar "side effects" of corporate funding. A common joke in the industry today is that PBS no longer stands for "Public Broadcasting Service" but "Petroleum Broadcasting Service" because so much of their funding comes from large oil corporations that place limits on what they can produce and broadcast using the funds they donate.

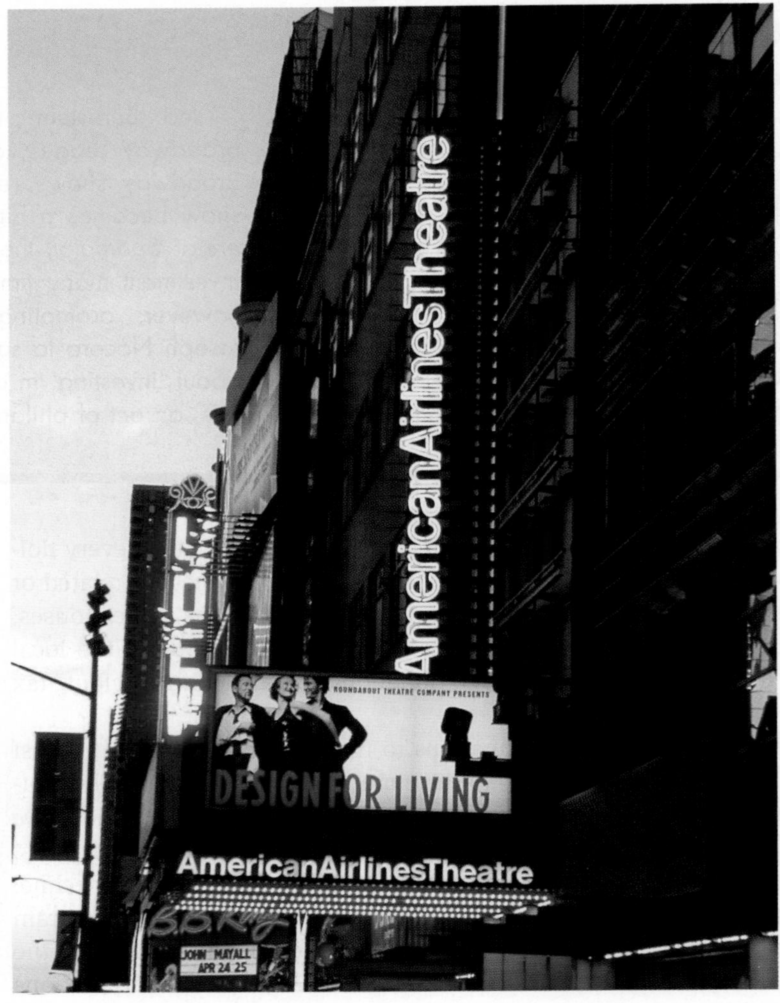

Walter McBride/Retna, Ltd.

Product placement is not common in the theatre but corporations that donate money to various theatres are seldom in it for purely altruistic reasons. Often they want their name prominently displayed; in other cases they want to control content. American Airlines paid millions to have the Selwyn Theatre on Broadway renamed.

Government funding, the money spent each year on the arts by federal, state, and local entities, is by far the most controversial method of maintaining a healthy arts community in the United States—even though we spend far fewer tax dollars on the arts than any other major industrialized nation. Here is a list of the dollar amount average taxpayers in ten countries pay per year to fund the arts:

Finland	$91.00	Netherlands	$46.00
Germany	$85.00	United Kingdom	$36.00
France	$57.00	Australia	$25.00
Sweden	$57.00	Ireland	$9.00
Canada	$46.00	United States	$0.46

The federal agency that disburses our arts tax dollars is the **National Endowment for the Arts (NEA)**, and it is one of the smallest of all the government programs. Funding for the arts takes up a very tiny part of the federal budget. Approximately 29 percent of the federal budget goes to support the military, 19 percent to pay the national debt, 4 percent for education, but only 0.01 percent to support the arts. In fact the amount of money Americans pay in federal tax dollars to support the NEA is less than they pay to support the United States Army marching bands. (In 2010 the budget for the NEA was $161.3 million; the budget for the United States Army marching bands was $198 million.) To be fair, it is important to point out that many of Europe's arts agencies are structured differently than

Before the NEA there was the Federal Theatre Project (FTP), established in the 1930s as part of Franklin Delano Roosevelt's New Deal social reforms. During its four-year existence, the Federal Theatre Project employed more than ten thousand theatre professionals and mounted more than one thousand productions. Many plays staged during this time highlighted the social ills of the nation, such as Triple-A Plowed Under, *which dramatized the plight of farmers, and* One-Third of a Nation, *which studied the problems of the homeless in America. These sorts of plays got the Federal Theatre Project into deep trouble. By 1939, charges began flying that the FTP was dominated by communists, and politicians accused it of portraying "un-American propaganda." Soon thereafter, funding was cut.*

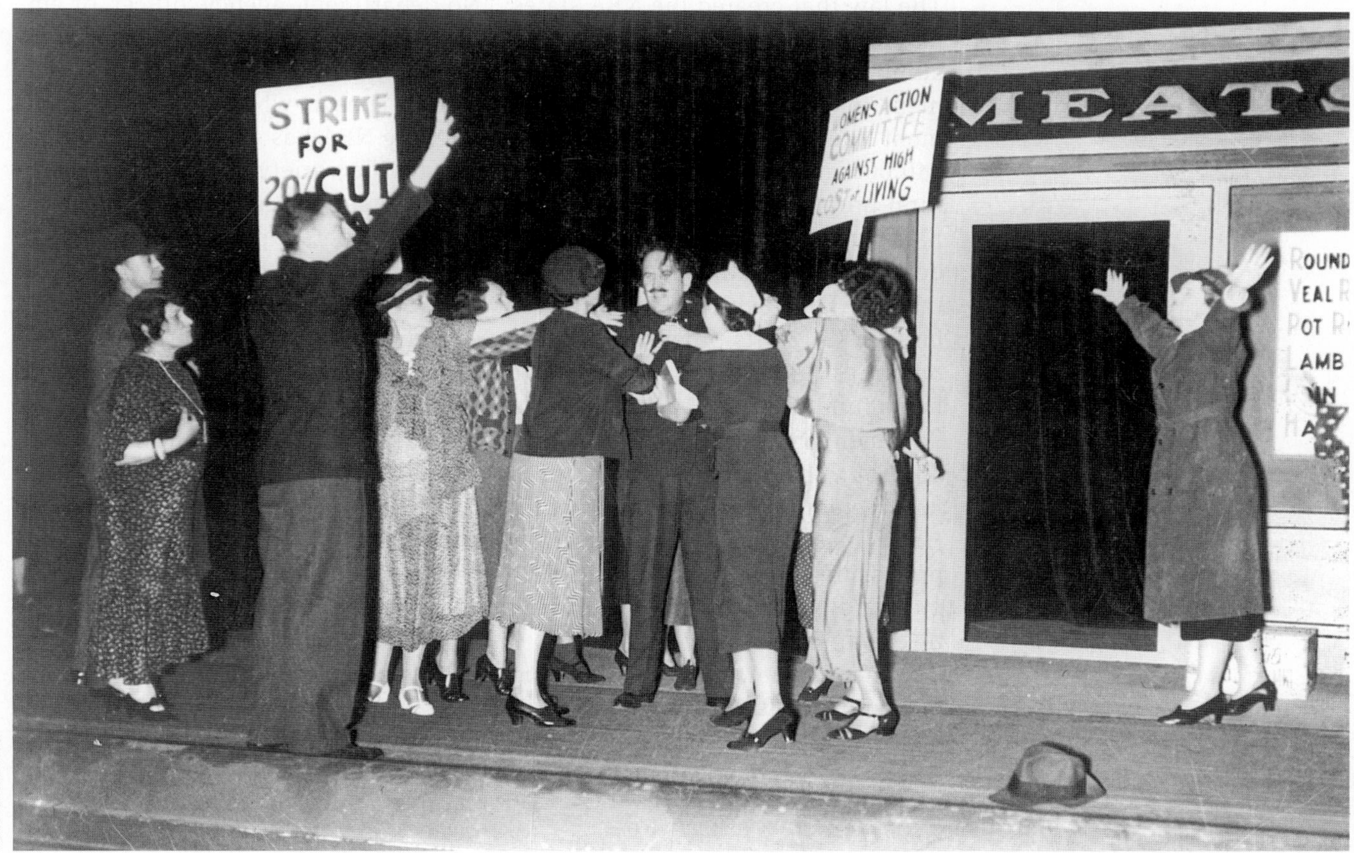

the NEA and have far more financial responsibilities. But if you include the federal tax dollars that go to the Smithsonian Institution, the Corporation for Public Broadcasting (PBS), the National Endowment for the Humanities, the National Gallery of Art, the Kennedy Center for the Performing Arts, the Advisory Council for Historic Preservation, the Institute of Museum and Library Services, and the money the departments of State and Education spend to support the arts, the total is still less than $8 per American.

President John F. Kennedy finally earned the bipartisan support needed to create the National Endowment for the Arts (NEA), but he was assassinated in 1963 before his dream could be realized. In September 1965, President Lyndon B. Johnson signed into law the bill that created the National Endowment for the Arts as well as the National Endowment for the Humanities. The bill states in part, "While no government can call a great artist or scholar into existence, it is necessary and appropriate for the Federal Government to help create and sustain not only a climate encouraging freedom of thought, imagination, and inquiry, but also the material condition facilitating the release of this creative talent." The first NEA grant went to the American Ballet Theatre and saved the nearly bankrupt ballet company from extinction. Over the next forty-five years, the NEA would become the largest single supporter of nonprofit art in America as it attempted to fulfill its mission "to foster the excellence, diversity, and vitality of the arts in the United States, and to broaden public access to the arts."

> We have agencies of the Government which are concerned with the welfare and advancement of science and technology, of education, recreation and health. We should now begin to give similar attention to the arts.
>
> ***John F. Kennedy,***
> President of the United States, 1961–1963

The NEA acts as an independent commission, and NEA panels do not have to get their decisions rubber-stamped by the Senate or the president. The law that created the NEA states: "No department, agency, officer, or employee of the United States shall exercise any supervision or control over the administration or operations of the NEA." It is to be an independent government institution, thereby facilitating artistic speech while limiting government interference and censorship. To date, the NEA has given out more than 140,000 grants and provided funding for a wide variety of artistic and cultural programs across the United States. It has supported concerts, theatres, film festivals, dance performances, orchestras, operas, poetry readings, and downtown renewal projects. It has helped museums with travel costs so that they can take exhibitions to inner cities and rural areas. It has invested millions in K–12 arts programs nationwide. It gives money to preserve historical paintings and public monuments. It helps showcase Native American art, helps fund the PBS *Great Performances* series, and even helped with the PBS documentary on the history of the American music creation known as rock and roll. The NEA has funded projects ranging from the design of the Vietnam Veterans Memorial in Washington, DC, to the acclaimed documentary *Hoop Dreams* about two inner-city Chicago youths and their quest to become professional basketball players. When a symphony orchestra played at the memorial service for the victims of the Oklahoma City bombing, it was aided by a grant from the NEA.

The relatively minuscule funding our government invests in the NEA helps the national arts community pump nearly $37 billion into the economy and generates more than $5 billion in revenue for federal, state, and local governments. Few, if any, other governmental programs can boast such a high return on such a small investment.

Control: Who Pulls the Strings?

The picture we have painted so far portrays those who control screen entertainments as being far more interested in the audience's values than in the artist's voice. Theatre, on the other hand, has been shown as more interested in the artist's voice than in the audience's values. However, there is no exact dividing line between them. Some commercial theatre productions, such as Disney's stage versions of its films *The Lion King* and *Beauty and the Beast*, are sometimes called **bourgeois theatre** because they pursue maximum profits by reaffirming the audience's values just as rigorously as any big-budget Hollywood film, and many art and independent films stress the artist's vision as much as any noncommercial theatre. But generally speaking, Hollywood more often produces entertainment, and theatre more often creates art. This becomes even clearer when you look at the organizations that produce and fund—and therefore control—entertainment and art.

> Television technology is inherently antidemocratic. Because of its cost, the limited kind of information it can disseminate, the way it transforms the people who use it, and the fact that few speak while millions absorb, television is suitable for use only by the most powerful corporate interests in the country. They inevitably use it to redesign human minds into a channeled, artificial, commercial form that nicely fits the artificial environment.
>
> ***Jerry Mander,***
> *Four Arguments for the Elimination of Television*

William Missouri Downs

Hollywood movies often use star power to sell tickets. On the other hand, most theatres do not have the resources to hire big name actors. When a star does accept a contract with a theatre, it is often at a drastically reduced salary and he or she performs mostly for the love of being on stage. Here the Wenham's theatre in London headlines Academy Award Winner Holly Hunter.

SPOTLIGHT ON We Hate You (But Please Keep Sending Us *Baywatch*)

The Writers Guild of America (WGA) recently held a panel discussion entitled "We Hate You (But Please Keep Sending Us *Baywatch*)," which looked at the influence of American screen entertainments on world culture. Like its fast food, America exports its entertainment worldwide. For example, Hollywood movies can easily reach as many as 2.6 billion people and even the soap opera *The Bold and the Beautiful* is watched by 450 million people in 98 countries. In Britain, U.S. movies account for 95 percent of the box-office revenues, with an average of nine of the top ten films at any Cineplex coming from America. The numbers are similar in Germany, Spain, and Italy. Even in Afghanistan, where only 19 percent of the people now have televisions and censorship laws require that a woman's bare midriff must be electronically covered, American television is prevalent, with Kiefer Sutherland's show *24* being one of the most popular. The bikini-filled *Baywatch* was cancelled after one season on NBC because of low ratings, but continues to play in syndication in 140 countries and in 195 major cities around the world.

On average Hollywood movies make about 50 per cent of their ticket sales from overseas markets. But not all American films translate well to other cultures. For example, comedies like *Anchorman: The Legend of Ron Burgundy* and *Talladega Nights: The Ballad of Ricky Bobby* fared poorly in international markets, but action movies such as *Spider-Man* and *Pirates of the Caribbean* do well. Trying to make a film that plays in a multitude of global markets can be problematic. Hollywood directors and editors often adhere to the unofficial maxim that if a movie is to be shown to Europeans, cut the violence; if it is to be shown to Asians, cut the sex scenes; and if it is to be shown to Americans, cut both.

Hollywood moviemakers have also learned that satirizing—even in a good natured, well-intentioned manner—various peoples around the world is a

William Missouri Downs

A movie poster for Iron Man *in China.*

The Big Picture

With combined revenues in the hundreds of billions, most Hollywood screen entertainment companies are owned by some of the largest multinational corporations in the world. These multinational corporations have holdings in agribusinesses, airlines, transportation companies, banks, insurance companies, coal and oil producers, defense contractors, rocket and jet engineering firms, hotel chains, medical technology companies, and companies that build nuclear power plants and nuclear weapons. In contrast, smaller companies, independent producers, and even mom-and-pop theatre companies produce the lion's share of theatre in the United States.

In 1975, about fifty corporations owned 90 percent of American entertainment companies. Today, because of *deregulation*, the number is down to six:

quick way to reduce international profits. For example the Mike Myers movie *The Love Guru* satirized Hinduism, which lead to an uproar in India and an international boycott of the film. The same is true of the sitcom/cartoon *The Simpsons*, which has been accused of including derogatory stereotypical characters like Apu, the convenience store owner from India who is the father of octuplets. In fact, in India the word "Apu" is used to mean any stereotypical perceptions of Indians.

Hollywood movies can also lead to stereotypes of Americans. Most of the world's population knows Americans only through Hollywood movies and television shows. A Council on Foreign Relations report, "Public Diplomacy: A Strategy for Reform," examined polls by Gallup, Zogby, and the U.S. State Department and found that "foreign perceptions of the United States are far from monolithic, but there is little doubt that the stereotypes of United States citizens as arrogant, self-indulgent, hypocritical, inattentive, and unwilling or unable to engage in cross-cultural dialogue are pervasive and deeply rooted." Margaret Tutwiler, former under secretary for public diplomacy and public affairs at the U.S. State Department, said, "By allowing our society to be represented overseas by popular art that portrays us as secular, violent, undisciplined and obsessed by sex, we are only making it easier for extremists to recruit. . . ." The effect Hollywood has on the world, and the world's perception of the United States, must be considered if any major attempt is ever made to change that perception.

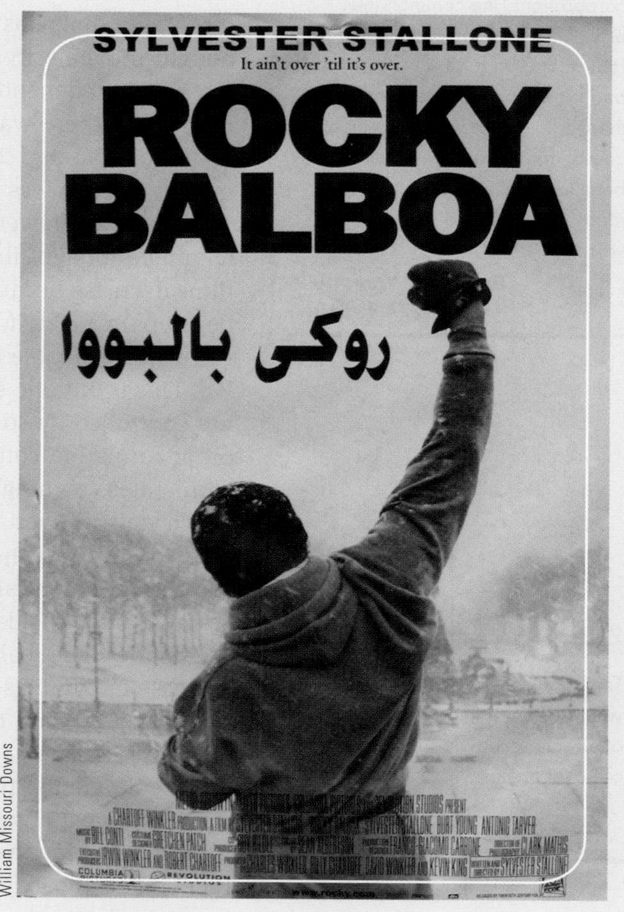

William Missouri Downs

A movie poster for Rocky Balboa *in Egypt.*

General Electric, Viacom, News Corporation, Disney, Time Warner, and Sony. Not only do these companies control our news and entertainment but they also export American entertainments around the world. See the Spotlight "We Hate You (But Please Keep Sending Us *Baywatch*)." As discussed in Chapter 1, entertainment companies make money by reaffirming the audience's values. Yet there is another motive for the decisions about the content of our entertainment: As the media moguls have gained more control, they have become increasingly interested in reaffirming their own values over those of their audiences.

Here is a small example of what can happen when only a few huge corporations gain control of our screen entertainments. In the mid 1960s, when numerous companies were competing for our entertainment dollars, approximately one out of every twenty major movies shown in the United States was a foreign

> Because control of the media is concentrated among a few similar corporations, the common interests of the corporations further reduce the range of perspectives and life experiences reflected in the media. The palpable result of consolidation on TV writers has been to reduce them to only those ideas acceptable to the corporate voice.
>
> ***Patric M. Verrone,*** WGA President

film. American movie theatres periodically showed the films of acclaimed and influential artists such as Akira Kurosawa, Satyajit Ray, Federico Fellini, and Ingmar Bergman. Twenty-five years later, only about one in every one hundred major films in the United States is foreign. It would seem that America's appetite for foreign films has waned, right? But the truth is that huge media corporations bought the majority of the movie screens and built huge megaplexes that drove the small, independent movie theatres out of business. These media moguls found that there was less profit in showing foreign films, so they loaded their mammoth 12- and 24-screen theatres with their own movies. Even if their own movies were in less demand, their costs were lower, so their income was higher. The result was fewer and fewer foreign movies available to us. The next group to eliminate foreign films was movie rental stores, which saw demand for foreign films decrease because the new generations attending movies were not seeing or developing a taste for them. Instead, huge corporations dictated what entertainment was available and the public simply followed.

This is but one small example of what happens when screen entertainments are controlled by so few, and it is minor in comparison to what is happening to other forms of "content" and information. If this same handful of media conglomerates, owning both entertainment and news services, can control what world perspectives we see by filtering out movies from other countries, it can also control what news we see from other countries—and even what news we see about ourselves! Mark Crispin Miller, director of the Project on Media Ownership, said, "The danger of media concentration lies not in the risk of prices getting higher. The real danger is much subtler. You're talking about an exponential increase in conflicts of interest. You're talking about few interests having greater market power. You're talking about the rise of trivial programming."

> The heads of major corporations will have more impact on values of people worldwide than heads of governments.
>
> ***Norman Lear,*** TV writer and producer

As a consumer you do have some small, yet authoritative, power against the media giants: there is a power-off button on your TV remote control, and there is almost always a legitimate stage not far away where theatre professionals are plumbing the depths of the human condition for you to laugh at, rave at, rage at, weep over, boo, or applaud where it makes a difference.

The Theatre Next Door

Although screen entertainments tend to be commercialized and globalized and have concentrated ownership, most theatre is less commercialized, more provincial, and locally controlled. But this does not necessarily mean that artists at a given theatre have the financial or civic freedom to produce any play they wish. For thousands of years the powerful and elite have subsidized theatre, from monarchs and czars to wealthy citizens and the church. Those who control the funding have a tendency to control content. In short, the theatre has always been a pawn for whoever controls the purse strings, and those who do not control the money often charge those who do with censorship. Joan E. Bertin, executive director of the National Coalition Against Censorship, points out that the impulse to suppress ideas comes from both sides of the political spectrum: "The left complains about art that is critical of feminists, civil rights advocates, and gay activists. The right usually objects to artworks that include nudity, have sexual or antireligious themes, or denigrate patriotism or the American flag." The battle to control the funding of the theatre goes much deeper than government leaders and citizens worried about how tax dol-

> Theatre could have been rendered obsolete years ago, but it hasn't yet. There's still an elemental need to sit around the campfire and tell stories.
>
> ***Allison Narver,*** Artistic director of the Empty Space Theatre

T. Charles Erickson/Courtesy Berkeley Repertory Theatre

Because legitimate theatres are locally controlled and funded, they can often present a wider diversity of views than do Hollywood movies. Here, Kevin Jackson and Kecia Lewis star in Zora Neale Hurston and Dorothy Waring's Polk County, *directed at the Berkeley Repertory Theatre by Kyle Donnelley.*

lars are spent. The core of the issue is who will control content and who will be able to promote his or her point of view and censor those who disagree. But unlike screen entertainments that are dominated by a small handful of executives in massive companies with similar political agendas, theatre is liberated by a multitude of diverse, smaller, independent production companies. Hundreds of differing political points of view are promoted by thousands of theatres across the United States. As we stated in Chapter 1, art is political. Art conveys messages about how an artist thinks the world is or should be. A play contains an artist's opinions, values, and political views. Add this to the thousands of actors, playwrights, and directors in America, each working in theatres owned by different producing organizations with different funding sources, and you have a greater possibility that a wealth of diverse points of view will be expressed. Therefore, when you go to the theatre, you can see patriotic musicals and radical anti-government plays; stories that promote traditional family values and stories that champion diverse values; themes that endorse communism and themes that uphold capitalism; plays that glorify Christianity and plays that sing the joys of atheism. Some theatre companies promote African American, Latino, and Asian points of view, and others stage plays with gay, lesbian, and feminist themes. As long as theatre remains locally funded and controlled, a wealth of opinions can be expressed. (For more discussion on these topics, see Chapter 3.)

In short, a particular theatre may be controlled by corporate or local funding that restricts content, and groups may succeed in censoring, delaying, or even canceling a given production. Yet with so many different theatres located in diverse areas and with diverse funding, more information, more points of view, and more diverse content can be disseminated. Theatre, therefore, has a much greater chance of being a forum for debate and controversy and providing a voice to those parts of our society about which the massive screen entertainments are silent.

Ownership: Copyrights and Cash

There are striking dissimilarities between a typical Hollywood screen entertainment and the theatre when it comes to who owns the words, ideas, or content. A **copyright** is a legal guarantee granted by the government to authors, playwrights, composers, choreographers, inventors, publishers, and/or corporations that allows them to maintain control and profit from their creative works. A copyright is similar to a patent. When you patent an invention, the U.S. government grants you "the right to exclude others from making, using, offering for sale, or selling" your particular invention without your permission. A copyright, unlike a patent, protects the form of expression rather than the subject matter. When you copyright something, you affirm your exclusive right and ownership of your words, music, photographs, paintings, drawings, computer software, CDs, DVDs, MP3s, or other form of expression.

Playwrights copyright their plays, published or not. This means that in order to stage a play by a playwright who is living or has died within the last seventy years, you first must get written permission from the playwright or the playwright's agent, publisher, or estate. When a play is produced, a **royalty payment** must be made to the playwright or the playwright's estate. This payment is like rent, except that instead of renting property such as a house or a car, you are renting the playwright's intellectual property. Also, because a play is copyrighted, directors, producers, actors, or anyone involved with the production cannot change, rewrite, or rearrange a script without permission from the playwright or the playwright's agent, publisher, or estate. Therefore, playwrights have the right to say who will perform their plays, the right to make money from the production or publication of their plays, and the right to decide what changes, if any, will be made. This gives playwrights one power: Their words, and therefore their thoughts, themes, and messages, cannot be altered without permission. So when a high school or community theatre cuts all the dirty words from a play in order not to offend their audiences, they are guilty of breaking the copyright laws of the United States. (See the Spotlight "Copyright Law: Infringement, Public Domain, and Parody.")

Rewriting is the intrusion of another mind, another personality, another ego, another ethos. Sometimes it is done with good intentions, good will, and sometimes it will seem to improve the script. But it is a violation of what lies at the heart of authorship and that's why . . . I was never happy writing for screen or for TV. I met some nice people, had some fun, and made some money, but was never satisfied.

David Karp,
Hollywood screenwriter

Things could not be more different for Hollywood screen and television writers. They, unlike playwrights, do not retain the copyright but instead sell their

Richard Feldman

Playwrights copyright their work, so when producers, directors, or theatre companies want to stage a living playwright's work, they must get the playwright's permission first. Sometimes playwrights grant permission initially, but then object to script changes, unusual casting, or a particular interpretation of the play. For example, in 1984 playwright Samuel Beckett objected strongly to director JoAnne Akalaitis's decision to set his Endgame *in a decrepit subway station rather than in the "bare interior" he'd specified in his stage directions. This production featured Ben Halley, Jr.*

words outright. They are known as **writers for hire**. This means that instead of an individual writer owning her intellectual property, usually the Hollywood production company owns it and can hire other writers to change, rewrite, or rearrange the script however they see fit without the original writer's permission. Unlike the art of playwriting, which is dominated by solo writers who develop and own their words, Hollywood movies and television shows are often written by groups of writers who are hired to do the corporation's bidding and fired if they fail to measure up. Writers for hire are able to make considerably more money than playwrights. However, they usually make money by catering to the needs of the media conglomerates, not by sharing their own artistic visions of the world.

Unlike writers for hire, playwrights seldom make a living by writing plays. When a play is produced by a college or amateur theatre, the playwright might get as little as fifty dollars per performance. Professional productions often pay a percentage of the gross box-office take (5–10 percent is common), which can lead to payments of several hundred to several thousand dollars per week, but these payments only last for a matter of weeks—until the play closes. If a big Broadway theatre produces the play, payments can rival or exceed a Hollywood screenwriter's paycheck, but this is extremely rare. Often, less successful

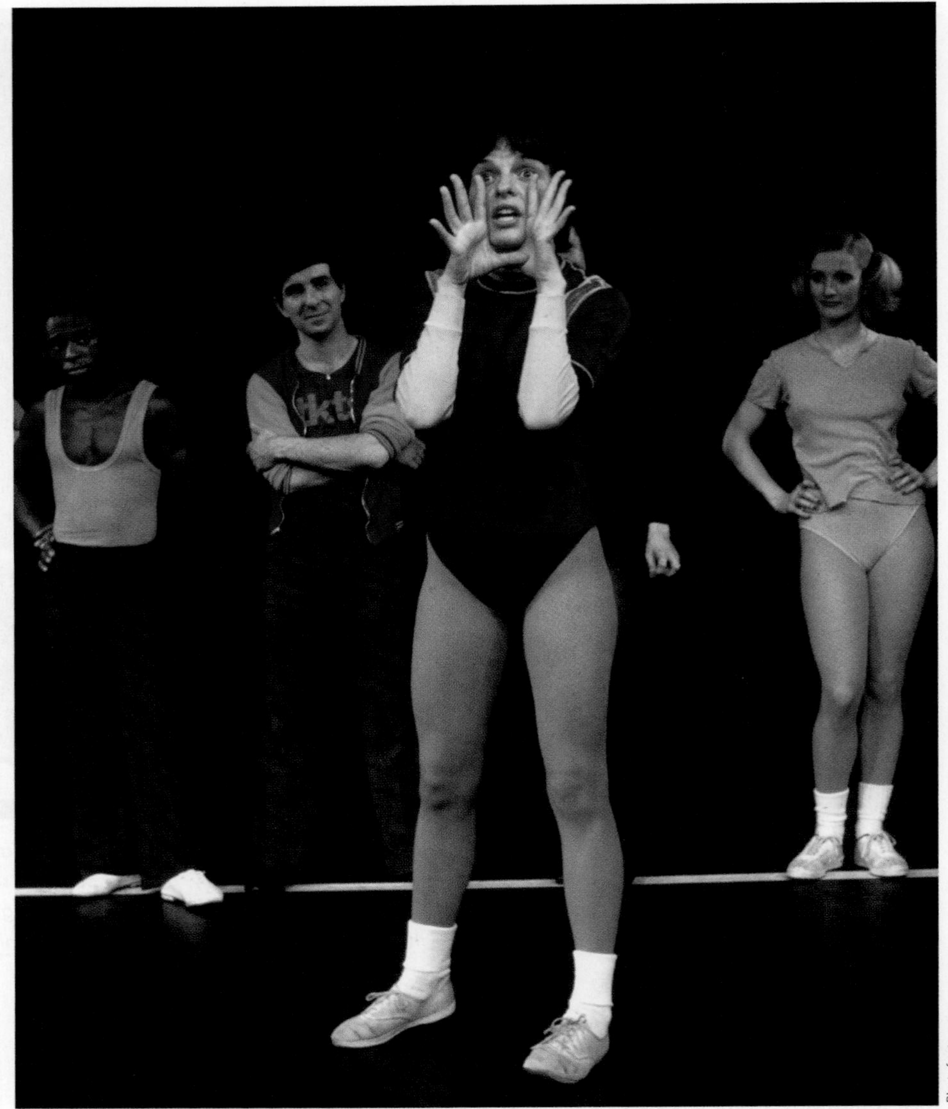

When a high school in Utah wanted to do the musical A Chorus Line, they decided to cut the gay character and rewrite some of the lyrics to please a more conservative audience. What they didn't take into account is that writers copyright their work, which means that no one is allowed to rewrite scripts without the copyright holder's permission. If the writer has been dead for fewer than seventy years, permission must be obtained to make any alterations. Pictured here is the cast of the original 1975 production of A Chorus Line.

playwrights agree to have their plays produced for no pay whatsoever in the hope of being discovered and therefore produced more regularly.

The playwright stands alone, has sole creative control of the script, and decides what can be changed. From the original idea to first draft to finished product, playwrights own their intellectual property. When you see a play, you are hearing the voice of the playwright, not of a committee. Emanuel Azenberg, the Broadway producer, said, "The wonderful thing about the theatre is the writer. Who writes a movie? The theatre is the writer's place." Unlike screenwriters, playwrights see their work produced as written. Unlike screenwriters, playwrights can be part of the total creative process, and unlike screenwriters, playwrights can know the joy that lies at the heart of authorship. When you see a play on stage, you are likely to be experiencing a story that is true to the author's voice rather than one that has been rewritten to please the audience, the producers, or a multinational corporation.

SPOTLIGHT ON Copyright Law: Infringement, Public Domain, and Parody

The copyright laws of the United States can be complicated and in some cases contradictory. But one thing is certain: copyright infringement is a real problem. Dan Glickman, the president of the Motion Picture Association of America, estimates that American companies lose around $18 billion worldwide every year because of copyright infringement. These losses include movies that are copied without permission, illegal downloading of songs, and TV shows that are aired without paying royalties.

Copyright infringement also includes altering copyrighted material without permission. For example, the company CleanFlicks took Hollywood movies and edited out all of the sex, violence, and nudity. They removed Kate Winslet's nude scene from the movie *Titanic*, for example, and eliminated all the violent moments from Jackie Chan's kung fu movies. Several Hollywood directors challenged CleanFlicks in court, saying that not only do these edits violate the integrity of their work but that they are also a violation of the copyright laws of the United States.

In the end, the court ruled in favor of the Hollywood directors, reaffirming that if you want to edit a movie for your own personal use, that is allowable under the fair use clause of the Copyright Act, which allows alterations to copyrighted material for teaching, news reporting, comment, scholarship, research, or criticism. However, if you turn around and sell or rent a movie that you've altered without the creator's permission, you are profiting from someone else's intellectual property and therefore breaking the law.

Another example of copyright infringement is a high school theatre group that decided to produce the musical *A Chorus Line*, but felt that some of the language (including the song "Dance Ten, Looks Three," a comic number about a dancer getting breast augmentation) was inappropriate, so the group rewrote it. In doing so, the high school had broken the copyright laws and was ordered to do the musical as written or close the show. The high school theatre group could write its own musical, but it couldn't alter a copyrighted musical and publicly perform it without permission.

One loophole in the copyright law that does allow alteration of copyrighted material is **parody**. Parodies are exaggerated imitations that are done for comic effect or political criticism. For example, the rap group 2 Live Crew rewrote the Roy Orbison song "Oh, Pretty Woman" without permission. In their parody, the pretty woman became a "bald-headed woman." The publishing company that held the copyright sued 2 Live Crew for copyright violation. The case went all the way to the Supreme Court, which ruled that parody is allowed under the fair use clause. This means that the high school in the previous example could have rewritten "Dance Ten, Looks Three" if it had been performing a parody of *A Chorus Line*. However, because the school chose to rewrite *A Chorus Line* with the intent of improving or altering the content rather than parodying the content, they broke the copyright owned by James Kirkwood, Jr., Nicholas Dante (book), Edward Kleban (lyrics), and Marvin Hamlisch (music).

A copyright only lasts the lifetime of the creator plus seventy years. This means that seventy years after the creator dies, the copyrighted material passes into the public domain and the copyright no longer applies. Songs, plays, pictures, etc. in the **public domain** are owned by the general public, and everyone has the right to produce or change them, without permission or payment to the creator. The plays of William Shakespeare (1564–1616) are in the public domain and can be produced free of charge and extensively rewritten or altered without permission.

Curtain Call

Far more separates theatre from screen entertainments than most people take into account. True, one is live and the other only "shadows on a screen," but those shadows have far more financial power and it's concentrated in only a few hands. The media moguls of massive corporations have a huge effect on

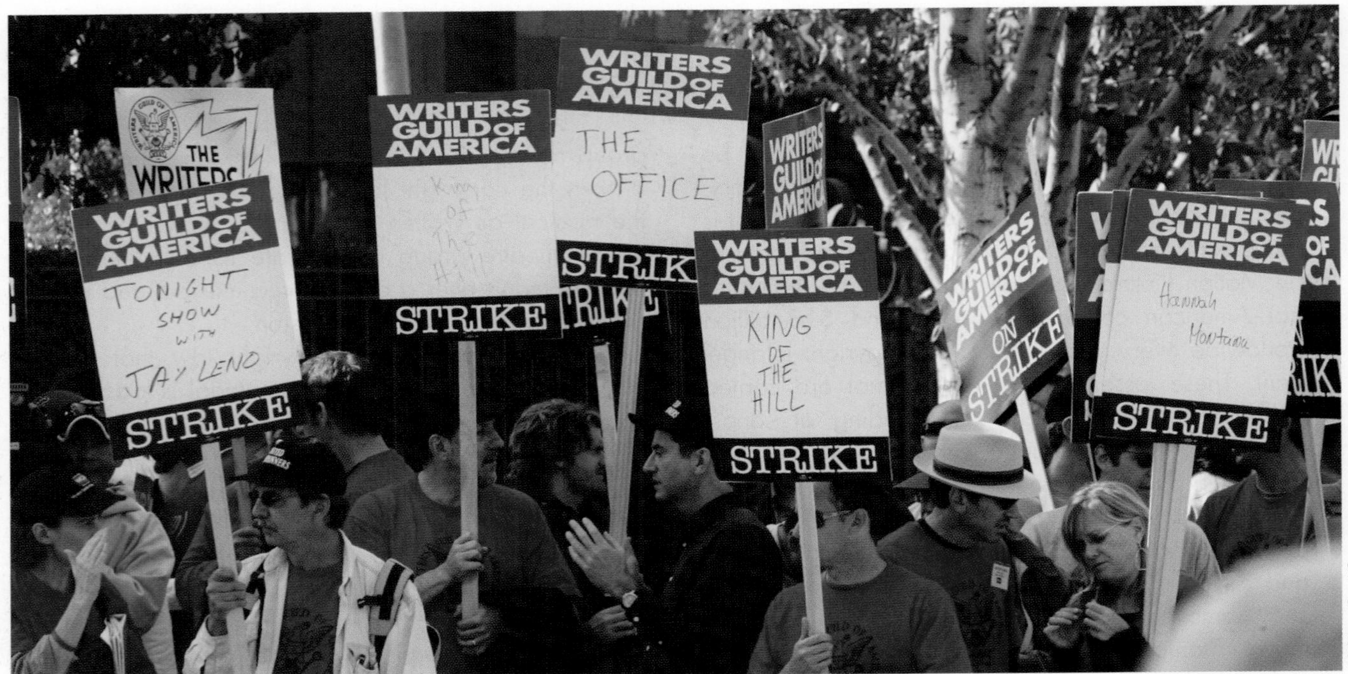

AP Photo/Reed Saxon

In late 2007, the 12,000-member Writers Guild of America (WGA) went on strike against the Alliance of Motion Picture and Television Producers (AMPTP), a trade organization representing the interests of the majority of American film and television producers. Unlike playwrights, screen and television writers have a closed shop union, which means they can band together and demand better wages.

our lives. Not only do they reflect our values more often than questioning them, which is problematic in itself, but they color their evening news programs, their newspapers, their movies, and their television shows with their corporate values or the values of other corporations that have the millions needed to buy air time.

This influence happens on several levels. Not only do corporations add their political points of view to the scripts, they also push their politics through their product advertisements. For example, major health care companies have hired agencies such as William Morris to help improve their image in television dramas and movies. These few media moguls have so much power they can influence laws in Washington, DC, and in foreign countries. They have driven legislation through Congress that increases their profits and makes them less accountable to the general public. And what do these huge corporations want from you, the audience? They want you to be good consumers. Theatres, by and large, seek to challenge you, not to make you "brand loyal."

The theatre is little, much smaller than it once was, but is it dying? Has it been defeated by the forms of screen entertainments that grew out of it during the early part of the last century? No. It is still very much alive, but its voice is a whisper compared to the roar of endless TV channels and megaplex cinemas. Yet, as long as it is funded and uncensored, sometimes a whisper can change the world.

Summary

There are many differences between screen entertainments and the theatre. In terms of societal impact, one of the most important is that theatre attracts a relatively small audience. A play can run on Broadway for thousands of performances and still not be seen by as many people as watch a popular television show on a single night. Another key difference between theatre and screen entertainments is that theatre is a live, relatively interactive medium. When you watch a movie or a TV show, communication flows only one way: from the screen to you. In contrast, when you watch a play, you and the actors share communication—you each have a direct influence on the other. This is why theatre is called a living art.

Because it is live, theatre is a risky business. Many unfortunate surprises can occur in a live setting, but the show still must go on. As such, stage actors usually need plenty of rehearsal time in order to avoid making mistakes during a performance. Often, they also must be skilled in singing and dancing as well as acting. In contrast, screen actors are provided a safety net in the form of multiple takes, dubbing if they can't sing, and editing if they're not talented dancers.

In film, directors often have a lot of power and can directly influence what the audience will see. They control many aspects of the movie-making process because they can rewrite a script, influence the actors' performances, and dictate the editing of a movie. Stage directors usually do not have as much power or control. Because playwrights copyright their work, directors must obtain the playwright's permission to change a script, unless it is in the public domain. In addition, directors can do nothing to control the actors' performances once the curtain goes up on a performance. Similarly, directors of television programs have limited power over a production and are sometimes even subservient to the writers.

Theatre and screen entertainments also differ in how they are funded and in how profitable they are. Screen entertainments are often controlled by mega-corporations that expect their products—movies and TV programs—to make a profit. To help ensure that these products are profitable, corporations use test audiences to make sure movies and TV shows are appealing and entertaining. These mega-corporations export American entertainment all around the world, open movies in dozens of theatres at once to maximize ticket sales, sell movies to home audiences in the form of DVDs, and sell movie rights to lucrative overseas markets. Although some blockbuster plays and musicals turn a profit, many theatres cannot rely on ticket sales to cover the many costs of putting on a production. Consequently, most theatres seek additional funding from individual patrons, corporations, and government agencies (such as the National Endowment for the Arts) in order to make ends meet. Yet, because theatre is often locally controlled and funded, it can often present a wider diversity of subject matter and ideas than screen entertainments do.

The Art of Theatre ONLINE

To access this chapter's interactive theatre workshop activities, along with many other learning tools, log onto your Theatre CourseMate. Access is available at cengagebrain.com.

Key Terms

bourgeois theatre / 39
copyright / 44
corporate funding / 34
government funding / 37
National Endowment for the Arts (NEA) / 37
parody / 47
patrons / 34
public domain / 47
royalty payment / 44
writers for hire / 45

Top Girls, written by Caryl Churchill, directed by Casey Stangl, Guthrie Lab, 2003, featuring (l to r) Bianca Amato, Eunice Wong, and Sally Wingert. (The inset features Eunice Wong.) This play depicts the challenges working women face in the contemporary business world and society at large.

Photos on this spread Michal Daniel/Proofsheet

CHAPTER 3

Theatre and Cultural Diversity

OUTLINE

We've all heard the age-old philosophical question "If a tree falls in the forest and no one is around to hear it, does it make a sound?" Philosophers have argued over this question for centuries, but substitute the theatre for the tree and the argument becomes moot: If a play is performed and no one attends it, then the play has no effect on society, provides no entertainment, and makes no statement. In order for theatre—or, for that matter, communication—to take place, there must be someone to express an idea and someone to respond. In short, even if you have the ability and the freedom to speak, you don't have a voice in the political, social, or cultural arena unless someone can hear you.

Though we often think of theatre in terms of stars and spotlights, this chapter will focus on the **theatre of the people**, where there are few stars or spotlights. This type of theatre provides a forum for everyday people to express themselves; it gives a voice to those who are seldom heard in the mainstream media. This goal is possible because of the very characteristics that distinguish theatre from television and film entertainments: at its most basic, theatre can be relatively low-tech, so it can be done anywhere, anytime, and at a low cost. Expensive lights, costumes, sets, and professional actors are *optional*. Additionally, local organizations often control theatre at the regional level, which means that theatre can represent the concerns of the *people*, not the government, the powers that be, or multinational media corporations. (See the Spotlight "Could Technology Create a Cultural Divide?") In this chapter we will explore theatre that gives a voice to the voiceless.

Critical Mirror: Art and Entertainment Reflect Culture

> We're all grappling with this idea of entertainment versus intellectual complexity. How can we introduce new forms and ideas to an audience that has a shorter attention span and is increasingly dominated by a need for the familiar? It's our job as leaders to fight this trend when we can and to articulate how we rub up against the values of the dominant culture.
>
> ***Tony Taccone,***
> Artistic director of Berkeley Repertory Theatre

The word *culture* often pops up in our society. Our newspapers and television are filled with references to culture wars, multiculturalism, counterculture, pop culture, cultural relativism, and corporate culture. **Culture** is composed of the values, standards, and patterns of behavior of a particular group of people. It can include habits, traditions, languages, prejudices, superstitions, religions, rituals, customs, preferences, manners, assumptions, and lifestyle—anything that affects a group of people's particular way of thinking about the world. We all come from a culture and yet we are not always aware of it, particularly if we come from the dominant culture. Only when our culture is celebrated, denied, or contrasted with another culture do we become conscious of how much it affects our daily lives.

We are not born with cultural knowledge. We learn about our culture by watching and imitating the behaviors of others and listening to their stories. The process by which we learn about our culture is called **enculturation**. Throughout history and in many societies, art and entertainment have often been sources of enculturation; they are tools for demonstrating culture.

> I wrote my first play, *Uncommon Women and Others*, in the hopes of seeing an all-female curtain call in the basement of the Yale School of Drama. A man in the audience stood up during a post-show discussion and announced, "I can't get into this. It's about girls." I thought to myself, "Well, I've been getting into *Hamlet* and *Lawrence of Arabia* my whole life, so you better start trying."
>
> ***Wendy Wasserstein,***
> Playwright

Sometimes art and entertainment can suggest change rather than simply reflect existing culture. For example, in 1965 African American playwright Douglas Turner Ward (b. 1930) wrote the play *Day of Absence*, about a small town from which all the black people suddenly disappear. The play satirizes the dominant culture of the day by depicting the white characters as suddenly adrift because they have no one to wash their clothes, take out the trash, and clean their yards. This biting satire did not support enculturation. Instead, it questioned the dominant culture of 1965 and helped change how Americans thought about race. More recently, the movie *A Day without a Mexican* (2004) considers what might happen if one day all the Latinos disappear from California. As the movie progresses, the state begins to deteriorate and it becomes apparent that the "California dream" is fueled in large part by Latino domestics, gardeners, farm and construction workers, athletes, and professionals. This movie makes the point that *all* cultures, not just the dominant culture, contribute to the well-being of a society.

SPOTLIGHT ON Could Technology Create a Cultural Divide?

In his book *Art, Inc.*, Bill Ivey, former head of the National Endowment of the Arts, writes that there is a new division in American Society between those who have access to cultural diversity and those who do not. Today the vast majority of our "culture" is provided to us by digital media through massive multinational corporations, which means you have to pay for it. If you do not have the funds you may be limited to standard cable, fewer books, no newspapers, only big budget mainstream Hollywood movies, and consequently miss out on the wealth of information and experiences available. This *digital divide* may also cause a cultural divide because the more money you have, the more access you have to experiences unlike your own. You might say that the Internet contains all the information anyone could ever need about cultural diversity, but in order to use that information you must be aware of its existence and seek it out. When few people are exposed to such information, or cannot afford access to it, few seek it out.

You might also say that money has always been a factor between the haves and the have-nots. The wealthy can buy better homes, safer cars, better educations, and expose themselves to more cultural diversity. But when it is cultural information that people do not have access to, the divide is not only a dilemma on a personal level but also on the national: the very idea of democracy calls for people with diverse points of view to work together and understand each other. Individuals with little access to information outlets such as the Internet often have limited access to cultural information. Bill Ivey writes, "Armed with state-of-the art equipment, adequate time, and an ability to pay through the nose for high-speed access, the savvy few can find their way to more and more choices (although they often land variations of what the search engine thinks it knows they already like). But for those who get their television over the air, who shop at Wal-Mart (not online), see blockbuster films at the Multiplex, and listen to Clear Channel–owned radio in the car, the options are increasingly bleak and seem to be getting worse."

While it is possible to see cultural programming on television, often such shows are not included in basic cable. Because of this many Americans are not exposed to films like *When the Levees Broke*, Spike Lee's take on the Katrina disaster, or *Angels in America*, Tony Kushner's political epic about the AIDS crisis during the mid-eighties, or alternative sources for news and entertainment. In his book *Four Arguments for the Elimination of Television*, Jerry Mander writes that television is not democratic: "There are still no poor people running television, no Indians, no ecologists, no political radicals, no Zen Buddhists, no factory workers, no revolutionaries, no artists, no communists, no Luddites, no hippies, no botanists, to name only a few excluded groups."

The theatre (along with PBS and the NEA) can be a way to give a voice to those whose ideas about life, liberty, happiness, family, economics, and society are seldom heard in the mainstream media. But these are lonely voices in a world where true understanding of cultural diversity takes time and money. We are only now beginning to understand the consequences of this digital divide.

LWA/ Dann Tardif/Getty Images

Could digital media be causing a cultural divide between those who can afford access and those who cannot?

More often, though, art and entertainment reflect the voice of the dominant culture. In its long history, theatre has not always given a voice to all people or reflected the many cultures in any society. Instead it has generally been controlled by the dominant culture: those in power, members of the upper class, government, religious institutions, and, in particular, men. For thousands of years, the dominant culture has controlled playwriting, directing, design, and acting through racism, sexism, discrimination, economic power, and social and religious customs. Throughout the centuries, women and minority racial and ethnic groups have usually been forced to stand on the sidelines. During most of Western and Eastern theatre history, not only was it considered improper for religious, social, or cultural reasons for women to write plays, but women were also not allowed to set foot on stage. Instead, men and boys played women's roles in drag. In England a few centuries ago, women were arrested for participating in theatre productions. In 1611, Mary Frith was arrested for acting on a public stage in London and charged with, among other things, "swearing & cursing & . . . usually associat[ing] her selfe [*sic*] with Ruffinly swaggering & lewd company." Today in the west there are still more parts written for male characters than there are females.

With few exceptions, female playwrights were not part of the theatre until just three hundred years ago. Even in our time, males dominate the art. The most recent numbers show that women write only about one out of every five

As they get older, most women in Hollywood struggle to find substantial and interesting movie roles, whereas men are offered leading roles even into their sixties and seventies. Women also struggle to find directing jobs—in 2004, women directed only four of the top one hundred Hollywood films. Many older women turn to the stage or independent movies, such as Titus, *directed by Julie Taymor and starring Jessica Lange in the lead role of Tamora. Older women are having greater success as movie executives. In 2005 women held top creative decision-making roles in four of the six top studios, including Universal, Paramount, Sony, and Buena Vista.*

plays today. And women of color write only about one out of every fifty plays. The numbers are not much better in Hollywood. Martha Lauzen, a professor of communication at San Diego State University, found that the number of women working as directors, writers, producers, and editors in Hollywood is only about 15 to 16 percent. She estimated that the number of female studio executives is around 20 percent. According to the Writers Guild of America, male writers outnumber female writers in Hollywood by about five to one in feature film and by four to one in television. In addition, only 4 percent of Hollywood writers are minorities.

Theatre of the people attempts to correct the biases and address the stereotypes, rather than simply reflecting the dominant culture. Let's take a closer look at this forum for people traditionally left out of the mainstream.

AP Photo/ Reed Saxon

In Hollywood only 25 percent of screenwriters and 20 percent of executive producers are women. A few of these female executive producers are Lynda Obit, Wendy Finerman, Amy Pascal, Jana Sue Memel, Denise Di Novi, Paula Wagner, and Kathleen Kennedy. Pictured here with Christine Lahti is Jana Sue Memel (right), who produced the Oscar-winning short movie Lieberman in Love. *She has also produced dozens of movies and television shows.*

Theatre Outside the Dominant Culture

The purpose of the theatre of the people is to promote cultural awareness by giving a voice to all members of society and by increasing multiculturalism. **Multiculturalism** is the endeavor to overcome all forms of discrimination, including racism, sexism, and homophobia, so that people can coexist peacefully and attempt to achieve a pluralistic society. One of the fundamental conflicts of human existence is the difference between how we perceive ourselves and how others perceive us. Whether at the individual, group, or national level, we have a basic view of who we are and spend a great deal of time trying to convince others that our self-perceptions are correct. We demand that others understand us, but we seldom take time to understand others. Instead, we often view others as stereotypes. **Stereotypes** are shortcuts in thinking that attribute a generalized identity to people who are not like us. In the United States stereotyped characters include Mexican bandits, bigoted Southern sheriffs, Korean grocers, drunken Indians, and dumb blondes. Stereotypes tend to diminish when communication among groups, races, and cultures increases.

The theatre of the people attempts to increase communication by celebrating our differences, by highlighting our similarities, and by allowing everyone a voice. There are three basic types of theatre of the people:

- *Theatre of identity* promotes a particular people's cultural identity and invites members of that culture and other cultures to experience that culture's joys, problems, history, traditions, and point of view.
- *Theatre of protest* objects to the dominant culture's control and demands that a minority culture's voice and political agenda be heard.
- *Cross-cultural theatre* mixes different cultures in an attempt to find understanding or commonality among them.

Of course, these types of theatre are not always separate. One play can include the characteristics of more than one type of theatre of the people.

> If there's specific resistance to women making movies, I just choose to ignore that as an obstacle for two reasons: I can't change my gender, and I refuse to stop making movies.
>
> ***Kathryn Bigelow,***
> Oscar winning director

Theatre of Identity

Theatre of identity promotes a particular people's awareness of themselves and their experiences, traditions, and culture. The plays of theatre of identity are written by members of a particular culture and staged by actors from that culture. This type of theatre gives a voice to a people and encourages audience members to reflect on, analyze, or reinvent their own self-perceptions. It gives a voice to groups that the dominant culture ignores or silences. This type of theatre is not closed to outsiders. On the contrary, theatre of identity often welcomes people of other cultures even though they might not completely understand the sensibility in these productions. Theatre of identity can present sugar-coated images of a culture, but it can also feature that culture's defeats and regrets. Images of imperfections are meant to strengthen the bonds of the community as it gives audience members of that culture a self-definition not available from the dominant culture. Cultural identity plays are performed in streets and small theatres in China, India, Latin America, Poland, and Nigeria—anywhere there are people who do not have a voice but have enough freedom to gather and form an audience. You'll read more about world theatre in Part 3. In this chapter, we'll focus on American theatre.

Theatre of Identity allows us to learn about various people's traditions, culture and experiences. This rendition of The Wizard of Oz *was produced by PHAMALY, The Physically Handicapped Actors & Musical Artists League*

In the United States, the theatre of identity grew out of the wide variety of traditions that make up our diverse population. People fleeing the French Revolution in 1789 started the French American theatre. One of the first African American theatres was founded in New York City in 1821, and some Spanish-language theatres were acquired with the conquest of the Southwest. In the 1800s German, Polish, Chinese, Norwegian, and Swedish theatres were founded across the country. These theatres reached their peak in the opening decades of the twentieth century, providing art and entertainment for millions of new immigrants whose cultural and language differences, as well as outright discrimination, kept them out of mainstream American life. By the 1900s Finns in Oregon had the Astoria Socialist Theatre; Italians in San Francisco had their own theatre; and in New York City, Second Avenue was known as the **"Yiddish Broadway"** because so many Jewish theatres were located there. The first half of the twentieth century was also a time when the absence of plays written by women playwrights began to be corrected. Zona Gale (1874–1938), Georgia Douglas Johnson (1880–1966), Susan Glaspell (1876–1948), Edna Ferber (1885–1968), Ruth Gordon (1896–1985), Lillian Hellman (1905–1984), and many others were writing plays that presented women as successful scientists, businesspeople, legislators, and screenwriters who dealt with or fought against the male-dominated culture.

Hulton Archive/Getty Images

The Second Avenue Theatre is one of the theatres in New York City that featured Yiddish plays in the early part of the twentieth century. There were so many of these theatres on Second Avenue that the area became known as the "Yiddish Broadway." Initially many of these theatres premiered European Yiddish works that appealed to New York's many Jewish immigrants. Later they featured new works based on the Jewish experience in America.

One of the strongest forms of theatre of identity in the United States is that of black Americans. Theatre performed by African Americans has been around for hundreds of years, but legitimate plays written by blacks, about blacks, and for blacks were rare until the twentieth century. Before that, black characters were mainly stereotypes written by whites and even performed by whites. (See the Spotlight "Blackface, Redface, Yellowface.")

Willis Richardson (1889–1977) was the first black playwright to have a play on Broadway that was not a musical; his play *The Chip Woman's Fortune* appeared in 1923. Richardson went on to write about black historical heroes including Crispus Attucks, who was killed in the Boston Massacre; Alexandre Dumas *père*, the biracial French playwright; and biblical characters such as Simon the Cyrenian, who carried the cross for Jesus. Richardson felt that too many plays by black writers were only about how black people were treated by whites. He said, "Still there is another kind of play: the kind that shows the soul of a people; and the soul of this people is truly worth showing." A few years later, in 1926, poet Langston Hughes said, "We younger Negro artists now intend to express our dark-skinned selves without fear or shame. If white people are pleased, we are glad. If they are not, it doesn't matter. We know we are beautiful. And ugly too." This comment summarized the black struggle for artistic independence that took place during the 1920s and 1930s, in the period known as the **Harlem Renaissance**. This was a time when black artists, actors, poets, musicians, and writers converged in Harlem to tell the stories of their lives, their history, and their people, contrary to white stereotypes of blacks.

SPOTLIGHT ON Blackface, Redface, Yellowface

For most of U.S. theatre and film history, blacks, Native Americans, and Asians were discriminated against and even banned from appearing on stage or in films. As a result, whites played "ethnic" characters by wearing heavy makeup, which led to one of the most bizarre forms of theatre: the **minstrel show**. Minstrel shows originated in the nineteenth century and lasted well into the twentieth. These performances contained comic scenes, dance interludes, and sentimental ballads, all based on white people's perceptions of black life in the South. Black music was popular, but it was considered improper for whites to go to a theatre to hear black musicians, so whites would put on black makeup, called **blackface**, and perform as black people. Minstrel shows often contained skits with illiterate and foolish exchanges that made fun of blacks. Blacks did not attend minstrel shows; they were entertainment for white people only.

For many years in Hollywood films, it was considered acceptable for whites to play blacks as well as Native Americans and Asians. The first talking picture, *The Jazz Singer*, was about a Jewish boy (Al Jolson) who becomes a jazz singer. In the movie's final scene he performs in blackface in a minstrel show. In the 1950s, whites playing blacks finally fell out of favor, but the tradition of whites playing Asians and Native Americans continued into the 1970s; for example, David Carradine played the lead in the TV show *Kung Fu*. Katharine Hepburn, Fred Astaire, John Wayne, and Marlon Brando are some of the stars who played Asian roles in Hollywood films.

White domination of ethnic roles was challenged when the British producer Cameron Mackintosh (*Cats, Phantom of the Opera*) announced that the white British actor Jonathan Pryce was going to play the Asian male lead on Broadway in the hit musical *Miss Saigon*. Asian actors protested that they weren't even given a chance to audition. Actor B. D. Wong said, "If Asian American actors aren't good enough to play Asian roles, what are we good for?" At first, the actors' union protested. Asian actors announced that they would not allow "taped eyelids and yellowface" on a white actor. But when Mackintosh threatened to cancel the production, throwing many actors out of work, the union backed down. In the end, Pryce played the role, but he did not wear the eye prosthetics he had worn when he played the role in London. After he left the show, an Asian actor took over the part.

Is it right for whites to play blacks, or for Filipinos to play Chinese, or for Jews to play Italians? (The practice of casting actors regardless of their race is called *color-blind casting*. For more on this topic, see Chapter 8.) The actors' union said, "Jews have always been able to play Italians, Italians have always been able to play Jews, and both have been able to play Asians. Asian actors, however, almost never have the opportunity to play either Jews or Italians and continue to struggle even to play themselves." As recently as 1995, a book on stage makeup listed "ethnic appearances" including "Caucasian to Oriental" and "Caucasian to Indian," complete with before-and-after photos of a young white model made up to look like Fu Manchu. White to black makeup was not included. Today, the question remains: should the theatre be color-blind or color-conscious?

Joan Marcus/Photofest

British actor Jonathan Pryce originated the Asian lead role in the London run of the musical Miss Saigon. *His casting caused controversy when the play transferred to the United States, where the Actor's Equity union initially refused to allow Pryce to continue in the part because "it would be an affront to the Asian community." After pressure from the play's producer, Pryce joined the Broadway production. However, he agreed to perform without the eye makeup he had used in London to appear Asian.*

During the civil rights movement of the late 1950s and 1960s, theatre of identity continued to grow. In 1959, Lorraine Hansberry (1930–1965) became the first black woman playwright to be produced on Broadway. It would take another twenty-five years for another African American playwright to succeed on Broadway. However, black playwrights, although they were still locked out of the mainstream commercial theatre, were finding a voice. Some of these playwrights were Amiri Baraka (b. 1934), whose *The Slave* (1965) deals with an interracial couple; Adrienne Kennedy (b. 1931), whose *Funnyhouse of a Negro* (1964) focuses on the human unconscious and the search for meaning and truth; and Douglas Turner Ward, whose *Day of Absence* mocks minstrel shows by having a black cast dress up in whiteface and play white characters.

By 1968 there were forty black theatre companies in the United States, and twenty years later there were more than two hundred. However, many of these theatres struggle for funding because their major purpose, unlike the mainstream commercial theatre, is not to make money but rather to promote cultural awareness and tolerance. Some of the plays created by these influential theatres have even become mainstream Hollywood movies: *The River Niger* (1976), which starred James Earl Jones; *Ceremonies in Dark Old Men* (1975) with Glynn Turman; and Charles Fuller's Pulitzer Prize–winning *A Soldier's Play* (1981), which became the movie *A Soldier's Story* (1984) with Adolph Caesar and Denzel Washington.

Today, perhaps no two playwrights represent the growing diversity of the American theatre scene more than August Wilson (1945–2005) and Suzan-Lori Parks (b. 1964). Wilson grew up in the Hill District of Pittsburgh, Pennsylvania. He left school after daily barrages of racial epithets. Rather than tell his mother that he had dropped out, Wilson spent his youth at the public library, where he gave himself an education. In 1984 he had his first big writing success with *Ma Rainey's Black Bottom*, a play about black musicians struggling with their white bosses in the 1920s. The play was first produced by the Yale Repertory Theatre and later on Broadway. His second play, *Fences*, opened on Broadway in 1987. It was set in the 1950s and tells the story of Troy Maxon, a garbage collector who has become embittered by the white-controlled system that has denied him the

> We have never said that white reviewers cannot understand black theatre—if you can understand Duke Ellington and Ray Charles, you can understand black theatre.
>
> ***August Wilson,***
> Playwright

> We're not beyond race in this country. We have a lot to learn about existing in a very colorful society.
>
> ***Tisa Chang,***
> Founder of the Pan Asian Repertory Theater

Don Ipock Photography/Kansas City Repertory Theatre

August Wilson's Two Trains Running *uses sharp-edged humor and cutting social analysis to reveal the conflicts that African Americans face. Set in Pittsburgh in 1969 after the assassinations of Martin Luther King, Jr., and Malcolm X, the characters find themselves at a crossroads as they try to come to terms with their pasts and find self-respect in an inequitable world. This 2005 production featuring (l to r) Adolphus Ward, E. Milton Wheeler, James A. Williams, and Erika LaVonn was directed by Lou Bellamy at the Kansas City Repertory Theatre.*

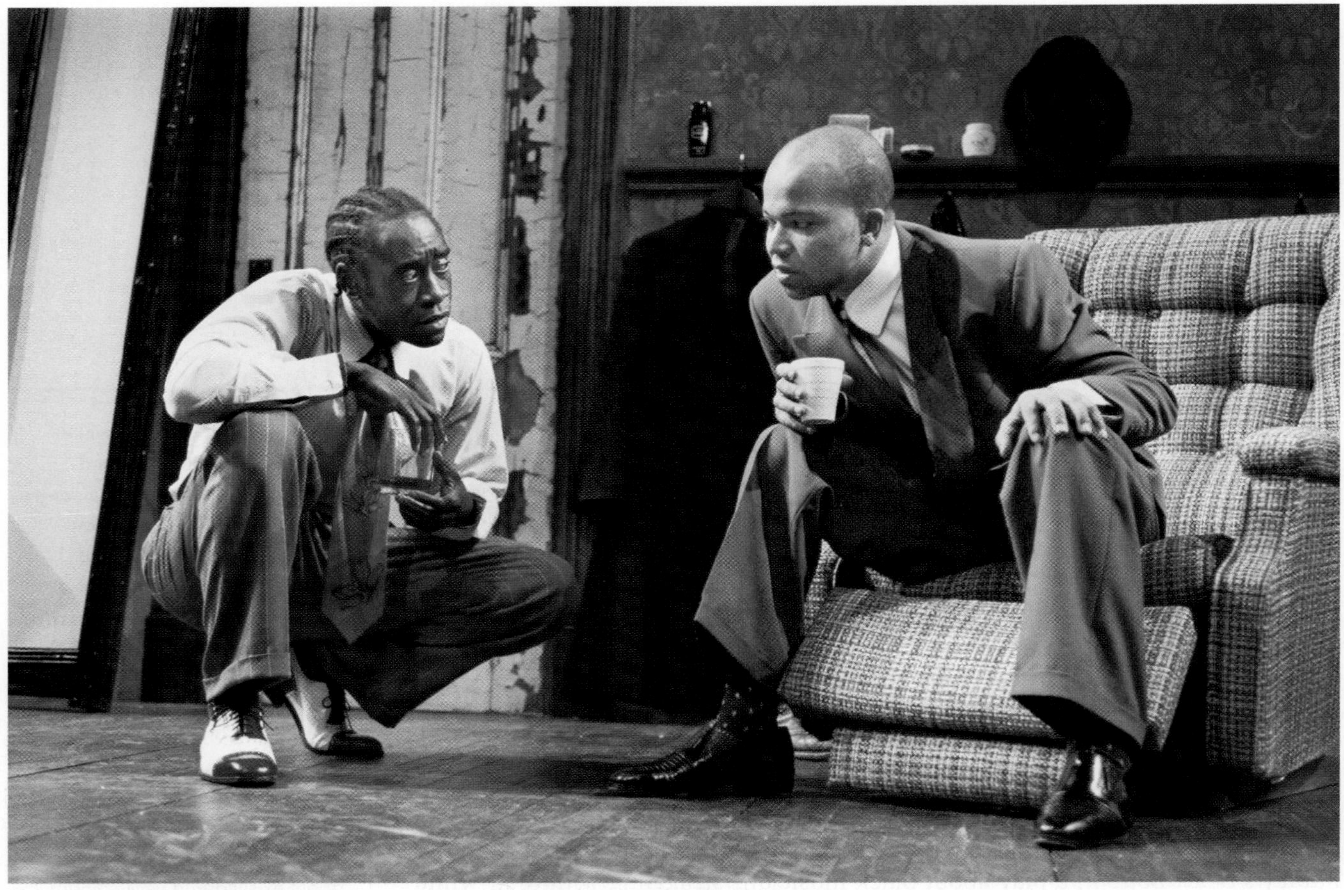

Michal Daniel/Proofsheet

Topdog/Underdog by Suzan-Lori Parks is the dark comic tale of two brothers who vie with each other to come out on top. The brothers, named Lincoln and Booth by their father as a joke, experience an intense sibling rivalry and come to understand their shared history only through their obsession with the con game three-card monte. This 2001 Off-Broadway production featured Don Cheadle as Booth and Jeffrey Wright as Lincoln and was directed by George C. Wolfe at the Public Theatre in New York.

baseball stardom he feels he deserves. For this play, Wilson won the Pulitzer Prize. The following year he returned to Broadway with *Joe Turner's Come and Gone*, the story of a black man who was unjustly imprisoned in 1910. Then came *The Piano Lesson*. Set in the 1930s, it is the story of a man who wants to buy the land in Mississippi where his ancestors once worked as slaves. But in order to raise the money, he must sell the family heirloom, a piano. This play earned Wilson his second Pulitzer Prize for Drama. In Wilson's plays the white world is a major character but remains almost entirely offstage. Wilson said, "Blacks know the spiritual truth of white America. We are living examples of America's hypocrisy. We know white America better than white America knows us."

Suzan-Lori Parks represents a generation of playwrights who are not waiting for the mainstream commercial theatre or the dominant culture to recognize their plays. Born in Fort Knox, Kentucky, she lived the transient childhood of an "Army brat." This allowed her to experience many different worlds, but friendships were hard to maintain, so she entertained herself by staging puppet shows. Her life changed when she took a creative writing class from James Baldwin, who suggested that she was a natural playwright. After graduating from college with degrees in English and German literature, she moved to New York and started staging her own plays wherever she could find an empty space. Once, when she couldn't find a stage, she even used a garage at a gas station. To those who run into barriers she says, "To get a play done, you go to a place and do it, or you work your day job and then you do a play; you produce it yourself." Within a few years, she had graduated from garages to such notable theatres as the Public Theatre in New York City and the Arena Stage in Washington, DC, and in 2001 her play *Topdog/Underdog* was produced on Broadway. A dark comedy about sibling rivalry between two brothers, Lincoln and Booth, *Topdog/Underdog* deals with oppressive systems within society. With this play, Parks became the first African American woman to win the Pulitzer. Parks succinctly summed up the ideas behind theatre of identity when she said, "I know where I am and who I am and what I do."

Theatre of Protest

The second type of theatre of the people could be called theatre of social agenda or theatre of militancy, because its purpose is protest and change. **Theatre of protest** vents hostility toward the ruling class, race, or culture. Protest plays date back to the ancient Greeks. For example, Aristophanes' comedy *Lysistrata* (411 BCE) is often called the first anti-war play. Twenty-four hundred years later, similar anti-war plays were produced during the 1960s and early 1970s as American students demonstrated against inequality and the Vietnam War. The French director Antonin Artaud (1896–1948) summed up the purpose of protest plays when he said, "The action of theatre, like that of plague, is beneficial, for, impelling men to see themselves as they are, it causes the mask to fall, reveals the lie, the slackness, baseness, and hypocrisy of our world." In other words, this type of theatre isn't presented to entertain but rather to demand justice.

One such theatre is El Teatro Campesino ("farmworkers' theatre"), founded in 1965 by Luis Valdez (b. 1940). Spanish-speaking theatre has existed in America since the late sixteenth century, but El Teatro Campesino became a new type of theatre that did more than celebrate Latino culture—it protested social injustice. Valdez and his theatre improvised plays to support Filipino and Chicano migrant farmworkers who, led by Cesar Chavez (1927–1993), were on strike against California grape growers. Performed on the backs of flatbed trucks, these plays were often cast with striking workers, which narrowed the line between performer and audience and made audience participation critical. The dialogue in *The Conscience of a Scab* and other plays was drawn from real conflicts the strikers experienced. The stories focused on the strikers' meager pay and poor working conditions, highlighting the oppressions perpetrated by the white growers. Valdez went on to write plays that addressed not only immediate local issues but also cultural identity and national issues. He has written about members of the Chicano community who deny their heritage as they attempt to blend into the American melting pot and has attacked Mexican stereotypes found in mainstream theatre, television, and film. He has

Luis Valdez's play Zoot Suit dramatizes the powerful racial tensions of 1940s Los Angeles. Shown here is Edward James Olmos playing the part of El Pachuco in a 1979 production of the play, directed by Valdez at the Winter Garden Theatre in New York. The first Mexican American playwright to be produced on Broadway, Valdez observed that "until we [Mexican Americans] had the artists who could express what the people were feeling and saying, we wouldn't really register politically. Art gives us the tools of that expression."

written that El Teatro Campesino's purposes are to "replace the lingering negative stereotype of the Mexican in the United States with a new positive image created through Chicano art, and to continue to dramatize the social despair of Chicanos living in an Anglo-dominated society."

Valdez's most famous play is *Zoot Suit* (1978), which is based on the Sleepy Lagoon murder trial and the famous Zoot Suit Riots, now often called the Sailor Riots. These riots occurred when American military personnel claimed that Mexicans wearing zoot suits had attacked them while they were on leave in Los Angeles during World War II. (A "zoot" is a flamboyant suit with wide lapels and oversized pleated pants popular among Mexican American youth in the 1940s.) In response to the allegation, more than two hundred uniformed white sailors stormed into the heart of the Mexican American community in East Los Angeles and attacked anyone wearing a zoot suit. The police did nothing to stop the sailors' riot. After several days of rioting, when the Navy feared it had a mutiny on its hands, military authorities finally took steps to end the melee. None of the sailors were ever prosecuted, but many of the Zoot Suiters were.

> We are a lot more varied, as a country, than we like to pretend to be. I mean, we give sort of a nodding recognition that the country is multiracial, for instance, but do not do a lot to really integrate, in a cultural-artistic sense, the real currents that flow in this country. That sort of thing has to happen of itself through the daily life of the people, through the daily cultural life.
>
> ***Luis Valdez,***
> Playwright

Zoot Suit takes place in front of a giant newspaper that serves as a drop curtain. The headline reads "Zoot Suiter Hordes Invade Los Angeles. U.S. Navy and Marines Are Called In." The newspaper's fallacious headline becomes a symbol of Anglo racism. The play tells the story of Chicano consciousness and cultural survival in a country in which racism and violence are advocated by the press and the state. *Zoot Suit* ran for more than eleven months in Los Angeles. It was also the first Chicano play to be produced on Broadway, and Valdez was the first Mexican American to direct on Broadway. Since *Zoot Suit*, Valdez has gone on to write many more plays and direct popular movies including *La Bamba* (1987).

Another example of theatre of protest is the modern performance art of Karen Finley (b. 1956), who tours the country performing one-woman plays about sexual abuse, violence against women, prejudice, censorship, AIDS, suicide, and the male domination of politics. Her most notorious piece, *We Keep Our Victims Ready* (1989), satirizes national events, questions the definition of obscenity, and confronts the dehumanization of women that reduces them to sexual objects. She also attacks the idea of a sole deity whose image is masculine, monolithic, and absolute, which she says results in a masculine-dominated society. Her performance includes a scene where she covers her naked body in chocolate and yams, almost like a tar-and-feathering, in order to symbolize the bruising abuse women suffer in our society. Taken out of context, these symbolic acts earned her the epithet "the chocolate-smeared woman." But Finley says, "My critics are people like Jesse Helms. The attacks don't come from people who have actually seen my work." Those who have seen her work, such as critics from the *New York Times*, praise her "highly visceral, startling monologues" in which she confronts pressing social issues. Theatre of protest is often censored or marginalized by the dominant culture, which doesn't want its views or traditions questioned. Such was the case when Finley was denied a grant from the National Endowment for the Arts because of what the head of the NEA called "certain political realities." Finley took her fight all the way to the Supreme Court. (See the Spotlight "Diverse Beliefs and Values: Karen Finley and the NEA.")

> The National Endowment for the Arts was funding work by those who were once rendered invisible by economic, ethnic, or gender differences. What previously had been a private, almost sequestered world, existing only within academia or in galleries, became public. People who had never had the same access that white, middle- or upper-class men have traditionally had were suddenly given means to create.
>
> ***Karen Finley,***
> Performance artist

Cross-Cultural Theatre

Cross-cultural theatre borrows contrasting ideas from diverse cultures and joins them into a single work. At its most basic, cross-cultural plays borrow staging

SPOTLIGHT ON Diverse Beliefs and Values: Karen Finley and the NEA

In the last few years several complaints have been lodged against the National Endowment for the Arts (NEA) concerning the social and moral concepts behind the works of art it funds. (For more on the NEA, see Chapter 2.) With all the controversy, one might think that thousands of so-called questionable or obscene works of art must have been funded with federal tax dollars. But the truth is that fewer than fifty out of 140,000 works of art funded over thirty years have received complaints. Compare this to American television, which through the FCC (Federal Communications Commission) has received as many as one million complaints in a single year. Why would so few works of art—including Karen Finley's *We Keep Our Victims Ready*—cause such a stir? In his book *Culture Wars*, artist and writer Richard Bolton points out that many believe that artists are trying to introduce a progressive agenda into society, "an agenda based upon multiculturalism, gay and lesbian rights, feminism, and sexual liberation" that is intended to destroy traditional American values. Somehow this "objectionable" handful of artistic projects funded by the NEA—less than 0.1 percent of all the projects it has ever funded—is seen as a serious threat to the power structure of the United States.

In the 1990s Senator Jesse Helms tried to stop this "progressive agenda" with a law stating that every art grant given by the NEA has to take into consideration the general standards of "decency and respect for the diverse beliefs and values of the American public." Some said that the new law, when properly interpreted, had no practical effect. Others felt it was a far-reaching attack on the First Amendment's guarantee of freedom of speech. Finley, who was denied an NEA grant under the new law, immediately challenged the law in court. She felt that it discriminated against nontraditional artworks and that the "diverse beliefs and values" clause unconstitutionally suppressed ideas that challenged the general public's sensibilities.

David Cole, a professor at Georgetown University Law Center and a lawyer for the Center for Constitutional Rights, represented Finley before the Supreme Court. He argued that "one would be hard-pressed to find two people in the United States who could agree on what the 'diverse beliefs and values of the American public' are, much less on whether a particular work of art 'respects' them. . . . Decency is likely to mean something very different to a septuagenarian in Tuscaloosa and a teenager in Las Vegas." In the end the Supreme Court ruled eight to one to uphold the new law. Everyone from Speaker of the House Newt Gingrich to President Bill Clinton claimed it to be a victory, whereas many people in the arts felt it was censorship and an attack on cultural freedom. Actor and former head of the NEA Jane Alexander said, "It is in decisions such as the Supreme Court's that liberties in our society are whittled away slowly and incrementally. Doors to diversity and variety silently close." Theatre producer and critic Robert Brustein said, "The channels that support serious advanced expression are quickly drying up. The big cultural dinosaurs will probably survive and some theaters and dance companies may hang on if they fill their schedules with the equivalent crowd-pleasing holiday shows like *A Christmas Carol* and *Nutcracker*, but high art in America is dying and dying along with it are our hopes for a still significant civilization."

The arguments before the Supreme Court raised many provocative issues: Does the government have the right to favor certain points of view? Does the NEA have the right to exclude grant applicants because they are not in tune with the dominant culture? Is it even possible to make a work of art that respects all of the "diverse beliefs and values of the American public"?

Terry Ashe/Time Life Pictures/Getty Images

Actor Jane Alexander, former head of the NEA, answers charges in front of a congressional committee. Of the 140,000 works of art funded by the NEA in its nearly forty-year existence, there have been only fifty complaints. But this was enough for some members of Congress to slash the NEA's budget and call for its demise. Although they succeeded in reducing its budget, the majority of their colleagues voted for its continued existence.

Joan Marcus

Today one of the best-known plays of the theatre of protest is Eve Ensler's The Vagina Monologues *(1996). Its monologues about female sexuality deal frankly with childbirth, sex, and rape.* The Vagina Monologues *continues to be performed around the world, often in connection with the V-Day initiative, a movement to end violence against women and girls throughout the world. On a local level, benefit performances of* The Vagina Monologues *are organized and performed by volunteers to raise awareness and funds for anti-violence groups.*

techniques from another culture to create a unique piece of theatre. At its highest level, cross-cultural theatre is an attempt to fuse various cultural rituals, myths, and styles in order to find parallels between cultures, including those of the writers and performers and those of each audience, and merge them in a performance that celebrates our diversities and similarities and promotes cultural pluralism. As Nigerian writer Ben Okri (b. 1959) said, "Literature doesn't have a country. Shakespeare is an African writer. . . . The characters of Turgenev are ghetto dwellers. Dickens's characters are Nigerians. . . . Literature may come from a specific place, but it always lives in its own unique kingdom."

Cross-cultural plays have been a part of the Western theatre experience for hundreds of years. Irish poet and dramatist William Butler Yeats (1865–1939) was influenced by the masks, mime, and dance techniques of Japanese Noh drama for his poetic dramas *Four Plays for Dancers at the Hawk's Well* (1916). American playwright Thornton Wilder (1897–1975), who spent part of his childhood in China, adopted Chinese staging methods in his masterpiece *Our Town* (1938), a drama about life and death in a small New England town. In the play, Wilder used the character of a stage-manager/narrator to invoke the imagination of the audience, just as the Beijing Opera uses the character of the property man. Yet historically, many other Western cross-cultural plays have done little to promote understanding between cultures. For example, Gilbert and Sullivan's musical *The Mikado* (1885) and Puccini's *Madama Butterfly* (1904) were both influenced by Asian theatre but did little to portray nonstereotypical Asian characters or to promote cultural understanding.

Cross-cultural plays remain a part of the contemporary theatre. Japanese director and theorist Tadashi Suzuki (b. 1939) set the Greek tragedy *Trojan Women*, about the destruction of the ancient city of Troy, in post-World War II Japan, and used both classical Japanese theatrical styles and modern Western staging. The play includes traditional Japanese music and Western punk rock, kimonos and sweatshirts, and a script spoken in both English and Japanese. One critic described the performance as "a controlled crash that celebrates both East and West and finds a common language." Similarly, the Contemporary Legend Theatre of Taiwan creates performances that fuse four-hundred-year-old Shakespeare plays, two-hundred-year-old staging techniques from the Beijing opera, and verse written in Mandarin (performed with English subtitles) into a single production. Another example is Japanese director Shozo Sato, who stages Western classics such as *Medea*, *Faust*, and *Macbeth* in Japanese Kabuki style. Sato uses a multiracial cast of men and women, although Kabuki traditionally uses only men, and he adds a dash of "Kabuki soy sauce" in order to create what one critic called a "dramatic tension between the stylized beauty of the Kabuki tradition and the visceral action of Western stories."

The purpose of cross-cultural theatre is often to join people of diverse cultural backgrounds. This can mean that the performers come from one culture and the audience largely from another. For example, the play *Black Elk Speaks* (1994), which was adapted from an oral biography of a Sioux holy man, tells the story of white America's westward expansion from the Native American perspective. It is a story of broken promises, war, and the white man's quest for land and gold. When the play was originally produced at the Denver Center for the Performing Arts, it employed a cast of Native American actors, dancers, and singers from twenty North American tribes, but it drew an audience that was largely non-American

> "What has the modern artist done to deserve the violent epithets . . . ? Essentially what he has done is to say—here is the way I see contemporary reality, this is the way I wish to work, these are the things I present for you to see, this is what I believe about art, this is what I have learned, I intend to go on working this way, consider it, look at it, enjoy it, with my compliments. As far as I can see, the conduct of the artist is impeccable. . . ."
>
> **Harold Tylor,**
> Philosopher

Denver Center for the Performing Arts

Black Elk Speaks is an example of theatre as a vehicle for cultural interaction. Dramatizing the life of Black Elk, a Sioux holy man, and the struggles of Native Americans against the policy of Manifest Destiny, the play brings together the Native Americans who perform the play and the largely non-Native American audiences. This 1994 production featured Ned Romero as Black Elk and was directed by Donovan Marley at the Denver Center for the Performing Arts.

Indian. The play's purpose was to bring people together. As the director, who is white, said, "If *Black Elk* is saying anything, it is that the categorization is not red, white, yellow, and black . . . and all four have to live in this world together."

Other cross-cultural plays expose the complexities among cultures by putting them on stage side by side. Such is the case with *M. Butterfly* (1988) by David Henry Hwang (b. 1957). This play explores the Western psyche and its stereotypical views of Asian culture, race, and gender. Hwang's play combines plot elements of *Madama Butterfly*, an Italian opera, with a story about a French diplomat who, after ten years, discovers that his Chinese mistress is not only a spy but also a man. This play uses a modified Japanese Kabuki stage and choreography from the Beijing Opera as it attacks the cultural blindness that pervades so much of the world—a blindness that reveals itself in many ways.

Michal Daniel/Proofsheet

David Henry Hwang's plays often blend Eastern and Western styles of theatre. This production of his play M. Butterfly was directed by Peter Rothstein and staged at the Guthrie Theater in Minneapolis.

> I think one of the big problems, ultimately, in the efforts towards cultural diversity in the theater is whether the white establishment is willing to give up control. There have been a lot of well-meaning people, a lot of people trying to do things, but if you look at the administrative staffs of theaters, the decision makers there, nothing much has changed with them. As a result, tokenism remains far too prevalent.
>
> ***David Henry Hwang,***
> Playwright

Cross-cultural theatre does have its critics. Some feel that cross-cultural plays mix cultures without grasping their ideological dimensions. These critics charge that intercultural borrowing merely reduces culture to an interesting stage technique. For example, the great-grandson of Black Elk was bluntly critical of the inclusion in *Black Elk Speaks* of non-Lakota songs, incorrect choreography, and sacred images that should not be put on stage. Other critics have charged that Shozo Sato's Kabuki versions of Western classics trivialize Japanese theatre because the Western actors lack traditional training and so cannot comprehend Japanese content or culture. But from another viewpoint, Ping Chong, a Chinese American creator of avant-garde dance-theatre who often employs Chinese and Japanese aesthetics, says, "I'm not going to allow myself to be ghettoized as an Asian American artist. I'm an *American* artist. The irony is that we are now ghettoizing ourselves by choice. I understand that this act is an affirmation of one's identity. That's important. But we cannot lose sight of the fact that we all live in a society where we have to coexist. It doesn't mean that I have to like your culture. But we have to be *sensitive* to each other's cultures."

Theatre as a Way of Seeing through Another's Eyes

We all see the world from our own point of view, and most people tend to think that their take on it, as seen through their culture, is the correct view. This phenomenon is called **ethnocentrism**. English philosopher Francis Bacon (1561–1626) called ethnocentrism the "idols of the cave" because we often assume that our own social or cultural group is superior to others, that our sheltered and secluded "cave" is better than someone else's. Writer Dinesh D'Souza, who is a Fellow at the Hoover Institution at Stanford University, said, "To some degree ethnocentrism is unavoidable, because human beings have no alternative to viewing the world through some background set of assumptions and beliefs. If ethnocentrism cannot be completely overcome, however, the scope of its errors can be reduced and minimized. The way to do this is to turn assumptions into questions." Most would agree that all cultures should be allowed to express themselves, but what happens when cultures are so different that they come into conflict in their attempt to define a nation's cultural identity? How do we turn assumptions into questions?

Several years ago the mayor of New York City, Rudolph Giuliani, threatened to terminate the funding and possibly take over the Brooklyn Museum of Art because it displayed a painting by English artist Chris Ofili called *Holy Virgin Mary*. The painting depicted a woman representing the Virgin Mary. Attached to the painting were clumps of elephant dung, which prompted some critics to call it sacrilegious and obscene. In fact, a retired schoolteacher found it so offensive that he smuggled a container of latex paint into the museum and threw it on the painting. The painting insulted his culture and he reacted, but he failed to take the time to understand the artist's cultural perspective and intention. Few people did. The public debate over freedom of speech, obscenity, and the painting raged in the national news media for weeks. Yet a closer look at Ofili's background reveals that he is a Roman Catholic of Nigerian descent. Although the elephant dung may shock us in the West, he meant it as an affirmative interpretation of Christianity: Because elephant dung fertilizes the soil of Africa, to Africans it is a symbol of all

© Martha Swope Photography

Terrence McNally's Love! Valour! Compassion! *is the story of eight gay men who have come to a house in the country to celebrate summer holidays. Populated with complex characters and energized by witty and passionate dialogue, the play is notable for its straightforward depiction of gay middle-class relationships. This 1995 production featured (l to r) John Glover, Anthony Heald, and Nathan Lane and was directed by Joe Mantello at the Walter Kerr Theatre in New York. Of the thousands of plays written about the gay and lesbian experience,* Love! Valour! Compassion! *is one of the few to be made into a Hollywood film.*

that is good and nurturing. When cultures come into conflict, it is often a test of how well society as a whole tolerates alternative points of view.

Many plays attempt to combat or minimize ethnocentrism, including Milcha Sanchez-Scott's (b. 1955) *Roosters* (1987), a play about a generational feud between a proud, headstrong Hispanic father and his equally determined son; Anna Deavere Smith's (b. 1950) series of one-woman plays, *On the Road: A Search for American Character* (1983 to the present), which confronts racial and gender identity issues; and Regina Taylor's (b. 1964) *Watermelon Rinds* (1992), a seriocomic exposé of African American family politics. Currently, perhaps the most famous cultural-awareness play is Tony Kushner's (b. 1956) Pulitzer Prize–winning *Angels in America* (1992), a play in two parts that was adapted for television by HBO in 2003.

> People have waged a war against art in the name of decency, in the name of civic stability, in the name of God. But censoring art, even indecent art, isn't decent; it's thuggish, it's unconstitutional, undemocratic, and deeply unwise.
>
> **_Tony Kushner,_**
> Playwright

Kushner grew up Jewish and homosexual in the turbulent South of the 1960s. He said that he had had "fairly clear memories of being gay" since he was six but he did not come out until after he tried psychotherapy to change his sexual orientation. *Angels in America* tells the interwoven stories of several gay men. One is Prior Walter, a young man dying of AIDS who is visited by a frightening and mysterious angel; another is a Mormon, Joe Pitt, who comes to terms with his homosexuality despite its being forbidden by his religion; and another is Roy Cohn, a powerful attorney who denied his gay lifestyle in public and collaborated with Senator Joseph McCarthy in the 1950s persecution of "un-Americans." *Angels* is a perfect example of a play that challenges an audience to think and calls their values into question. By doing so it transmits knowledge, and with knowledge comes understanding.

Just as Ofili experienced with his painting, artists who attempt to produce plays that promote cultural awareness also sometimes come into conflict with the dominant culture. In 1993 when Terrence McNally's play *Lips Together, Teeth Apart*, which includes positive portrayals of gay men, was produced by a theatre in Cobb County, Georgia, the County Commission attempted to

L. Mueller/Staff/The Charlotte Observer

The controversial subject matter of Tony Kushner's Angels in America *has ignited protests since it premiered in 1991. Here, citizens for and against the play protest in 1996 in front of the Charlotte Repertory Theatre in North Carolina. Most recently, Alabama state senator Gerald Allen attempted to ban the Tony Award–winning play and all other literature with homosexual themes and characters from public school textbooks and libraries.*

silence any further such productions by establishing a "family values" criterion for funding local art. When that proved to be difficult to defend in court, the commission simply eliminated all art funding for the entire county. A similar incident occurred in 1999 when the theatre department at Kilgore College in Longview, Texas, staged *Angels in America*. On the sold-out opening night the building had to be surrounded by police because there were so many protesters. The play received a standing ovation, but a county commissioner revoked $50,000 worth of support to the Texas Shakespeare Festival, which was hosted by Kilgore College (but not by the theatre department). The commissioner said that county funds should not be used to support the arts because the "arts are always controversial." The arts are not always controversial, but they can be when they attempt to foster understanding of differing cultures within society. As Tony Kushner put it in a letter to the cast and crew at Kilgore College, "A healthy state needs vigorous, lively, pluralistic debate, not enforced acquiescence to a bullying majority."

Keeping the Theatre of the People Alive

Public opinion polls show broad public support for the arts and artists. The majority of Americans feel that the arts and humanities contribute to the economic health and well-being of society and that they are important to education. Yet today public funding for art that expresses a minority's point of view is sometimes questioned. At the center of this debate has been the National Endowment for the Arts, whose primary purpose has always been to give a voice to all cultures as it "increases the public awareness of our cultural heritage." This policy has put the NEA into conflict with some people who feel that all cultures are not equal. These people seem to believe that Americans must decide which culture is *the* American culture and government policies and funding must reflect that decision. Others feel that the government should stay out of arts funding altogether. Still others feel that without government assistance only those with the loudest voices—representatives of the dominant culture with the most private funding—will be heard.

The U.S. government does have a long history of guaranteeing freedom of speech by financially supporting viewpoints that might otherwise be drowned out. For example, it restricts monopolies by allowing smaller companies access to the marketplace, thereby guaranteeing them a voice. It provides funding for numerous political candidates. It gives tax-exempt status to tens of thousands of organizations, including hundreds of different religions. But should the government simply *allow* for freedom of speech or should it *guarantee* it? And how far should the government go to ensure that all voices are heard? The answers to these questions will continue to be debated as long as what one group calls their culture, another group calls blasphemous or obscene. Richard Bolton says in his book *Culture Wars*, "In the end, censorship of the arts reveals the failure of democratic institutions to articulate and defend the complexity and diversity of the American public. The NEA debate contained many lessons about art's relationship to society, but it also raised many questions about the future of American democracy."

Curtain Call

Today, the East/West Players, El Teatro Campesino, Ujima Theatre Company, Repertorio Español, Puerto Rican Traveling Theatre Company, the Hispanic American Arts Center, Pan Asian Repertory, Teatro de la Esperanza, San Diego Black Ensemble Theatre, and many more culturally specific theatres are opening up opportunities for culturally diverse actors, designers, directors, playwrights, and theatre practitioners. In addition, countless theatres have been formed to highlight gay and lesbian themes, as well as to advocate feminist ideas and stories written by women, about women, and for women.

The battle over cultural diversity around the world and in the United States continues. Some would agree with this statement in UNESCO's *Universal Declaration on Cultural Diversity*: "Cultural diversity is as necessary for humankind as biodiversity is for nature." Others would agree with William Bennett, the chairman of the National Endowment for the Humanities under President Ronald Reagan,

When Henrik Ibsen's A Doll's House *was first performed in 1879, a protest ensued, similar to those staged against* Angels in America. *Victorian audiences were outraged because the play did not reinforce the family values of the day, which dictated that women stay home to love and amuse their husbands. This play illustrates the need for artists to be free to explore ideas that conflict with mainstream values. This 2000 production at the University of Wyoming featured Aimee Callahan and Michael Childs and was directed by William Missouri Downs.*

who said that to keep a country together, it must share a common culture, which is our "civic glue" and serves as a kind of "immunological system." Without a doubt our cultural differences will continue to be a source of celebration and conflict and the theatre will be part of both. Recently, playwright David Henry Hwang wrote, "American theatre is beginning to discover Americans: black theatre, women's theatre, gay theatre, Asian American theatre, Hispanic theatre." American theatre, like its audience, is diverse. The only way to fully appreciate it is to see and study its many forms, not just those that reflect our own culture and beliefs.

Summary

We often think of theatre in terms of stars and spotlights, but theatre of the people, where artists outside the dominant culture express themselves, also thrives. This type of theatre is what Brazilian director Augusto Boal calls the "theatre of the oppressed." In its long history the theatre has seldom given a voice to all the people or reflected the many cultures in any society. Instead it has been controlled by the dominant culture through racism, sexism, discrimination, economic power, and social and religious customs. Theatre of the people attempts to give a voice to all members of society as it increases multiculturalism and reduces stereotyping.

There are three types of theatre of the people. Theatre of identity promotes a particular people's cultural identity as it strengthens the bonds of the community. It can also invite members of other cultures to experience that people's joys, problems, history, traditions, and point of view. Theatre of protest objects to the dominant culture's control as it demands that a minority culture's voice and political agenda be heard. Cross-cultural theatre mixes different cultures in an attempt to find understanding or commonality among cultures.

Most people see the world from their own point of view, and they tend to think that their take on things, as seen through the lens of their culture, is the correct view. This ethnocentrism leads to a great deal of conflict between cultures. The theatre of the people attempts to lessen this conflict by raising the cultural consciousness of audiences. Government organizations, such as the National Endowment for the Arts, try to promote cultural understanding by funding art created by non-mainstream cultures and allowing all voices to be heard. These attempts sometimes fail, especially when members of the dominant culture see them as threats to the nation's cultural identity. Yet in order for societies to evolve and progress, artists must be free to voice ideas that challenge mainstream views and values.

The Art of Theatre ONLINE

To access this chapter's interactive theatre workshop activities, along with many other learning tools, log onto your Theatre CourseMate. Access is available at cengagebrain.com.

Key Terms

On the closing night of the hit Broadway musical Hairspray *the audience jumped to its feet for a standing ovation.*

Photos on the spread James Estrin/The New York Times/Redux Pictures

CHAPTER 4

Experiencing and Analyzing Plays

OUTLINE

People go to the theatre for a variety of reasons: Some want to be amused, others desire to be challenged; some want philosophy, others want magic. Theatre can be a vehicle to make us feel, think, and learn, and perhaps motivate us to discuss, analyze, or even take action on what we've experienced. To have ample opportunities to do all these things is in our best interest as audience members and as a society. When we support playwrights, directors, and actors in expressing themselves, not only do we increase our own awareness, but we also fuel public dialogue, which sometimes can help us change our world.

This chapter will explore the dynamics of the audience, what to expect when you go to the theatre, and what is expected of you as an audience member. It will also look at a special kind of audience member, the critic, and explain how to go beyond your own opinion to analyze a play and understand what the theatre artist is trying to convey. Finally, it will explore how the right to freedom of speech applies to the arts and how it affects what audiences see.

The People Who Watch

> In a theatre, actors and audience meet each other at the moment of performance; they share the experience and each contributes something towards it. Real actors, acting in the presence of a real audience: This is the essence of theatre.
>
> ***Stephen Joseph,***
> Theatre director, producer, and designer, in *New Theatre Forms*

Theatre is a group activity. Unlike television, which usually is watched alone or with a few family members or friends, theatre is designed to be experienced with a sea of strangers. In fact, unlike television or the movies, without an audience there can be no theatre. Remember the quote from the British director Peter Brook in Chapter 1: At its most basic, theatre requires someone to walk across an empty space while someone else watches. Theatre artists have studied their audiences for thousands of years and have learned to manipulate their feelings, reactions, and even their thoughts. This manipulation is possible primarily because of three factors: group dynamics, the suspension of disbelief, and aesthetic distance.

Group Dynamics

Group dynamics is simply the functioning of humans when they come together into groups. Whether those groups are gangs, families, church congregations, or theatre audiences, studies have shown that people act and react differently when they are in a group than when they are alone. We become less intellectual and more emotional, less reasonable and more irrational, less likely to react as individuals and more likely to react as a group. Perhaps our desire to fit into a group can be traced back to the prehistoric need to belong to a tribe because there was safety in numbers. Television producers know we like to be part of a group, so most sitcoms include a laugh track; as we sit alone in our living rooms, we hear other people laughing. Because of group dynamics, we have a tendency to join in and laugh. The old saying "laughter is infectious" is true, but only if someone else is laughing. That's why comic movies do not use laugh tracks; they are intended to be viewed with an audience, so there is no need to add the illusion of other viewers.

Theatres take advantage of group dynamics by selling tickets to seat all audience members next to one another. So even if the play doesn't sell out and the theatre is half empty, the audience will be seated as a group, increasing the chances that they will be influenced by group dynamics. Theatres reason that if the people around you are enjoying the play, there is a good chance you will too. Some theatres even go so far as to **paper the house**. In theatre lingo, *house* is the auditorium, and in this case *paper* means tickets. So to "paper the house" means to give away a lot of free tickets to the families and friends of cast members in order to make it appear as though the performance is well attended. Theatres are most likely to paper the house on opening night when they know a critic is attending. They hope that an audience's positive response to the play will rub off on the critic, who may then write a favorable review. One of the most famous cases of using group dynamics to manipulate an audience happened in 1964 when the Beatles visited the United States for the first time and appeared on *The Ed Sullivan Show*. To sell John, Paul, George, and Ringo to audiences, the show's producers hired young girls to scream and faint during the performance. Soon, young women throughout the country were screaming and fainting for the band.

Suspending Disbelief

When we go to the theatre, or watch a television show or movie for that matter, we must enter into a **willing suspension of disbelief**. We admit that what is happening is not real and so we don't need to rush up and save the actor who is being attacked or call the police to stop the actor playing the criminal. When suspending our disbelief, we put aside our concerns about everyday reality and agree to accept the *play's* particular quasi reality, which communicates some *perception* about everyday reality.

If an artist crosses the line and we don't know if the moment is real or make-believe, it can make for a very powerful performance, but the audience may feel violated. For example, in 1994 performance artist Ron Athey famously broke the audience's willing suspension of disbelief during a performance at the Walker Art Center in Minneapolis. In his piece, which was based on African tribal traditions and was about the spread of AIDS, Athey purposely nicked the skin of another actor—with the actor's permission of course—and blotted the blood onto a paper towel that he then showed to the audience.

Sygma/Corbis

Dreamworks LLC/The Kobal Collection/James, David/Picture Desk

Performance artist Ron Athey (left) famously broke an audience's willing suspension of disbelief when he nicked the skin of another actor and blotted the blood onto a paper towel. His audience was shocked and disturbed because they knew that what was happening onstage was real. In contrast, during this disturbing scene from the World War II saga Saving Private Ryan *(right), audience members did not feel they needed to save the little girl because they willingly suspended their disbelief and understood that what was happening onscreen was not reality. Yet the scene was real enough to allow the audience to feel empathy, give the events serious consideration, and even lose themselves in the story.*

People get nicks all the time; they cut their skin shaving, cleaning the yard, or playing sports. But because this nick happened in front of a live audience, it sent shock waves through the auditorium and across the country. When Senator Jesse Helms of North Carolina heard about the performance, he sent a letter to the then head of the National Endowment for the Arts, Jane Alexander, accusing her agency of funding a work in which HIV-positive, "blood-soaked towels" were sent "winging" over the audience. None of this was true; the blood was not HIV positive, nor did it come into contact with the audience. The Minnesota Department of Health affirmed that the Walker Center had taken appropriate safety precautions, but that wasn't enough to squelch the commotion. It's interesting to compare the impact of a few droplets of real blood on stage in front of a live audience to the dozens of bloody and severed limbs in summer blockbuster movies like Quentin Tarantino's *Kill Bill* (Volumes 1 and 2). One type of performance set off a political firestorm; the other simply seems to sell more tickets. What's the difference between the two? A movie audience knows it isn't real blood.

Athey's performance made a powerful statement about AIDS, but he also blurred the lines between art and life. Theatre artists are always attempting to manipulate the audience's willing suspension of disbelief, sometimes engulfing them in total fantasy and at other times taking them to the edge of reality. Suspension of disbelief allows the audience to laugh at a painful beating during a farce, or come so close to real life that they are moved to tears. For example, the smash Broadway success *Spamalot* (2005), the musical based on the movie *Monty Python and the Holy Grail* (1975), creates a hilarious fantasy world that demands an audience suspend their disbelief in order to find the slapstick violence funny. In contrast, Marsha Norman's play *'night, Mother* (1982) details the last ninety minutes of a woman who has decided to commit suicide. The set of this play features functioning clocks and the actors perform in real time, highlighting the sense of reality for the audience. Yet, because the audience members suspend their disbelief while watching the play, they know the actress is not really going to kill herself, and so don't try to stop her.

Distancing Yourself

Closely tied to the suspension of disbelief is **aesthetic distance**, the audience's ability to remove themselves from a work of art just far enough so that they can contemplate it—or even judge it. If we allow ourselves to be immersed in a play, movie, or television show to the point that we forget ourselves, then we have no aesthetic distance. We are simply using the show as a vicarious experience. For example, we want to live a more exciting life, so we go to an action movie or play a video game and feel that we have been on a mini-escapade. But most artists don't want the audience to totally forget themselves; they want the audience to distance themselves from the work just enough to be semi-objective but not indifferent. This way, the audience can have a vicarious experience, feel empathy for the characters, and be entertained, yet they can also think about the play's themes and meaning and even its artistic merit.

Some writers and directors go further and challenge or even alienate an audience. The German playwright Bertolt Brecht (1898–1956) believed that an audience's emotional involvement in the characters and story could cloud their grasp of the play's message. He sneered at what he called "culinary theatre,"

Kevin Berne/Courtesy American Conservatory Theater

The very nature of theatre encourages audiences to maintain a certain aesthetic distance, keeping us from completely losing ourselves in a story. Some plays ask audiences to maintain more distance than others. For example, the character of the Stage Manager in Thornton Wilder's Our Town *acts as an omniscient narrator, interacting with both the audience and the play's characters. Similarly, Mark Hollman and Greg Kotis's* Urinetown, the Musical *(shown here) also features a narrator, Officer Lockstock, who addresses the audience directly. In addition* Urinetown *spoofs traditional musicals, allowing the audience to laugh at this art form while also enjoying a funny story. This 2003 production was directed by John Rando at San Francisco's American Conservatory Theater.*

theatre that does not provoke socially meaningful thought but rather feeds us illusion and leaves us feeling content and emotionally satisfied, as we do after a good meal. In his "epic theater" style, he tried to shatter traditional stage illusions and continually remind the audience that they were sitting in a theatre watching a performance. In this way, Brecht did not allow the audience to lose themselves in the play. Instead he consciously urged them to think about the play's message. (For more on Bertolt Brecht and his plays, see Part 3.)

Levels of Participation

Group dynamics, suspension of disbelief, and aesthetic distance also affect the level of audience participation. Audience participation can be divided into two basic levels: active participation and sitting quietly in the dark. The two types of theatre that correspond to these levels of participation are sometimes called *presentational* and *representational*.

Presentational theatre makes no attempt to offer a realistic illusion onstage, and the actors openly acknowledge the audience and sometimes even invite

Playwright Bertolt Brecht often took pains to remind his audience that what was happening onstage was a performance. During the play he did not want them to lose themselves, but rather to think critically and objectively about the issues raised. In this production of his Mother Courage and Her Children *(1941), the set designer took a Brechtian approach, letting the audience know they were watching a play, not reality, by exposing the lights and using highly stylized set pieces.*

Richard Feldman

members to participate. When Peter Pan begs the audience to clap their hands to help Tinker Bell, that's presentational theatre. In **representational theatre** actors never acknowledge the audience and go about their business as if there were no audience present. Almost all movies and TV shows are representational (an example of an exception is *High Fidelity*, in which the main character often addresses the audience directly), but in the theatre plays are either presentational or representational, and audiences either sit quietly in the dark or are asked to participate. To maximize your and your fellow audience members' theatregoing experience, you need to know what is expected of you for both types of plays and what etiquette you should follow.

> In its essence, a theatre is only an arrangement of seats so grouped and spaced that the actor—the leader—can reach out and touch and hold each member of his audience. Architects of later days have learned how to add conveniences and comforts to this idea. But that is all. The idea itself never changes.
>
> ***Robert Edmond Jones,*** Theatre set designer

Sitting Quietly in the Dark

Sitting quietly in the dark to watch a play is a relatively new behavior for theatre audiences. It started in the late 1850s but did not become popular until Edison invented the lightbulb. Electric lights allowed designers to control the illumination of the stage and to completely dim the house during performances; before this, the audience was as well lit as the stage. But the major reason for a passive audience was **realism**, a style of theatre that attempts to portray life as accurately as possible. (For more on realism, see Part 3.) By the late 1800s, realism had become the dominant form of theatre in the West, and the idea of an actor talking with an audience was considered passé. Asides, prologues, and epilogues were dropped, and the performers began acting as though the audience didn't exist. The actors' "reality" incorporated a **fourth wall**, an imaginary wall between the actors and audience. In this form of theatre, the audience had to sit quietly. In short, the rules of theatre etiquette had changed.

> You would think after all this time people would walk into the theater with their cell phones turned off.
>
> ***Robert Falls,*** Broadway director

Audience Etiquette

Etiquette includes the conventions of behavior prescribed for a particular occasion. Rules of etiquette at performances differ from one type to another. People who talk during a movie will get dirty looks and perhaps a "shh," but in a theatre they will probably get evicted. In a theatre, people are expected to be on their best behavior and to be considerate of others. Here are some basic rules of etiquette for theatre-goers in the United States, especially for plays that require the audience to sit quietly in the dark. (We will cover the exceptions to these rules in the next section.)

1. **Turn off phones and beepers.** A mobile phone ringing (or merely vibrating) not only bothers the actors but other audience members. Doctors or parents who must be available during the performance can leave their phones or beepers at the box office or coatroom. If the phone should ring or the beeper beep, an usher will come get its owner.
2. **Do not text or tweet during the play.** The actors may not see you using Twitter but it can be very distracting to other audience members. The bright light of your handheld device is extremely visible to those around you.
3. **Do not talk.** Even whispering can bother other audience members and the actors. At a musical, all talking should end when the lights dim or the conductor enters; the overture is part of the performance. However, vocal responses to the play itself, such as gasping or laughing, are okay.
4. **Try not to cough.** If you have a cough, then you should bring cough drops (unwrapped before the show starts, see rule 6) and do everything in your power to suppress the cough until scene changes or the intermission. One cough can obscure a crucial word of dialogue and ruin a scene.
5. **Do not be late.** Latecomers edging down a row to their seats are very distracting. If you arrive late, you will probably have to wait to be seated

Polite behavior is required in a theatre. Talking and other disruptive behaviors will not only ruin the play for the audience but may also affect the actors. In the Neil Simon play The Good Doctor, *pictured here, one audience member sneezing on another is the source of a great deal of comedy, but is not so funny in real life. This production was staged by the National Theatre Conservatory.*

until a break in the performance. You may be required to stand in the back or sit in a different seat until intermission.

6. **Do not eat.** In most U.S. theatres, food is not allowed (although each theatre is different). Cough drops should be unwrapped before the performance begins. The crinkling of cellophane wrappers distracts audience members and actors.
7. **Be courteous.** Do not kick or put your feet on the seat in front of you, fidget, squirm, or constantly wiggle in your seat. Do not sing or hum along with the music or make any other disruptive noises.
8. **Go light on the perfume or cologne.** In the theatre you sit close to other audience members; heavy perfume or cologne may bother them or even trigger an allergic response.
9. **Do not leave until the intermission or until the end.** The only reason to leave during a performance is an emergency. Leaving a performance because it bores you or insults you is discourteous and will ruin the play for those who do not find it boring or insulting.
10. **No photos or recording devices allowed.** Not only is the noise distracting, but the flash can disorient the actors. In the past, actors blinded by a flashbulb have actually fallen off the stage. Moreover, taking pictures or recording a performance is a violation of copyright laws. Your ticket allows you to attend the performance once, not to own a copy of it. (For more on copyright, see Chapters 2 and 6.)

Although many of these rules of etiquette apply when you attend a movie, they are even more important when you attend a live theatre performance. Actress Mary-Louise Parker, the Emmy-nominated lead actress from Showtime's *Weeds*, famously said, "People think they're watching television. What they don't know is that when you're onstage, one Tic-Tac coming out of the box sounds like an avalanche."

Not Sitting Quietly in the Dark

Not all plays require the audience to sit complacently in the dark. For some types of theatre, the audience is supposed to express themselves and even participate in the play. These productions do not allow the audience the safety of the fourth wall, and in some cases the actors embrace or confront the audience during the play. Interactive theatre comes in many forms, from Japanese Kabuki theatre to children's shows to comedies such as *Tony n' Tina's Wedding*, a popular satire of an Italian American wedding in which audience members participate in the ceremony, the champagne toast, and the cutting of the wedding cake. The most extreme example of audience participation is the musical *Rocky Horror Show* (1973) or the movie based on the play, *The Rocky Horror Picture Show* (1975), where audience members dance the Time Warp, throw buttered toast, water, rice, and toilet paper at the actors or the screen, and even speak lines of dialogue. You don't go to "see" *Rocky Horror Show*; rather, you "experience" it. In short, when attending the theatre, knowing and obeying the basic etiquette improves the experience for everyone, but you can seldom predict what will be expected of you. Keep an open mind and play along.

Going to the Theatre

Now that you know how to conduct yourself at the theatre, let's explore what you need to know to find a play you want to see, buy a ticket, choose what to wear, and use the program.

Finding a Play

Unless you live in a small town, finding a play is easy; your local paper probably carries ads, reviews, or a list of local theatres and what is playing. The Internet is also a great resource for information about plays. Most theatres now have websites where you can find a description of what is playing and purchase tickets. Reviews almost always give a bit of the story, which can help you decide whether you are likely to be interested in a play. However, it is also important to take a chance on plays that you suspect might challenge you. They may give you new interests or help you explore your values. It can pay to be adventurous.

Getting Your Tickets

Theatre tickets must almost always be reserved in advance by calling or visiting the box office or buying tickets online. When you buy your tickets by phone or online, the tickets will be mailed if there is enough time or you can pick them up at the box office before the performance. Many theatres have a "**Will Call**" window for those who are picking up tickets they have already paid for. Be sure to pick them up at least fifteen minutes before **curtain** (the start of the show), or the theatre may assume you are not coming and sell them to someone else.

NILS JORGENSEN/Rex USA/BEImages

Theatre today is often considered an upper-class affair, where the rules of etiquette demand an audience be behaved, quiet, and passive. That is not the case with The Rocky Horror Show, and its filmed counterpart The Rocky Horror Picture Show, during which the audience is encouraged to sing, chant, dance, and throw rice, toast and hotdogs. This production was staged by the Wimbledon Theatre in London.

Once you have purchased your tickets, you usually cannot return or exchange them. Some theatres may offer an exchange of tickets for another performance or play, but most will not. Because you have purchased your seat in advance, the theatre cannot sell it to anyone else and cannot afford to give you a last-minute refund. The same no-refund policy is true if you misplace your ticket or are dissatisfied with the play. Just as with a fishing license, you can't get your money back if you fail to catch any fish.

Saving Money

If you want to save a little money, be sure to ask at the box office if student tickets are available. Often theatres sell high school and college students discount tickets if they have a valid student ID. The availability of these tickets can be limited and sometimes they don't go on sale until the afternoon of the performance. If you are seeing theatre in New York City, then you can get bargain tickets the day of the performance at the TKTS booth in Times Square (or visit **http://www.tdf.org/tkts**). Sometimes you have to stand in line for several

SPOTLIGHT ON Broadway Is Not the Only Place to See Great Theatre

Fifty years ago there were only a handful of professional theatre companies outside of New York City. Today, thanks to the National Endowment of the Arts and patrons, there are hundreds. Some are **road houses** where touring companies perform Broadway plays and musicals; others are professional theatre companies known as LORT theatres (**League of Resident Theatres**). These large regional theatres have companies of professional actors and fill their seasons with traditional comedies, dramas, and musicals, as well as challenging new plays. In addition, there are now nearly 1,800 smaller professional and semi-professional theatre companies throughout the United States, not counting hundreds of community and college theatres. You don't have to travel far to see a good play.

Here is a list of a few of the major regional theatres across the United States:

ACT Theatre, Seattle WA
Actors Theatre of Louisville, Louisville, KY
Alabama Shakespeare Festival, Montgomery, AL
Alley Theatre, Houston, TX
Alliance Theatre, Atlanta, GA
American Conservatory Theater, San Francisco, CA
American Repertory Theatre, Cambridge, MA
Arden Theatre Company, Philadelphia, PA
Arena Stage, Washington, DC
Arizona Theatre Company, Tucson/Phoenix, AZ
Arkansas Repertory Theatre, Little Rock, AR
Asolo Repertory Theatre, Sarasota, FL
Barter Theatre, Abingdon, VA
Berkeley Repertory Theatre, Berkeley, CA
Capital Repertory Theatre, Albany, NY
Centerstage, Baltimore, MD
Center Theatre Group, Los Angeles, CA
Cincinnati Playhouse in the Park, Cincinnati, OH
City Theatre Company, Pittsburgh, PA
Clarence Brown Theatre Company, Knoxville, TN
The Cleveland Play House, Cleveland, OH
Court Theatre, Chicago, IL
Dallas Theater Center, Dallas, TX
Delaware Theatre Company, Wilmington, DE
Denver Center Theatre Company, Denver, CO
Florida Stage, West Palm Beach, FL
Florida Studio Theatre, Sarasota, FL
Ford's Theatre, Washington, DC
Geffen Playhouse, Los Angeles, CA
George Street Playhouse, New Brunswick, NJ
Georgia Shakespeare, Atlanta, GA
Geva Theatre Center, Rochester, NY
The Goodman Theatre, Chicago, IL
Goodspeed Musicals, East Haddam, CT
Great Lakes Theater Festival, Cleveland, OH
The Guthrie Theater, Minneapolis, MN
Hartford Stage Company, Hartford, CT
Huntington Theatre Company, Boston, MA
Indiana Repertory Theatre, Indianapolis, IN
Intiman Theatre, Seattle, WA
Kansas City Repertory Theatre, Kansas City, MO
Laguna Playhouse, Laguna Beach, CA
La Jolla Playhouse, La Jolla, CA
Lincoln Center Theater, New York, NY
Long Wharf Theatre, New Haven, CT
Maltz Jupiter Theatre, Jupiter, FL
Manhattan Theatre Club, New York, NY
Marin Theatre Company, Mill Valley, CA
McCarter Theatre, Princeton, NJ
Merrimack Repertory Theatre, Lowell, MA
Milwaukee Repertory Theater, Milwaukee, WI
Northlight Theatre, Skokie, IL
The Old Globe, San Diego, CA
Pasadena Playhouse, Pasadena, CA
The People's Light and Theatre Company, Philadelphia, PA
The Philadelphia Theatre Company, Philadelphia, PA
Pittsburgh Public Theater, Pittsburgh, PA
PlayMakers Repertory Company, Chapel Hill, NC
Portland Center Stage, Portland, OR
Portland Stage, Portland, ME
The Repertory Theatre of St. Louis, St. Louis, MO
Roundabout Theatre Company, New York, NY
Round House Theatre, Bethesda, MD
San Jose Repertory Theatre, San Jose, CA
Seattle Repertory Theatre, Seattle, WA
Shakespeare Theatre Company, Washington, DC
Signature Theatre Company, Arlington, VA
South Coast Repertory, Costa Mesa, CA
Syracuse Stage, Syracuse, NY
Theatre for a New Audience, New York, NY
TheatreWorks, Palo Alto, CA
Trinity Repertory Company, Providence, RI
Two River Theater Company, Red Bank, NJ
Virginia Stage Company, Norfolk, VA
The Wilma Theater, Philadelphia, PA
Yale Repertory Theatre, New Haven, CT

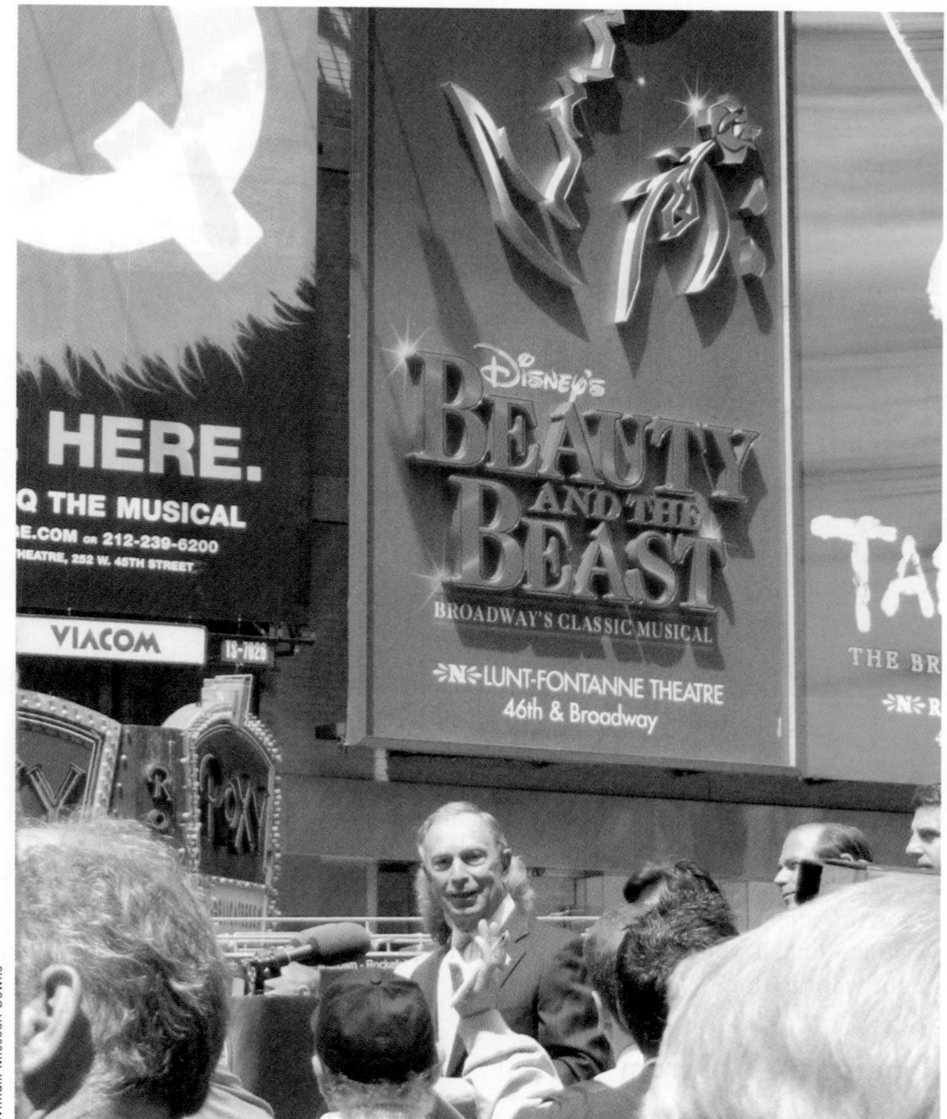

William Missouri Downs

Mayor Michael Bloomberg of New York City announces the construction of a new TKTS booth in Times Square. For 35 years TKTS has offered day-of-performance tickets to Broadway shows for 25 to 50 percent off.

hours, but in the end you can save as much as 25 to 50 percent. Another way to get discount Broadway tickets is through the School Theater Ticket Program (**http://schooltix.com**), which offers discount tickets for students.

Preview performances, for which tickets are usually half price, offer another way to save money. Previews are performances open to the public before the play officially opens and are common in the professional theatre but rare in college, community, and amateur theatres. Finally, if you're willing to volunteer your time helping with the production or by being an usher, you may be able to get free admission at college, community, and amateur theatres.

Dress Codes

In the United States you're expected to dress up a little or a lot when you go to the theatre. Unlike movie audiences, theatre audiences are made up of people intending to attend a special event. If you go to the professional theatre, you'll

William Missouri Downs

Going to the theatre is a special event. People often dress up, go out to dinner before, and stay after for talkbacks or panel discussions. If you treat theatre attendance as you would a movie, you are missing some of the magic.

be out of place if you dress the way you do for college classes. Unless you are attending the opera, formal or semi-formal attire is not required, but you will need to reach farther into your closet for something clean and pressed. In other words, vintage T-shirts and old tennis shoes are inappropriate. But there are exceptions: If you are attending an outdoor performance of Shakespeare, then dress for the weather. And if you are attending a performance of *Rocky Horror Show*, you might want to dress in costume.

Reading the Program

Once you enter the theatre, an usher will give you a program and show you to your seat—unless it's "general seating," in which case you can sit anywhere you like. In the United States programs are free, but in some countries, such as England, programs must be purchased. Try to arrive early enough to spend a few minutes reading the program before the play begins. Programs feature information that will help you better understand the performance, such as the location and time of the scenes and the cast of characters. Some programs also include a **director's note** or a **playwright's note** that explains what he or she intended to accomplish with the play. You might also find historical information about the play, playwright, or style of production. Some larger professional theatres sell **souvenir programs** that have more pictures and information about the cast and production. You don't have to buy one unless you really want a souvenir.

After the Show

Occasionally a theatre will sponsor an audience **talk-back**, a post-performance discussion where you get a chance to meet, and perhaps ask questions of, the

SPOTLIGHT ON Ovation Inflation

The play ends, the curtain call begins, and the audience claps. Then an enthusiastic patron, perhaps an actor's mother, stands and a few seconds later someone else stands—before you know it, everyone feels compelled to stand. You have been sitting for a while so it feels good to stretch, but did the performance really deserve a standing ovation? Today, standing ovations, which were once reserved for the most outstanding actors and productions, are becoming commonplace. Blogs, theatre critics, and audience members have all voiced concerns about the frequency of ovation inflation.

Some feel that this surplus of standing is because the theatre is too expensive, so people want to supersize the experience. And it is expensive. The *Wall Street Journal* recently pointed out that four full-price tickets to a Broadway show could cost more than an iPad. In addition, some directors stage plays so that the audience has no choice but to stand. For example during the last number in the Broadway musical *Mamma Mia*, the audience tends to get up and dance, which means that they just happen to be on their feet as the curtain call begins.

There is also the emotional pressure of the group dynamic. (See "Group Dynamics" in this chapter.) If everyone around you is standing it is hard to not follow the crowd's lead, if for no other reason than to get a better view of the curtain call. Jesse McKinley wrote in "The Tyranny of the Standing Ovation" (*New York Times*), "Whatever the motivation, the effect of the rampant increase in standing ovations has been accompanied by—as with any other form of inflation—a decrease in value. If almost every performance receives one, then it ceases to be a meaningful compliment."

You don't have to stand. If you do not feel it was an exceptional performance, then it is perfectly acceptable to sit while you applaud—even if the friend/date/spouse/family member next to you is standing. If anyone questions you about not standing, let them know that you are a soldier in the fight against ovation inflation.

RICHARD PERRY/The New York Times/Redux Pictures

Audience members give a standing ovation to the hit Boradway musical The Book Of Mormon.

director, actors, and sometimes the playwright. If the play is issue-oriented, the theatre might even have experts there to discuss the play's theme. For example, recently the Broadway producers of David Mamet's play *Oleanna* held such audience talk-backs after every performance. *Oleanna* deals with charges of sexual harassment between a female student and a college professor, so the producers had criminal defense lawyers and professional mediators present to discuss the problem. Such talk-backs were once limited to smaller theatres, but today they are held at theatres of any size; with certain particularly evocative plays, talk-backs have become a regular and expected part of the theatregoing experience as an outlet for the audience to express themselves. "I think talk-backs are being embraced more and more by commercial theatre because we producers sense that when people connect to a show, they want to prolong that experience as much as they can," said Jed Bernstein, one of the producers of the Broadway production of *Oleanna*.

Not all theatres sponsor talk-backs, and when they do, they don't always hold one for every performance. In addition, just because the theatre is holding a talk-back, that doesn't mean you have to attend. However, when you leave the theatre you should have your own talk-back where you and your friends discuss the play's merits, shortcomings, and meaning.

Play Analysis

> [The critic's job is to] improve theatrical standards by educating an audience to a level of taste more receptive to ambitious theatre and less tolerant of mediocrity.
>
> ***Richard Palmer,***
> Theatre professor, director, and author, in *The Critics' Canon*

As a beginning theatre student, you'll probably not only attend plays but also read plays and write about what you've seen and read. To fully appreciate a play and analyze it thoughtfully, it's important to understand the differences between a review, which is an opinion, and criticism, which is a detailed analysis. An opinion tells you what someone thinks about the play, but educated, thoughtful, and justified criticism will most often lead you to a greater understanding of a play. Let's take a look at what constitutes a review, what constitutes criticism, and how to analyze a play.

Everyone Is a Critic

Reviews, sometimes called *notices* in theatre lingo, are evaluations of a production, often published in newspapers or magazines. They can also be broadcast on television, on the radio, and over the Internet. In a sense, everyone who has ever expressed an opinion about a dramatic performance is a reviewer, whether or not they have published or broadcast that review to a large audience. The reviewer's main goal is to inform the potential audience members whether a play is, in the reviewer's opinion, worth attending. A reviewer assesses the production and gives it a "thumbs up" or "thumbs down," or may rate a production, for example, by giving it three stars out of four. Reviews are a sort of consumer report or comparative shopping guide that rates a performance.

One of the oldest examples dates back to about 1800 BCE, when the Egyptian actor Ikhernofret wrote in hieroglyphics his opinions about a ritual play in which he had performed—he gave himself a positive review, four stars out of four. Today, however, many reviewers' number-one desire is to sell newspapers, so their reviews must above all grab readers' attention. A few years ago, an actor in Denver was mugged and beaten by a gang as he walked home after his performance. The next day, a newspaper reviewer wrote that perhaps the gang had seen the actor's performance and were on a mission of revenge. The reporter was later forced to apologize.

Although some reviews can be insensitive or even as mean-spirited as that example, regularly reading reviews can help you discover which reviewers' tastes you share. And you'll know that when certain reviewers pan a play, you'll probably love it. In any case, reviews generally do not provide a deep, scholarly analysis of a play, the artists, or the production—that level of analysis is left to dramatic criticism.

Dramatic Criticism

Dramatic criticism, sometimes called *literary criticism* or simply criticism, is not meant to draw people to a particular production or warn them away from it, nor

AP Photo/Mary Altaffer

The rock musical Hair *is considered by some to be a great example of counterculture art, whereas others consider it obscene for its nudity and antiestablishment messages. This production was performed at the Union Square Theatre in New York City.*

is it based solely on opinion. Instead, criticism offers the reader a discriminating, often scholarly interpretation and analysis of a play, an artist's body of work, or a period of theatre history. Criticism appears in literary quarterlies, in academic books, and in more sophisticated magazines and newspapers. Academics and theatre professionals often study criticism when they research a particular play, playwright, historical movement, or genre. Students of theatre find reading criticism often allows them a greater understanding of the plays they read and see.

Criticism comes in many forms. It can examine the structure of a play; it can compare a play with others of its genre; or it can analyze a play's effectiveness. Criticism can judge a play in relation to a particular period or style of theatre. It can challenge or support a play's philosophical or sociological perspective. Or it can chronicle how the play was created and how history and the artist's background and conscious or unconscious motives affected it. Criticism can also attack or endorse other works of scholarly criticism. In short, criticism has less to do with rating a particular production than with delving into a play's aesthetic effect, history, and dramatic structure.

Being More Than a Reviewer

For beginning theatre students, writing an opinion paper about a production is a lot like writing a review. Often such papers say more about the critic than they do about the play: if you prefer musical theatre, you may not enjoy a tragedy; if you like serious plays, you may not care for farce. Such an essay is a nice exercise, but only when you know the basics of analyzing a play can you take the first steps toward dramatic criticism and analysis. Of course, the greater your knowledge of theatre, the deeper you can delve into the subject. And the more you know about playwriting (Chapter 6) the better you'll be at analyzing a play's structure, theme, and story. The more you know about acting (Chapter 7) the better you'll be at analyzing the actors' performances and the play's characters, emotions, and motivations. This also applies to

SPOTLIGHT ON Audiences Behaving Badly: The Astor Place Riot

On the evening of May 10, 1849, demonstrators gathered outside the Astor Place Opera House in Manhattan to protest the appearance of the English actor William Charles Macready (1793–1873). The Astor Place was an opulent theatre with ticket prices of $1 per seat, four times what other theatres in New York City charged, and Macready was considered by average Americans to be a symbol of English aristocracy. It had been only thirty years since the English had last invaded, and anti-English feelings in America were still running high. But the demonstrators were protesting more than just Macready's being English; they also didn't like his acting. They preferred the acting style of the American-born Edwin Forrest (1806–1872), who was appearing just a few blocks away in a play about the gladiator Spartacus. Forrest was an "American-style" actor. He was a big presence with a strong voice, and his acting was described as "heroic" and "robust," in contrast to the more restrained and dignified Macready.

A war of words broke out between the two actors. It started when the London critics panned the American when he was acting in England. Forrest blamed his poor reviews on Macready and took revenge by attending Macready's performance of *Hamlet* and hissing from the audience. When Macready came to New York City to play Macbeth, the newspapers reported the charges and countercharges of their war of words. On the night of May 8, 1849, some "shiftless" young men, who had accused the Astor Place theatre of being "elitist" because its patrician dress code required white kid gloves and silk vests, infiltrated the audience. On cue, they began booing Macready. When this didn't stop the play, they pelted the stage with eggs, apples, potatoes, and a bottle of asafetida, a brownish, foul-smelling liquid once used in medicines. Macready's response was mock expressions of fear, which only enraged the young men even more. They threw chairs and wooden shingles at the stage, and Macready finally called off his performance. This was not the first time lower-class Americans had thrown things at him; in Cincinnati someone even pitched half a sheep's carcass on the stage. Only when the owners of the Astor Place promised police protection did Macready agree to return to the stage. But this time it would end in death.

On May 10, the rowdy young men once again managed to get in the theatre, but this time the police were waiting. When they interrupted the performance, they were thrown out. They began pelting the theatre with bricks from a nearby construction site and attracted a crowd, which grew to more than fifteen thousand protesters. When the police failed to disperse the crowd, they fired a volley over the crowd's heads, then at their feet, and then into them. When the smoke lifted, twenty-two people lay dead or dying and more than one hundred were wounded, all because, as the *New York Tribune* reported, "Two actors had quarreled."

The *Philadelphia Public Ledger* concluded, "It leaves behind a feeling to which this community had hitherto been a stranger . . . a feeling that there is now in our country, in New York City, what every good patriot had hitherto considered it his duty to deny—a high and a low class."

Bettmann/Corbis

One of the bloodiest theatre riots in history took place at Manhattan's Astor Place Opera House in 1849, causing twenty-two deaths and more than one hundred injuries—all because "two actors had quarreled."

directing (Chapter 8), design (Chapter 9), and theatre history (Part 3). But you don't have to be a theatre expert to a write meaningful criticism after seeing a performance or after reading a play (for more on reading plays see the Spotlight "Why Read Plays?"). The key is to ask the right questions and always include examples from the play itself that lead you to your answers or conclusion.

Three of the most productive questions for analysis were proposed by the great German romantic playwright, philosopher, and critic Johann Wolfgang von Goethe (1749–1832):

1. *What is the artist trying to do?* This question will help determine the direction of your essay. If you understand the intention of the artist, you will understand the reasons for his or her choices. Put aside your opinion of the play and identify the artist's purpose. What is the artist trying to express? What is the artist's goal? What was the artist trying to accomplish? Can you explain why the artist chose to bring this particular work into being?
2. *How well has the artist done it?* By answering this question, you judge the degree of success the artist achieves toward the goal you identified in answer to the first question. How do the artist's techniques, methods, and talents help to achieve the goal? How effective is the production in fulfilling the artist's intention?
3. *Is it worth doing?* The final question is whether the finished work of art was worth the artist's and the audience's time and effort. Does the play have new, interesting ideas? Will it help us understand the world, or understand it in a new way? If it didn't communicate to you, did it communicate to anyone else?

Goethe's simple formula has been used for hundreds of years and can lead to a well-structured, intelligent assessment of a play that is useful to audience members as well as to the artist. Another way to evaluate a play, which can be done separately or combined with Goethe's method, is to break the play into its basic components and analyze the effectiveness of each one. An excellent, time-tested definition of a play's elements is derived from Aristotle's *Poetics*. More than twenty-three centuries ago, Greek philosopher Aristotle deconstructed plays into six elements: plot, thought, character, diction, spectacle, and song. (For more on Aristotle and *Poetics*, see Chapter 1 and Part 3.) A clear and cohesive analysis of a play can be written by investigating how each element works by itself and in relation to the others. Here is a brief description of each element, followed by questions to which you might respond when analyzing it.

- ***Plot***

  Aristotle defined *plot* as a unified "arrangement of the incidents" in which characters, meaning, language, and visual elements come together to comment on a single subject. In other words, plot is what happens. Plot is the main story of a play. Because Aristotle believed that a story does not copy but, rather, imitates nature, it is not "real life" logic that determines the order of events but rather the requirements of the story. The action must be both probable and essential to the story.

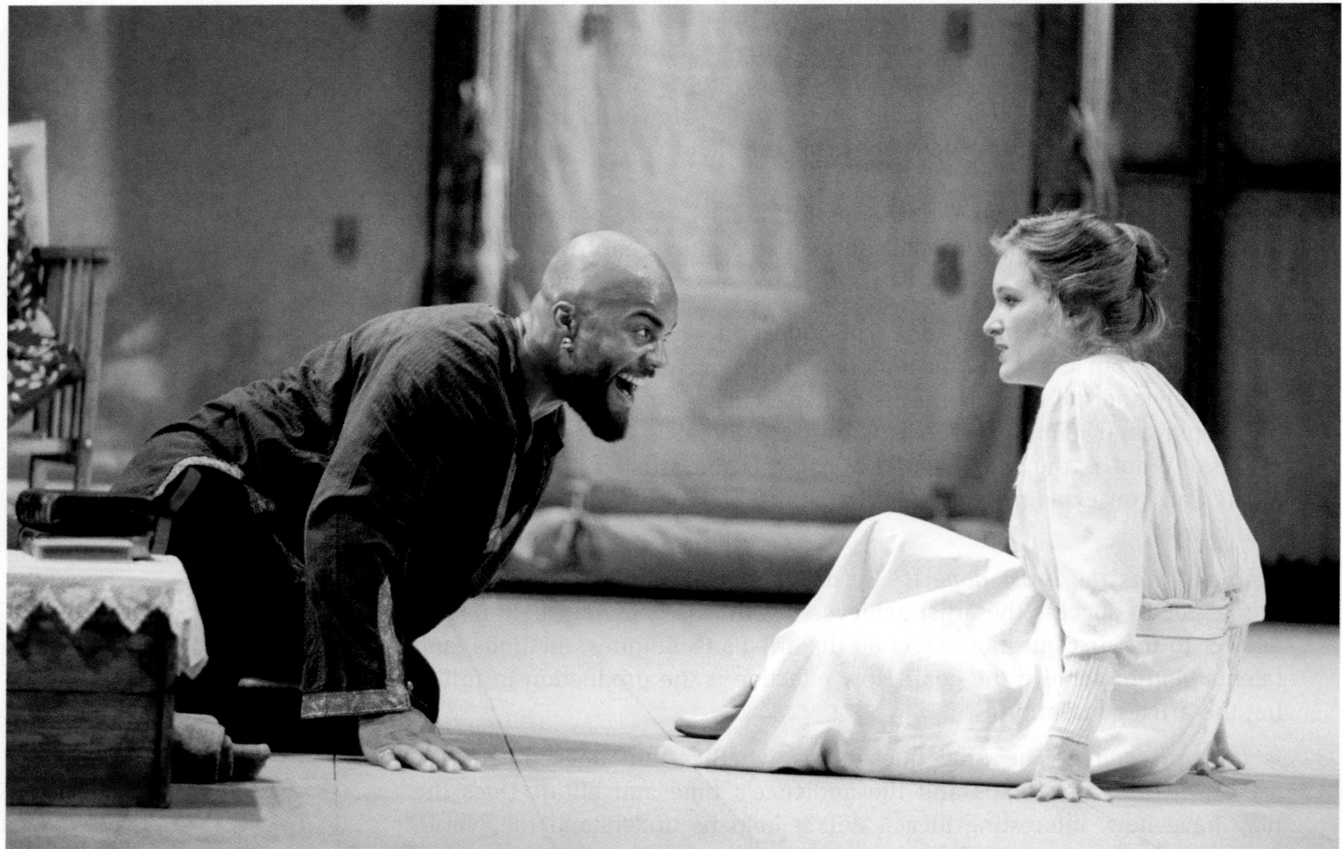

Donald Cooper/Photostage Ltd.

Understanding a character's motivations is critical for actors such as Ray Fearon and Zoe Walker, playing Othello and his wife, Desdemona, in this scene from Shakespeare's Othello. *Why does Othello believe his wife has been unfaithful? Why is he so enraged that he is willing to kill her for her supposed crime? Why is Desdemona unable to convince Othello of her innocence? To analyze a play effectively, you must ask similar questions. This 2001 Royal Shakespeare Company production was directed by Michael Attenborough at the Barbican Theatre, London.*

1. Are all the parts of the plot essential?
2. Are any parts of the plot unclear and why?
3. Is the story told in a linear or nonlinear way and why? That is, does it follow chronological order or jump around?
4. What are the main conflicts of the play, and how are they resolved or left unresolved and why?
5. Why does the playwright make the story a comedy instead of a serious play or a serious play instead of a comedy?

- ***Character***

  Character is about the personalities of the story. Characters are made up of motivation and action. We are what we do.

1. Which character is the protagonist (the main character around whom the story revolves, and without whom the play could not take place), and why do we care about him or her?
2. Which character is the antagonist (not necessarily the villain but rather the person who blocks the protagonist from getting what he or she wants)?
3. Are the characters' action and behaviors motivated?
4. What are the characters' objectives?
5. How does each character advance the play's plot?

6. How does each character advance the play's theme?
7. What is the psychological makeup of each character?
8. What are the characters' relationships?
9. Are the characters well developed, or are they caricatures that lack depth or are exaggerated?

- ***Thought***

Thought is what the play means, the ideas it's trying to communicate, and its themes or message. If plot is the series of actions in the play, thought asks what the sum of those actions mean. For some plays, thought is a complicated philosophy; for others, it is simply a question or idea about the universal human condition. Usually the meaning of a play is implied, not stated directly.

1. What is the play's thought, theme, or message?
2. How does the play's thought, theme, or message apply to today's social, cultural, or religious climate?
3. What events in the playwright's life motivated him or her to include this thought, theme, or message?
4. To what degree do you agree or disagree with the play's thought, theme, or message, and why?
5. Is the play's thought, theme, or message universal? Does it apply to human beings of any social class in any period? Why?
6. What does the play's theme say about human nature?
7. What do other criticisms say about the meaning of the play?

- ***Diction***

Aristotle describes *diction* as "modes of utterance." It is the dialogue used to create the thought, character, and plot. It is the playwright's mode of expression. From beautiful rhyming couplets to guttural grunts, diction comprises the human sounds that communicate the play.

1. How does the playwright use language to advance the plot?
2. How does the playwright use language to reveal the characters?
3. How does the characters' language reveal their background, education, or social class?
4. How do imagery and symbolism help or hurt the dialogue of the play?
5. What are the most memorable lines of the play and why?
6. How does the dialogue reveal the characters' identities?

- ***Spectacle***

Spectacle is the performance's set, costumes, and effects—the sensory aspects of the production. Aristotle said that spectacle is the least important element of any play, but he lived long before electric lights, recorded sound effects, and indoor theatres in which the environment could be controlled.

© P. Switzer

Plays such as Arthur Miller's The Crucible *have themes that can be applied to generation after generation, regardless of the setting.* The Crucible *concerns the 1693 Salem Witch Trials but is also an allegory to the McCarthyism of the 1950s as well as contemporary attempts to intimidate and censor alternative ideas. This production was produced by the Arvada Center for Arts and Humanities in Colorado.*

1. How do the set, lights, sound, and costumes help tell the story? How do they help set the mood?
2. How does the setting tell you about the characters?
3. Why does the playwright set the play where he or she did?
4. How does the director's staging advance the story, characters, and/or theme?
5. What is the style of the production? (For more on style, see Chapter 9.)

- ***Song***

Portions of ancient tragedies were sung, so Aristotle included *song* as a standard part of any play, but today song is optional. However, if you are analyzing a musical or a drama that incorporates music, you will certainly want to consider song.

1. How do the songs and music advance the plot, characters, or thoughts of the play?
2. How do the songs and music help set the mood?
3. Are all the songs and music necessary? If not, which ones and why not?

Using Goethe's and Aristotle's methods, you can break a play into its elements and specify how and why it does or doesn't work. Analyzing a play can also increase your understanding and open your mind to new points of view and forms of expression in the theatre.

Because plays often appeal to smaller audiences than movies and television do, they are more likely to express ideas outside the mainstream. Consequently, Goethe's last question, "Is it worth doing?" is more often asked in regard to plays. When some group takes a negative response further and insists the play *shouldn't* be done, criticism turns into censorship. The right to freedom of speech affects all of us, but theatre artists and critics are particularly concerned about it. Theatre practitioners rarely make a consistent living writing, producing, directing, or acting in plays, so it isn't money that drives them. What motivates many of them is having a forum for expressing ideas they are personally invested in. In the United States, the right to freedom of speech protects that expression.

The Right to Speak: Freedom of Speech and the Arts

We live in a society bristling with consumer warnings. Everything from power tools to children's toys has an inventory of warnings and dangers printed on labels. Even the entertainment industries have been pressured to come up with ratings systems and warning labels that let consumers know what age group the

Tony Savino/The Image Works

Artists often highlight a society's problems, cultural short comings, religious hypocrisy, and corporate greed, and so there are many groups that wish to censor them. Here a protester with the 1st Amendment etched into his t-shirt, protests in front of the United States Supreme Court.

producers think a particular program or product is suited for and what questionable content is to be expected. There is also the V-chip, which allows consumers to block any program they wish from their televisions. On top of this the FCC (Federal Communications Commission), which regulates radio and television, can impose fines of up to $325,000 on stations that broadcast over the public airwaves anything that does not meet its decency standards—standards that are not particularly well-defined and therefore often force filmmakers, PBS, and other broadcast companies to self-censor to avoid a possible penalty. No such warning labels or consumer protections exist in the theatre. A play may be advertised as a children's play or a theatre may choose to warn theatregoers that a particular production is inappropriate for children, but no government institution such as the FCC regulates the theatre. Instead, audience members must take responsibility for researching a play if they want to know its content before viewing it. The fact that there is no rating system for theatre can lead to problems regarding the right to express ideas freely. Some members of the public want not only to be warned about the content of a particular play, but also to restrict the content of plays so that certain ideas will never be heard, even by those who desire to hear them.

Free speech is most often contested when unpopular or controversial ideas are being expressed. Yet if only popular ideas were protected, there would be no need for the First Amendment, which states, "Congress shall make no law respecting an establishment of religion, or prohibiting the free exercise thereof; or abridging the freedom of speech, or of the press; or the right of the people peaceably to assemble, and to petition the Government for a redress of grievances." **Censorship** is the altering, restricting, or suppressing of information, images, or words circulated within a society. It can take the form of banning or altering books, periodicals, films, television and radio programs, video games, content on the Internet, news reports, theatrical productions, or any other expression

> Without censorship, things can get terribly confused in the public mind.
>
> ***General William Westmoreland,***
> commenting on the Vietnam War as the first war without censorship

of thought that someone finds objectionable or offensive. Even though freedom of speech has been a part of America's tradition since its beginning, some people still call for censorship, particularly in the arts.

> If the printed word facilitates the working of the imagination, then the staging of dramatic scenes in a public auditorium by presenting these images to our senses in much stronger colors makes a much deeper impression on the spectator and stirs their passion more violently.
>
> ***Czar Nicholas I,***
> Russian ruler, justifying censorship of the stage

You Can't Say That on Stage!

Theatre has been censored for thousands of years. Records of censorship go back to antiquity. In 493 BCE, the playwright Phrynichus presented his tragedy *The Capture of Miletus* at the Theatre of Dionysus in Athens. The play was about the fall of the Greek city Miletus, which had been sacked by the Persians the year before. The government felt that the play reminded the citizens of their misfortunes, so it banned the play and fined the playwright. The Roman emperor Caligula ordered actors and playwrights who offended him to be burned alive. In the late Middle Ages and the Renaissance, the church banned or condemned opposing ideas with papal edicts, the Inquisition, and the *Index of Forbidden Books*.

In 1737, the **Licensing Act** was passed in England. This law placed the censoring of plays under the authority of the Lord Chamberlain, one of the officials of the royal court. Any plays that contained negative comments about the king or queen, unorthodox opinions, or statements considered heretical or seditious could be censored; the term *legitimate theatre* comes from this period. In 1817 Shakespeare's play *King Lear*, about a king who slowly loses his mind rather than believe that his daughters have betrayed him, was banned for several years in England because officials were afraid the audience might associate it with the madness of King George III. In 1818 Thomas Bowdler published *The Family Shakespeare*, in which he had edited out of Shakespeare's plays all words and expressions "which cannot with propriety be read aloud in a family." The result was Shakespeare without the bawdy jokes, playful banter, or any mention of sexuality. This is where the term *bowdlerize* originated. To **bowdlerize** means to remove any possibly vulgar, obscene, or otherwise objectionable material before publication.

For almost eighty-five years the Comstock Act (1823) was used to censor mail in the United States. If Post Office inspectors decided a book, picture, play, or other item was indecent, they would seize all copies and arrest both the sender and the receiver. The list of items banned from the mail included information on birth control, anatomical drawings, anything written by atheists, agnostics, or freethinkers, and information about cures for venereal disease. They even seized copies of pictures of Egyptian belly dancers that were mailed from the Chicago World's Fair. J. D. Salinger's *The Catcher in the Rye* has the distinction of being the most frequently censored book in the United States since its publication in 1951, primarily because the main character, teenager Holden Caulfield, takes the Lord's name in vain 295 times.

Hollywood has also long been a target of censorship. In the 1930s, complaints by religious leaders were so numerous that Hollywood producers "voluntarily" submitted to the Hays Code, which stated, "No picture shall be produced that will lower the moral standards of those who see it." The Hays Code banned any scene that contained homosexuality, adultery, or sex. It even limited the length of a screen kiss to three seconds. The code also banned a long list of words and phrases, including *fairy, goose, madam, pansy, tart, in your hat*, and *nuts*. The Hays Code was in force until 1968, when the modern rating system took over.

The theatre has almost always been the first of the arts to be censored because it can rouse emotions, create empathy, hide subliminal messages, and stir groups of people to action. A novel may stir emotions but it does so for only one reader at a time—the theatre does it en masse. Another reason the theatre has been heavily censored is the problem of interpretation. The dialogue of a play might appear harmless on the page, but it can be interpreted by an actor to have new meanings. Unlike a film or a novel, a play can be changed from one performance to the next. A wink, a change in vocal inflection, or the slightest gesture can change the meaning. In Poland during the Soviet occupation, every theatre performance had to hold seats for censors so that every performance could be monitored. This is still true in many countries. For example, in Egypt a censorship committee must first see all plays before any can open to the general public.

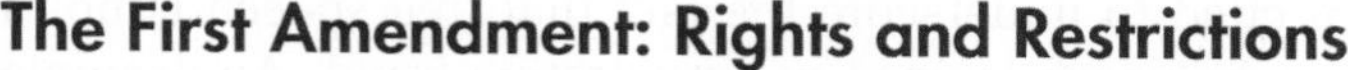

The First Amendment: Rights and Restrictions

Photofest

Although Lucille Ball and Desi Arnaz were married in real life, societal standards dictated that they could not be shown sharing a bed during the run of their 1950s sitcom I Love Lucy. Even when Lucy was expecting their first child, network officials prohibited the scriptwriters—who had written the birth of the baby into the show—from using the word "pregnant."

The First Amendment protects our right to express ourselves not only with words but also with nonverbal, visual, and symbolic forms of expression. A silent candlelight vigil is protected by the First Amendment as freedom of speech. Symbolic gestures are also protected, such as burning the American flag—as long as the flag is your property and you obey local fire codes. Satire of public figures is protected as well. In 1988 the Supreme Court ruled in *Hustler Magazine v. Falwell* that satirical portraits of public figures, such as presidents, religious leaders, and movie stars, are protected under the First Amendment even if the satire is insulting, vulgar, or false. However, freedom of speech is not guaranteed in all situations. Exceptions include defamation; expression that causes a breach of the peace, sedition, or incitement to crime; expression that violates the separation of church and state; and obscenity.

Defamation Freedom of speech does not cover the publication or statement of alleged facts that are false and harm the reputation of another. This exception to freedom of speech is difficult to apply because the expression of an opinion that is false is allowed. In other words, you have the right to express a factually wrong or politically incorrect opinion. Let's say a theatre critic writes a highly negative review about a play and says that the acting is horrible and the playwright is an execrable writer. Even though none of his opinions are accurate, audiences stay away and the producer has to declare bankruptcy. The critic cannot be sued because the review is his opinion and is covered under the First Amendment. But if the critic publishes a false negative statement, such as a made-up quotation from the city inspector saying that the theatre is unsafe, then the producer can sue because a false statement was published as fact.

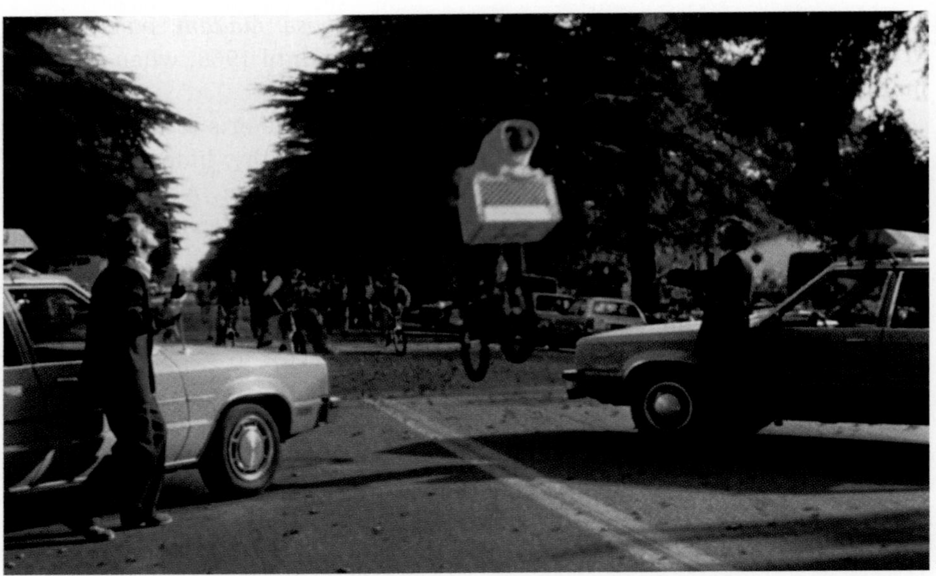

Photofest

Although there is no longer a Hays Code restricting what can be said and done in movies, a rating system does exist, and some artists and watchdog groups charge that these ratings result in a form of censorship. For example, top directors are contractually obligated to edit their films to avoid the most restrictive rating, NC-17, and movie theatres located in shopping malls are often contractually prohibited from showing NC-17 films. Some directors even censor themselves to better appeal to family-friendly markets. In the 2002 re-release of the movie E.T., this scene depicting police officers trying to capture Elliott and E.T. was digitally altered to show the officers with walkie-talkies instead of the guns that appeared in the original movie.

Breach of the Peace In 1919, Supreme Court Justice Oliver Wendell Holmes wrote, "The most stringent protection of free speech would not protect a man in falsely shouting fire in a theatre and causing a panic." This famous maxim has often been cited to underscore the fact that free speech is not a viable defense when such speech is used to perpetrate a fraud. An example is Orson Welles's *War of the Worlds* radio broadcast. On the night of October 30, 1938, Welles, famous for his movie *Citizen Kane*, broadcast to more than one hundred radio stations in the eastern United States a play version of H. G. Wells's novel *War of the Worlds*. In order to make this story of an alien invasion of the earth more realistic, Welles interrupted another show with seemingly real "breaking news" reports about meteors landing on earth and huge mechanical monsters emerging from the debris. Some people who heard the fake bulletins panicked. The newly created FCC (Federal Communications Commission) reprimanded the station and passed rules to prevent such a pseudo-event from happening again.

Sedition and Incitement to Crime The Supreme Court has affirmed that freedom of speech does not cover unlawful conduct against the government or speech that advocates the violent overthrow of the government. This point can be difficult to argue because we all have the right to criticize the government and demand change. You can write a play in which you advocate "throwing the bums out," but you cannot write a play in which you unequivocally urge the audience to assassinate the president.

This exception to freedom of speech also applies to the laws of the land. If your words incite someone to commit a crime, the First Amendment does not protect your words. This exception to freedom of speech has been used for several years in an attempt to silence gangsta rap artists, most notoriously Ice-T and his band Body Count. Their 1992 track "Cop Killer" was condemned by law enforcement officials, who claimed that the song incited crime against police officers. The same charge has been applied to some movies, such as Oliver Stone's *Natural Born Killers*, a story about a young couple who commit a series of ruthless murders. In the mid 1990s, a family in Ponchatoula, Louisiana, sued Stone and Time Warner Entertainment for damages after a family member was shot by two teenagers. The family claimed that the teenagers' shooting spree was inspired by repeated viewings of Stone's movie. The case was dismissed in 2001 because the family's lawyers couldn't prove that Stone intended to incite violence.

Bettmann/Corbis

In 1938 Hollywood writer and director Orson Welles broadcast a dramatization of H. G. Wells's alien invasion story, War of the Worlds. *The program was so realistic that Welles eliminated the audience's aesthetic distance and broke their willing suspension of disbelief. As a result some radio listeners panicked, believing that an actual Martian invasion was taking place. The broadcast caused such a commotion that the FCC passed rules to prevent future such breaches of peace.*

Separation of Church and State The part of the First Amendment that states "Congress shall make no law respecting an establishment of religion" is known as the "establishment clause." It means that the government cannot endorse, or appear to endorse, any religion. This is a sensitive point to many people who view the clause as a violation of their personal freedom of speech. This controversy was highlighted when the National Endowment for the Arts (NEA; see Chapter 2) funded an exhibition of work in 1990 by artist David Wojnarowicz. The exhibition, titled "Tongues of Flame," included a painting that attacked prominent religious and political figures and accused them of being indifferent to the suffering caused by AIDS. A lawyer filed a lawsuit against the NEA, alleging that the exhibition displayed "hostility toward religion" and that the art caused him to suffer "spiritual injury" because it was offensive to his "religious sensibilities." He also charged that, because the art was partly funded by the government through an NEA grant, it violated the establishment clause. The idea was that if the government cannot endorse religion, then it should not be allowed to support art that attacks religion.

The court ruled that there is a difference between spiritual injury and physical or economic injury. Freedom of speech can be suppressed if it causes physical or economic injury, but cannot be suppressed if it causes spiritual injury. In other words, you cannot deny someone an opinion just because it makes you feel bad, such as a critic's negative review. But what about the second part of the lawsuit, that the government should not fund art that insults religion? The court ruled that Congress does not directly decide how the NEA funds are to be spent, because the NEA is an independent government agency; nor is the NEA simply administering Congress's wishes. Thus the government was not directly attacking religion and the grant did not violate the establishment clause. This decision highlighted a fascinating loophole in the establishment clause: not only is it legal for the NEA to fund art that criticizes or insults religion, but it can also fund art that promotes an appreciation for religion, which it has done on many occasions.

Obscenity Freedom of speech does not apply to obscenity, but the courts have long struggled to define the word *obscene*. The word means many different things to different people. In 1973 the Supreme Court (*Miller v. California*) established a three-pronged test for obscenity:

1. Whether the average person, applying contemporary community standards, would find that the work, taken as a whole, appeals to the prurient interest;
2. Whether the work depicts or describes, in a patently offensive way, sexual conduct specifically defined by the applicable state law; and
3. Whether the work, taken as a whole, lacks serious literary, artistic, political, or scientific value.

These standards remain in effect today but are still surrounded by controversy. The Court basically said that each community could adopt its own idea of what is obscene, but how do we define *community* in the age of the Internet? A web page that may be acceptable to someone in Los Angeles, California, might be grounds for arrest if it were downloaded in Opp, Alabama. And who decides what is of "serious literary, artistic, political, or scientific value"? Many feel that the Court has not solved the problem of defining obscenity but has only made it more complicated, so obscenity prosecutions are rare.

Despite these exceptions to the First Amendment, there is much room for freedom of speech in the arts. But there are also many people who still wish to limit speech and control content. For example, in 2005 Ted Stevens, chairman of the Senate Commerce Committee, proposed banning what he considered foul language on cable and satellite television. He was speaking specifically of the profuse use of "four-letter words with participles" in the HBO series *Deadwood*, the story of a rowdy gold-rush mining town in the Dakota Territory in the late 1870s. However, unlike network television, cable and satellite television are not subject to the same FCC standards because they are not broadcast over the public airwaves. In addition, *Deadwood* is probably quite accurate in its portrayal of this slice of American history, obscene language and all.

Today, people who want to censor seldom use the word *censorship*. More often, they hide behind such terms as *speech code, political correctness, decency*, and *morals*. And people who want to restrict speech seldom see themselves as censors; more often they believe that they are protecting basic social institutions and values, such as religion, patriotism, the war effort, or children. The critical questions remain: Who decides what will be censored and what will not? Is it possible to create a society in which the audience is never offended? And what happens if we succeed? One possibility is that we become less tolerant of other people's opinions and right to express themselves.

Curtain Call

Powerful forces are at work when people join together into a group, and many, including the artists, would like to control those forces. The power of the audience may come from being in a group, but every audience is made up of individuals who must decide if a given work has meaning. Too often today, audience members dismiss a play because it isn't to their liking, but if they knew how to analyze plays beyond simple opinion, they could come to a deeper understanding of the work. Only when audiences learn to analyze and artists are free to create does the theatre become a powerful work of art. As Czech playwright Václav Havel said, "[I]f theatre is free conversation, free dialogue, among free people about the mysteries of the world, then it is precisely what will show humankind the way toward tolerance, mutual respect, and respect for the miracle of Being."

Summary

There are as many reasons to attend the theatre as there are audience members. But even though each member of the audience is unique, when they join together in a group, there are forces at work that can change how they feel and react. These forces include group dynamics, the suspension of disbelief, and aesthetic distance.

When you go to the theatre, you never know exactly how much you will be asked to participate. Some plays require you to be active, and others require you to sit quietly in the dark. Depending on what type of play you are seeing, the rules of etiquette change. These rules cover everything from how to behave to what to wear. Attending the theatre is also different than attending a movie; not only are you expected to behave differently, but tickets are harder to get and there are fewer performances to see. Going to the theatre requires more of an effort than going to movies or watching television, so going to the theatre takes a little more planning.

Once you see or read a play, it is important that you think about it and learn to evaluate it with more than a simple "I liked it" or "I didn't like it." In order to become a connoisseur of the theatre, you must learn to justify your critical thoughts by asking these three questions: What is the artist trying to do? How well has the artist done it? Is it worth doing? Plays can also be analyzed in terms of plot, character, thought, diction, spectacle, and sometimes even song.

Who controls what the audience sees and hears? In a few ideal cases the artist controls content, but usually other entities are involved. The government, corporations, religious institutions, or even the audience themselves can demand, legislate, or enforce censorship. Freedom of speech is important because self-expression is at the core of all works of art. However, limitations are placed on artists by the Constitution and the courts, including defamation, breach of the peace, sedition and incitement to crime, separation of church and state, and obscenity.

The Art of Theatre ONLINE 

To access this chapter's interactive theatre workshop activities, along with many other learning tools, log onto your Theatre CourseMate. Access is available at cengagebrain.com.

Key Terms

aesthetic distance / 76
bowdlerize / 94
censorship / 93
curtain / 81
director's note / 84
dramatic criticism / 86
fourth wall / 78
group dynamics / 74
League of Resident Theatres (LORT) / 82
Licensing Act of 1737 / 94
paper the house / 74
playwright's note / 84
presentational theatre / 77
preview performances / 83
realism / 78
representational theatre / 78
talk-back / 84
reviews / 86
road houses / 82
souvenir programs / 84
Will Call / 81
willing suspension of disbelief / 75

Without makeup the actors' faces would appear flat and washed out under the high-intensity theatrical lighting. Here actors Nick Linn, Katrina Despain, and Rachel Rosenfeld prepare for the evening's performance.

Photos on this spread Jim West/PhotoEdit; William Missouri Downs

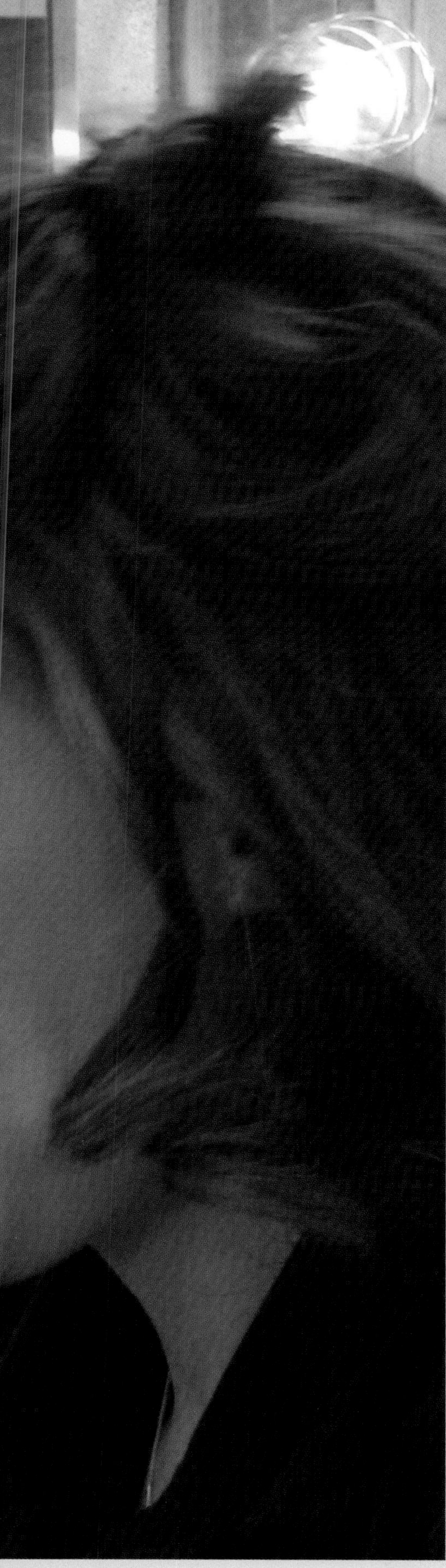

CHAPTER 5

A Day in the Life of a Theatre

OUTLINE

9 AM: Entering Springfield Ensemble Rep by Ghost Light
10 AM: Checking Wardrobe and Planning for Next Season
11 AM: Rehearsing and Building a Show
NOON: Fund-Raising, Designing, and Sewing
1 PM: More Rehearsing
2 PM: Creating Sets and Sounds, and Advising the Director
3 PM: Attending Meetings and Creating a Mission Statement
4 PM: Publicizing a Play and Fitting Costumes
5 PM: Brainstorming a Concept
6 PM: Preparing for the Evening Performance
7 PM: Opening the House
8 PM: Performing the First Act
9 PM: Performing the Final Act
10 PM: Clearing Out
11 PM: Bringing Out the Ghost Light
Curtain Call

Theatre is a hybrid art. More often than not it is brought to you by an **ensemble**, or dozens of artists and technicians, including playwrights, actors, directors, and designers, as well as painters, carpenters, drapers, stagehands, and electricians, who join together to make it appear as if a performance were the product of a single creative mind. In order for a production to be successful, a theatre must have a well-organized power structure (see Figure 5.1) that allows for unfettered communication as well as a delineation of duties, which gives each member of the ensemble the freedom to create as they share the same artistic vision.

The *ensemble* is so important that many theatre companies—such as the West Coast Ensemble and the Boulder Ensemble Theatre Company—include the word in their name.

To understand how theatre works, let's look at a day in the life of a typical large repertory theatre. The word **repertory** means a group of plays performed by a theatre company during the course of a season. For example, the Colorado Shakespeare Festival's repertory might include *A Midsummer Night's Dream*, *Hamlet*, and *Romeo and Juliet*. Many theatres include the word repertory in their name, such as the Milwaukee Repertory Theater, the Seattle Repertory Theatre, and the San Jose Repertory Theatre. Often these theatres shorten the word repertory to "Rep,"

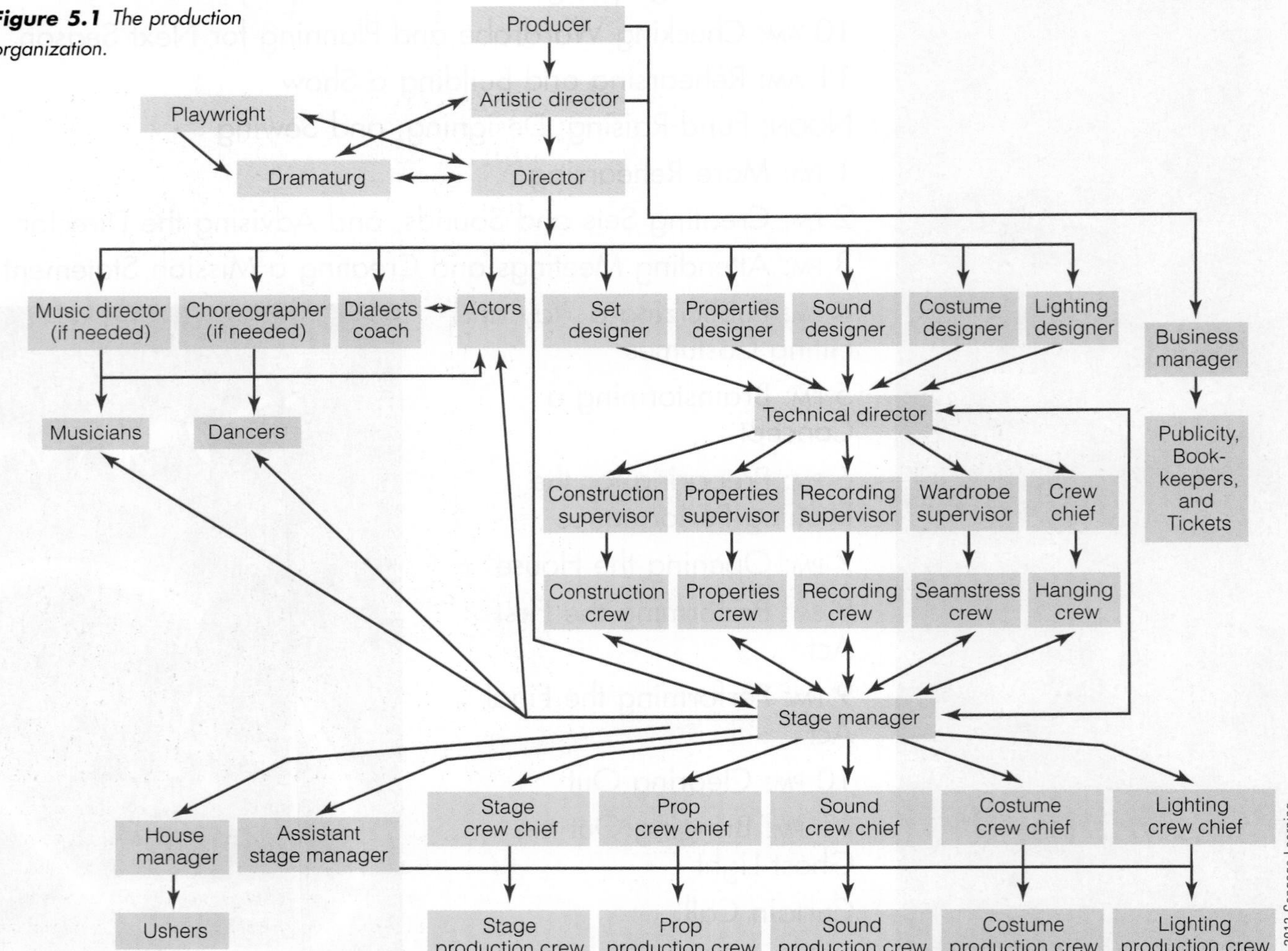

Figure 5.1 *The production organization.*

as in "The Seattle Rep." For the purposes of this chapter, we will call our imaginary theatre the Springfield Ensemble Rep and explore, hour by hour, the ensemble of people who contribute to the work done on stage and behind the scenes during a day in the life of a theatre.

9 AM: Entering Springfield Ensemble Rep by Ghost Light

The otherwise dark stage is lit by a single bare lightbulb mounted on a portable pole. This solitary illumination is known as the **ghost light**, which was rolled out on stage the night before as a safety precaution. Walking into a jet-black theatre and trying to find the light switch can be dangerous, so the ghost light is left burning all night in the middle of the stage. The flickering of the naked bulb throws long, spooky shadows. Add this to its rather eerie name, and you can see why there have been many superstitions concerning ghost lights. The custodians are first to turn on the work lights at the beginning of a new day to clean the theatre after the previous night's performance.

Bob O'Connor/Getty Images

Finding a light switch in a dark, empty theatre can be difficult and dangerous, so a single "ghost light" is often left burning near center stage.

Meanwhile, the staff arrives at the adjoining offices of the theatre. The Springfield Ensemble Rep has several administrative assistants, literary staff to read plays, bookkeepers to pay the bills, and box-office staff to sell tickets. Some theatres find it too expensive to run a box office, so they subcontract to companies like Ticketmaster, but the Springfield Ensemble Rep has a big enough staff to handle the workload. Ticket sales roll in through the Internet and by phone.

10 AM: Checking Wardrobe and Planning for Next Season

In the **costume shop**, crews are washing the costumes from last night's performance. A typical costume shop has rows of sewing machines, fabric-cutting tables, fitting rooms, and laundry facilities. Acting under the hot theatrical lights for several hours means that most costumes can seldom be worn for more than one performance without first being washed and pressed. Costume crews are also looking for any stains and making minor repairs. If actors wear just a few costumes each in a simple contemporary play, such as the one currently showing at the Springfield Ensemble Rep, then there may be less work for the costume shop. However, if it is a large, complicated show requiring sequined costumes and wig maintenance, the process can be time-consuming. For example, the Broadway musical *Titanic* needed five wig

Bruce Gilkas/FilmMagic/Getty Images

What you see on stage takes hundreds of hours of rehearsal and the talent and time of wig makers, costume designers, drapers, and stitchers. It also takes several backstage assistants to clean, repair, and maintain costumes and wigs between performances. Here, Aubrey O'Day and Karen Mason perform a scene from the Broadway musical Hairspray.

dressers to care for the show's seventy-one wigs, and fourteen wardrobe people to repair, wash, starch, and press the 180 costumes between performances. In all, *Titanic*'s costume maintenance required more than 275 hours a week.

In the literary department the **literary manager** has begun another day of reading and evaluating new scripts for next season. The literary manager is a liaison between playwrights, agents, and the theatre. Also, this person often writes grant applications to help support new play development and stage readings of new plays. The literary department at even a moderately well-known theatre can receive up to one thousand scripts a year from struggling playwrights. Notoriously understaffed, the literary manager and assistant (if there is one) cannot possibly read all the scripts. This is why they commonly ask playwrights without agents to send only sample pages, a synopsis, and cover letter; if the literary manager likes the sample, she requests a copy of the full script. The office is stacked with hundreds of scripts yet to be read—plays by famous playwrights submitted through agents, and by lesser-known playwrights who have been queried to submit plays in their entirety. Because such a backlog is common, some playwrights wait as long as a year to get a rejection letter. The literary department rejects a vast majority of scripts, but chooses perhaps one hundred a year for closer scrutiny. In the end, the literary manager only forwards a few dozen scripts to the artistic director for possible inclusion in a future season.

What prepared me for the artistic director job? Everything and nothing. . . . One of the biggest problems I face is when to be pragmatic in solving a problem and when to just insist on the art.

Irene Lewis,
Artistic director of the Center Stage in Baltimore

A few doors away, the artistic director of the theatre is in a budget meeting with the producing director. In the theatre a **producer** or a **producing director**

Oscar-winning actor Cate Blanchett is known for her powerful performances in movies like Elizabeth *(1998),* Oscar & Lucinda *(1997), and* Notes on a Scandal *(2006). She also serves as the co-artistic director of the Sydney Theatre Company in Australia.*

Patrick Riviere/Getty Images

SPOTLIGHT ON The Producers

The word *producer* has different meanings depending on how it is used. For a Hollywood movie as for a play on Broadway, the producer is the person in charge of the business and managerial side of a production. For a television sitcom or hour-length drama, the producer is usually a staff writer who may have a title such as associate producer, producer, or executive producer. However, for other kinds of television shows, the producer has the same business-managerial role as the producer for motion pictures or the theatre. Just to make the definition even more confusing, in England the word producer is often used to denote the person who directs a play.

In the American theatre, producers may be individuals who put up their own money or control an investor's money to finance a production—or they may be institutions such as universities, churches, or community organizations that handle the business side of the production. Depending on the size of the production, the financial responsibilities can range from small to large, sometimes involving millions of dollars. If the theatre is nonprofit, the producer—often called a producing director—must manage all the aspects of the theatre's budget to meet government regulations for nonprofit organizations. If a play is performed for profit, the producer assumes financial responsibility for any losses but also pockets any profit. Because money is involved, the producer or producing organization is one of the most powerful positions in the theatre. It is the producer's responsibility to raise money, negotiate contracts, keep financial records, pay taxes, and hire the creative, production, and construction teams.

AP Photo/Paul Sancya

A well-known and prolific director in the theatre, Woodie King, Jr. (pictured at right, with Morgan Freeman and Ruby Dee) has also produced many plays, including For Colored Girls Who Have Considered Suicide When the Rainbow Is Enuf *and* Reggae.

is someone who financially backs the theatre or orchestrates funding through grant money and ticket sales (see Spotlight "The Producers"), and the **artistic director** is in charge of the overall creative vision or goal of the ensemble. The artistic director will often choose which plays to produce, who will direct them, and who will design them. A director is in charge of a single play, whereas the artistic director is in charge of an entire season of plays. He or she needs to find a repertory that includes tried and true audience favorites, but he or she also needs to introduce the audience to plays they don't know. The artistic director also manages the ensemble by making sure that all its members work together and have the same artistic goal. On top of this, the artistic director is an ambassador to the community, a fund-raiser, and the theatre's chief promoter. The position of artistic director is so important that it sometimes attracts world-famous stars to the job: the Oscar-winning actors Cate Blanchett and Kevin Spacey are both artistic directors, of the Sydney Theatre Company in Australia and the Old Vic Theatre in London, respectively.

11 AM: Rehearsing and Building a Show

In one of the rehearsal halls, the director and actors are rehearsing the next play in the repertory. Though not as visible, one of the most important people in the room during rehearsal is not the director or actors but the **stage manager**, also known as the SM (and sometimes known as the PSM, for "production stage manager"). The stage manager not only runs the show during the performance but also helps the director throughout the rehearsal process by taking notes, recording blocking (the movement of the actors on stage—see Chapter 8), scheduling rehearsals, and assisting during auditions. The stage manager has many responsibilities, from getting coffee (although this is often done by the assistant stage manager or ASM) to enforcing safety rules, and therefore she often requires the help of several assistants (see the Spotlight "Managing the Stage").

> *In theatre it's about emotion. It differs every night and it's the stage manager's job to respond to what's happening on stage and in the audience. The actor says something, the audience responds, and the stage manager responds. At the end of the show, when the audience applauds—yes, of course they're applauding the actors, but they're also applauding everyone backstage who made the production possible.*
>
> **Alan Hall,**
> Stage manager of the Tony Awards

Down in the scene shop, the set construction crew is building the set for a play that opens in two weeks. Most theatres have well-equipped scene shops with a variety of metalworking and woodworking tools; an electric shop with equipment to maintain, repair, and hang lights; and a paint shop, where paint is stored and mixed. Theatres also have a great deal of storage space for all the costumes, props, wood, platforms, and flats that are used during a production. A **flat** is the standard scenery unit made of wooden frames covered with canvas, muslin, or thin plywood. Most flats are from twelve to sixteen feet tall and one to six feet wide. Some flats are plain wall units, whereas others are built to accommodate doors, windows, and fireplaces. Other scenery units include platforms, steps, and staircases, fake fireplaces, doors, and window frames.

In many small theatres, designers are forced to build their own designs, but in larger professional theatres like the Springfield Ensemble Rep the designers turn over their drawings, paintings, blueprints, scale models, and sketches to the **technical director**, or TD. The TD supervises the construction crews, which include painters, carpenters, electricians, stitchers, wig makers, and others who are often collectively known as the "tech crew." The technical director has authority over all the crew chiefs, such as the master carpenter and the chief electrician, and answers only to the director, the designers, the budget office, and the artistic director. Depending on the size of the production, the tech crew can be made up of a few people or dozens.

William Missouri Downs

Building the set and hanging lights are labor-intensive processes that can take weeks. Here, crews hang lights at the Vienna Opera house in Austria.

Noon: Fund-Raising, Designing, and Sewing

At a local restaurant, the artistic director is having lunch with a wealthy business owner, trying to subtly convince her that supporting the Springfield Ensemble Rep is good for the community and her company. Most theatres make only about 50

SPOTLIGHT ON Managing the Stage

One of the most important positions in the theatre is that of the stage manager. From auditions to closing night, the stage manager is involved in every aspect of the play. The stage manager's job starts in pre-rehearsal meetings with the director and designers. For the audition process, she will post audition announcements, reserve audition and rehearsal spaces, prepare the room for auditions, and assist the director during auditions. Once rehearsals start, the SM maintains contact sheets, obtains rehearsal props, schedules rehearsals, and generates and keeps a **prompt book** in which every aspect of the production is recorded. This book includes light cues, blocking, technical notes, and director's notes. Sometimes the prompt book is called the production's "bible" because everything that is important is recorded in it.

At the end of each rehearsal, the stage manager stays after to write up a **rehearsal report**, which is then e-mailed to everyone involved with the production. This report lets the entire ensemble know how rehearsal went and informs designers about any concerns or ideas that came up that affect the set, lights, props, or costumes.

Once a play is up and running, the stage manager becomes the production stage manager, or PSM. The director usually leaves and the PSM takes over. The PSM, often with the help of several **assistant stage managers** (ASM), conducts the technical rehearsals, authorizes when an understudy goes on instead of a primary cast member, calls for brush-up rehearsals, and continually gives friendly reminders to everyone about where they have to be and when.

During a performance the PSM sits in the control booth and calls all the cues: instructing the light board operator when to change the lights, the sound board operator when to play music, and the backstage crew when to move scenery. At the end of a performance, the PSM gives notes to the actors and crew and also writes a detailed **performance report** that includes any problems that occurred and what needs to be fixed before the next performance.

In short, the stage manager is the conduit and facilitator of the whole process, something akin to a conductor or maestro. Stage managers must be well organized, know how to communicate with artists as well as backstage crews, and possess the rarest of all qualities—the ability to stay calm in a crisis.

William Missouri Downs

A stage manager typically has so many responsibilities that she or he will often need one or two assistants. Here, stage manager Danielle Fullerton and assistant stage manager Leean Kim Torske go over a checklist before an evening performance.

percent of their budget from ticket sales, so fund-raising goes on seven days a week (see Chapter 2).

Meanwhile, back in the costume shop, drapers and stitchers are making the costumes for the play that opens in two weeks. A **draper's** job is to study the costume designer's drawings and renderings (see Chapter 9) and then find a way to cut fabric into patterns that realize the design. A few feet away the **stitchers** sew the fabric patterns together creating the full costumes. They also build or find **rehearsal costumes**, used temporarily during rehearsal so that the actors get a feel for the actual costumes long before they are ready. For example, if an actress must wear a long Victorian skirt in a play, then the costume shop sews a long rehearsal skirt of plain muslin. Actors seldom get to put on the real costume until just days before a play opens.

The technical director supervises the various construction crews to ensure the designer's visions are realized. Here, tech director Larry Hazlett guides traffic as various construction crews work.

William Missouri Downs

In a nearby shop, the **prop master** is busy working on the props for the next production. **Prop** is theatre lingo for "properties" and includes hand props or any objects actors handle while on stage, such as pens, fans, cigars, and umbrellas. There are also set props, which include sofas, chairs, beds, etc. Prop masters find and buy props for productions, and they often design and build them. The prop master is also in charge of **rehearsal props**. Just as with rehearsal costumes, these props are used during rehearsals to represent the real property that the actors will not be able to use until the last week of rehearsals.

Typically, actors don't wear their costumes in rehearsal until just days before a play opens. In order to get a feel for the costume, the costume shop often builds rehearsal costumes. Here, actors Megan Antles, Katrina Despain, and Rachel Rosenfeld model their rehearsal skirts and corsets. The corsets are worn on the outside during rehearsal so that they can be easily removed during breaks.

William Missouri Downs

1 PM: More Rehearsing

Back in the rehearsal halls, work on the next production is slowed due to problems with space allocation. The next play is to be a musical that takes place during the Restoration, which will require several simultaneous rehearsals. In one rehearsal hall, the musical director is teaching the actors their songs. The **musical director** supervises all aspects of a musical and conducts the orchestra during performances. In another hall the **choreographer** has created new dance numbers and is teaching the steps to the dancers. In still another, the **movement coach** is showing the actors how people moved during the Restoration—a time when graceful mannerisms were the norm. Starved for space, the **fight director** is forced to hold his rehearsal in a hallway. Fight directors are experts at staging safe, realistic, make-believe fights. Stage combat, such as fistfights and swordplay, must be carefully choreographed and can be time-consuming to create. Every thirty seconds of a staged fight can take many hours to rehearse. Finally, upstairs the voice and dialect coach has found an unused office for her rehearsal. The **vocal coach** helps the actors with speech clarity, volume, and preservation of their voices for the long run of

Drew Farrell/ArenaPAL/Topham/Image Works

Prop masters spend their days researching, designing, and building properties. Properties are built to endure the run of the show and must often be historically accurate. In this shot, Rachel George builds miniature dolls for an opera at the Festival Theatre in Edinburgh, Scotland.

AP Photo/Keith Srakocic

There are many types of rehearsals, including fight, dance, blocking, and singing. At this movement rehearsal, students from Point Park University practice for Bill Nunn's experimental dramatization of African folktales.

Damon Winter/The New York Times/Redux Pictures

Musicals require dozens of special rehearsals for the actors to learn their parts. Here, musical director Robert Bass works with actors Dwayne Croft and Emily Pulley.

The sound designer selects or creates every sound you hear during a performance. Here, sound engineer Gabriele Nicotra works the sound mixing board at the Little Sicily Stage in Malmesbury, England.

Louise Wilson/Getty Images

a show. If the character requires a particular accent, the coach will also give the actors lessons on how to speak realistically with that accent.

2 PM: Creating Sets and Sounds, and Advising the Director

> A lot of what sound designers do is detective work. The ability to figure out what's needed and then find it.
>
> **Rob Milburu,** Sound designer

In the sound booth, the **sound designer** is working with various effects recordings as she synthesizes the sounds, so that everything from the pre-show music to the sound of a doorbell is exactly right (for more on sound design see Chapter 9). In a nearby office, the **set designer** boots up his computer and uses a CAD (computer aided design) program to design a set for a production that will not be needed for several months. Designers often work many months in advance and on several sets at a time (see Chapter 9).

Back in the literary department, the director of the next play is meeting with a dramaturg for advice on the production. The duties of a **dramaturg** can be difficult to define because no two theatres use them in exactly the same way. In some theatres the dramaturg is a literary advisor and expert in theatre history who helps the director understand specifics about a play's performance history, the historical period in which the play is set, as well as the play's style and verse. At other theatres they serve as a literary manager, whereas in others they assist with a play's development by setting up workshop productions and staged readings to help the play find its final form. A common joke is that dramaturgs often spend a significant portion of their time responding to the question "What is a dramaturg?" Dramaturgs are still relatively rare in the theatre, and only a few theatre organizations can afford the help of a dramaturg (for more on dramaturgy, see Chapter 8).

3 PM: Attending Meetings and Creating a Mission Statement

The various crew chiefs now take a moment for a **production meeting**. In this meeting all aspects of the production are discussed and evaluated. The director, stage manager, and technical director are all present along with the heads of the various crews. Every aspect of the next production is discussed, including lights, set, props, and costumes. The purpose of the meeting is to report on the progress of the crews and make sure any small problems are circumvented.

In his office, the artistic director has just finished a meeting concerning next year's season and is writing a new mission statement. A theatre's **mission statement** declares in clear and concise terms the theatre's purpose and key objectives. These objectives can include quality, diversity, and accessibility. It can also state what type of theatre is to be produced—from comedies and classics to thought-provoking, socially relevant plays or perhaps even new plays by up-and-coming playwrights. A theatre might state, for instance, that its goal is to bring cultural enrichment to the community or give a voice to a wide range of artists and visions.

4 PM: Publicizing a Play and Fitting Costumes

The **publicity department** is working on promoting the next play. Today they are setting up an interview with the director at the local radio station. They are also arranging times for actors to tour area schools as a part of the theatre's outreach program. Additionally, they must design print, radio, and television ads. Advertising is expensive and budgets are limited, so they must decide which venues will give them the best return on the investment. Not only do they want to entice their patrons to see a play, but they also hope to reach out to people who generally do not attend the theatre in order to further build the audience.

A few doors down, the costume shop manager is doing fittings. One at a time, the actors come in and try on their new attire while a stitcher pins and tucks the fabric to make sure everything fits just right. One costume might require several fittings, so the costume shop is always busy.

> Strictly speaking, there is only one creative artist in the theatre. It is the playwright, the one who makes something out of nothing. The rest of us—directors, designers, actors—are interpretive artists. We take what the playwright has created and demonstrate to the audience what we think the playwright's creation looks and sounds like.
>
> ***Terry McCabe,***
> Director

5 PM: Brainstorming a Concept

The various shops are cleaning up for the day and getting ready for the evening performance. But before they can head home, the designers are called to a concept meeting for a play that will be produced three months from now. A **concept meeting** is an artistic gathering held long before the play is cast or the sets and costumes designed. During this meeting the director and designers brainstorm, research, and experiment with different set, costume, and light possibilities as they interpret the playwright's script. There can be dozens of concept meetings in which the director synchronizes all the aesthetic elements and talents needed to produce theatre.

6 PM: Preparing for the Evening Performance

As the literary staff, bookkeepers, and administrative assistants head home through the front doors of the theatre, the actors arrive for the evening performance via the stage door. The **stage door** is usually located behind the theatre and has a little lobby where there is a notice board. Here the actors can check for any messages and sign in, letting the stage manager know that they are in the building. The time the actors arrive at the theatre is known as their **call**, and the time the play starts is called **curtain**. If they have a lot of makeup to apply, the actor's call might be several hours before curtain; if they have little hair or makeup to apply, call may be as little as forty-five minutes beforehand. Actors spend the time before the performance warming up their body and voice, doing their hair, and putting on makeup and costumes.

Backstage the prop master is making sure that all the props needed that night are on the prop table. The **prop table** has each prop laid out and clearly labeled. Few things can be more disastrous than an actor losing a prop, so actors are not allowed to leave the backstage area without putting the props back on the table. The prop master is also making sure each prop is in working order: if a production requires a gun, for example, it must be test fired. If food is needed during a play, a prop crew must prepare it.

On stage, the light crew begins checking each light to make sure that it is working. The high-intensity bulbs used in theatrical lighting can burn out at any time, even when they aren't being used, so each light, one at a time, must be raised and lowered while a technician checks that it is still properly aimed. Meanwhile the **sound board operator** is running various sound cues and making sure all the speakers, mixer, amplifiers, backstage monitor, and intercom are working.

7 PM: Opening the House

It is now getting busy backstage. All the actors have arrived. The costume shop, dressing rooms, and makeup rooms are buzzing with people. The stage manager calls out, "One hour until curtain." That means that the house will open

Hanging theatrical lights often requires a large crew. Each light must be individually hung, circuited, focused, and aimed. Once the lights are flown into position, the crew must make dozens more adjustments before opening night. Here, lighting designer Larry Hazlett works with Michael Earl and Jessi Sundell to hang the lights.

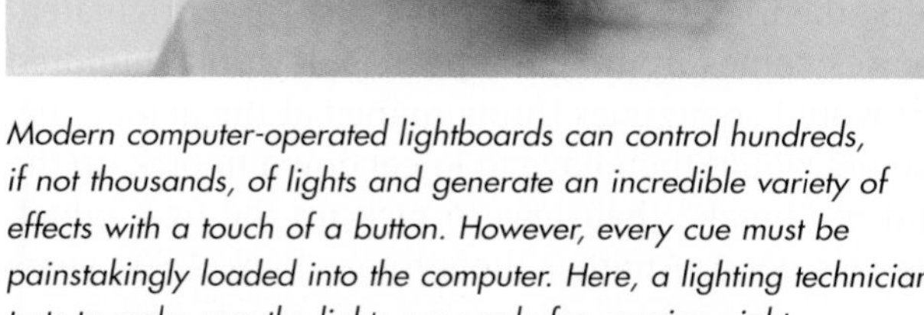

Modern computer-operated lightboards can control hundreds, if not thousands, of lights and generate an incredible variety of effects with a touch of a button. However, every cue must be painstakingly loaded into the computer. Here, a lighting technician tests to make sure the lights are ready for opening night.

Prior to making her entrance as Feste in Idaho Rep's production of Shakespeare's Twelfth Night, *actor Claudine Mboligikpelani Nako checks her makeup.*

in thirty minutes. The **house** is theatre lingo for place where the audience sits. Once it opens the actors will no longer be allowed to walk on stage, so if they want to warm up in the theatre they must do it now. The actors make their way to the stage to do a **prop check** just to ensure everything is where it needs to be. Tonight's play also has a fight sequence, so two actors practice their fight choreography one last time. They rehearse on stage because they want to recreate exactly what they will do tonight.

Nearby, the house manager is making final checks before letting the audience enter the theatre. The **house manager** is in charge of all the ushers. It is his job to deal with any seating problems and to make sure the audience find their seats and that the play begins on time. If the ushers encounter a problem seating people, the house manager may tell the stage manager over a headset or intercom that they need to "hold" until the audience is ready.

Half an hour before curtain, the stage manager orders the actors off the stage. Sound and light checks are finished and the house opens. Backstage, the stage manager walks through the dressing room, makeup, and greenroom announcing, "The house is now open." The theatre's microphone system is turned on so that everything that happens during the play will be broadcast in the dressing rooms, makeup rooms, and even the bathrooms backstage. This way the actors can hear the performance and not miss their entrances. It also means that the actors who are not on stage can clearly hear the audience entering, talking, or laughing.

The stage manager announces, "Ten minutes to curtain!" The actors now make the final adjustments to their costumes and makeup. Nerves can be a real problem, even for experienced actors; many of them are doing deep breathing or relaxation exercises. Moments later the stage manager shouts, "Places!" This is the actors' final warning. Those who enter at the top (beginning) of the show now take their places backstage, while others gather in the greenroom. The **greenroom** is the place where actors wait before their entrances. The term *greenroom* has been around for about three hundred years and there are several theories as to its origin. Some say that it comes from the green color this room used to be painted in order to soothe the actors before they made their entrance. Others think it comes from the old fashioned practice of calling the stage "The Green," hence the room that's just off stage is the "green room." However, no one really knows where the term comes from. Some modern greenrooms have television monitors allowing the actors to watch the production, but one thing they usually all have in common is that greenrooms are seldom fancy and rarely painted green.

Because theatre is live, a lot can *and will* go wrong. As a result, several theatrical superstitions have developed over time (see the Spotlight "If It Can Go Wrong, It Will"). It is considered bad luck, for example, to wish an actor "good luck" before a performance. Instead, actors wish each other bad luck by saying "break a leg." There are several theories as to where this expression originated. One of the most popular theories comes from Shakespeare's day, four hundred years ago, when the audience would sometimes throw money at the actors' feet during the curtain call. The actors would then have to kneel down to pick up the money—in other words, bend or "break" their legs to pick up the tips, which meant that their performance was good. Another theory goes back 2,500 years

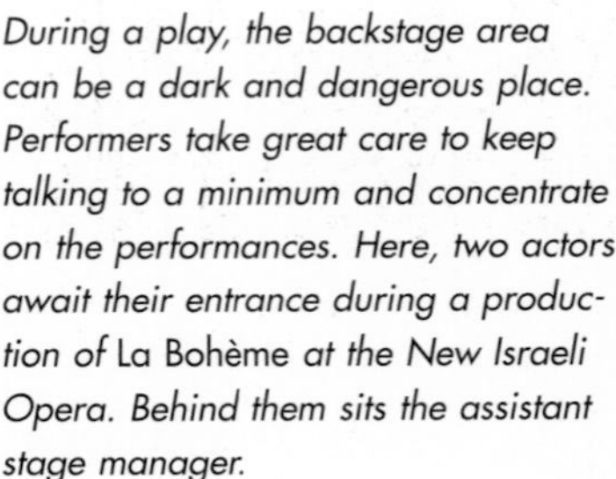

During a play, the backstage area can be a dark and dangerous place. Performers take great care to keep talking to a minimum and concentrate on the performances. Here, two actors await their entrance during a production of La Bohème *at the New Israeli Opera. Behind them sits the assistant stage manager.*

O. Rotem/Lebrecht/Image Works

SPOTLIGHT ON If It Can Go Wrong, It Will

Murphy's law is alive and well in the theatre, proving the old adage true: "If it can go wrong, it will." And because theatre is a live medium, when things go wrong it generally happens in front of the audience. Often mistakes are minor. For example, an actor stumbles on a line, a bulb burns out, a doorknob falls off, etc. But there have been times when a performance turned into a disaster, as in the Broadway musical *Spider-Man: Turn Off the Dark,* in which several actors sustained serious injuries.

Apocryphal stories abound, including the actor who got hungry during a performance of a Stephen Sondheim musical so he decided to order a pizza and have it sent to the greenroom. Coming in the back door of the theatre, the delivery person made a wrong turn and ended up walking on stage in the middle of a tender love ballad. At another theatre, the stage manager mistakenly called for the phone to ring just moments before the end of the play. The stunned actors didn't know what to do. So one of them answered the phone, turned to the other actor on stage and said, "It's for you."

In another case, during a production of the musical *West Side Story*, the gun that Chino uses to kill Tony failed to fire. The poor actor pulled the trigger over and over—nothing but "click, click, click." The audience began to snicker. Finally, the actor ran over and kicked Tony, who fell down, playing dead. Chino then turned to the audience and said, "Poisoned shoes." That night the prop master worked for hours to make sure the gun would never fail again. He cleaned and oiled it to ensure it would fire with the slightest touch. During the next performance the gun went off without a hitch and the prop master breathed a sigh of relief. But moments before the end of the play, when Maria points the gun at the Jet and Shark gang members, the gun accidentally fired. It was pointed at one of the members of the Jet gang . . . so he fell and played dead. That night the play ended with Maria being taken away in handcuffs, charged with murder.

Unlike a movie, when things go wrong on stage there is no second take. As actor Willem Dafoe said, ". . . acting for film is like a musician playing in a recording studio and acting in the theatre is like playing live in concert. . . ."

Sara Krulwich/The New York Times/Redux Pictures

It is often said that what can go wrong, will go wrong. In the theatre, it goes wrong in front of the audience. During a performance of the musical The Pajama Game *(starring Michael McKean and Roz Ryan), two desks moving on stage collided, injuring Ms. Ryan. The play had to be stopped for twenty-seven minutes.*

to the ancient Greeks. In those days some scholars think that the audience didn't clap at the end of the performance but stomped their feet instead. Thus, "break a leg" meant that the performance was so good that audience members would break their legs while stomping.

8 PM: Performing the First Act

The Springfield Ensemble Rep's stage manager now arrives in the control booth to work beside the light and sound board operators. It is from here that the SM will call all the cues and run the show. The house manager pops in to say

During a production, the assistant stage manager sits in the wings to ensure that everything backstage runs smoothly. Communication with all of the other members of the stage crews is maintained through headsets. Generally, it is an uneventful job punctuated by moments of panic.

Mike Goldwater/Alamy

that the audience is seated and the doors are closed. It's time to start the play. The sound board and light board operators, as well as the backstage crews, are now on headsets. Nowadays, these headsets are wireless, which allows crews to move around freely. Over headsets the stage manager says, "House lights to half." The light board operator brings the house lights halfway down for a few moments to let the audience know the play is about to start. "Fade out pre-show music, house lights out, go." The house is plunged into darkness. "Lights 1, sound 1, go." The play begins. During the show there is very little talking over the headsets. Most of the time there is only one-way communication from the stage manager to the assistant stage manager, the light board operator, the sound board operator, and the stage crews. Usually the only time anyone else speaks is when there is a question or problem.

> What you don't see backstage is what really controls the show.
>
> ***Sarah Sutton,***
> Actress of stage and screen, (*Doctor Who*, 1981–83)

Meanwhile, in the greenroom there is also little talk. Most actors are listening to the play over the speakers (or watching it on a monitor) and judging the audience's reaction. Other actors waiting for their entrances are reading the newspaper, relaxing, playing cards, running their lines, etc. One actor comments on a joke that always gets a laugh but didn't tonight. "It's a dead audience," he says. "We'd better pick up the pace." Actors always talk about the audience behind their backs. If it is going well they might say, "We're killing them." If the play is going poorly they might say, "Let's just run for curtain." The latter comment means that there is no hope for a positive response to the play, so they may as well get the play over with as fast as possible.

About five minutes before their entrance, the actors leave the greenroom and go backstage. Here they are met by the assistant stage manager. It is the assistant stage manager's job to make sure that everything runs smoothly during the scene. Getting around backstage is an obstacle course. The actors

O. Rotem/Lebrecht/The Image Works

Scene shifts are done with the help of stagehands, often referred to as running crews. Pictured here is an act break at the New Israeli Opera. With the curtain down, crews rush to change the set for the next act.

must find their way around braces holding the walls of the set, electrical cables taped to the floor, as well as backstage crew and other actors waiting to make their entrances. Even though light from the performance spills off the stage, it is still quite dark. To help actors and crew find their way, dim red or blue running lights have been clamped to the prop table and set braces. During blackouts in the play, moving can be an even bigger problem, so obstacles have been marked with glow-in-the-dark tape to give actors and crews a faint reference point to guide them through the shadows. To make sure the audience can't hear the actors moving around backstage, crews have screwed strips of old carpeting to the floor.

> We are also artists and give a performance every night.
>
> ***Cindy Toushan,***
> Stage manager

During a play anyone helping out backstage is a part of the **running crew**, which includes **stagehands** who shift scenery and generally set up the play for the next scene. Moving scenery around in the dark is one of the most potentially dangerous things in the theatre, and each crew member must be well rehearsed in order to avoid accidents. Stagehands can move scenery using wagons, platforms on casters, a revolve (a large turning platform often powered by electric motors), or elevators that raise and lower segments of the stage. The running crew also includes **dressers** who help actors make quick costume changes. When actors must change in a great hurry in order to make it back onstage, they will have an appointed dresser just offstage; when the actor leaves the stage, they will work with the dresser in quick and well-rehearsed movements to change from one costume to the next. Modesty is not allowed. The running crew usually has some **riggers**, also known as "flymen," who mount and operate all curtains, sets, and anything else that must move via the fly system above the stage. Most theatres also have a variety of curtains that can be used to frame the set and conceal offstage spaces. The curtains used on the sides are called **legs**, and those that frame the top of the stage are referred to as **teasers**. Open-mesh gauze curtains, called **scrims**, are used to make the stage appear opaque when a scene downstage (in

SPOTLIGHT ON Making a Living as an Artist

The United States Census Bureau estimates that more than two million Americans work as artists. From painters to dancers to writers and actors, artists certainly get a great deal of joy from their work. But earning a living is not so easy. A recent study commissioned by the artist support organization L.I.C. (Leveraging Investments in Creativity) found that two-thirds of artists earned less than $40,000 a year in total income. In addition, even though a majority of artists have college degrees, only about 6 percent earn more than $80,000 per year. The L.I.C. study found that about 40 percent of artists said they earned 20 percent or less of their total yearly income from their art, while only 28 percent said their creative work accounts for more than 80 percent of their income. This means that most artists must supplement their income with second jobs; the study found that 66 percent of artists hold at least one additional job, and 21 percent have two more additional jobs.

The recent economic downturn was of great concern to many artists. They worried about their health care—many must buy their own—the loss of income, and retirement plans. But they also were concerned about the loss of arts grants and a downturn in audience numbers that corresponded with the general population squeezing their spending on arts down to a bare minimum. Despite these obstacles, most artists tend to be positive about the future: According to the study, 89 percent of artists believe they have a special role in their communities, and 75 percent believe it is an inspiring time to be an artist.

front) of it is lighted, and transparent or translucent when a scene upstage (behind) the scrim is lighted. The **cyclorama**, often shortened to *cyc* (pronounced "psych"), is a large, stretched curtain suspended from a U-shaped rod. It makes a background that curves around the back of the stage to suggest unlimited space. Cycloramas are usually neutral in color, but lighting designers can turn them into almost anything, from a symbolic collage of colors to a starry sky.

9 PM: Performing the Final Act

During intermission the actors make their way back to the dressing and makeup rooms. Here they often compare notes on how the play is going, change costumes, touch up their makeup, and drink lots of water. Acting under the hot lights can take its toll and actors must keep their vocal cords moist.

When the play begins again, the stage manager watches the performance and calls every cue from the control booth. Each theatre has its own protocol as to how cues should be called, but generally it's done by calling "warning," "standby," and "go." The SM gives a "warning" over the headsets to alert crews a few minutes before the cue to make sure everyone is where they need to be. The SM calls "standby" just before the cue and "go" the moment the cue is to be executed. To reduce confusion, each cue is numbered. Talk over the headsets might sound something like this: "Standby lights 32. And go." The light board operator presses a button on the light board, and the computer automatically changes the lights. "Standby sound 15 and lights 33; warning scene change." The sound board operator makes sure that sound cue 15 is ready and set to the

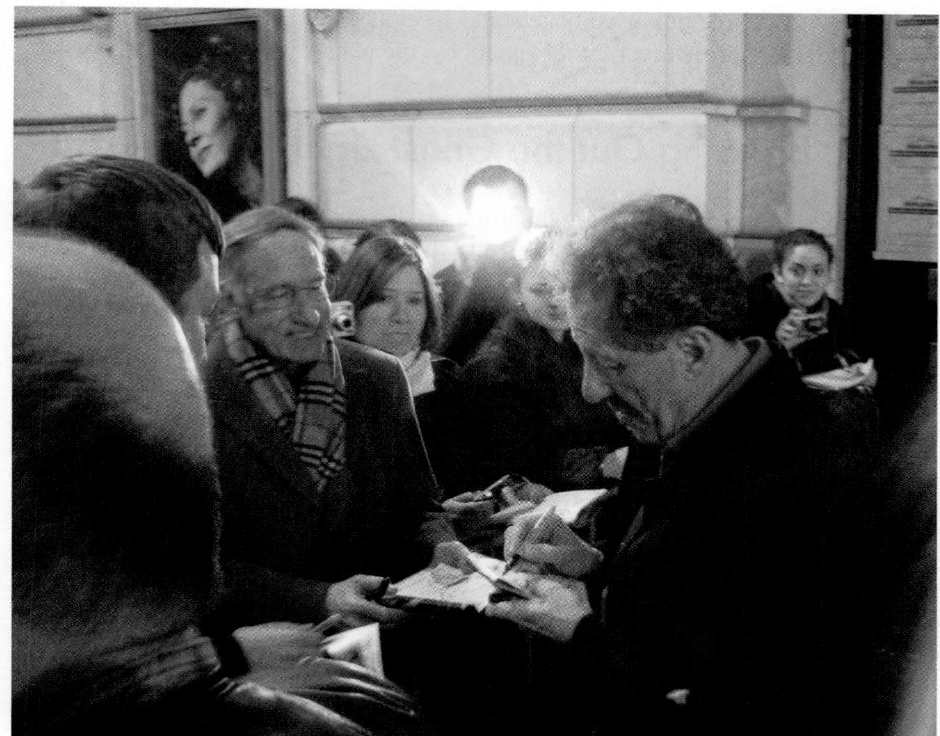

William Missouri Downs

After the play, some audience members will gather at the stage door in the hope of meeting the stars. Here Academy, Tony, and Emmy Award winner Gregory Rush signs autographs after performing on Broadway in Eugene Ionesco's absurdist comedy Exit the King.

correct volume. The light board operator checks to make sure the light board computer has the correct cue up, while backstage crews take their places for the next scene change. Sometimes there can be so many warnings, standbys, and cues given that the stage manager must double up by saying something like, "Standby lights 25 through 28, standby sound 15 through 18. Lights 25, go. Lights 26, go. Sound 15, go."

10 PM: Clearing Out

After the curtain call the actors work their way up to the dressing rooms and begin hanging up their costumes and removing makeup. Usually the stage manager stops in to share a few notes and make any announcements, such as the need for a brush-up rehearsal.

Even before the audience has left the theatre, backstage crews are cleaning up. The prop master begins putting away the props. The running crews are stowing equipment. When the last audience member has left the house, the theatrical lights shut down and the bland white work lights pop on. Crews clean the stage and check for any damage or problems, which are reported to the stage manager. The stage manager then writes the performance report that is e-mailed to the entire artistic staff and crew, informing them of any problems or concerns.

Twenty minutes after the show is over, the actors are out of makeup and heading home. At the stage door they meet a few friends and fans. Meanwhile the folks in the box office are adding up tickets and receipts as they account for every seat. As the last audience member leaves the lobby, the ushers head home after them.

11 PM: Bringing Out the Ghost Light

The last of the running crews are finishing up. Everything is now powered down. The last person to leave the theatre rolls the ghost light out on stage, and the theatre is locked. Once again, as the famous set designer Robert Edmond Jones said, "the stage is lonely, and forlorn and as silent as midnight."

Making a living in the theatre requires hard work and grueling hours, and the pay is often very limited. (See Spotlight "Making a Living as an Artist.") However, for theatre people the joy of doing a job they really love outweighs the drawbacks. Playwrights, actors, directors, stage managers, artistic directors, and designers seldom see their work as just a job, but rather as a creative outlet. Their work is intensive, but for them, there is nothing more satisfying. Nothing beats a life in the theatre.

Curtain Call

When theatre, or almost any work of art for that matter, is at its best, it appears to be almost effortless. In the theatre this effortlessness is an illusion. From inception to fruition, theatre requires thousands of hours of labor and the talents of many trained, creative, and hard-working individuals. When theatre succeeds, it does so because every member of the ensemble understands his or her duties, yet is also allowed to solve problems, express opinions, use the techniques of his or her trade, and be creative. On the other hand, the director or artistic director who micromanages a production, just like the corporate executive who micromanages a company, will limit the potential for creativity and in the end produce a well-controlled but sterile product. As director Terry McCabe says, a good director sees the creative team "as valuable colleagues precisely because they might enlarge the director's own sense of the play."

Summary

In the theatre, as in many other professions, creativity often occurs within an ensemble. The key to working within an ensemble is to ensure that all the members of the group are allowed to be creative but that they also work in unison toward the same artistic vision. A theatre's ensemble can be divided into four categories: administrative, creative, construction, and production. The administrative team includes accountants, box-office staff, administrative assistants, fund-raisers, grant writers, publicity personnel, and producer(s) who run the business aspects of any theatre. The creative team is the artists who invent the play and stage the production, specifically the playwright, the director, the actors, and the designers. The team can also encompass assistant directors, dramaturgs, musical directors, conductors, vocal coaches, understudies, dancers, and choreographers. The construction team includes the technical director(s) and crew chief(s) who supervise a company of stitchers, contractors, and laborers who hang the lights, build the sets, fabricate the props, and stitch the costumes. The production team includes stage manager(s), house manager(s), and ushers, as well as the lighting, set, and costume crews who work behind the scenes during the performances. In fact, large productions can have far more people behind the scenes than on stage: the Broadway musical *Titanic* needed seven prop people, fourteen carpenters, three follow-spot operators, two computer operators, three riggers, and four stage managers for every performance. At nearly any time of the day, members of the ensemble are hard at work on the elements that create contemporary professional theatre.

The Art of Theatre ONLINE

To access this chapter's interactive theatre workshop activities, along with many other learning tools, log onto your Theatre CourseMate. Access is available at cengagebrain.com.

Key Terms

artistic director / 105
assistant stage manager / 107
call / 111
choreographer / 108
concept meeting / 111
costume shop / 103
curtain / 112
cyclorama / 118
dramaturg / 110
draper / 107
dresser / 117
ensemble / 102
fight director / 108
flat / 106
ghost light / 103
greenroom / 114
house / 113
house manager / 113
legs / 117
literary manager / 104
mission statement / 111
movement coach / 108
musical director / 108
performance report / 107
producer or producing director / 104
production meeting / 110
prompt book / 107
prop / 108
prop check / 113
prop master / 108
prop table / 112
publicity department / 111
rehearsal costume / 107
rehearsal prop / 108
rehearsal report / 107
repertory / 102
rigger / 117
running crew / 117
scrims / 117
set designer / 110
sound board operator / 112
sound designer / 110
stage door / 111
stage manager / 106
stagehand / 117
stitcher / 107
teasers / 117
technical director / 106
vocal coach / 108

Pulitzer Prizing winning playwright Suzan-Lori Parks is one of America's more prolific playwrights.

Photos on this spread Todd France/Corbis Outline

CHAPTER 6

The Playwright and the Script

OUTLINE

Theatre begins with the playwright, the artist who conceives the theme, the characters, the dialogue, and the story. The root word *wright* in playwright comes from the Middle Ages and means "one who builds." A shipwright was someone who built ships; a wheelwright was someone who built wheels. So it follows that a playwright is someone who builds plays. Playwrights are so important to the process that many theatre professionals call them the "primary artist." The playwright Moss Hart said, "The writer is the person who was there when the paper was white." Yet when a play is produced, it is unlikely that the director, actors, or designers will ever meet

I created *Tracers* with a group. In the workshop process I pushed for "Truth" more than anything else. Most of my writing tends to be autobiographical with poetic license—Hopefully unmasking, honest, and most importantly theatrical. I think of it as mythologizing my life.

John DiFusco,
Playwright

the playwright. In fact, the playwright is the only member of the ensemble of a production who can be long dead.

In this chapter we will look at the artists who build plays and the techniques they use to express themselves. We will also examine the elements that make up a play and how playwrights combine these elements to craft a script. Studying the elements of playwriting will help you better analyze performances and the written words upon which the contributions of all other theatre artists depend.

The Playwright's Life and Words

Unlike the other artists in the theatre, who usually work within the ensemble, the playwright typically works alone (which, incidentally, accounts for why she didn't make an appearance at the Springfield Ensemble Rep, featured in Chapter 5). The exception is for scripts conceived through workshops or improvisations, as was the case with Caryl Churchill's *Cloud Nine* (1978), a dark comedy about gender roles and sexuality. Churchill wrote the script but then participated in workshops with actors who improvised some of the dialogue. Similarly, John DiFusco's play *Tracers* (1980), which recounts eight veterans' tours of duty in Vietnam, was created by a group of actors, directors, and writers who contributed lines and ideas. More recently, director and playwright Moisés Kaufman and fellow members of the Tectonic Theater Project collaborated on *The Laramie Project* (2001), about the 1998 murder of Matthew Shepard, through workshops and interviews with the residents of Laramie, Wyoming. But as a rule the playwright labors alone for months, if not years, to write a play. In fact, playwriting is the most time-consuming of all the arts of the theatre. The combined number of hours it takes the actors to rehearse, the designers to design, and the director to direct does not come close to the amount of time it takes the playwright to conceive and write the play. This, along with the fact that playwrights are the primary artists, is why playwrights get top billing in the program, even above the director, in contrast to Hollywood movies, where the director gets top billing.

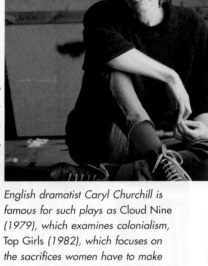

David Montgomery/Getty Images

English dramatist Caryl Churchill is famous for such plays as Cloud Nine *(1979), which examines colonialism,* Top Girls *(1982), which focuses on the sacrifices women have to make to achieve success, and* Seven Jewish Children *(2009), which dramatizes the conflict in Israel.*

As we mentioned in Chapter 2, playwrights do not sell their copyright. Consequently, they retain control of the script and technically no director, actor, designer, producer, or anyone else can change the script without permission from the playwright or the playwright's lawyer, publisher, or estate. We say "technically" because sometimes members of the ensemble do change the script without seeking the playwright's permission. They just slip the changes in and hope that the playwright doesn't find out. (For more on copyright, see "Copyright Law: Infringement, Public Domain, and Parody" in Chapter 2.)

In the case of the text, in theater (unlike the movies) the writer is the final arbiter.

Tom Stoppard,
Playwright

Owning the copyright means that playwrights retain a lot of power over their plays, but they do not necessarily make a lot of money from them. One of the reasons they don't make much money is that they are not employees of the theatre and so are not allowed to form closed-shop unions and strike for better compensation. A **closed-shop union**, sometimes called a union shop, is a union to which all employees *must* belong and which the employer formally recognizes as their sole collective bargaining agent. The advantage to closed-shop unions is that the employees can call a strike if their demands go unmet. Television and screenwriters have a powerful closed-shop union called the **Writers Guild of America (WGA)**. As a result, staff writers on television shows can earn five to ten thousand dollars or more a week, and a single screenplay can sell for hundreds of thousands if not millions of dollars. In fact, according to *Written By*, the WGA magazine, Hollywood producers pay screen and television writers about $1 billion a year to write, rewrite, and develop new scripts. Screen and television writers are allowed to form a closed-shop union because they sell their copyright, giving up their power to control the script, the production, or the final product. This makes them "writers for hire" or "employees." The exception to this would be screenwriters who direct their own work, make independent films, or write small films that are seen only online. These writers often retain their copyright and thus creative control. For example, Woody Allen (*Annie Hall*, *Midnight in Paris*) writes and directs his own movies and is not a writer for hire.

William Missouri Downs

Many theatres in the United States specialize in the development of new plays. One of the most famous is Playwrights Horizon in New York City. Hundreds of playwrights have had their new scripts developed here and the theatre boasts numerous world premieres.

Playwrights, because they retain the copyright, are not writers for hire. Instead, they are considered "management," and U.S. law does not allow managers to form closed-shop unions. Playwrights' only option is a weak **open-shop union**. In an open shop, membership is optional, so meaningful strikes are impossible. The playwrights' union, the **Dramatists Guild of America (DGA)**, can champion the rights of playwrights but can do little to demand higher pay. Because of this, few playwrights make a living from their art. A recent study by the nonprofit Theater Development Fund found that 62 percent of playwrights make less than $40,000, and nearly one-third pull in less than $25,000.

Rather than sell their scripts, playwrights rent them to theatres and are paid a royalty. These royalties can amount to a few dollars per performance for a small, sub-professional theatre to many thousands of dollars a week for a professional, regional, Off-Broadway, or Broadway production—though big money in playwriting is rare. Sometimes playwrights can't even keep the few royalties they do earn because theatres occasionally demand that the author give the theatre *subsidiary rights*. This means that the playwright must pay the theatre a percentage (usually 10 percent) of any royalties that the play earns for the next ten years. It is ironic that the one who creates the play is often the lowest paid member of the theatre. Inadequate compensation is one of the major reasons playwrights must find outside employment to make ends meet, or seek out higher paying writing jobs in Hollywood. Although there was once a time when playwrights considered it to be "selling out" to write for television, more and more of today's playwrights are paying the bills by writing for movies and television.

Even world-famous playwrights often turn to more commercial work. For example, Sam

One of America's most famous playwrights is David Mamet. His plays include Sexual Perversity in Chicago *(1974), which dramatizes dating in the Windy City;* American Buffalo *(1976), which explores three petty crooks and their plan to steal a coin collection; and* Glengarry Glen Ross *(1984), which examines the lives of real estate agents. He also has written the screenplays for several movies, including* The Postman Always Rings Twice *(1981) and* The Untouchables *(1987).*

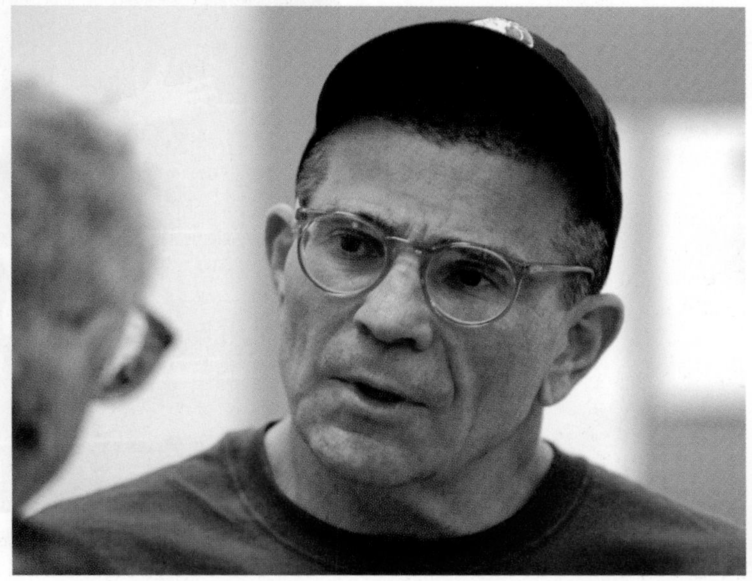

AP Photo/Kathy Willens

Hal Horowitz/WireImage/Getty Images

British playwright Sir Tom Stoppard is famous for such plays as Rosencrantz and Guildenstern Are Dead *(1966), an absurdist tragicomedy about two minor characters in Shakespeare's* Hamlet, *and* Rock 'n' Roll *(2006) about a young Czech Ph.D. student and the repressive regimes that control his life. He also co-wrote the screenplays for the movies* Brazil *and* Shakespeare in Love.

Shepard (b. 1943), famous for writing such plays as *Curse of the Starving Class* (1978), *Buried Child* (1979), *True West* (1980), *Fool for Love* (1982), and *Simpatico* (1995), has also written screenplays and teleplays and has acted in more than forty movies, including *The Right Stuff* (1983) and *Black Hawk Down* (2001). Similarly, playwright David Mamet (b. 1949), famous for such plays as *American Buffalo* (1976), *Glengarry Glen Ross* (1984), and *Oleanna* (1992), has also written several screenplays, including *The Verdict* (1982), *The Untouchables* (1987), and *Wag the Dog* (1998), and he is the creator of a popular television show about a special forces military squad called *The Unit*.

The reward for low pay and long hours is that playwrights, unlike most screenwriters, see their work presented as written. Their unique voices remain pure and their ideas about how the world is or should be are communicated to audiences without alteration. When it comes down to it, all that playwrights have are their words, and to playwrights, their words are far more valuable than any paycheck. Playwright Sir Tom Stoppard wrote in his play *The Real Thing* (1982) that words build bridges across incomprehension and chaos. Words, he said, "deserve respect. If you get the right ones in the right order, you can nudge the world a little." And all playwrights, rich or poor, want to nudge the world. (For more on a playwright's life, see the Spotlight "The Life of a Playwright: Sarah Ruhl.")

The Art of Playwriting

Playwriting is a limited form of storytelling because a play script is limited to dialogue, stage directions, and an occasional parenthetical. Unlike a novelist, for example, who can describe a character's inner world to readers, the playwright must make that inner world known through what the actors outwardly

Geraint Lewis / Alamy

One of Tom Stoppard's most clever plays is Arcadia, *which merges the early nineteenth century with the present to tell a story about literature, epistemology and sex. David Leveaux directed this production.*

SPOTLIGHT ON The Life of a Playwright: Sarah Ruhl

Growing up in Chicago, Sarah Ruhl loved to read. Her favorites were short stories by Virginia Woolf and Katherine Mansfield, and poems by Elizabeth Bishop and Wallace Stevens. She also loved to read plays by Maria Irene Fornes and William Shakespeare. She went on to earn her MFA (Masters of Fine Arts) from Brown University, and it was there that she fell in love with playwriting. When her first play was produced at Brown's new play festival she remembers thinking, "Oh, there's no turning back at this point. I'm completely in love with this job, vocation, hobby, whatever you'd like to call it."

When she works on a new play Ruhl often gets her story ideas from ordinary incidents in everyday life. "I mean, of course work emerges out of extraordinary moments of loss and ecstasy and all that," Ruhl said, "but it also emerges from day-to-day observations." For example, one of her most famous plays came from a chance comment she overheard during a dinner party. A doctor said, "My cleaning lady is depressed and won't clean my house. So I took her to the hospital and had her medicated. And she still won't clean!" That one remark gave birth to the comedy *The Clean House*, the story of a Brazilian maid looking for the perfect joke while working for an obsessive family. *The Clean House* was produced all over the world and was a Pulitzer Prize finalist.

Ruhl's other plays often celebrate what she calls "the pleasure of heightened things." For example, her play *Dead Man's Cell Phone* is about a woman who repeatedly asks a man sitting next to her in a coffeehouse to answer his ringing cell phone, only to discover that he is dead. This event leads to a play about love and death in the digital age. "Cell phones, iPods, wireless computers will change people in ways we don't even understand," Ruhl said. "We're less connected to the present. No one is where they are. There's absolutely no reason to talk to a stranger anymore—you connect to people you already know. But how well do you know them? Because you never see them—you just talk to them. I find that terrifying."

Ruhl often writes quirky comedies, but comedies about deeply serious subjects. She feels that one should have the ability to step back and laugh "at horrible things even as you're experiencing them." At this writing she is only in her 30s, so audiences can look forward to new Ruhl plays for many years to come.

Joseph Marzullo/WENN Photos/Newscom

Playwright Sarah Ruhl

say and do. **Dialogue** is the spoken text of the play, the words the characters say. Playwrights write everything the actors say, including fillers such as "ah," "so," and "uh-huh." Finding the right words for each character takes many rewrites and an acute sensitivity to how people express themselves. To help the actor or the reader interpret a particular line of dialogue, a playwright sometimes adds **parentheticals**, short descriptions such as (*lovingly*), (*angry*), or (*terrified*). To distinguish them from dialogue, parentheticals are enclosed in parentheses and are usually italicized. The playwright also writes the **stage directions**, which are notes that indicate the physical movements of the characters. The director and actors decide the majority of the movements, so a

> I believe that whatever a character says is true. So I write down everything the character says—pages and pages. Then, the trick is weeding through all that and finding the story that is really buried in there. And sometimes you really have to dig.
>
> ***August Wilson,***
> Playwright

playwright usually limits the stage directions to short notes such as "with a smile" or "closing the door." Not all the stage directions in a published play are necessarily written by the playwright. Occasionally a publisher includes stage directions taken from a stage manager's notes in order to help amateur companies with the staging of a play. Within these script parameters, a playwright builds a play using the basic tools of playwriting, including theme, characters, conflict, language, and plot.

What Does It Mean? The Theme

Playwrights are philosophers in that they search for meaning in the world and attempt to understand human nature. Their search results in a statement about life, a central idea, or a moral; this is the play's **theme**. For example, the theme of David Henry Hwang's play *M. Butterfly* is the blinding effects of racial stereotyping. The theme of a play is more often implied than directly stated, because playwrights rarely sit down to write a play about a particular theme. Instead, the theme usually reveals itself during the writing process. American playwright Arthur Miller said that he often didn't know what his plays were about until the second or third draft. Even then, playwrights rarely state the theme, because themes that are explicitly stated are less powerful than those that are revealed through action. In other words, the playwright tries to make the theme clear without spelling it out. Consequently, the theme is often open to interpretation by audiences and readers.

Characters in Action

> Drama cannot deal with people whose wills are atrophied, who are unable to make decisions which have even temporary meaning, who adopt no conscious attitude toward events, who make no effort to control their environment.
>
> ***John Howard Lawson,***
> Playwright, screenwriter, and author

Playwrights love to study people. As a matter of fact, all plays are about human beings and their emotions and actions. Playwrights build all their characters from what they know about people via their own experience or through observation and intuition. A playwright's ability to write good characters is based on an ability to examine and understand people's motivations and emotions. For this reason, playwrights often write about people they know and understand, including themselves.

Yet not all characters are good material for the stage. Stage characters are different from those written for novels, poems, or short stories, because they must be able to express themselves and take action. For thousands of years playwrights have used the word *action* to define character and story. **Actions** are the characters' deeds, their responses to circumstances, which in turn affect the course of the story. In other words, the situation of a play is what happens but action is what the characters *do* with what happens. Characters in plays come to life not by what they *feel* and *think* but by what they *say* and *do*.

In real life, most people rarely take action. We receive an unjust parking ticket and we pay it rather than fight it in court; our boss treats us unfairly and we bear it rather than file a complaint; a huge corporation or the government cheats us and we accept it rather than deal with the red tape. Most people would make horrible characters in a play because dramatic characters must be willing to take action. Romeo must be willing to endanger his life to proclaim his love; Oedipus must be willing to seek the king's killer even though there may be dire consequences; and Lena (Mama) Younger in *A Raisin in the Sun* must be willing to take a stand to change her family's lives. If these

SARA KRULWICH/The New York Times/Redux Pictures

Sarah Ruhl's Passion Play *follows three different communities in different historical periods who are mounting different productions of plays concerning Christ's death and resurrection. The New York production pictured here featured Kate Turnbull, front, and Dominic Fumes.*

characters were not willing to take action, there would be no story and no play. The writer Peter Thorpe said, ". . . virtually all respectable novels, plays, and poems deal with change: falling in love, falling out of love, growing up, growing old, winning, losing, moving, moving, moving, in every conceivable way—physically, geographically, sociologically, spiritually." Once playwrights know the action (or change) that they want to show, they must next find what is standing in the characters' way, for every play is full of roadblocks and obstacles called *conflict*.

Conflict as Catalyst

Unfortunately, conflict is one of the constants of human existence. Hardly a day goes by that we are not involved in some major or minor conflict with ourselves or each other; this is true for individuals, families, societies, and nations. Historians Will and Ariel Durant write in their book *The Lessons of History* (1968) that in the last 3,420 or so years of recorded history, only 268 have seen no war. And in all those thousands of years, there has never been *one single day* without conflicts among individuals, families, and societies. A play is essentially the history of a particular conflict. Plays are not about people who have idyllic lives; they're about people who have unfulfilled needs and desires and the obstacles or opponents preventing them from obtaining what they want. The result is conflict. It's a simple equation: desire + obstacle × lack of compromise = conflict.

Here are some examples:

Desire: Romeo loves Juliet and Juliet loves Romeo.

Obstacle: Their families will not allow them to see each other, let alone marry.

Photostage

"O Romeo, Romeo! wherefore art thou Romeo? / Deny thy father and refuse thy name; / Or, if thou wilt not, be but sworn my love, / And I'll no longer be a Capulet." These lines by Shakespeare give voice to Juliet's willingness to enter into the conflict that drives the story of Romeo and Juliet. *In order to drive the story forward, playwrights must use language to let audiences know what characters think, feel, want, and intend. This 2004 production featured Tom Burke as Romeo and Kananu Kirimi as Juliet. Directed by Tim Carroll, Shakespeare's Globe, London.*

Reason compromise is not an option: They can't live without each other.

Desire: Oedipus wants to find the killer of the King of Thebes.

Obstacle: He is blind to his own shortcomings.

Reason compromise is not an option: A terrible plague haunts the city of Thebes. Oracles have said that if the killer is not found, many more will die.

Desire: Lena Younger wants to give her family a better home.

Obstacle: The white homeowners association will not allow a black family to live in its neighborhood.

Reason compromise is not an option: If she does not move her family, they will lose their dreams and fall into depression and self-doubt.

Notice that the third element, the reason compromise is not an option, is what makes the story possible. The playwright can write a play because the characters are not willing to compromise and must take action. In the process, they cause conflict. Once playwrights know what the conflict is and why the characters must take action, they must write characters who express themselves with language. Language helps audiences comprehend what characters are thinking, feeling, wanting, or intending to do. Characters use language as action or to promote or enhance action. They use language to drive the story forward.

The Art of Language

Words are the playwright's paint. When mixed properly, they can glance or glaze, collide or clip to reveal the heart of a character. Yet dialogue does not begin with words; it begins with the need to talk. We talk because we want. If we want nothing, we say nothing. Even small talk about nothing in particular can be traced to our need for companionship. As infants, we cry when we want to be fed or changed. As we grow, our needs become more complicated and we learn language in order to communicate. The need for a bottle or a fresh diaper is replaced by the needs for friendship, for justice, and for protection of our ego. As we mature, our strategies to get what we want through speech become more complicated. We learn to manipulate language in order to provoke, settle scores, find love, defeat enemies, and satisfy our wants without announcing them directly. Sometimes, when our deepest wants go unfulfilled, they seep into our subconscious, coloring our speech with secondary meanings and concealed desires. Dialogue is a combination of what the character needs to say and what the character is compelled to say. It's simple communication colored by the character's environment, history, emotions, and situation. Let's look at a few of the tools playwrights use to write dialogue: subtext, listening, imagery, rhythm, tempo, and sound.

Subtext A line of dialogue has two levels: what the character says (the text) and what the character consciously or subconsciously means (the subtext). **Subtext** is the hidden meaning behind the words, the real reason a character chooses to speak. In other words, dialogue is like an iceberg; only part of the meaning can be seen above the waterline. For example, when a playwright adds subtext, the simple line "I hate you" can take on any of hundreds of possible meanings, from "I love you" to "I miss you" to "I wish I were you." When King Lear speaks the famous line "Blow, winds, and crack your cheeks. Rage, blow!" he is not talking about the weather but about his own troubled life and madness. The subtext makes the line memorable.

> People may or may not say what they mean . . . but they always say something designed to get what they want.
>
> ***David Mamet,***
> Playwright

Listening Another way of looking at subtext is to realize that playwrights are psychologists in that they are constantly analyzing human character. One way to understand a character, or another person for that matter, is to understand *how* they hear, because what is said and what is heard can be very different. More often than not, people filter what they hear through their own needs, emotions, and prejudices. People ignore, misinterpret, or read special meanings into just about everything. We project our own thoughts and emotions onto other people. For example, look at a simple exchange between two people:

BETH: Honey, where's the coffee?

SHANE: In the cabinet near the fridge.

BETH: And the sugar?

SHANE: Right beside it, on the left.

This is boring dialogue because both characters hear each other perfectly and respond obviously. But look what happens when the characters hear something different from what the other is saying. In this next example, simple questions are heard but misinterpreted, adding depth and subtext to an otherwise mundane exchange.

BETH: Honey, where's the coffee?

SHANE: You don't think I know, do you?

BETH: And the sugar?

SHANE: Are you testing me?

Obviously, what Shane hears is quite different from what Beth is saying, so we learn something about Shane's psychological makeup. Playwrights know that how someone listens and responds reveals a lot about who they are and what they are thinking.

Imagery In a movie it's easy to show images. What the screen can show is almost limitless, so screenwriters love to write scenes that let the audience see all manner of things firsthand. Playwrights, on the other hand, are limited by the confined space of the stage and small budgets. So they must be more like poets and write dialogue that allows the audience to see things in the mind's eye. They do this by writing dialogue full of imagery, picture-making words that allow the audience to see into their imaginations. A classic example comes from Eugene O'Neill's *Long Day's Journey into Night*, when the character Edmund recounts his days at sea.

In contrast to movies, plays create imagery with words rather than photography, special effects, or action sequences, so playwrights work hard to find the right words for each character and scene. For example, in Eugene O'Neill's classic Long Day's Journey into Night, *Edmund's monologue about his days at sea is necessarily as powerful as any movie scene. This 2003 production featured Robert Sean Leonard and Brian Dennehy. Directed by Robert Falls, Plymouth Theatre, New York.*

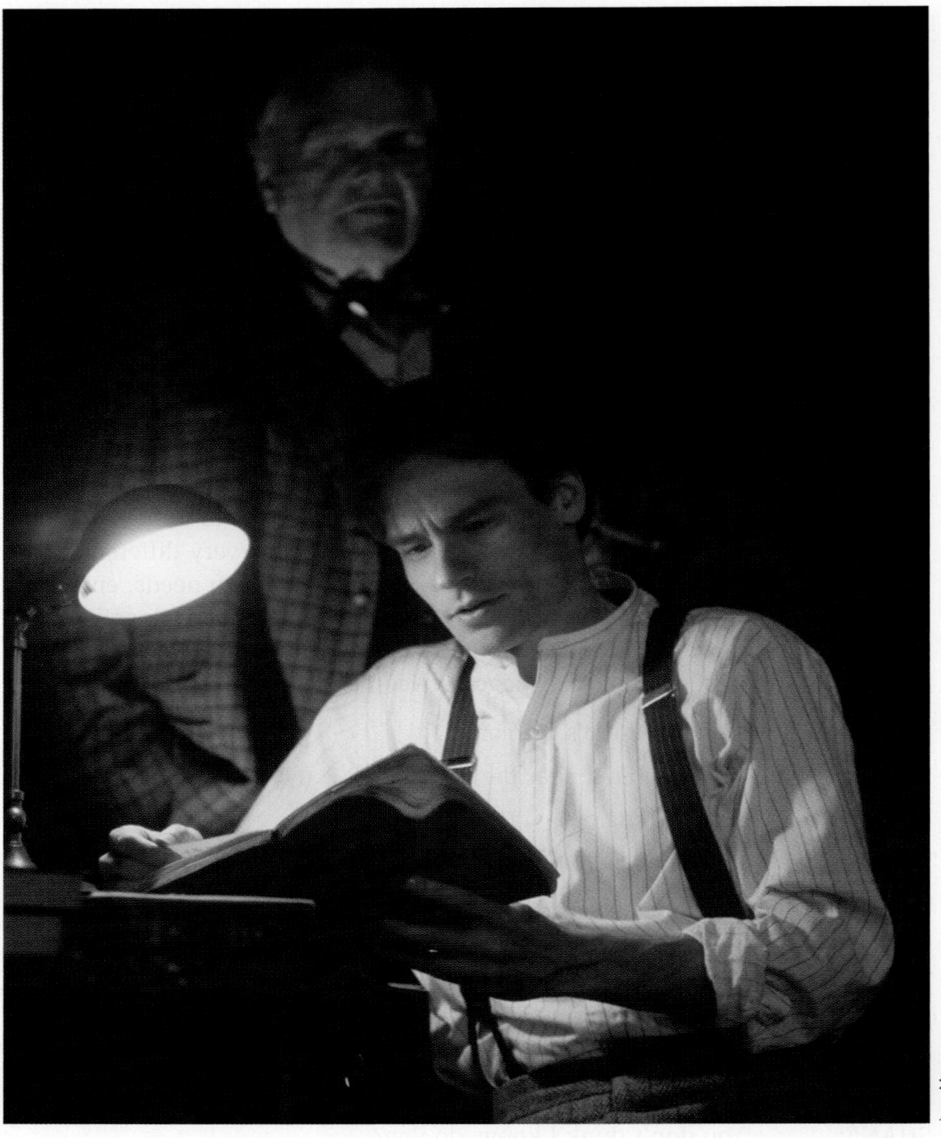

Joan Marcus

> A play is as personal and individual a form of self-expression as a poem or a picture.
>
> ***Oscar Wilde,***
> Poet and playwright

EDMUND: I was on the Squarehead square rigger, bound for Buenos Aires. Full moon in the trades. The old hooker driving fourteen knots. I lay on the bowsprit, facing astern, with the water foaming into spume under me, the masts with every sail white in the moonlight, towering high above me. I became drunk with the beauty and singing rhythm of it, and for a moment I lost myself—actually lost my life. I was set free! I dissolved in the sea, became white sails and flying spray, became beauty and rhythm, became moonlight and the ship and the high dim-starred sky! I belonged, without past or future, within peace and unity and a wild joy, within something greater than my own life, or the life of Man, to Life itself! To God, if you want to put it that way. Then another time, on the American Line, when I was lookout on the crow's nest in the dawn watch. A calm sea, that time. Only a lazy ground swell and a slow drowsy roll of the ship.

> The passengers asleep and none of the crew in sight. No sound of man. Black smoke pouring from the funnels behind and beneath me. Dreaming, not keeping lookout, feeling alone, and above, and apart, watching the dawn creep like a painted dream over the sky and sea which slept together. Then the moment of ecstatic freedom came. The peace, the end of the quest, the last harbor, the joy of belonging to a fulfillment beyond men's lousy, pitiful, greedy fears and hopes and dreams!

If this were a scene from a movie, the scriptwriter could take us to the crow's nest and show us the flying spray and the black smoke. One shot might be enough to convey the thoughts and feelings of the character. But the playwright is limited by the stage and must verbally communicate the thoughts and images critical to the story. Shakespeare often used verbal scene-painting in which the characters describe their environment so that elaborate (and expensive) sets were unnecessary. (For more on set design, see Chapter 9.)

Rhythm, Tempo, and Sound Playwrights love the music of language; they write dialogue that has a particular rhythm, tempo, and sound. By not only

Jennie Franks

Public readings of new plays give playwrights a chance to test their narratives long before theatres produces them. Here a new play is read by Barbara Betts, Nicolas Day, and Lily Sullivan at the Telluride New Play Festival in Colorado.

choosing the character's words carefully but also adjusting the sounds, a playwright can reveal a character's feelings. For example, in Tennessee Williams' *Cat on a Hot Tin Roof* (1955), Maggie describes her sister-in-law, her rival for Big Daddy's money, as a former "Cotton Carnival Queen." The hard sound of each of the first letters gives the character a chance to show jealousy and contempt without being too obvious. Sounds are combined to create "rhythm." As in music, *rhythm* in dialogue is a variation of sounds that creates a pattern, which prompts an emotional response. The characters each have their own rhythm, which manifests itself in the dialogue. The rhythm of dialogue is much more subtle than the rhythm of poetry. It's a gentle adjusting of the lines' sounds and stresses. Given the needs of the moment, dialogue should pulsate or flow, jingle or swing, oscillate or tranquilize. To understand rhythm, look at the following line:

> The right word in the right place.

Its rhythm comes from the repetition of the *r* sound juxtaposed with the soft ending word, *place*. Now compare the following lines, which have the same meaning but different rhythms:

> The perfect word perfectly placed.
> An accurate word in its correct location.
> A proper expression placed with perfection.

Rhythms and sounds convey particular *tones* and evoke particular character types. The first line, "The perfect word perfectly placed," is dominated by the percussive sound of the *p*'s but also contains the soft consonants *th* and *w*. This gives the line what some might call a comfortable sound—perhaps we see a young woman saying the line as she laughs in her lover's arms. "An accurate word in its correct location" is more formal and harder sounding with the *c*'s and *t*'s; it might bring to mind a business executive praising a subordinate. "A proper expression placed with perfection" is dominated by a rhythmic pattern of soft *p*'s; we might envision a retired English professor describing a favorite line of poetry. No two people talk the same way or use the same rhythms. A playwright adjusts each line so that the words reveal each character's inner rhythm.

Dialogue is also designed to be spoken at a particular speed, or *tempo*. A good line of dialogue has an internal clock that makes the tempo unmistakable to the reader or actor. For example, Shakespeare masterfully uses Leontes' tempo and rhythm to expose Leontes' true nature in *The Winter's Tale*:

> Is whispering nothing?
> Is leaning cheek to cheek? Is meeting noses?
> Kissing with inside lip? stopping the career
> Of laughter with a sigh? (a note infallible
> Of breaking honesty). Horsing foot on foot?
> Skulking in corners? Wishing clocks more swift,
> Hours minutes, noon, midnight? And all eyes
> Blind with the pin and web but theirs; theirs only
> That would unseen be wicked? Is this nothing?

Here, Shakespeare gives the usually even-tempered King Leontes a fervent, fanatical tempo as he wonders whether his wife has committed adultery. The many short, almost half-asked questions reveal thoughts tumbling out at breakneck speed, suggesting a jealous temper.

Plotting the Story

Playwrights are always trying to plot the stories of life. Although we often use the words *plot* and *story* interchangeably, there is a difference between the two. *Story* is everything that happens, and **plot** is how it all fits together. The plot gives the story a particular focus. For example, "the king died and the queen died" is a very basic story. But "the king died, and the queen died of grief" is plot. This example comes from novelist and critic E. M. Forster, who, in his book *Aspects of the Novel* (1927), said that story is the chronological sequence of events and plot is the causal and logical structure that connects events. A play generally has only one story but may have a main plot and a subplot or a multitude of plots. Playwrights may start developing a play with the characters and the conflict, but soon they must get down to plotting the story.

Plotting the story means finding its structure. Real life is raw and disorganized; a play structures life into a unified whole. **Plot-structure**, as it is sometimes called, is the playwright's selection of events to create a logical sequence and as a result to distill meaning from the chaos of life. Even a play written to argue that life is meaningless must be logically structured. Plotting the structure of a story is not easy, because thousands of factors can change the sequence of events. The character's deepest motivations must be taken into account, but the playwright must also consider believability, style, and the norms of the particular genre. **Genre** is a category of an artistic work that has a particular form, style, or subject matter. (For more on genre, see the Spotlight "Genre.") Sometimes playwrights create a unique plot-structure; at other times they use a conventional plot-structure.

> The narrative impulse is always with us; we couldn't imagine ourselves through a day without it. . . . We need myths to get by. We need story; otherwise the tremendous randomness of experience overwhelms us. Story is what penetrates.
>
> ***Robert Coover,***
> Novelist

Formula Plots

Playwrights don't come up with a new plot every time they tell a story. Sometimes they depend on formula plots. A formula plot is one that follows a blueprint. Today, formula plots prevail in most big Hollywood movies and many plays.

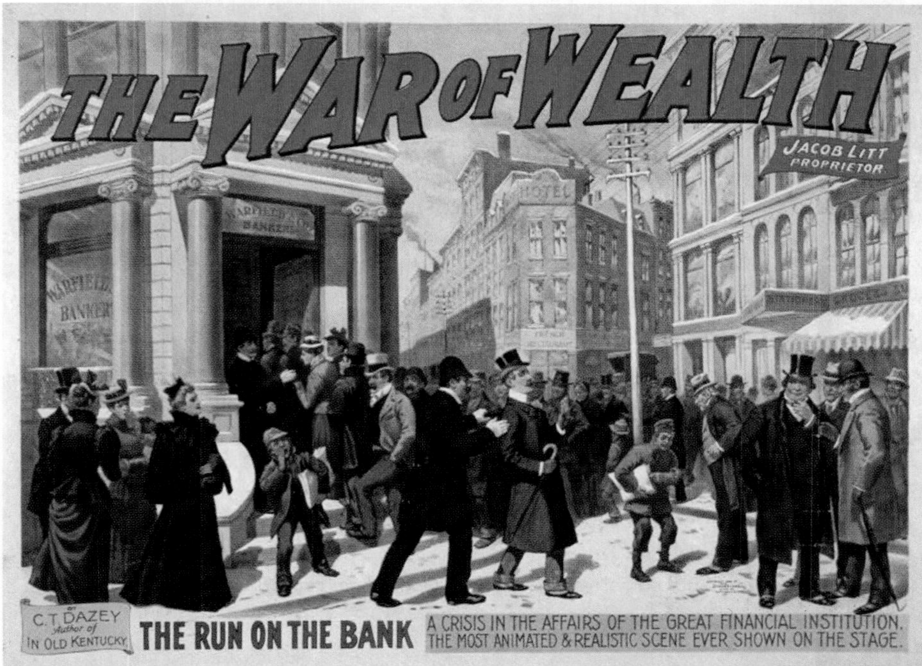

World History Archive/Alamy

Many modern plays, movies, and television shows follow a melodramatic structure with simple formula plots, and good versus evil storylines. Melodrama has been around for over one hundred and fifty years. This poster is from The War of Wealth, *an 1896 melodrama based on the economic panic of 1893.*

SPOTLIGHT ON Genre

Playwrights often write plays of a particular *genre*, or type of story. The most common genres are comedy and tragedy. Other genres include melodrama, realism, romanticism, expressionism, and absurdism. Each genre may also have subgenres. For example, a subgenre of comedy is sentimental comedy, which takes an entertaining look at the troubles of everyday people. *The Dining Room* (1982) by A. R. Gurney and *The Man Who Came to Dinner* (1939) by Moss Hart and George Kaufman are examples of sentimental comedies. Another subgenre of comedy is farce, such as *Noises Off* (1982) by Michael Frayn, in which the characters are caught in a fast-paced story and broadly satirical circumstances. Situation comedy, called "sitcom" on television, is a subgenre that takes a light look at comic situations, such as the TV show *Seinfeld* (1990–1998). Dark comedies, such as *Little Murders* (1966) by Jules Feiffer and the movie *Eternal Sunshine of the Spotless Mind* (2004), allow the audience to laugh at the bleaker or absurd side of life.

Working within a genre means obeying its rules. A playwright who sets out to write a realistic play cannot include supernatural events or dream sequences, because such moments would not be realistic. Romantic plays have protagonists who set out against impossible odds simply because they know in their hearts they're right. Expressionist plays use highly stylized methods to show the characters' inner feelings rather than external realities. Absurdist plays have stories that show the world as cruel, unjust, and meaningless. In Part 3 of this book, you will learn more about the many genres and how they came into being.

Sometimes playwrights deliberately mix genres in an attempt to shock the audience, to increase irony or comic effect, or to express ideas that can't be limited to a single genre. For example, in *Macbeth* (1606) Shakespeare follows the tragic scene where Macbeth returns from killing King Duncan with a broadly comical scene with a drunken porter. By juxtaposing a serious scene with a comic scene, he creates ironic moments and powerful dramatic effects. Playwrights may also mix genres to show different points of view. For example, Arthur Miller's *Death of a Salesman* (1949) is a realistic play but switches to expressionism when it enters into the mind of the main character, Willy Loman, thus allowing the audience to gain greater understanding of the troubled salesman.

Chris Bennion

One of the most popular types of comedy is farce, a fast-paced story in which characters are caught up in improbable situations. Some farces are called "door-slamming farces" because the characters enter and exit so many times. One of the most famous door-slamming farces is Noises Off *by Michael Frayne, a broadly comical look at what goes on backstage during a play. This 2004 production featured Bradford Farwell, Lori Larsen, Mark Chamberlin, Bhama Roget, Michael Patten, and Suzanne Bouchard. Directed by Richard Seyd, Seattle Repertory Theatre.*

Formula is nothing new; it is, in fact, as old as humanity. In his book *The Hero with a Thousand Faces*, Joseph Campbell examines myths and storytelling throughout the ages. He found that most myths have a similar structure no matter what country, culture, or century they come from; they all follow similar formulaic plotlines. Storytellers from ancient Greece to Kenya to China to Hollywood often use the same formula. In fact, the first bedtime story you were told as a child was probably a formula story.

To study formula, let's compare the structures of several plays and movies:

- *Marvin's Room* (1992), a play written by Scott McPherson, is about estranged sisters, Bessie and Lee, who attempt to heal old wounds when they discover that Bessie has been diagnosed with cancer; the movie version starred Diane Keaton, Meryl Streep, and Leonardo DiCaprio.
- *A Raisin in the Sun* (1959), an award-winning play written by Lorraine Hansberry, chronicles an African American family's fight against poverty and segregation; the most famous movie version starred Sidney Poitier in 1961.
- *Romeo and Juliet* (ca. 1595), by William Shakespeare, is a classic story of forbidden love.
- *Oedipus Rex* (ca. 431 BCE), a play written by Sophocles in Greece 2,400 years ago, is about a king who kills his father and mistakenly marries his mother.
- *Star Wars* (1977) is a sci-fi adventure movie written and directed by George Lucas.

As unlikely as it may seem, these stories share a similar formulaic structure, just as a grand cathedral and a plain box-like office building can share the same skeletal design. First we will identify the basic structural elements and then use a grid to show how each of these works follows the formula.

The basic sections of a formula plot are beginning, middle, and end. By pinpointing the moment one section of the story ends and the next begins and by defining the components of each section, we can discover the mechanics of a formula plot.

> The very impulse to write, I think, springs from an inner chaos crying for order, for meaning, and that meaning must be discovered in the process of writing or the work lies dead as it is finished.
>
> ***Arthur Miller,***
> Playwright

In the Beginning

In the beginning of most plays, the playwright sets up the characters and the basic situation, which includes the time and location, character relationships, and some exposition. **Exposition**, sometimes called **back story**, lets the audience in on what happened to the characters before the play began and what happens between the scenes and offstage. For example, if two characters talk about what happened the night before, that's exposition.

At the beginning of a play, the playwright also introduces the protagonist and antagonist. The **protagonist** is the central character who pushes forward the action of the play. The protagonist can be a hero or a severely flawed soul, as long as the audience can identify with, care for, and even root for him or her. The **antagonist** is what the ancient Greeks called the "opposer of action." It's the adversary who stands in the way of the protagonist's goals. An antagonist may be a one-dimensional villain, a complex character, an element of nature such as a storm or a huge whale, or even an aspect of the protagonist's own character such as alcoholism or self-doubt.

This information about setting and characters is conveyed through the structural components of the beginning of a formula plot: event, disturbance, point of attack, and major dramatic question. (See Table 6.1.)

TABLE 6.1: The beginning of a formula plot

Play	Event	Disturbance	Point of attack (decision)
Marvin's Room	Bessie goes to the doctor because she's not been feeling well.	Bessie discovers she has leukemia.	Bessie decides to communicate with her sister, to whom she hasn't spoken in years.
A Raisin in the Sun	The poor African American family is excited about a large check that's to arrive in the mail.	The check for $10,000 arrives.	Mama decides to trust her son Walter Lee to manage the money.
Romeo and Juliet	Young men from the warring Capulet and Montague families engage in a street brawl.	Romeo, of the house of Montague, and Juliet, of the house of Capulet, fall in love, despite their families' feud.	Romeo and Juliet decide to marry, despite the obstacles they face.
Oedipus Rex	The citizens of Thebes gather at the palace of Oedipus.	Oedipus learns that the plague upon his city will not end until the murderer of King Laius is found and punished.	Oedipus decides to investigate the crime, find the guilty party, and punish him.
Star Wars	Luke Skywalker meets the Jedi master Obi-Wan Kenobi.	Luke's family is killed.	Luke decides to join Obi-Wan, become a Jedi knight, and fight for good.

Event Most plays begin with an **event**, an unusual incident, a special occasion, or a crisis in the characters' lives. This unique moment could be a wedding, a funeral, a homecoming, or preparation for a party. With the event, the playwright draws the audience into the play.

Disturbance At the beginning of a play, the basic situation often has equilibrium. In other words, the lives of the characters have achieved a certain stasis, or balance—a balance that must be disturbed if there is to be conflict. The **disturbance** is an inciting incident that upsets the balance and gets the action rolling by creating an opportunity for conflict between protagonists and antagonists.

Point of Attack The disturbance causes the situation to deteriorate to the point where the protagonist must make a major decision that will result in conflict. This moment is called the **point of attack**. It is the moment in the plot when the fuse is lit. This decision defines what the play is about; it states the protagonist's goal. It's the core action of the play, sometimes called the *through line*, for at that moment we know what the play is about.

The disturbance and the point of attack cause a **major dramatic question**, sometimes called **MDQ**. This is the hook that keeps people in the theatre for two hours because they want to know the answers. It is the major dramatic question, not the theme of the play, that causes curiosity and suspense. For example, if the major dramatic question in *Romeo and Juliet* is "Will love triumph over hate?" then the theme would be a broader statement about the nature of love.

TABLE 6.2: The middle of a formula plot

Play	Conflict, crises, and complications	Dark moment
Marvin's Room	Bessie must convince her sister, Lee, to stay. She must convince Lee's son, Hank, to have a bone marrow test.	Hank says he won't help Bessie by giving her a bone marrow transplant. He runs away.
A Raisin in the Sun	Walter Lee discovers that his friend is really a con man and has run off with his money.	Walter Lee falls into a deep depression. He thinks that the only way out is to sell his mother's new house back to Karl Lindner, the white homeowners' association representative.
Romeo and Juliet	Tybalt, Juliet's beloved cousin, challenges Romeo to a fight, but Romeo refuses to fight back—until Tybalt kills Romeo's friend. (Tybalt is now Romeo's kin because Romeo and Juliet have secretly married.)	Romeo kills Tybalt and is banished from the city.
Oedipus Rex	Oedipus accuses Creon of being guilty, but he begins to suspect himself.	Oedipus learns that he is in fact the murderer of King Laius.
Star Wars	Luke must join forces with the less-than-trustworthy Han Solo; they are caught by the evil Death Star and wind up facing death again and again, such as when they are nearly crushed by an enormous garbage compactor.	Han Solo refuses to help. As part of the Republic's fighting force, Luke attacks the Death Star. All his fellow fighters are killed. The evil Darth Vader is about to kill Luke.

In the Middle

The middle of a formula play consists of conflict and crisis. Until the final climax, in fact, there's a string of these conflicts or crises. The characters and the story are in a constant state of flux. This instability is governed by **rising action**, which means that each conflict, crisis, and complication is more dramatic and more serious than the ones before. In other words, the middle of a play follows *the path of most resistance*. Any moments of apparent success always lead to an even greater undoing. As film director Alfred Hitchcock said, "Drama is life with the dull parts left out." The components of the middle are conflicts, crises, and complications, and the dark moment. (See Table 6.2.)

Conflicts, Crises, and Complications The middle of a formula play is full of conflicts, crises, and complications, which are the hurdles that the protagonist must clear to achieve the goal. *Conflict* is the struggle of opposing forces in the play; *crises* are events that make it necessary for the characters to take action; and *complications* are roadblocks that stand in the way of success. Conflicts, crises, and complications are what make a story interesting, for no one wants to see a play about what UCLA writing professor Richard Walter calls "the village of the happy people."

TABLE 6.3: The end of a formula plot

Play	Enlightenment	Climax	Denouement
Marvin's Room	Hank returns home and agrees to the bone marrow transplant.	Bessie learns that Hank's bone marrow doesn't match hers. He can't save her life.	The family is reunited. Bessie discovers that she has been lucky because she's had so much love in her life.
A Raisin in the Sun	Walter Lee realizes his family's pride is more important than the money.	Walter Lee throws Karl Lindner, the spokesman for the white community, out of his house.	The family moves out of their flat and into the better neighborhood. There are still hard times ahead, but they are ready.
Romeo and Juliet	Friar Laurence mixes a potion that causes Juliet to fall into a deep sleep. Her parents, thinking she's dead, transport her to the family tomb, where Romeo goes to save her.	Thinking his love dead, Romeo commits suicide. Juliet awakens and, finding her lover dead, also takes her life.	The grief-stricken Montagues and Capulets promise to end their long feud.
Oedipus Rex	Oedipus is proved to be the killer.	Oedipus blinds himself as punishment.	Oedipus is exiled, thus freeing the city of the plague.
Star Wars	Han Solo comes to Luke's rescue.	In another attack on the Death Star, Luke feels the Force and is able to blow the Death Star to pieces.	Princess Leia rewards Luke and Han Solo for their service and bravery.

The Dark Moment The middle of a formula play ends with the **dark moment**, when the protagonist fails for internal or external reasons, the quest collapses, and the goal seems unattainable.

Where It All Ends

The end of a formula play is usually the shortest part. Here, the playwright adds up the events and comes to some sort of conclusion. Although the ending may not have been predictable at the beginning, by the end, in retrospect, it must appear to have been inevitable. The components of the end are enlightenment, climax, and denouement. (See Table 6.3.)

Enlightenment **Enlightenment** occurs when the protagonist comes to understand how to defeat the antagonist. Enlightenment can come in many forms: the protagonist may join forces with someone; a revelation may shed light on the problem; or the protagonist, after falling into an emotional abyss, may now see the error of his or her ways. The enlightenment is often closely tied to the theme of the play, because the manner, the cause, and the type of enlightenment often reveal the playwright's philosophy.

Climax Enlightened, the protagonist is ready to defeat the antagonist. For the first time the protagonist is able to resolve the conflict with the antagonist. The **climax** is the point of the greatest dramatic tension in the play, the moment the antagonist is defeated. The climax doesn't have to be violent or horrible. It can be quiet, even subtle. Whatever its quality, the climax must be a direct result of the protagonist's actions.

Denouement The **denouement** is the final outcome of the play, a short final scene that allows the audience to appreciate that the protagonist, because of the preceding events, has learned some great or humble lesson. The scene also often hints at the future for the characters, as balance returns. This new balance enables the protagonist to comprehend why he or she suffered and take charge of or accept destiny. The denouement also allows audience members to feel catharsis, or purging of emotions. They may leave the theatre believing, if only for a moment, that someday their lives too might include a moment of understanding, forgiveness, or triumph.

Although these works have different characters and stories, they all follow the same basic formulaic structure. The fundamental elements—event; disturbance; point of attack; major dramatic question; conflict, crisis, and complications; dark moment; enlightenment; climax; and denouement—all occur in exactly the same order. This formula can be used in full-length plays or ten-minute plays (see the Spotlight "How Many Acts? How Many Intermissions?") and in big Hollywood action-adventure flicks or small independent films. In fact, formula storytelling is so common that there are even software programs such as Final Draft and Movie Magic to help writers build formulaic stories. But not all plays or Hollywood movies follow the formula. Sometimes playwrights use nonformulaic structures.

Plots Outside the Formula

When playwrights or screenwriters abandon formula, they allow the story to grow naturally from the characters' actions, motivations, and needs. Writers who abandon formula are often trying to look at life the way it *is*, or as they perceive it, rather than trying to fit it into a standard structure. Many writers who create character-driven stories believe that formula plots do the audience a disservice because they don't require them to confront the chaotic and ineffectual parts of life. In real life we seldom defeat our antagonists, confront our problems, risk it all, refuse to compromise, or have enlightening experiences.

A good example of a nonformulaic movie is Quentin Tarantino's *Pulp Fiction* (1994), starring John Travolta and Samuel L. Jackson, which cleverly interweaves the stories of several characters involved in varying degrees of criminal behavior. This movie is unique in the highly fragmented telling of its stories, whose ties are revealed only at the end. An example of a nonformulaic play is Marsha Norman's Pulitzer Prize–winning *'night, Mother* (1982). It is about a woman, Jessie, who explains to her mother, Thelma, why she's decided to kill herself as she goes through the house tying up the loose ends of her life. The play has no clear-cut protagonist or antagonist, nor is there an opening event or disturbance. Jessie's decision was made before the play begins and not as a reaction to any event that happens on stage. There is a great deal of crisis and conflict as

SPOTLIGHT ON How Many Acts? How Many Intermissions?

Modern plays can be anywhere from a few seconds to many hours long. Most long plays are divided into sections called *acts*, which are separated by short breaks called *intermissions*. The practice of taking an intermission originated about four hundred years ago during the Italian Renaissance, when indoor theatres were introduced. At the time, theatres were lit with candles; performances had to be halted at regular intervals so that the spent candles could be replaced and lit. For most plays the candles had to be replaced four times, so plays were divided into five acts. When you read a Shakespeare play, you'll notice that they have five acts. Interestingly, the division into acts was added after Shakespeare's day—his plays were performed outdoors during the daytime, so he included no intermissions. Later, as candle technology improved, four-act plays with three intermissions became the norm. Today, indoor theatres are no longer lit by candles, but most long plays still have at least one intermission as a relic of the Italian Renaissance and a chance for audience members to stretch their legs. Most plays today are staged in one of the following formats.

Three-act full-length play: The three-act format is not as common today as it was fifty years ago. The double intermission makes the play longer and more formal. Tracy Letts' Tony Award–winning play *August: Osage County* (2007) is an example of a contemporary three-act play.

Two-act full-length play: This is the most common way to divide a full-length play. The intermission is generally taken just after the middle of the story. Most modern plays, such as Caryl Churchill's *Top Girls* (1982), follow this format. However, when directors stage older plays, they often break for only one intermission. For example, today Shakespeare's plays are often staged as two-act plays.

Full-length one-act play: There is no intermission in this type of play, so the beginning, middle, and end flow without interruption, much like a movie. Because people cannot sit for too long without a break, full-length one-act plays are generally shorter than two- or three-act full-length plays (usually between 1 hour 20 minutes and a maximum of 1 hour 35 minutes). *Art* (1996) by Yasmina Reza is an example of a full-length one-act play.

Short one-act plays: These plays can be anywhere from several seconds to about an hour long. Often, several short one-acts are produced on a single night with an intermission after each play. Some playwrights even write several short one-act plays as *companion pieces*, designed to be performed on the same night. By doing this, the playwright doesn't have to share the evening with other short one-acts. Companion pieces can have related or unrelated themes and stories. Examples of related one-acts are *Lone Star* (1979) and *Laundry & Bourbon* (1980) by James McLure. Examples of unrelated one-acts are Christopher Durang's *Sister Mary Ignatius Explains It All for You* (1979) and *The Actor's Nightmare* (1981).

Ten-minute plays: Ten-minute plays are a relatively new format and are growing in popularity. Theatres that produce these tiny plays will stage as many as ten in one evening. Often there is no formal intermission between ten-minute plays, but there may be a short pause while the set is changed. The Actors Theatre of Louisville, a major regional theatre, is often credited with pioneering this format as a way to introduce new voices in playwriting during their new-play festival each year.

Thelma tries to talk Jessie out of her decision, but there are few complications and nothing makes Jessie reconsider. The play ends at the point of its greatest dramatic tension; there is no denouement.

Russian playwright Anton Chekhov neatly alluded to the power of nonformulaic plays when he said, "Let everything on the stage be just as complicated and at the same time just as simple as it is in life. People eat their dinner, just eat

Joan Marcus

When playwrights abandon formula, they allow stories to grow naturally from the characters, often presenting a "slice of life." Marsha Norman's Pulitzer Prize–winning play 'night, Mother *is one such nonformulaic play. This 2004 revival starred Brenda Blethyn and Edie Falco. Directed by Michael Mayer, Royale Theatre, New York.*

their dinner, and all the time their happiness is being established or their lives are being broken up." When you attend a nonformulaic play, expect the playwright to take you on a journey that, just like real life, is unpredictable.

Curtain Call

Playwrights are philosophers, psychologists, poets, and storytellers all rolled into one. They write because they have a deep desire to tell stories that change or entertain the world. They are often solitary people who search their life experiences for interesting stories and characters with the hope that they reveal a bit of truth about human nature. They are also opinionated and want to express themselves. So great is their need to communicate their thoughts about how life is or should be that they often accept low pay in order to find an audience. But in return for their low pay and hard work, they can create worlds and can try to find truths about our relationships and our problems as well as our successes. An old saying in the theatre is "Playwrights write to get well." If they are well, so is the world.

> We're one of the last handmade art forms. There's no fast way to make plays. It takes just as long and is just as hard as it was a thousand years ago.
>
> ***Steven Dietz,***
> Playwright

Robbie Jack/CORBIS

Existentialist playwrights are famous for their adherence to nontraditional plot structures. Samuel Beckett's Waiting for Godot *(1953) consists of two clownlike tramps waiting on a barren plain for a mysterious character who never comes. In this funny and disturbing existentialist classic, Vladimir and Estragon are determined not to take action. As a result they never move toward enlightenment. This 1991 production featured Adrian Edmondson and Rik Mayall, Queen's Theatre, London.*

Summary

The playwright is the artist who conceives the theme, characters, conflict, dialogue, and plot of a play. So important to the theatre are playwrights that they are often called the primary artist. Yet playwrights are often not a part of the theatre ensemble; in fact, most members of an ensemble never meet the playwright whose play they are producing. Playwrights often have trouble making a living because they are self-employed artists. They can join a union that will champion their rights, but because theirs is an open-shop union, they cannot strike to negotiate better compensation. However, because they own the copyright for their work, they are able to control how their plays are presented and they get top billing in the program. A playwright's life may be difficult, but each one knows the joy that lies at the heart of sole authorship and finds great satisfaction in communicating his or her ideas without alteration.

In a sense, playwriting is a very limited form of writing. Plays consist only of dialogue, stage directions, and parentheticals. But playwrights do have many tools with which to construct a play, including theme, character, conflict, language, and plot. With these tools, playwrights can create stories of dramatic power, full of action and insight.

Playwrights may create unique plots or use formula plots, which are based on myths and stories that have been told for centuries. The basic elements of a formula plot are event; disturbance; point of attack; major dramatic question; conflict, crisis, and complications; dark moment; enlightenment; climax; and denouement. When playwrights create their own structures, the plot grows naturally from the characters' motivations and needs, not from a formula's predetermined requirements.

The Art of Theatre ONLINE 

To access this chapter's interactive theatre workshop activities, along with many other learning tools, log onto your Theatre CourseMate. Access is available at cengagebrain.com.

Key Terms

action / 128
antagonist / 137
back story / 137
climax / 141
closed-shop union / 124
dark moment / 140
denouement / 141
dialogue / 127
disturbance / 138
Dramatists Guild of America (DGA) / 125
enlightenment / 140
event / 138
exposition / 137
genre / 135
major dramatic question (MDQ) / 138
open-shop union / 125
parenthetical / 127
plot / 135
plot-structure / 135
point of attack / 138
protagonist / 137
rising action / 139
stage directions / 127
subtext / 131
theme / 128
Writers Guild of America (WGA) / 125

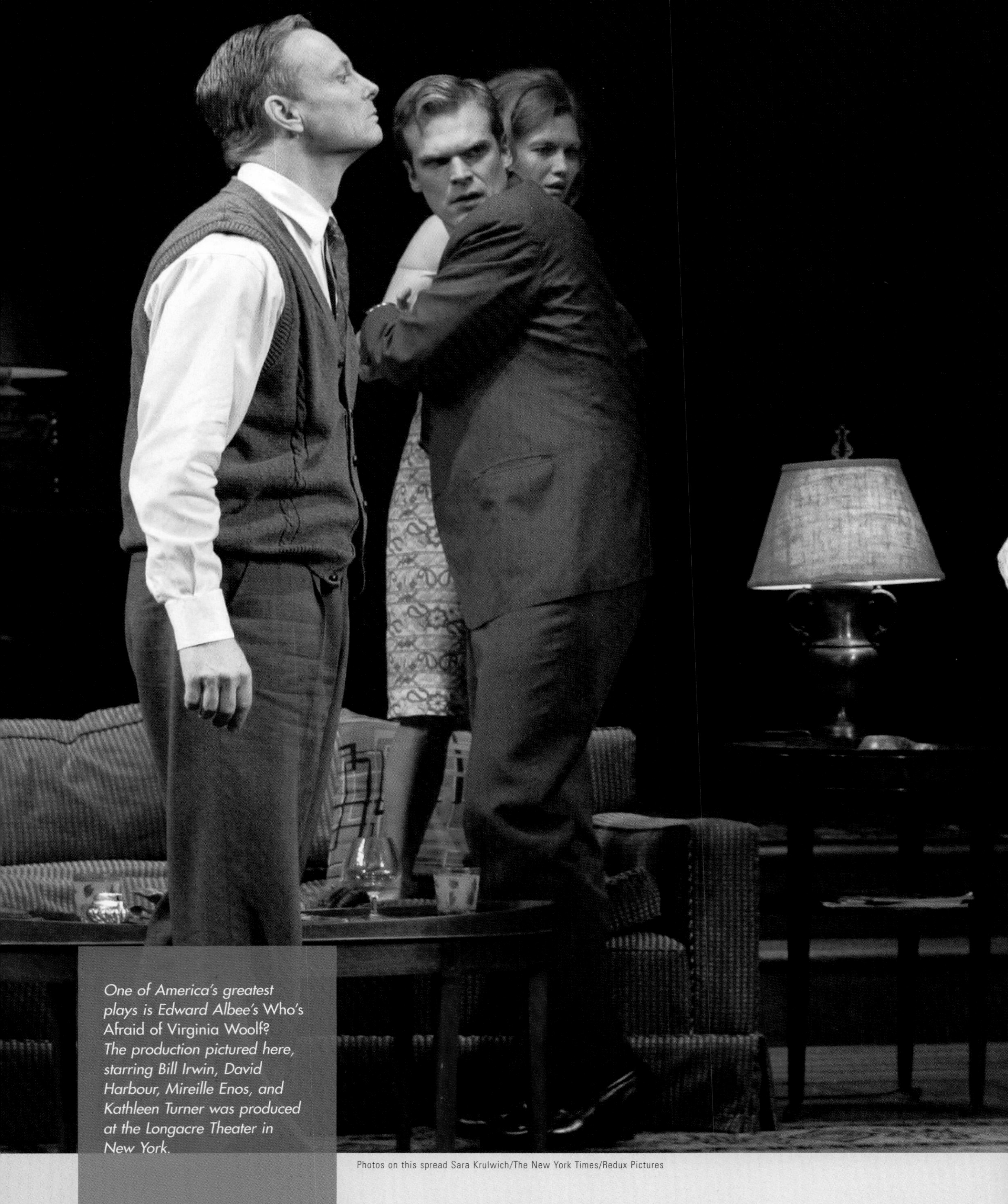

One of America's greatest plays is Edward Albee's Who's Afraid of Virginia Woolf? *The production pictured here, starring Bill Irwin, David Harbour, Mireille Enos, and Kathleen Turner was produced at the Longacre Theater in New York.*

Photos on this spread Sara Krulwich/The New York Times/Redux Pictures

CHAPTER

The Art of Acting

OUTLINE

The actor has perhaps the most romantic role in the theatre. On the opening night of a new play, the playwright goes unnoticed, nervously pacing the lobby; the director sits unseen in the audience; and backstage dozens of stagehands labor incognito. Unlike these offstage members of the theatre ensemble, the actor takes center stage on opening night and is the play. Who among us hasn't dreamed of being an actor or a movie star? It would be a charmed life, speaking great speeches, commanding the attention of admiring audiences, and winning critics' hearts—in fact, even actors dream of such a life. Yet for all its rewards, acting is hard work. The applause comes only after months of rehearsal and years of training. And actors rarely land a role before they have failed tens of dozens of auditions and struggled for months if not years with little or no income. (See the Spotlight "The Life of an Actor: Terri White.")

In this chapter, we will examine the training and life of actors. We'll also look at the techniques actors use to analyze and play characters, especially the techniques that apply to everyday life as well as the stage. Basically, acting is performing a part, something we all do. As Shakespeare said, "All the world's a stage and all the men and women merely players." You may never direct or write a play, but at some point in your life you'll need to play a part.

Training to Be an Actor

Some people just have a natural talent for acting. They have the charisma and stage presence that make them interesting to watch. They can even make the art of acting appear effortless. However, good acting on stage or in film or television requires a lot of training. Yet for most of theatre's history there were no acting schools. The only way to learn acting was by becoming an apprentice at a theatre. Apprentices helped out backstage and sometimes played what are jokingly called "spear-carrier roles." These are the small roles such as servants, attendants, or soldiers that seldom have any lines. After years of service to a theatre, if the apprentice had proven himself, he might be allowed to take a larger role. Today, actors in the United States and Canada usually start their training in a conservatory, university, or college. Undergraduates can earn a BFA (Bachelor of Fine Arts) in acting, and many graduate schools offer an MFA (Master of Fine Arts) in acting. An MFA in acting takes two to three years and includes intense training in voice, dialects, movement, singing, dancing, auditioning, characterization, theatre history, dramatic literature, acting styles, and much more. (BFAs and MFAs are also available in directing, design, playwriting, and other theatre arts.)

Once an actor leaves academia, it takes determination, imagination, and most of all stamina to live the actor's life, but it is seldom the end of the training. When actors are not struggling to find an acting job or working a second job to make ends meet, they are often taking classes to improve their body, voice, and mind—what actors call their "instruments."

Training the Body

Actors, like athletes and dancers, train for years in order to learn greater physical control. This training can include dance, martial arts, and yoga to enhance movement and relaxation; gymnastics, fencing, and stage combat to prepare for realistic-looking fight scenes; and even circus-arts training such as clowning and juggling to prepare for physically demanding roles in broad comedies. They also learn to reduce body tension as they focus on the physical characteristics, mannerisms, and body language of a character or of a particular style of acting.

Training the Voice

An actor's vocal training can be divided into two broad categories: breathing and speaking. At its most basic, the act of breathing simply ensures an adequate supply

SPOTLIGHT ON The Life of an Actor: Terri White

A life in the theatre is easier said than done. Employment seldom lasts more than a few months so actors are continually auditioning, trying to find their next "gig." The on-again-off-again lives of actors mean that one moment they are taking a bow in front of hundreds of adoring fans, and the next they might be counting their tips after a long night of waiting on tables. No actor's life demonstrates the harsh realities of a career in the theatre more than that of the Broadway actor and singer Terri White.

Ms. White was born into a family of traveling performers, and took to the stage herself when she was only eight years old. She learned to tap-dance and often performed to her theme song "Nobody Knows When You're Down and Out." Soon she was acting on Broadway, singing with Liza Minnelli, and, between gigs, performing at nightclubs around New York City. She even acted with five-time Academy Award nominee Glenn Close in the Tony-nominated musical *Barnum* (about P. T. Barnum, the great showman of Barnum & Bailey Circus fame). But then her luck ran out.

After several years of not being able to find work, Ms. White was evicted from her apartment and forced to sleep on a friend's couch. When her money ran out, not wanting to burden her friends, she began sleeping on a bench in Washington Square Park near NYU. "I didn't go to a shelter because there was a certain pride in myself," Ms. White said. "I didn't want to take a pity home." She never mentioned to her fellow homeless that she had once been a star on Broadway.

One night she was recognized by a police officer who helped her find a place to live and get her life back on track, and soon thereafter, her luck began to change. A year later, Ms. White was cast in the Broadway musical *Finian's Rainbow* at the same theatre she had last performed with Glenn Close many years before.

Asked about her future as an actor she said, "I didn't dream I was going to be homeless, and a year ago, I didn't think that I was going to be back on Broadway, so I can't figure out what's happening after *Finian's*." A life as an actor can be highly rewarding, but it is a life filled with nonstop competition, heartbreak, and few safety nets. It is not a life well suited to a fragile ego, those who are easily daunted, or those lacking great personal discipline and devotion.

Walter McBride/Corbis

Terri White takes a bow on Broadway.

of oxygen to the blood. But actors must learn to allow the body to breathe in the most tension-filled moments. No matter what is happening on the stage, the actor must know how to permit the body's air pressure to support the voice so that it can be heard at the far corners of the theatre. To do this without amplification takes training—years of rigorous exercises and techniques designed to allow speech without rigid shoulders, braced knees, a tense back, or any of the other posture problems that can make nonactors appear ill at ease when they speak in front of crowds.

> Acting is simply my way of investigating human nature and having fun at the same time.
>
> ***Meryl Streep,***
> Stage and screen actor

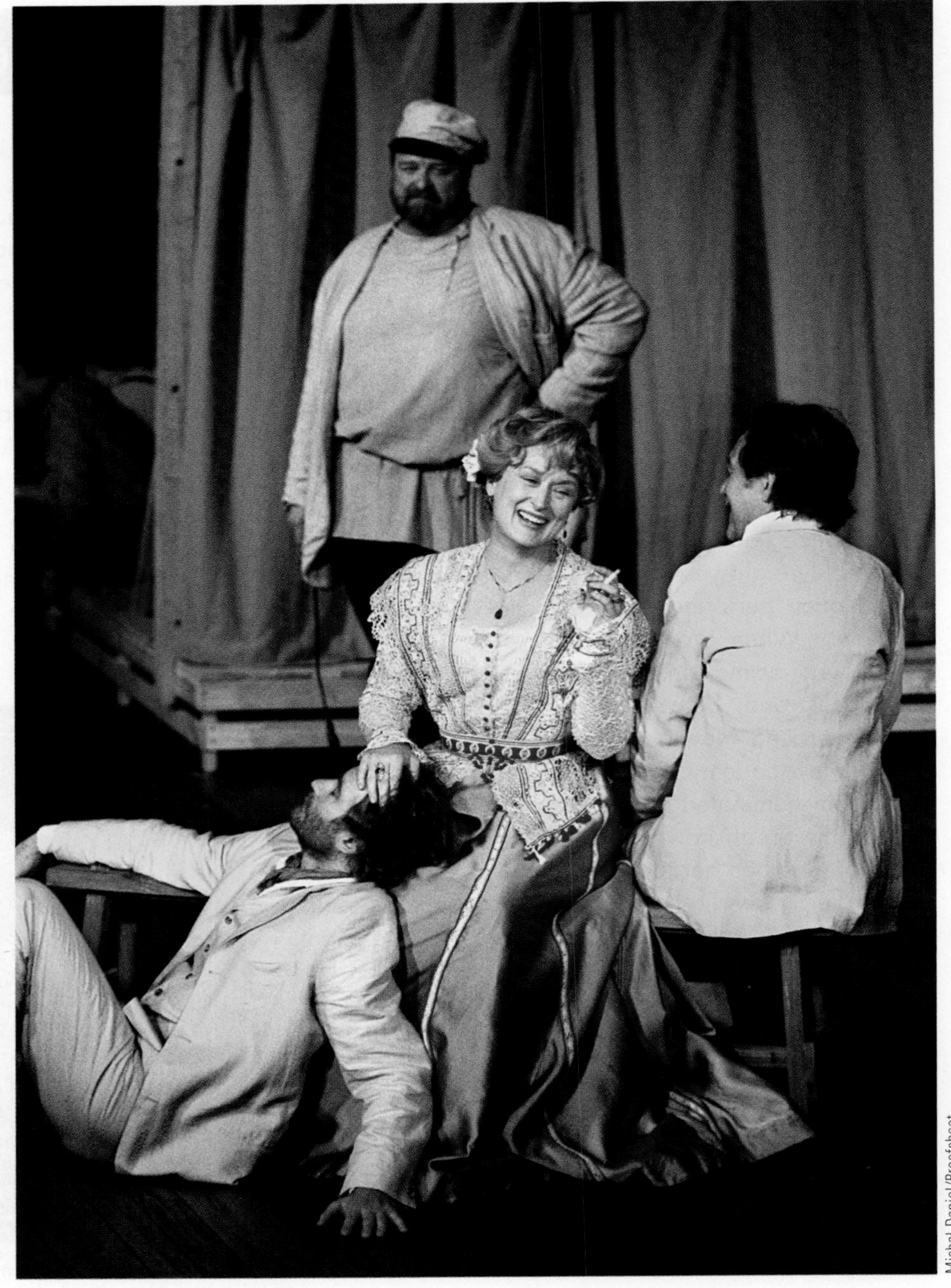

Michal Daniel/Proofsheet

Meryl Streep, who began voice lessons at the age of twelve and continued her training at Yale's School of Drama, is known for her ability to take on almost any accent and apply it convincingly in her film and stage roles. Here she plays the actress Arkadina in Chekhov's The Seagull *in a 2001 production at the Delacorte Theater, Central Park, New York. New version by Tom Stoppard. Directed by Mike Nichols.*

Like singers, actors take years of voice training in order to learn to control their pitch, volume, and resonance. They must also learn to project their voices night after night without becoming hoarse. In addition, actors may learn a variety of dialects so that they can be cast as a character who speaks with a French, Italian, Southern, or other accent on a moment's notice. In order to learn an accent and to speak clearly, actors often use the **International Phonetic Alphabet (IPA)**. IPA is a system for transcribing the sounds of speech; it is independent of any particular language but applicable to all languages.

With training an actor can build a flexible, dynamic, articulate voice with which to flesh out a character, focus on the sounds and images of the playwright's words, and sound natural show after show while being heard by thousands of people.

Training the Mind

It takes concentration and discipline to perform in the theatre. Actors train their minds to memorize thousands of lines of dialogue in a short period of time, as well as to think on their feet. They must be involved with the needs of their characters but never forget that they are acting in imaginary situations. This duality means that actors must have unwavering focus but also be aware of everything going on around them. In fact, acting may be the ultimate multi-tasking. In order to train their minds, actors use improvisation, game-like acting exercises, and even yoga to help build their self-confidence and ability to concentrate even in the most difficult situations. (See the Spotlight "An Actor's Nightmare—Forgetting Lines.")

> The actor's basic problem has remained the same throughout the ages. He is the only artist whose basic raw material is himself; he uses his own muscles, brain, emotions, voice, speech, and gestures to identify with and create another human being.
>
> ***Lee Strasberg,***
> Acting teacher

Gurus and Mentors: Acting Teachers

The need for actor training has given birth to countless acting schools and teachers who each expound particular methods for helping actors tap into their creativity and train their body, mind, and voice. Some of the most famous acting teachers are Stella Adler, Sanford Meisner, Uta Hagen, Michael Chekhov, and Lee Strasberg. Some acting teachers have created actor-training methods for the needs of their own styles of theatre; these teachers include Jerzy Grotowski, Bertolt Brecht, and Tadashi Suzuki. Almost all modern actor-training methods trace their heritage, at least in part, to one of the greatest of all acting teachers, Konstantin Stanislavsky (1863–1938). Often called the father of modern acting, Stanislavsky was the cofounder of the world-famous Moscow Art Theatre. He also wrote several books that revolutionized the world of acting, including *An Actor Prepares* (1926) and *Building a Character* (1949). Throughout his life, Stanislavsky advocated many different approaches for training actors. One of his most famous techniques taught actors to be more natural onstage by recalling their own emotions and transferring those feelings to their characters, thereby finding a detailed emotional identification with the characters they played. This individualized, psychological approach to acting became known as the **Stanislavsky system**, or **method acting**.

> An actor lives, weeps, laughs on the stage, but as he weeps and laughs he observes his own tears and mirth. It is this double existence, this balance between life and acting that makes for art.
>
> ***Konstantin Stanislavsky,***
> Acting teacher and director

In January 1923, members of the Moscow Art Theatre arrived in America for a tour. By the time they left in the spring of 1924, they had changed U.S. acting forever: in their productions even the tiniest spear-carrying role was fully thought out and played as a multidimensional individual with deep motivations. Shortly thereafter, Stanislavsky's ideas about acting would revolutionize the American theatre.

American acting gurus such as Stella Adler (1902–1992) and Lee Strasberg (1899–1982) developed Stanislavsky's methods, and new theatres such as the Group Theatre and the Actors Studio, both in New York City, promoted variations of Stanislavsky's methods. Marlon Brando, James Dean, Rod Steiger, Geraldine Page, Dustin Hoffman, Jane Fonda, Robert De Niro, Paul Newman, Jack Nicholson, Christopher Walken, Gene Wilder, Anne Bancroft, and Al Pacino are some of the actors trained in Stanislavsky's methods at the Actors Studio.

Acting teacher Konstantin Stanislavsky is best known for his revolutionary approach to acting, which advocated that actors identify emotionally with their characters rather than simply playing "types."

SPOTLIGHT ON Tadashi Suzuki

Not all modern actor-training methods trace their heritage to Konstantin Stanislavsky. One exception is Tadashi Suzuki's actor-training system, which became popular in the United States in the early 1980s. Suzuki was enthralled with the traditional Japanese forms of theatre, Noh and Kabuki. Noh acting and its more popular version, Kabuki, take years of training and discipline to master. In fact some Japanese Kabuki actors train from childhood. Others learn the art from their fathers, who learned it from their fathers in a process that goes back many generations. Some Kabuki actors in Japan are even declared "national treasures," in the same way that important sites and structures in the United States are put on the National Register of Historic Places. (For more on Noh and Kabuki see Chapter 11.)

Suzuki decided to form his own theatre that would embody the stamina and concentration of traditional Japanese theatre. He began training actors in techniques ranging from modern Western ballet to Indian Kathakali dancing (a traditional form of folk drama) in order to develop their ability to control their body. Suzuki said that his rigorous training was designed to temper and shape the body so that the actor can bring to the stage a "brilliant liveliness" that takes into account the "tiniest details of movement." He wanted to free the actors to express the character in every way possible.

An example of Suzuki's attention to the details of movement is his work with actors' feet. Traditional Japanese plays are performed in tabi, white divided-toe socks that put a focus on the feet and thus make them an important part of the performance. Suzuki developed complex exercises so that actors could discover how their feet could express character. He even named a chapter in his book *The Way of Acting* "The Grammar of the Feet." By putting so much attention on a part of the body that is often ignored by modern Western actors, he teaches actors that there is more to characterization than just circumstances, objectives, and character analysis. In fact, sometimes the most complex understanding of character comes when actors free their body and thus find power and control.

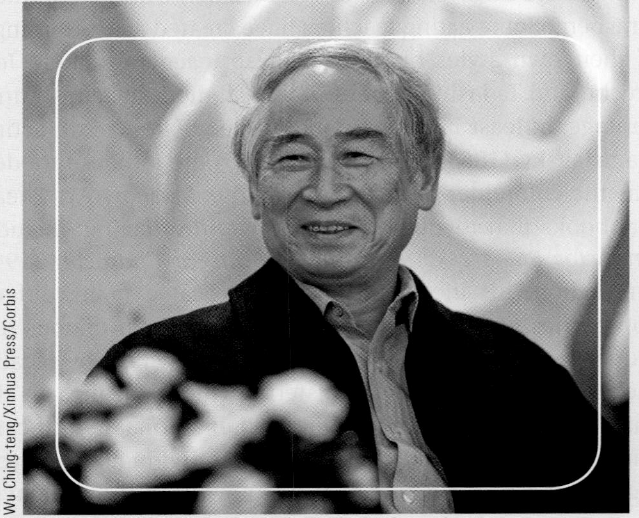

Wu Ching-teng/Xinhua Press/Corbis

Acting coach Tadashi Suzuki

Even Marilyn Monroe studied there when she got tired of playing the ditzy-blonde roles that had made her famous. Today, Stanislavsky's influence in the United States still predominates; nearly all actors and actor-training programs borrow from his system. (One of the few actor-training methods that does not is the one devised by Tadashi Suzuki. See the Spotlight "Tadashi Suzuki.")

Acting Techniques We All Can Use

Acting is not limited to actors. Every day we are confronted with situations that call for acting: The professor looks at us during a lecture and we stifle a yawn and feign interest; we're pulled over for speeding and try to act remorseful; we attend our cousin's wedding and heartily congratulate the bride even though we're convinced she is making a colossal mistake. Although we are told honesty is the best policy, we all learn how to act and hide our emotions at an early age—in fact, acting may even have been one of the reasons for our survival as a species. After all, human beings are woefully unprepared compared to other animals; our strength is meager, our skin is thin, our eyesight is below average, and our sense of smell is poor. Prehistoric hunters would have gone hungry if they had been honest with their prey. Instead, they used stealth to sneak up on a deer: they moved downwind, wore a costume made of deerskin, and acted as a member of the herd. By the time the deer knew an impostor, an actor, was in their midst, it was too late. Because acting, on some level, is common to all humans, we're going to look at acting techniques not only from the actor's point of view but also at how nonactors can use these techniques in everyday life.

Changing How You Feel: Outside/In and Inside/Out

Actors have known for thousands of years the two basic methods of controlling one's emotions. These methods go by many names, but, for simplicity, we'll label them "outside/in" and "inside/out." If you change yourself physically—in other words, on the outside—you can change how you feel on the inside, and if you change how you feel on the inside, you can change what other people see. The mind and body connection is a two-way street: change your body and you can affect your emotions; change your emotions and you can cause your body to react. For example, when you get ready to take part in a formal wedding, you clean yourself up, put on a fancy dress or tux and, as a result, feel more confident and attractive. The physical adjustments change how you feel.

The same principle is true for people who have makeovers on television shows; often participants say that their new look makes them feel more alive, sexy, or in control. In fact, the purpose of makeovers is not to change people's appearance but to change how they feel—in other words, to make them *act* differently. Changing your appearance is an obvious way to change how you feel, but you can also alter how you feel by manipulating the shape of your body or by, say, changing what you hold in your hand. You feel very different cradling a bouquet of flowers than you do when you clutch a gun. Actors have been doing this for thousands of years. In 400 BCE a Greek actor named Polus performed the title role in Sophocles's *Electra*. (Men played women's roles in ancient Greek theatre.) In the play, Electra grieves the death of her brother Orestes. In her hand is an urn, which she believes contains his ashes. In order to feel the true, deep emotions of the character and give a convincing performance, Polus put the ashes of his recently deceased son in the urn and held it on stage.

You may also be able to change how you feel by making a small physical change—try it yourself. The next time you feel upset, tired, or bored, force yourself to smile. It may take a few minutes, but if you're sensitive to it, the forced smiling may make you begin to feel better. The opposite is also true. Sometime when you are feeling good, force yourself to frown. After a few minutes, your emotions may follow the physical cue and you may start feeling a little sad.

This outside/in technique can be quite useful for nonactors. For example, several years ago a newly graduated law student was going to interview with a fancy law firm in Switzerland. The first round of interviews was to be held over the phone, and then the company would fly the three final candidates to Switzerland for face-to-face interviews. The new lawyer desperately wanted the job, or at least the free trip to Switzerland. The lawyer sat there in his apartment in tattered shorts and a frayed tee shirt waiting for the phone to ring, but he didn't feel right for the job; even though he passed the bar examination, he didn't feel like a lawyer. So he pulled out his best suit, shirt, and tie. He shaved, showered, and dressed for the interview as if it were to be face-to-face. He made himself feel the part of a capable young law-school graduate. Changing himself physically brought out that part of his personality that was good enough to get the job. During the phone interview, he easily played the part of the competent young lawyer because he felt like one.

Just as changing physicality can engender a mood or feeling, changing the way you feel can alter your physicality. Sadness causes your body to collapse slightly as your shoulders curve in and your head droops. Joy brings your shoulders back and your head up. By simply producing a feeling, you may change your outward appearance. But how does one *control* feelings, or choose which feeling to express? One method is through what Stanislavsky called **emotional memory**—also known as sense memory or affective memory. The idea is to think back over a certain incident and remember it well enough to relive the accompanying emotions. This process occurs all the time in daily life; we can get so caught up in telling a story that we relive the emotions. For example, as you are telling a friend about how your significant other dumped you and get to the moment when "good-bye forever" was said, suddenly the tears start flowing again. Your memory causes you to relive the emotions accompanying the event. Acting from the inside out is no different. We have all fallen in love, felt anger, or suffered the death of someone close. These emotions, if they can be recalled and controlled, allow an actor to make genuine connections with how the character feels and responds.

> Emotional power is maybe the most valuable thing that an actor can have.
>
> ***Christopher Walken,***
> Stage and screen actor

Nonactors can also make good use of this inside/out technique. Let's go back to our law school graduate who used the outside/in technique for the phone interview. A few weeks later he found himself in Switzerland awaiting the face-to-face interview. As he looked at the elegant brass and leather decor of the lobby, he was overtaken by a sense of inadequacy. He thought he wasn't good enough to work in such a fancy office. So he searched his emotional memory for a time when he felt confident and recalled his game-saving home run in college. He concentrated on the sights and smells of the ball field. He could almost see the stern look on the pitcher's face and then the fastball and hear the thwack of the bat as he connected. Rounding first, he looked up and saw the ball soar over the fence—the fans were going wild and his teammates were running out from the dugout. As he recalled the details of the event, he felt a sense of confidence come over him; soon his breathing calmed and his shoulders relaxed. During the interview, the trepidation returned a few times, but all he had to do was think "thwack!" and he felt, and therefore acted, confident. Was this job applicant lying to his future employers? No. His confident feelings were real, just as an actor's emotions can be real. He simply chose which emotions he was going to play rather than letting his emotions control him. In short, he was a good actor. By the way, he got the job.

An actor working from the outside in, concentrating on physical details, is often said to be using a **technical approach** to acting. An actor working from the inside out, finding the right memories to relive the needed emotions, is often said to be using method acting. Whichever system is used, and actors often use both, the intended result is feeling the needed emotions rather than being dominated by whatever emotions are naturally occurring. In short, acting isn't always *acting*; it is also *being*.

Acting is more than controlling emotions. It also is the ability to see ourselves in someone else's shoes. One of the highest forms of intelligence is the ability to see life from someone else's point of view. An actor playing a part must not only control emotions but also needs to understand life. Sometimes this means seeing life from the point of view of a character that has very different values and perceptions. Two methods actors often use to achieve this empathy are the "magic *if*" and substitution.

> The most important thing in acting is honesty. If you can fake that, you've got it made.
>
> ***George Burns,***
> Actor and comedian

Empathy and the Magic *If*: Sympathy Transformed

Sympathy is concern for another person, but empathy is more. **Empathy** is the ability to understand and identify with another's situation, feelings, and motives so completely that you feel you are experiencing that situation and those emotions. In other words, when you feel empathy, you're feeling yourself in the place of another. Empathy is as close as people can come to a shared experience. Many believe that actors cannot truly know a character without empathy. But this doesn't mean that actors must have experienced the death of a loved one before they can understand a character who is in mourning, or face death to understand how a terminal patient feels, or commit a murder in order to know the inner thoughts of a killer. Empathy is also possible when an actor vicariously stands in the shoes of another, builds a vivid image of the situation, and reacts.

Stanislavsky used a technique that he called the **magic *if*** to stimulate the imagination toward empathy. This technique is based on one question: "What would I do *if* I were this character in these circumstances?" The magic *if* is a springboard to the imagination; it allows actors to find similarities between themselves and the character and to explore the resulting emotions and thoughts. Of course, in order for the magic *if* to work, actors must spend many hours researching a character's motivation, situation, and back story. Empathy and

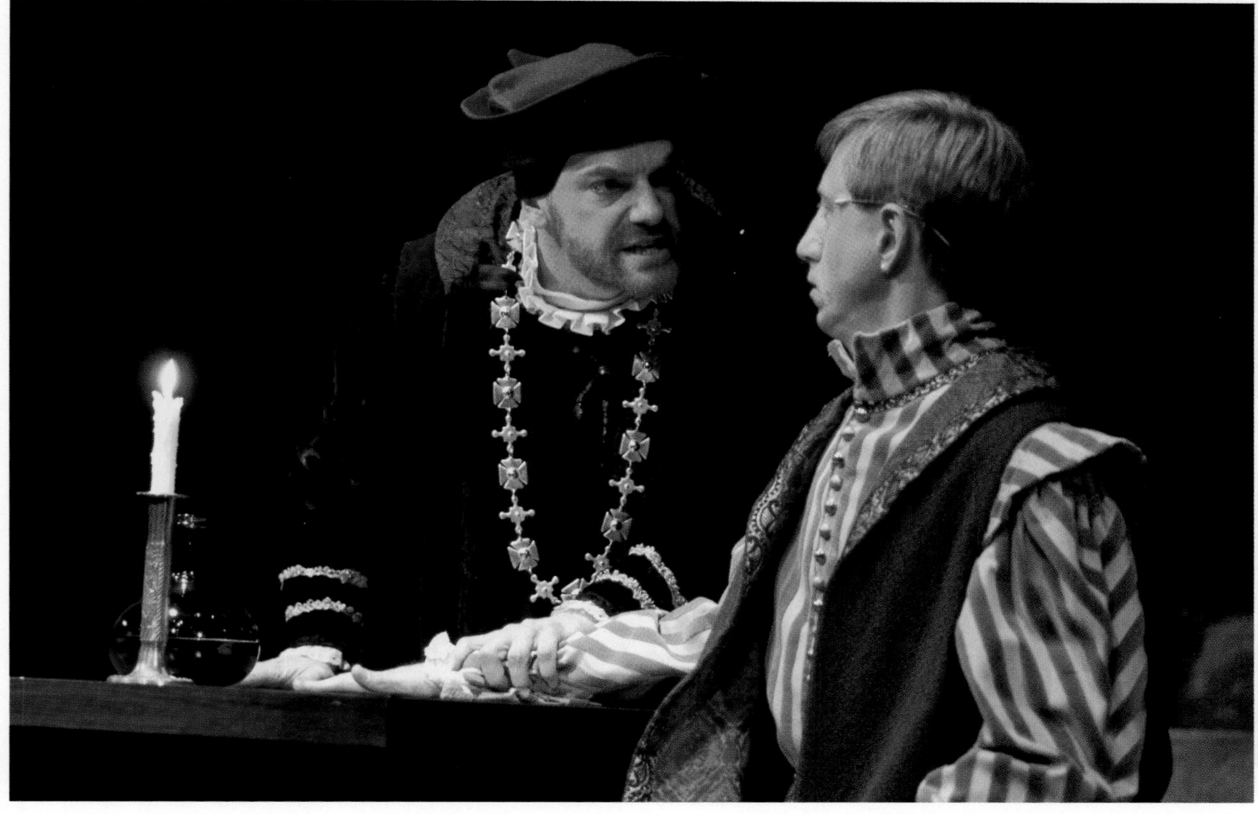

*Actors often use **substitution** to perform feelings from their own experiences that parallel the emotions called for in the script. Here actors perform a powerful scene from* A Man For All Seasons *at the Arvada Center for the Arts and Humanities.*

the magic *if* can lead to a deep personal understanding or to a flash of tolerance that can be mined for greater insight into the character. Stanislavsky said, "We must study other people and get as close to them emotionally as we can, until sympathy for them is transformed into feelings of our own." In other words, the actor must study the character until the actor has empathy. Needless to say, here is a great lesson that many nonactors—as well as many countries, races, and cultures—could stand to learn.

Substitution: It's All Yiddish to Me

Of course, no actor has the personal experience and understanding to quickly slip into every role. Occasionally, a play demands a character with which the actor has no experience or emotional bond. The solution is sometimes the actor's technique of **substitution**. When actors have little or no emotional bond with a character, they replace the character's emotions with unrelated but personal emotions of their own.

Robert Lewis tells a wonderful story about substitution in his book *Method—Or Madness*. Many years ago, an actor named Ben-Ami was in a Yiddish play in New York City. In one scene Ben-Ami's character had to attempt suicide.

He stood at the edge of the stage staring into the audience with a revolver to his head. During every performance, sweat would break out on his face and his eyes would seem to pop out of his head. Ben-Ami could keep the audience on

Occasionally, actors have the opportunity to play a character beyond their emotional knowledge and life experience. In this situation, they rely on the technique of substitution, replacing the character's emotions with unrelated emotions of their own. Here, David Morse and Mary-Louise Parker have most likely used that technique to play victim and victimizer in Paula Vogel's How I Learned to Drive *(1997), a play about the repercussions of sexual abuse.*

Carol Rosegg

SPOTLIGHT ON An Actor's Nightmare—Forgetting Lines

When actors forget their lines it is called "going up" or "blanking" and it can be a nightmare. Unlike movie and television where actors only need to memorize a few lines at a time, or have cue cards waiting just off camera to assist them, stage actors must memorize thousands of lines of dialogue and get them right night after night. Some stage actors swear that it is best to memorize just before they go to bed at night, claiming that their subconscious works on the lines while they sleep. Others seek out assistants to "run" their lines with them. In addition, directors occasionally hold special rehearsals where the actors "speed-through" their lines in an attempt to implant the words in their brain.

During rehearsals in the first few weeks the actors carry "the book"—which is the script, whether in booklet form or photocopied pages—with them on stage. But within a week or two the director will instruct the actors to go "off book," and leave the script behind. At this point the stage manager will follow along in the script waiting for the actors to forget a line, or to "go up" on a line. When she goes up, the actor simply says, "line" and the stage manager cues her by speaking the first few words of the dropped line until the actor again takes over. Knowing their lines perfectly is often considered the benchmark of professionalism for actors, but sometimes even the best have difficulty. A hundred years ago theatres often used a prompter, a stagehand who would sit near the stage during the performance, to feed the actors their lines should they go up.

Today prompters are rarely used, but when they are they're often high tech. For example, the Academy Award nominated and five-time Tony Award–winning actress Angela Lansbury once used a tiny wireless earpiece during a performance. But this does not always work. When the stage legend Mary Martin, famous for playing Peter Pan, tried the same trick she found that the earpiece not only picked up the voice of the prompter, but also taxi radios from the street. Actors have also been known to write their problem lines on the stage furniture, or hide it in the brim of their hat, but this is considered highly unprincipled, and in some cases such actors have been fired. Using earpieces and hiding lines are rare exceptions. Far more often actors have no help: if they go up, they are on their own. The stage is a risky business.

the edge of their seats for well over a minute without saying a word and hardly moving, as he debated whether he should pull the trigger. Finally he would say, "Ikh ken nit!" (I can't do it!), and the audience would bring down the house with cries of relief and applause. Night after night, he created such an emotional reality that soon he became the hit of Yiddish theatre. A young actor in the play asked him how he did it, but Ben-Ami said, "It's better for people not to know. . . . It'll spoil the show." On the closing night, Ben-Ami finally told the young actor how he pulled it off—he used substitution. Here is his explanation:

> My problem with this scene was that I personally could never blow my brains out. I am just not suicidal, and I can't imagine ending my life. So I could never really know how that man was feeling, and I could never play such a person authentically. For weeks I went around trying to think of some parallel in my own life that I could draw on. What situation could I be in where, first of all, I am standing up, I am alone, I am looking straight ahead, and something I feel I must do is making me absolutely terrified, and finally that whatever it is I can't do it? . . . I finally realized that the one thing I hate worse than anything is washing in cold water. So what I'm really doing with that gun to my head is trying to get myself to step into an ice-cold shower.

Ben-Ami found an emotional parallel that worked for him, one that allowed him to play the moment and to some extent find empathy. Through the use of empathy, the magic if, and substitution, it is possible to understand the emotions of another, even a character who is quite unlike yourself.

Understanding a Character

Centuries before the invention of psychology, actors were studying people's mental states and the motivations behind their behavior; playing a convincing character requires the ability to analyze personality. One key to analyzing stage characters is to treat them as if they were real people. Understanding character can also be of great help to nonactors; compassion can make our jobs and relationships more fulfilling. One way to start analyzing a character is to make a list of the character's traits by answering a series of questions about general, physical, sociological, and psychological traits (see Table 7.1).

This list of questions could go on for pages, but every single aspect of a character is too much for an actor, or a psychologist for that matter, to totally comprehend. A simpler method is to look at basic elements such as these: circumstances and objectives, public and personal sides, internal conflicts and character flaws, and motivation.

Circumstances and Objectives

When trying to analyze characters, or people for that matter, a good place to start is with the circumstances of their life: their situation, their problems, and the limits life has placed on them. Actors often call this approach to character analysis the **given circumstances**. It can include broad topics such as upbringing, religion, and social standing, but it can also include what happened to the character the moment before he or she entered the stage. For example, if the character has been fighting with a spouse, that particular given circumstance will certainly affect the character's emotional state and behaviors, such as tone of voice.

Next, it is important to understand the character's objective: what does he or she desire? Because characters may desire many things during the course of a play, a good actor often singles out the most important want, or the driving force that governs the character's actions throughout the entire play. This driving force is called the character's **superobjective**. For example, the character of Hamlet has many objectives during the course of Shakespeare's great tragedy—he wants to find his father's killer, he wants justice—but his superobjective, at least according to Stanislavsky, is to find God. Knowing the superobjective and given circumstances can take you a long way toward understanding a stage character, another person, or even yourself.

Public and Personal Images

There are two ways to view a character—or a person. One is from the public side, or what other people see. The second is from the personal side, or how we see ourselves. For example, from the outside, or the public image, a character might be described as:

- Irritating
- Perfectionist
- Hypercritical
- Anxious
- Work-centered
- Domineering
- Fault-finding

TABLE 7.1: Questions to help analyze a character

General Information	Sociological Traits
• What is the character's education? • What is the character's career or occupation? • What is the character's financial situation? • What are the character's talents? • What are the character's hobbies? • What are the character's tastes?	• What is the character's nationality? • What is the character's religion? • What is the character's class or status? • What are the character's family relationships? • What are the character's political views?
Physical Traits	**Psychological Traits**
• What is the character's age and sex? • What is the character's appearance? • What does the character wear? • What is the character's health status, including medical problems? • What are the character's mannerisms?	• What is the character's temperament? • What kind of childhood did the character have? • What are the character's hopes and ambitions? • What are the character's disappointments? • What are the character's fears and phobias? • What are the character's inhibitions? • What are the character's obsessions? • What are the character's superstitions? • What are the character's morals and philosophy of life?

Michal Daniel/Proofsheet

Fully understanding a character such as Richard III requires understanding his circumstances and objectives. What are his given circumstances? Born with a deformity that affects others' perceptions of him, he has learned to manipulate people to gain their sympathy; he is in line for the throne of England, but many are before him. What is his superobjective? He feels he deserves power—and the love that comes with it—as a reward for the bad hand that life has dealt him. This 2004 production of Shakespeare's Richard III *features Peter Dinklage. Directed by Peter DuBois, Public Theater, New York.*

You may recognize this description. It's the classic definition of an obsessive-compulsive. Here is another description:

- Fears disapproval
- Self-doubting
- Anticipates catastrophe
- Wants to be admired for ability
- Feels wounded when others don't value helpful hints
- Feels there is a right way and a wrong way
- Rarely feels support

Although this second set of characteristics sounds completely different, it is also a description of an obsessive-compulsive, but viewed from the inside, the personal image. To develop a strong, unique character, an actor must always look from both the public and personal images. How people or characters perceive themselves and how others perceive them is seldom harmonious and often results in conflict. This discrepancy between the personal and public views happens because stage characters, like people, have limited self-awareness. To make this point, playwright Arthur Miller used the story of *Oedipus*, the ancient Greek tragedy about a king who gouges out his eyes when he discovers he has unknowingly killed his father and married his mother (for more on *Oedipus*, see Part 3). If Oedipus had had more self-awareness, he would have seen that "he was not really to blame for having cohabited with his mother, since neither he nor anyone else knew she was his mother. He would have decided to divorce her, provide for their children, firmly resolve to investigate the family background of his next wife, and thus deprive us of a very fine play." Because Oedipus doesn't have clear, perfect knowledge of himself, discovery, growth, and a great tragedy are all possible. Limited self-awareness often causes some sort of flaw, vice, error in judgment, or internal conflict.

Inner Conflicts and Character Flaws

Another way to understand a character is to identify internal conflicts and character flaws. Powerful characters are often in conflict not only with others but also with themselves. This **inner conflict** can be a ghost from the past or some sort of unfinished business that is so compelling that it handicaps the character until it is confronted. In *Hamlet*, there is a literal ghost—the ghost of Hamlet's father. But Hamlet is also torn by the conflicts between his desire to seek revenge, his gentle nature, and his need to find an elusive God. A character's inner conflict can be an unresolved disagreement, a lost opportunity, a sense of inadequacy, or some other debilitating factor that preoccupies the character over the course of the play until he or she is able to put it to rest.

Plays are often about imperfect characters whose unfulfilled desires lead to inner conflict. In August Wilson's Fences *(1987), patriarch Troy Maxson feels he has been "fenced in" by discrimination. He once had a shot at playing major-league baseball, but now he toils at a dead-end job. He still dreams of being a ballplayer, but he is well past his prime. His broken dream colors every interaction with his family. In this photo from the original Broadway production, James Earl Jones plays Troy Maxson. Directed by Lloyd Richards, 46th Street Theatre, New York.*

If this inner conflict is powerful enough to affect the character's good judgment and cause the character to make unfortunate choices, then it's a **character flaw**, sometimes called a **fatal flaw** or **tragic flaw**. This personality imperfection cripples the character and prevents him from achieving his superobjective. Knowing a character's inner conflicts and flaws, as well as the given circumstances, superobjective, and public and personal images, will take you a long way toward understanding one of the most defining elements of character: motivation.

Motivation: Thinking in Positives

Motivation is the reason a character takes a particular action. It is embodied in the character's conscious or subconscious personality. It can come from some dark part of the character's past or simply be the desire to do the right thing. Wherever they come from, the motivations of characters are seldom complicated; the character may be complicated and the motivation may be hidden, but once it appears, it can usually be stated in a single sentence. For example, Juliet's motivation is that she is in love with Romeo and will do anything to be with him.

The key to understanding a character's motivation is to look at it from the character's point of view. A well-drawn character is always attempting to change negatives into positives—from his or her perspective. Characters, like people, may be misguided, even totally wrong, but they seldom see their motivations or the resulting actions as negative or evil. For example, if an actor studying the character of a father who abandons his child concludes that the father is "hateful" and "uncaring," he is not doing his homework. "Hateful" and "uncaring" are negative ideas coming from an external image and lead to a shallow interpretation of the father's motivations. Instead, the actor must find the positive motivation, the character's own reasons, for doing such a terrible thing as abandoning a child. After deeper analysis, the actor may discover that the father must think his actions are best for the child—perhaps he cannot provide for the child or he sees himself as too emotionally unbalanced to care for him or her. These would be reasons for thinking that abandoning the child would be best for the child; they are examples of positive motivations. A character can commit an evil act based on a strong "positive" motive. To truly understand a character, or another human being, you must find their positive motivations. Using your own morals or values to judge a character or a person seldom leads to true understanding.

> Actors are responsible to the people we play. I don't label or judge. I just play them as honestly and expressively and creatively as I can, in the hope that people who ordinarily turn their heads in disgust instead think, "What I thought I'd feel about that guy, I don't totally feel right now."
>
> ***Philip Seymour Hoffman,***
> Stage and screen actor

> I think very few people are interested in the craft of acting, which is actually to demask, to reveal what it is to be human.
>
> ***Cate Blanchett,***
> Stage and screen actor

These are just a few ways that actors analyze a character in order to gain a greater understanding. Good acting is far more than simple imitation. It is the ability to understand why characters think what they think, feel what they feel, and do what they do. Only when an actor can see life from someone else's point of view can he or she play a life on stage convincingly.

The Actor's Life

Like professional sports, acting is a business and, like athletes, actors need agents to help them find jobs, promote their careers, and negotiate contracts. There are also several labor unions that fight for actors' rights, including fair wages and safe working conditions. The union that represents stage actors is the **Actors' Equity Association**, often shortened to "Actors' Equity" or simply "Equity." The **Screen Actors Guild (SAG)** represents movie and television actors, and the **American Federation of Television and Radio Artists (AFTRA)**, which is affiliated with the AFL-CIO, represents talk-show hosts as well as announcers, singers, disc jockeys, newscasters, sportscasters, and even stunt people. Many actors join all three unions because they never know which medium their next job may come from.

The general public often assumes that actors are highly paid. This certainly can be true for big screen and television stars. For example, on the last season of his hit sitcom, comedian Jerry Seinfeld earned $2 million per episode, and Tom Hanks was reportedly paid more than $30 million to star in the movie *Saving Private Ryan*. But these fat paychecks are the exception; the vast majority of actors take home very little money for their efforts. In fact, according to the U.S. Department of Labor, the median annual income of actors in the United States is $23,470, whereas the average member of the Screen Actors Guild takes home less than $5,000 a year. There is so little money to be made at acting that a majority of actors do something in addition to acting to make ends meet—they are servers, administrative assistants, and delivery people. They take jobs that allow for a flexible schedule so they can attend acting classes and go to auditions. Their intermittent employment and lack of job security can make mortgages, insurance, and credit cards difficult to obtain. At least stage actors have one big advantage: unlike movie actors, they are indispensable to the art. (See the Spotlight "Synthespians versus a 'Poor Theatre.'")

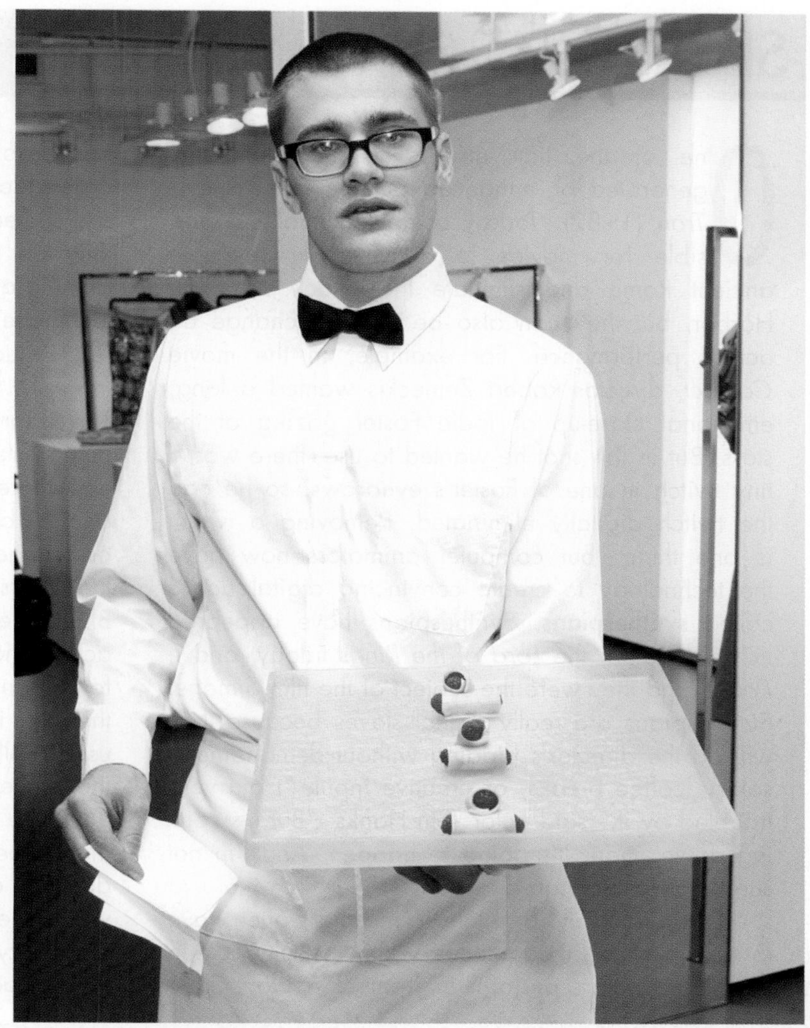

Getty Images

Few actors make a living at their art. In fact, 95 percent of actors must supplement their income by taking second jobs. Waiting tables is popular because the hours are often flexible, enabling actors to attend auditions and rehearsals.

Once actors land a job, seldom does it last more than a few weeks or months, after which they are back on the street auditioning for a new job. Competition at these auditions is fierce. There can be dozens if not hundreds of actors battling for the same part. Acting jobs are so scarce that Actors' Equity has created the **Equity waiver**, a loophole that allows its members to work for free in small productions. There are so few paying jobs that many actors act for free in order to sharpen their skills and in the hope of being discovered. Equity-waiver productions have to meet many qualifications. For example, the theatre must be fully insured, the play cannot have a long run, and the theatre must have fewer than one hundred seats. As a result, many Equity-waiver theatres have ninety-nine seats.

SPOTLIGHT ON Synthespians versus a "Poor Theatre"

One of the first movies to use computer-generated or enhanced actors was Disney's *Tron* (1982). Today, computers make it possible for movies to convincingly re-create ancient Rome and simulate the attack on Pearl Harbor, but they can also be used to change an actor's performance. For example, in the movie *Contact,* director Robert Zemeckis wanted a long, emotional close-up of Jodie Foster gazing at the stars. But in the shot he wanted to use, there was a tiny twitch in one of Foster's eyebrows, so he had the twitch digitally eliminated. Removing a twitch is one thing, but computer animators now have the technology to create convincing digital actors called **synthespians**. Synthespians have appeared in *Spider-Man,* the *Lord of the Rings* trilogy, and *I, Robot,* and they were the subject of the film *Simone*. Synthespians are really digital slaves because they will do the director's bidding without demanding a salary, coffee breaks, or creative input. "I am very troubled by it," said actor Tom Hanks. "But it's coming down, man. It's going to happen. And I'm not sure what actors can do about it."

In addition, film and television actors often have to act in synthesized scenes. With the blue-screen technique, actors perform in front of a blank blue backdrop, and digital backgrounds and characters are added in post-production. The resulting shots are so seamless that actors seem to be standing on the flight deck of an anthropomorphic spaceship or running away from fast-approaching dinosaurs. This technique has been used in any number of movies, including *Jurassic Park* (1993), *Men in Black* (1997), *Avatar* (2009), and *Inception* (2010). The actors are shot against a blue screen because human skin has very little blue in it, so a computer can more easily determine where the actor ends and the background should begin. Sometimes green or orange screens are used instead, depending on the colors of an actor's skin, makeup, and costume. Blue-screen acting requires actors to react to characters and things they cannot see and to work with few, if any, props. Often the actors don't know until the film is released if the acting techniques they used really worked. Blue-screen acting is so difficult that some film schools offer classes on the subject.

There are no synthespians or blue screens in the theatre because theatre is always live. Some theatre directors and acting teachers have gone out of their way to emphasize this. One of the most famous was Jerzy Grotowski (1933–1999), a Stanislavsky-trained actor and director who worked in Poland,

Pursuing the Part: Perpetual Auditions

There are as many types of auditions as there are plays, theatres, and directors. A common type of audition is the **cattle call**, also known as the "open call." Call is theatre lingo for "audition." During a cattle call, actors are generally given only about one minute to strut their stuff. If the director is impressed, the actor's name is placed on a **callback list** and allowed to come back for a second and perhaps a third and fourth audition as each callback narrows the field of candidates. Other auditions consist of **cold readings** of a script; in other words, the actors are not given a chance to prepare. For other auditions, actors can bring prepared scenes or monologues, or they might be asked to improvise, dance, or sing. The director can take the actors through a myriad of tests to look for vocal clarity, energy, stage presence, talent, and personal chemistry. Auditions are so important that some actors take more classes on how to audition than on how to act.

the United States, and Italy. In his book *Towards a Poor Theatre* (1968), he declared that theatre should not try to compete against the visual spectacle of film. Instead, theatre should concentrate on what makes it unique—the fact that it is live. So Grotowski stripped theatre down to its essence and created bare-bones plays that had no set, few props, no makeup, no special lights, not even a stage. He called this a "poor theatre" because it had none of what he called the superfluous elements. He felt that to act without a set, costumes, makeup, or computers that eliminate twitches—what he called "clutter" and "gimmicks"—actors require years of training. He wanted the actors' performances to be so real that they would make the audience uncomfortable. And so Grotowskian actors train for years so that their body and voice are all that is needed to make great theatre.

Warner Bros./Photofest

Tom Hanks and his synthespian counterpart in The Polar Express *(2004).*

Perfecting the Part: Rehearsals

Once the actors are cast in a play, they begin rehearsals. Normally rehearsals last from three to five weeks, but there are exceptions. Rehearsals for complex or experimental plays can last much longer—Stanislavsky once rehearsed a play for nearly a year—whereas rehearsals for a simple summer-stock play might be crammed into one week. However long the rehearsal process is, actors seldom rehearse on the stage until just a few days before a play opens. Most rehearsals take place in a rehearsal hall, which is an empty room approximately the same size as the stage. In the rehearsal hall, actors must use their creative imaginations because there is no finished set. They have to use simple rehearsal furniture and props. A plain folding chair can represent a grand throne, or a simple piece of wood may stand in for a king's jeweled staff. Costumes aren't generally ready until just a few days before the play opens.

Auditioning for a play can be stressful. An actor might be asked to cold read from the script, present prepared monologues, or sing and dance. The process can take days, and more often than not ends in failure for the actor. But for those lucky few who make it, a life in the theatre can be very rewarding.

Emmanuel Faure/Stone/Getty Images

Here is an approximately chronological list of the kinds of rehearsals:

- **Table work:** Some directors start rehearsals by having the cast read aloud through the play while seated around a table. After the reading, the director and actors discuss their thoughts about the characters and motivations and about the play in general. Sometimes the director invites the designers to the first table reading to make presentations about what the set, lights, and costumes will look like.
- **Blocking rehearsals:** This is a series of rehearsals during which the director and actors work out the basic movements, a process that is called "blocking."
- **General working rehearsals:** During these rehearsals the director and actors work on individual scenes and concentrate on understanding the characters' motivations, emotions, and personalities.
- **Special rehearsals:** If a play has fight scenes, musical numbers, or dance numbers, or if the characters have dialects, the director can call special rehearsals for each.

- **Off-book rehearsal:** During this rehearsal, the actors must have their lines memorized. It's called "off book" because the actors no longer have the script, or the "book," on stage with them.
- **Run-throughs:** During these rehearsals, the actors go through the entire play from beginning to end with as few interruptions as possible. A run-through gives the actors a feel for how the play works as a whole.
- **Tech rehearsals:** By this point, rehearsals have moved from the rehearsal hall to the stage. During tech (short for *technical*) rehearsals, the lights, sounds, props, and set are added.
- **Dress rehearsals:** These are the final rehearsals, only a few days before the play opens, when the costumes and makeup are added.
- **Final dress rehearsal:** This is the last rehearsal before an audience is invited. Ideally, the play is run as if it were a real performance.

Playing the Part: Performances

After the opening night, the actors settle in for the run of the play. A short run can be just a few performances, as is often the case with smaller theatres and university and community theatres; a long run can last for months or even years, as is the case in big Broadway theatres. In the professional theatre, plays are traditionally performed six nights a week. Actors may also have one or two matinee performances a week; on those days, they face the exhausting task of performing the play twice in one day. Mondays are typically **dark nights**, when the theatre is closed.

Plays run anywhere from just a few performances to years. For example, Cathy Rigby has now played Peter Pan more than 2,800 times. That is the equivalent of doing seven shows a week for seven and a half years without a day off. Keeping a play fresh for such long runs can be a real challenge, but Rigby points out that a long run has its advantages. "You get to a point when you can be alive in the moment, no white-knuckling it." Yet actors often get tired of doing the same show night after night and eventually leave the cast to explore new acting challenges.

Curtain Call

Perhaps the ability to act is in our genes. Children seem to pick the talent up quite early and practice it often. As adults, where would teachers, doctors, lawyers, salespeople, clerics, administrative assistants, servers, or, indeed, politicians be if they could not act? American playwright Arthur Miller said in *American Playhouse: On Politics and the Art of Acting*, "The fact is that acting is inevitable as soon as we walk out our front doors and into society."

But what happens when acting takes over every aspect of our lives? Some believe that with the invention of television we are so inundated with constant acting that we know few sincere moments. Miller points out that one of the oddest things about the lives of contemporary individuals is that today,

William Missouri Downs

Brian Seed

At left: *Moments before curtain, director Wolf Sherrill sits in the greenroom with nervous actors Mariah Everman, Andrew Franks-Ongoy, Keith Hull, and Brandon Taylor. Behind them, a stage manager goes over the final cues in the script. Most greenrooms are located just off the stage and are plainly furnished, but are rarely painted green.* At right: *Joan Allen (front) and fellow actors review a script during a table reading.*

as never before in human history, we are surrounded by acting. He said that "when one is surrounded by such a roiling mass of consciously contrived performances it gets harder and harder to locate reality. . . ." At its most innocent, acting is found in a child's game of make-believe; at its most important it's an instrument of survival; at its most sinister it is all the lies we tell each other and ourselves.

Summary

It may look easy, but becoming an actor takes dedication and years of training. That training usually begins at a conservatory, a university, or a college, but most actors go on to train for years after that in order to perfect their voice, body, and mind, or what they call their "instrument." The need for actor training has led to many acting schools and teachers who teach various acting systems. Most of these systems trace their heritage to the father of modern acting, Konstantin Stanislavsky, the founder of the Moscow Art Theatre and the Stanislavsky system, or what is often called method acting. Stanislavsky taught his actors to recall their emotions and then transfer those feelings to their characters in order to find a detailed emotional identification with them.

Actors use many techniques that can be useful to nonactors. These include outside/in acting, or changing physically in order to change emotions, and inside/out acting, or changing emotions in order to change physically. Outside/in acting is often referred to as the technical approach. Inside/out acting is often referred to as method acting. Other techniques actors use are empathy, the magic *if*, and substitution. In order to understand the characters they play, actors study the character's physical, sociological, and psychological traits. They also examine the character's public and personal images and the character's inner conflicts, flaws, and motivation.

An actor's life can be full of auditions, rehearsals, and performances. But it is also full of unemployment because paying acting jobs are scarce. The vast majority of actors work second jobs to make ends meet. Even when they find a job, they aren't always well paid. In order to protect their interests, performers have formed three unions to help win fair wages and safe working conditions: Actors' Equity, the Screen Actors Guild, and the American Federation of Television and Radio Artists.

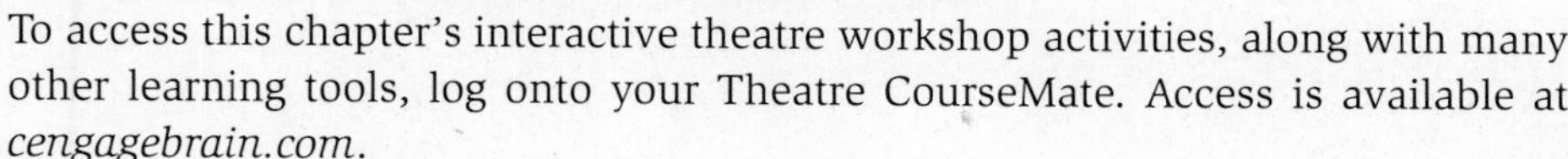

The Art of Theatre ONLINE

To access this chapter's interactive theatre workshop activities, along with many other learning tools, log onto your Theatre CourseMate. Access is available at *cengagebrain.com*.

Key Terms

Actors' Equity Association / 163
American Federation of Television and Radio Artists (AFTRA) / 163
blocking rehearsal / 166
callback list / 164
cattle call / 164
character flaw / 162
cold reading / 164
dark night / 167
dress rehearsal / 167
emotional memory / 154
empathy / 155
Equity waiver / 163
fatal flaw / 162
final dress rehearsal / 167
general working rehearsal / 166
given circumstances / 158
inner conflict / 161
International Phonetic Alphabet (IPA) / 150
magic *if* / 155
method acting / 151
motivation / 162
off-book rehearsal / 167
run-through / 167
Screen Actors Guild (SAG) / 163
special rehearsal / 166
Stanislavsky system / 151
substitution / 156
superobjective / 158
synthespian / 164
table work / 166
technical approach / 154
tech rehearsal / 167
tragic flaw / 162

Twelve Angry Men, by Reginald Rose. Directed by Scott Ellis, American Airlines Theatre, New York, 2004–5. This play, about a jury struggling to decide a capital murder case, provides a director with interesting opportunities for placing actors on a stage for maximum effect.

Photos on this spread Sara Krulwich/The New York Times/Redux Pictures

CHAPTER 8

The Art of Directing

OUTLINE

American playwright Tennessee Williams said that a play script is only the "shadow of a play and not even a clear shadow of it. . . . The printed script is hardly more than an architect's blueprint of a house not yet built." The **director** turns the printed script, the blueprint, into a production. To do this, the director must have the artistic vision and the talent to coordinate dozens of theatre artists, technicians, and other personnel to work toward that vision with a singleness of purpose. This coordination allows a production to speak with the unique voice of an individual artist. The director also represents the audience members, because the director

frames each moment of the play by deciding exactly what the audience will see. In order to turn these decisions into reality, the director must guide and persuade every member of the theatre ensemble and oversee all the artistic and technical aspects of the production. The director must synthesize the work of the playwright, the designers, and the performers into a unique theatrical event.

Although many major universities offer a Master of Fine Arts in directing, most directors start their theatre career as an actor, designer, playwright, choreographer, or critic. For example, one of America's most renowned directors, Elia Kazan, who directed the first production of Arthur Miller's *Death of a Salesman* as well as such great films as *On the Waterfront*, was an actor long before he started directing. Similarly, Robert Brustein, founder of both the Yale Repertory and American Repertory Theatres, started as a drama critic; Harold Prince, director of such Broadway productions as *The Kiss of the Spider Woman* and

SPOTLIGHT ON The Life of a Director: Tisa Chang

Born in China, Tisa Chang grew up in New York City, where as a child she learned to play piano and perform traditional Chinese dances and ballet. She attended the High School of Performing Arts and Barnard College at Columbia University. Soon she was dancing and acting in successful Broadway plays, including *Pacific Overtures, The Basic Training of Pavlo Hummel,* and *Lovely Ladies.* Then she started working at the Chinese Theater Group at La MaMa, an experimental theatre group in the East Village neighborhood of Manhattan, where she staged a bilingual adaptation of Shakespeare's *A Midsummer Night's Dream* set in China in 1000 BCE.

Corky Lee/Courtesy of the Pan Asian Repertory Theatre

Director Tisa Chang

In 1977 she founded the Pan Asian Repertory Theatre in New York City. The goals of the Pan Asian Rep are to celebrate professional Asian American artists and to present "Asian American masterpieces, adaptations of American classics, and . . . new work by Asian American writers, which reflect[s] the evolution of Asians in America." The Pan Asian Rep fast became one of the most influential Asian American theatres. Other Asian theatres in the United States include the East West Players in Los Angeles and The National Asian American Theater Company in New York.

Chang has directed intercultural productions such as *Return of the Phoenix*, which was adapted from the Peking Opera, as well as a Shogun *Macbeth*, Cambodian and Tibetan plays, and what Chang calls "the canon of Asian-American classics." "Beyond language and playwriting as the source . . . our theatrical production relies a great deal on the articulation. . . . We're talking about incorporating direction and design [that can] absolutely alter a script," says Chang. "I think that I would probably never direct a two-person play where people are sitting on chairs and talk to each

The Phantom of the Opera, was a producer; and Susan Stroman, director of the Broadway smash *The Producers*, began as a choreographer. Directors come from these many backgrounds because directing takes many talents. Directors must know how to inspire and coach actors, they must know how to communicate complex aesthetic ideas to designers, and they must understand the playwriting process. Directors also know how to create a cohesive, pleasant working environment. Moreover, an effective director has the ability not only to lead but also to inspire everyone involved with the play to be creative, to make decisions, and to add their talents to the production. The director must have the sensitivity of an artist, the fortitude of a good teacher, and the skills of an efficiency expert. (For more on the life of a director, see the Spotlight "The Life of a Director: Tisa Chang.") And yet, as important as directors are to the process today, they are relatively new to the history of the theatre.

It's our job to create an atmosphere of creativity that will stimulate the best work from the actor, to be a mirror, tell them what they are doing and what we see. Both for the playwright and for the actor, the director is the surrogate audience until the actual audience arrives.

Marshall Mason,
Director

other and expound. . . . I really love the magic and the latitude that we can have with direction and design and music and poetry."

About her directing style Chang says, "I don't like directors who over-impose or superimpose things onto a play. I just think all we [as directors] are doing is making the play clear and engaging." One of Chang's latest projects was to direct Elizabeth Wong's *China Doll*, a play that tells the life story of Anna May Wong (1905–1961), a Chinese American actress who starred in such early Hollywood movies as *The Thief of Bagdad* with Douglas Fairbanks, Sr., and *Shanghai Express* with Marlene Dietrich. Wong acted in Hollywood at a time when the vast majority of Asian roles were played by white stars in "yellowface." She spent her life trying to achieve stardom as she fought against Hollywood stereotypes. Chang, whose own work is often geared toward challenging stereotypes, has said, "I think the best theatre has a cohesive concept and a solid ensemble, and speaks to people on many different levels. And hopefully, the audience members leave the theatre thinking about what they saw."

Corky Lee/Courtesy of the Pan Asian Repertory Theatre

Scene from Elizabeth Wong's China Doll*, about Hollywood's first Asian American movie star, Anna May Wong. With Rosanne Ma as Anna May Wong, directed by Tisa Chang, Pan Asian Repertory Theatre, 2005.*

The Birth of Directors

For thousands of years, the role of director was not filled by a single person. The director's functions were simply tacked on to the duties of playwrights and actors. In ancient Greece, around 400 BCE, playwrights staged the plays they wrote. The term for these playwright-directors was ***didaskalos***, or "teacher," because they not only wrote the play but also instructed the performers and advised the designers and technicians. Two thousand years later, in Shakespeare's day, directing was quite simple, at least compared with today. Elizabethan plays were staged outdoors in the midday sun, so there was no need for a lighting designer. The actors wore costumes appropriate to their character's station and profession, but no one took into account the overall look or historical accuracy, so there was little need for a costume designer. And the stage set was virtually the same for every play, so there was no need for a set designer. Consequently, there was little need for a director to coordinate the designs. Playwright Ben Jonson, Shakespeare's contemporary, complained that directing a play was an exhausting job for which one did little more than prompt actors and yell at musicians. The job was so trivial that programs of the day have no mention of the position. When the first indoor theatres were built, they were lit with candles. The lighting was so inadequate that the actors would just try to find the brightest spot to stand in when the time came to speak their lines. Most of the directing at that time was done by an actor-manager, often the play's star, who told the other actors where to stand so that he could be seen in the best light.

The modern concept of a director did not come about until the nineteenth century, when a new genre of theatre called *realism* became popular. Realism called for psychologically complex characters, honest acting, and natural-looking sets. Realism also played off the worldwide scientific, social, and philosophical movements of the day. At the end of the century came the invention of electric lights, which made sophisticated lighting effects possible. Theatre was becoming a complex illusion, so there was a need for one person, a master coordinator, to oversee the various elements of production.

Georg II, the Duke of Saxe-Meiningen (1826–1914), the ruler of a small German state, is often credited as the first modern director. Being a wealthy monarch gave him the freedom and the resources to construct his own theatre and to organize and direct a resident company of actors and other artists. He was in a total leadership position, for he was the actors' literal ruler as well as their director—a power, no doubt, some modern directors wish they had. Duke Georg organized his actors, his subjects, into an ensemble in which there were no stars. He insisted on long rehearsal periods and ordered his actors to explore every psychological aspect of their characters. He also made many advances in staging. His crowd scenes were famous for looking like paintings, and his costumes, scenery, and props were fully integrated and authentic. Once he even used a real stuffed horse on stage in order to make a battle scene waged among fallen horses seem more real. One critic said that his production of Shakespeare's *Julius Caesar* was so real and so well directed that "one could believe that one was actually present at the beginning of the revolution."

From 1874 to 1890, the duke and his acting company toured Europe and gave more than 2,600 performances of forty-one plays. In the audience for one of these productions was Russian acting teacher Konstantin Stanislavsky (see Chapter 7). So impressed was Stanislavsky by the duke's staging that he used many of his directing techniques at the new **Moscow Art Theatre**. When Stanislavsky directed, he, like the duke, was concerned with every detail of the production, from the accuracy of props to the timing of special effects such as birdcalls and cricket chirps. He made copious notes about the characters, as well as detailed diagrams of the actors' movements. He also insisted on a rehearsal process that lasted for months rather than days or weeks, which was the norm for most theatre in that day. Like the duke, he spent a long time in rehearsals for even the smallest bit parts. (The Moscow Art Theatre is the source of the saying "There are no small parts, only small actors," meaning that every role is worthy of study and rehearsal.) Stanislavsky also felt that the director should lead the actors through a process of discovery rather than command them or treat them as his puppets.

AP Photo/Jerome Delay

The director is in charge of everything the audience sees. Here director Julie Taymor directs an actor during a rehearsal of the Lion King *at Pretoria's National Theater in Pretoria, South Africa. Ms. Taymor is the first woman to win the Tony Award for directing a musical.*

However, for Stanislavsky the new job of director was constantly evolving. After a lifetime of directing he wrote, "I used to think that the director was like a chef, whose job it was to mix the correct ingredients in the correct proportions; then I thought that the director was rather more like a midwife; and now I am not quite sure at all what a director is." Even though the specifics of their job were constantly changing, these early directors created the modern idea of the director as the person who interprets, organizes, and coordinates all the elements of a play into a meaningful, integrated whole.

Today, directors are an indispensable part of the theatre ensemble. They receive top credit in the program—only the playwright is listed higher. In Hollywood, movie directors have become so important that theirs is always the final name in the credits before the movie begins.

Before Rehearsals Begin

The director's job can be split in two phases: pre-rehearsal and rehearsal. Pre-rehearsal might be called the "paper phase" of the job because everything is on paper: designs drawn on paper, scripts written on paper, research in books, and notations in notebooks. During the paper phase, the director must discover what the play means and how the theatre ensemble might convey that meaning to the audience. The paper phase often lasts longer than the rehearsal phase. The paper phase includes script analysis, structural analysis, concept meetings, production meetings, and casting.

It All Starts with a Script: Script Analysis

The director's pre-rehearsal preparation begins with script analysis. Although studying a play can be as simple as using Goethe's play-analysis formula (see

Chapter 4), in order to direct a play, every character and every word of the script must be scrutinized. The director's analysis might include working with the playwright (if the playwright is alive and available) as well as spending countless hours rereading the script, combing newspaper archives, and researching the history and criticism of the play. The director's intensive analysis includes finding the script's strengths and weaknesses. For example, if a particular character is underdeveloped, the director may note that a particularly strong actor is needed to flesh out that part. The director must understand each character's motivations, desires, and given circumstances (see Chapter 7) as well as the play's mood and atmosphere and the moral and philosophical statements made by the playwright.

However, a director's analysis does not end with the script. In order to have a comprehensive understanding, a director must research previous productions—for it is a good idea to know how other directors have staged the play—and what the critics said about them. The director may also study the playwright's life. Often playwrights write about personal events and emotions, so knowing about the playwright can lead to a greater understanding of the play. The play's location, period, and historical background must also be carefully investigated, including the political trends and the social and moral codes that were in effect when the play was written.

Not doing this research can lead directors to mistaken interpretations of the characters. For example, a director who has not done the historical research might assume that Hedda in Henrik Ibsen's *Hedda Gabler* (1890) is a bit of a spinster. After all, she is in her mid- to late twenties and only recently married. But research would reveal that twenty-five was the average age of marriage for women in 1890 Norway. Without the research, the director might read into the character something the playwright never intended. This little bit of investigation could change the director's concept of Hedda, which in turn would affect the director's casting and staging decisions.

Script analysis is a crucial aspect of the director's job. Understanding the playwright's thoughts, philosophy, and opinions about a play is invaluable. Here, Robert Falls (right), artistic director of the Goodman Theatre in Chicago, is fortunate enough to be able to discuss a 2004 production of Arthur Miller's Finishing the Picture *with the playwright himself.*

Michael Brosilow/The Goodman Theatre

All this script analysis and research can be very time-consuming. For example, when Konstantin Stanislavsky directed Anton Chekhov's *The Seagull*, he spent a month and a half alone in a tower in the Ukraine studying. For help with the research process, some directors work with a *dramaturg*, a literary advisor and theatre-history expert. Dramaturgs can assist a director or theatre company in many ways. They can aid with the selection of plays, work with the playwright to help fully realize the script, and research the historical or literary background of a play in order to help directors, designers, and actors better understand the text. Armed with a strong background in theatre history, literature, and criticism, the dramaturg can serve as an information resource or as an integral part of the director's decision making. The dramaturg can make sure that the director's concepts and style stay within the standards of the theatre or are consistent with the ideas a theatre company wishes to express in a particular season of plays. Although common in other parts of the world, dramaturgs are still rather rare in U.S. theatre. Some directors feel that dramaturgs are an important part of the process, but others feel that what dramaturgs do is really part of the director's job. (For more on dramaturgy, see Chapter 5.)

Studying Even the Smallest Elements: Structural Analysis

While accumulating social, historical, and critical knowledge of the play, the director also studies the script's structure. This analysis often includes all the elements covered in Chapter 6, such as theme, characters, language, and plot, but it can also lead to the study of the smallest structural units within a play: french scenes and beats.

A **french scene** begins whenever a character enters or exits and continues until the next entrance or exit. For example, let's say a father and daughter are arguing and then Mom enters. Mom's entrance marks the beginning of a new french scene. If the father or mother or daughter exits, a new french scene begins. The length of each french scene varies, as does the number of french scenes within a play, act, or scene. A fast-paced farce may have dozens, but a play with no entrances or exits has only one. The idea of french scenes originated in, of course, France, when the printing press was still a novelty and quite expensive. To cut costs, actors were given only the pages on which they had lines rather than the full script. The most cost-efficient way of dividing a play was from one entrance or exit to the next entrance or exit. Although this did little to help the actors with character analysis and continuity, it did save a few precious pages. If you ever read a French neoclassical tragedy such as *Phaedra*, you'll notice that the script is split into french scenes. However, this antiquated method of dividing a play would have been long forgotten had it not been such a help in playwriting and directing. Because a french scene deals with only certain characters at a particular point in the play, it divides a play into small, workable units. The director treats each french scene as a mini-play that has the structural elements of a full play: beginning, middle, and end. With each entrance or exit, the play changes, the characters' attitudes shift, and the story moves forward.

A **beat** is the next smaller structural unit; it is a single unit of thought. It's a section of dialogue about a particular subject or idea. A change in subject or idea means the beginning of a new beat. A beat can be anywhere from a single word to several pages long. Beats are similar to paragraphs in other kinds of writing, but they are not signaled by indentations or any other typographical device. As an illustration, the following scene is divided into beats—but remember, beats

Beats and French scenes combine to form scenes and acts. For example, in the Tony Award winning play Equus*, a psychiatrist attempts to treat a young man who has a pathological fixation on horses. This play has hundreds of beats, dozens of French scenes but only 35 scenes and 2 acts. The photo is from a production staged by the National Theatre Conservatory.*

are never indicated in a real script. This scene, which has four beats, is about a woman who has returned home to take her elderly father to the hospital for what she thinks is a hernia operation.

BEAT ONE

DARLA: We gotta go. Where is she?

HENRY: Moonpie? She's out.

DARLA: Wish you wouldn't do that. Cats that wander don't live as long. How long she been missin'?

HENRY: She's not missin'. She killed a warbler two hours ago. Feathers everywhere.

DARLA: *(yelling out the window)*: Moonpie! Moonpiiiie!

HENRY: Absolute carnage. Apocalypse in the backyard. So she can't be far.

DARLA: M. P.! M. Peeee!

HENRY: If the cat don't know its name, what the hell makes you think it'd know its initials?

BEAT TWO

DARLA: You're feelin' better.

HENRY: Me? I feel terrible.

DARLA: Where the blazes is a double hernia anyway?

HENRY: I'd show you, but I'd be arrested.

DARLA: Are you sure it's a hernia?

HENRY: What do I know; pain is pain.

BEAT THREE

HENRY: I cancelled the papers and I'm havin' my mail forwarded to you.

DARLA: Why can't Mom pick up your mail?

HENRY: Your mother'll just lose it. Besides I think she sneaks over here and opens my mail. Tries to find out if I got a lover. I can't prove anything, but my Sears bill is missin'.

DARLA: I can only stay two days. I think it'd be better if she picked up your mail. She could read it to you in the hospital.

BEAT FOUR

HENRY: She can't read my mail.

DARLA: Why not?

HENRY: She had her cataract surgery.

DARLA: What? When? *(dialing the phone)* Why didn't you tell me?!
HENRY: I told her not to dilly dally. Told her, one eye at a time. Did she listen? Course not.
DARLA: She never lets it ring more than twice.
HENRY: Waited too long, so she had to get both eyes done at once. Got some nurse with her twenty-four hours a day.
DARLA: Did you send flowers?
HENRY: Why should I? She can't see 'em.
DARLA: Daddy, you should've told me.
HENRY: She's fine. Blind but fine. Got two huge silver patches on her face. Makes her look like some kinda massive gnat.

The word *beat* is misleading. It usually refers to a rhythmical unit. So why do theatre people use the word *beat* instead of *unit* or *section*? The explanation dates from the time when the disciples of Stanislavsky came to the United States to teach. Americans were supposedly confused by the Russians' thick accents, so they mistook the word *bit* for *beat*. If you say, "First you must split the play into little bits" with a Russian accent, you'll find some truth to this theory. Whether it's true or not, looking at "beats" as "bits" makes sense. A director, as well as actors and playwrights, divides dialogue into bits/beats to understand moment-by-moment changes in the characters' actions, conflicts, and motivations. This process is seldom as obvious as shown in Table 8.1, because directors often go through this process subconsciously, but the table illustrates how each beat reveals the moment's action, conflict, and motivation. Try it yourself—take a scene or a french scene from your favorite play and break it into beats. In doing so, you will find a deeper understanding of how the play was constructed and learn how the scene works moment by moment, just as a director does.

Meetings and More Meetings: Realizing the Production Concept

After spending weeks and even months researching and analyzing a script, the director gains a deep understanding of all the elements of the play. The next step is to devise a **production concept**. This is the metaphor, thematic idea, symbol, or allegory that will be central to the whole production. A director without a production concept is like a driver without a road map. However, for all the work that goes into it, the production concept is usually quite simple. For example, a director working on Ibsen's *A Doll's House,* a play about a woman who breaks free of her domineering husband, could envision the lead character, Nora, as a woman trapped in a beautiful birdcage. During the course of the play, Nora could come to see this birdcage as a terrible dungeon. With this concept, the director would be making a statement about how we allow ourselves to be trapped by our lives, seldom questioning our premises, rarely realizing that we are entangled by our own limited point of view. Once the director has a concept, it must be communicated to the designers through a series of production meetings. During these meetings the designers and director also discuss the play's philosophy, interpretation, theme, physical demands, history, and style. Between meetings, the designers attempt to realize the director's production

TABLE 8.1: Action, conflict, and motivation beat by beat

Beat	Action	Conflict	Motivation
1	Darla must find the cat before she locks up the house and takes her father to the hospital.	Her elderly father doesn't seem to care about the cat or the hospital.	Darla's parents are divorced, so she feels she must take care of them, including little details like the cat.
2	Darla asks her father about why he's going into the hospital.	He doesn't want to tell her the truth about his medical condition. He's dying.	Henry feels that a real man doesn't complain. Darla feels that real men are too secretive.
3	Darla and Henry disagree about who will pick up his mail.	Darla wants her parents to get back together and will do anything to make them have contact. Henry doesn't want to talk about his medical condition, so he changes the subject.	Darla feels that her parents are lonely and need each other. Besides, she wants some time for herself. Henry knows he has cancer and doesn't want anyone to know.
4	Darla learns that her mother is also in the hospital.	Darla must find out about her mother. She feels guilty because she hasn't called her in a few days. Henry is thrilled that the attention is off him.	Darla loves her mother, perhaps more than she loves her father. Henry wants Darla to know that there is no chance of his getting back together with her mother.

concept by drawing sketches of possible sets, costumes, and other designs. There can be dozens of production meetings held over a period of weeks, even months, before final designs are agreed upon. Only after the homework and production meetings are done is the director ready to cast the play and begin rehearsals. (For more on production concepts and meetings, see Chapter 9.)

Don't Call Us, We'll Call You: Casting the Right Actors

Casting the right actors is critical for the success of a play. A common theatre adage is that 90 percent of directing is casting. In fact casting is so important that some directors hire **casting directors**, who specialize in finding the right actor to fit the part—a practice that is common with Hollywood movies.

Actors are usually hired because they are stars and can draw an audience or because they have the talent to play the role, or a combination of the two. There is no fairness-in-casting law. Directors have the right to cast whomever they feel is the best person for the job; they don't have to give everyone a fair chance.

Directors can **cast to type**, or hire an actor who physically matches the role. In other words, if they are looking for a seventy-year-old Italian mother, they cast someone who looks just like, or is, a seventy-year-old Italian mother. Casting to type can also mean finding an actor who has a deep understanding of the character's emotions and motivations. Directors can also **cast against type**, or deliberately cast actors who are the exact opposite of, or very different from, what is expected. For example, the director might choose to cast an older-than-usual pair as the lovers in *Romeo and Juliet*, thereby making a statement about how love is right for all people, not just the young and beautiful. Directors also sometimes use **gender-neutral casting**, or casting without regard for the character's gender, and **cross-gender casting**, or intentionally casting men to play women's roles and women to play men's in order to study societal perceptions of gender identity. One of the most controversial forms of casting is **color-blind casting**, or choosing actors without regard for their race or ethnic background. (For more on color-blind casting, see the Spotlight "Color-Blind Casting.")

> What does the director do? He bears to the preparation of a play much the same relation as an orchestra conductor to the rehearsal of a symphony. But the symphony is performed by the conductor with each member of the orchestra playing under his leadership. He does not play the leading part. He does more. He interprets, shapes, guides, inspires the entire performance.
>
> ***Tyrone Guthrie,***
> Director

The Director's Role during Rehearsals

Once the paper phase is over, the director is ready to begin rehearsals. In a large production with a big cast, the director may have an **assistant director** to lend a hand. The first few days of rehearsal are critical because this is when the director must unite all the actors into an ensemble with a common goal. No two actors are alike; they have different methods and personalities. Some actors need reassurance, while others need a firm foundation. Some actors approach their roles through intellectual analysis, while others thrive on nothing but inspiration. Early in the rehearsal process the director must present a game plan and clear goal to all the actors. Initial rehearsals may be taken up with reading and analyzing the script, as well as improvisation. Then the director, with the help of the actors, begins blocking. **Blocking** is the movement of the actors on stage. At its most basic, blocking is simply making sure the actors don't bump into each other or the furniture, but it quickly becomes a complex set of movements that express the characters' emotions, thoughts, and relationships. Blocking is also how the director achieves focus and "picturization."

> When I create something, I usually have it completely created in pre-production. But then I go in and I feed off of the actors also, because that ultimately gives me the best result.
>
> ***Susan Stroman,***
> Director and choreographer

Directing the Audience's Eyes

Achieving **focus** in a movie is easy. Directors can simply point the camera at whatever they want the audience to look at. Close-ups and lingering camera angles can emphasize a tiny drop of incriminating blood on a killer's hand or a character's fleeting glance of guilt. On stage, focus is much more difficult because the audience is free to look wherever they like. The stage director must gain the audience's attention and direct their gaze to a particular spot or actor. This can be accomplished through lighting, costumes, scenery, voice, and movements. Focus can be gained by simply putting a spotlight on one actor, by having one actor in red and everyone else in gray, or by having one actor move while the others remain still. All these techniques will quickly draw the audience's attention to the actor whom the director wants to be in focus. There are also more subtle ways to lead the audience's eyes and pull focus. A few of these are body position, stage area, level, contrast, and triangulation.

SPOTLIGHT ON Color-Blind Casting

The opposite of ethnic-specific casting, color-blind casting ignores race and awards roles solely on the talent of the actor. This can lead to unexpected and illogical combinations of characters that the playwright never intended. Color-blind casting is often necessary at colleges and universities if few plays match the ethnic makeup of the theatre-major population. But it is also used in the professional theatre and in movies. For example, Denzel Washington was cast as Don Pedro in Kenneth Branagh's film version of Shakespeare's *Much Ado about Nothing*. He is black, but his brother in the play, played by Keanu Reeves, is white.

At a recent symposium sponsored by the Non-Traditional Casting Project, actors of a multitude of races presented roles traditionally played by white actors. For example, Hispanic actors performed a scene from Molière's *Imaginary Invalid*, a seventeenth-century French comedy. A black woman played Hedda in scenes from Ibsen's *Hedda Gabler*, a nineteenth-century Norwegian play.

During the symposium, several directors advocated color-blind casting as a way to ensure that all actors, regardless of skin color, have an equal chance of being cast, but others felt that trying to ignore skin color only makes for unbelievable interpretations and fundamental changes in the text and denies the racial conflicts in our society. Several audience members pointed out that 90 percent of all plays in the United States are written for white characters and that the way to ensure more roles for Hispanics, blacks, and Asian Americans is not color-blind casting but the creation of a library of new works by and for Americans of color. The late, great August Wilson, one of America's most respected playwrights, agreed. In his view, color-blind casting is not a substitute for plays about the black experience. Needless to say, the controversy over color-blind casting is not over. In the meantime, if you should see a play where the racial makeup of the cast doesn't correspond to the script, know that you are watching a play with color-blind casting and you are expected to accept it and devote yourself to the drama rather than being preoccupied by the race of the actors.

Joan Marcus

The choice of Whoopi Goldberg to play Prologus, a Greek actor, in a 1997 Broadway revival of A Funny Thing Happened on the Way to the Forum *is an example of color-blind (as well as gender-blind) casting. This practice has generated much controversy, although it is gaining popularity. Some feel it a fair way to ensure all actors are considered equally for a role, and others feel it masks the scarcity of roles for people of color in U.S. theatre.*

One of the most basic ways a director achieves focus is through actors' body positions. For example, in Figure 8.1 (A) the actors are **sharing focus**. They both have a shoulder thrown back (a position sometimes called "one-quarter" because the actors are turned a quarter away from the audience). Because the audience can see the actors equally, this position is used when what both actors are saying is of equal importance. In (B) the actor on the right takes focus because the actor on the left is standing in **profile**, or "half" away from the audience. The audience's eyes naturally go to the actor on the right because he is in the most "open" position. Perhaps at this moment in the play the character on the right is talking about how he knows his wife is cheating on him. The director feels that this speech is very important to the story and doesn't want the audience to

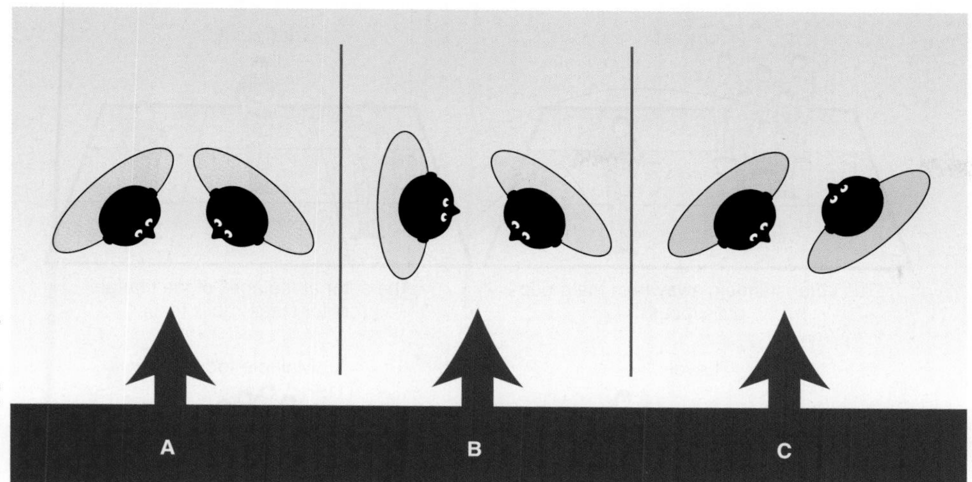

Figure 8.1 *Achieving focus through the actors' body positions.*

miss a word of it, so she has the actor on the left "close" himself by standing in profile. In (C) the actor on the right is standing in "three-quarters," an even more closed position than profile, so the actor on the left naturally demands a great deal of focus. Perhaps the character on the left is having an affair with the other character's "loyal" wife and the director wants the audience to see his guilty reaction, so the actor on the right gives the focus to the actor on the left.

Of course, all movements must be justified and fit into the action of the play. Actors mechanically turning to give and take focus would look silly, so motivated reasons for each individual movement must be found. During rehearsals actors are often asked to "open" themselves, to "share focus," to "give focus" or to "close" themselves in order to fit the focal demands of the moment. Actors who take focus when they aren't supposed to are said to be **stealing focus** or **upstaging** the other actors.

A director can also achieve focus by using different **stage areas** (see Figure 8.2). Each area is labeled from the actors' point of view as they face the audience; for example, "stage right" is to the audience's left. Using these labels, directors can easily ask the actors to move to a particular part of the stage or

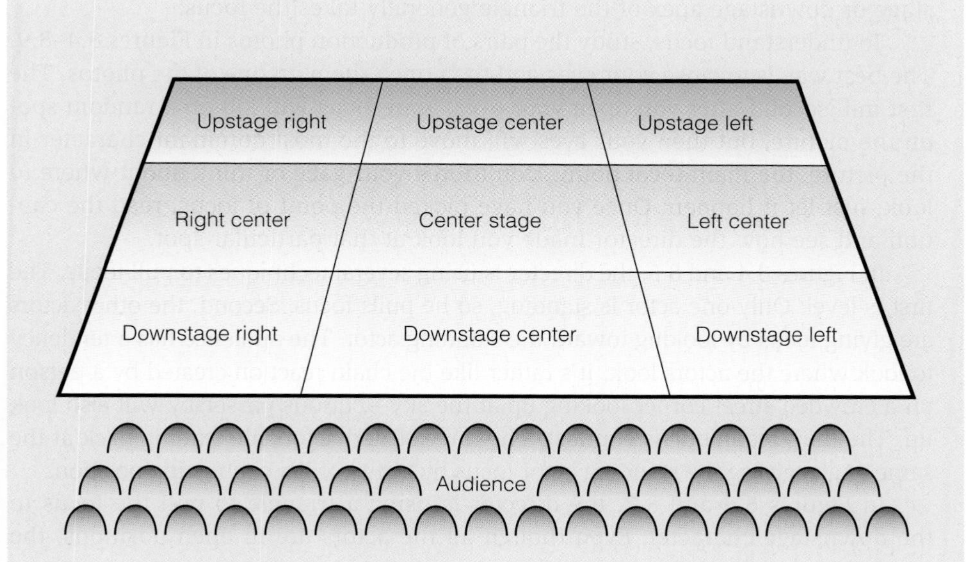

Figure 8.2 *Stage areas. To help with blocking, the stage is split into a grid and each area is labeled. Using these labels, directors can easily ask the actors to move to a particular place or look in a particular direction.*

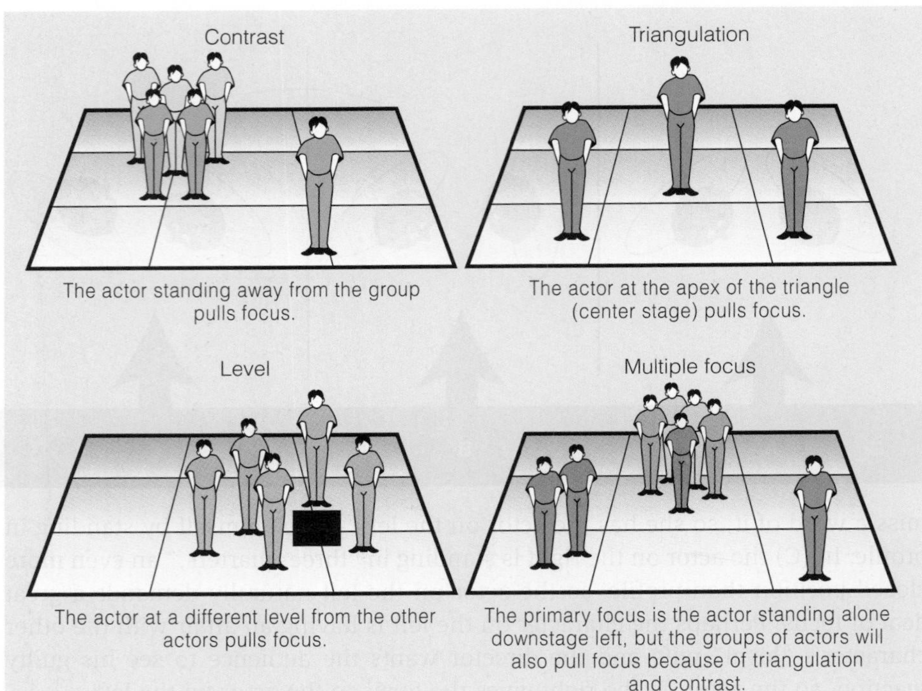

Contrast
The actor standing away from the group pulls focus.
Triangulation
The actor at the apex of the triangle (center stage) pulls focus.
Level
The actor at a different level from the other actors pulls focus.
Multiple focus
The primary focus is the actor standing alone downstage left, but the groups of actors will also pull focus because of triangulation and contrast.
© 2013 Cengage Learning

Figure 8.3 *Achieving focus through contrast, triangulation, and level.*

look in a particular direction. An actor who is center stage or downstage tends to draw the audience's attention more than actors in other areas.

Focus can also be achieved through level (see Figure 8.3). An actor who is at a different elevation than the other actors, either because he is on a platform of some kind or because he is standing while others are seated, tends to pull focus. The director can also use contrasting positions. An actor who is separated from the other actors always pulls the audience's focus. A contrast in movement also directs the audience's focus. The actor who is moving when the others are still or who is moving in a different direction will attract the audience's attention. Finally, one of the most common methods of drawing focus is **triangulation**. When there are three actors, or groups of actors on stage, whoever is at the upstage or downstage apex of the triangle generally takes the focus.

To understand focus, study the pairs of production photos in Figures 8.4–8.9. The best way is to close your eyes and then open them on one of the photos. The first millisecond after you open your eyes, your focus will fall on a random spot on the picture, but then your eyes will move to the most dominant character in the picture, the main focal point. Don't force your gaze or think about where to look; just let it happen. Once you have picked the point of focus, read the caption and see how the director made you look at that particular spot.

In Figures 8.4 and 8.5, the director is using several techniques to pull focus. The first is level: Only one actor is standing, so he pulls focus. Second, the other actors are giving focus by looking toward the standing actor. The audience has a tendency to look where the actors look. It's rather like the chain reaction created by a person on a crowded street corner looking up at the sky—curious passersby will also look up. The third technique is contrast: The three seated actors are leaning back at the same angle, giving the standing actor focus by virtue of his contrasting position.

In Figures 8.6 and 8.7, the director is using a triangle to pull the focus to the downstage character. Even though all the actors are in open positions, the

Figure 8.4

Figure 8.5 *Drawing focus with level, gaze, and contrast. From a University of Wyoming production of Edward Albee's* Who's Afraid of Virginia Woolf? *directed by Rebecca Hilliker.*

Figure 8.6

Figure 8.7 *Drawing focus with triangulation. From a University of Wyoming production of Henrik Ibsen's* A Doll's House, *directed by William Downs.*

Figure 8.8

University of Wyoming Archives

University of Wyoming Archives

Figure 8.9 *An example of double or triple focus. From a University of Wyoming production of Arthur Miller's* Death of a Salesman, *directed by William Downs.*

> The director must be the master of theatrical action, as the dramatist is the master of the written concept.
>
> ***Harold Clurman,***
> Director and theatre critic

focus is still taken by the downstage actor because he is at the downstage apex of the triangle. Also, the two upstage actors are looking at the downstage actor. The secondary focus is on the woman because she is the best lit.

In Figures 8.8 and 8.9, there is a double focus, perhaps even a triple focus. The two actors on the right are the first focus. The secondary focus is on the young woman sitting stage right, and then focus goes to the actor standing with his arms around the young women. Notice that if you look where any actor is looking and then to whom that actor is looking, and so on, your eyes eventually come to the man with his hand raised. Therefore, he takes the main focus.

Reinforcing the Story with Pictures

Words are a fine method of storytelling, but directors often go a step further by composing pictures with the actors that reinforce the story. This technique is called **picturization**. It uses many of the visual-art principles of painting and photography in order to express the characters' relationships, psychological situations, and moods at a glance. In real life people move without regard for where others are around them, groups of people seldom arrange themselves to tell a story, and there is randomness to crowds. For example, from a random photo of a bankruptcy auction on a farm in Iowa, we could probably tell that an auction was being held. The auctioneer might be in focus and around him would be dozens of farmers, but we'd know little else about the people or the situation. If the same scene were being shown on stage, the director would create pictures to help tell the story. From a single stage picture, we would be able to identify the members of the unlucky farm family. We'd know that this person is the mother, this is the father, and here stands the best friend. If a picture is well staged, we should even be able to tell what the characters' relationships are. We would know which of the farmers in the crowd had a vested interest in the proceedings and who were merely onlookers. We would also understand the mood of the moment, the sense of loss, and how the auction is the end of a way of life. A director arranging the actors to make these pictures is concerned not just with which characters are in focus but also with telling the story.

> The director builds a bridge from the spectator to the actor. Following the dictates of the author, and introducing onto the stage friends, enemies, or lovers, the director with movements and postures must present a certain image which will aid the spectator not only to hear the words, but to guess the inner, concealed feelings.
>
> ***V. E. Meyerhold,***
> Director and designer

If it is well staged, showing the purpose of the scene, the characters' objectives, and the mood of the moment, the picture can be given a title, like the title of a painting. One moment might be titled "True Love," the next moment "The Betrayal," and the next moment "The Confession." This title identifies the moment's main thrust or principal purpose. For example, in Figure 8.10, in a scene from a production of the comedy *Kosher Lutherans*, the placement of the actors creates a picture that tells a story. Without knowing any of the dialogue we could write a title such as "The show off" or "I win, you lose." Most of the time, the audience is unaware that they are seeing a succession of deliberate images. Yet when these stage compositions are well done, the audience might be able understand the play even if the dialogue was in a foreign language.

Figure 8.10 *Well-placed actors create a composition that tells a story. In this scene from the comedy* Kosher Lutherans *staged at the Bas Bleu Theatre, the director has created a stage picture that demonstrates the energy and mood of the scene without any need for dialogue.*

Different Types of Directors

Today, there are as many styles of directing as there are directors. Some directors are authoritarian leaders who micromanage every aspect of the play. Others are more like creative coaches who guide and inspire as they orchestrate the play in a democratic style. Every director has unique philosophies and methodologies about this highly individual process. But when it comes to working with an existing script, directors all fall somewhere in the spectrum between interpretive and creative.

Interpretive Directors

Interpretive directors attempt to translate the play from the page to the stage as accurately and faithfully as possible. They are not slaves to the playwright, but they make every attempt to realize the playwright's words and actions in a style that is true to the script. Directors inevitably impose their individual style on a production, but interpretive directors attempt to stage the play in a manner that they feel would please the playwright. Of course, an exact translation from page to stage is impossible—every line an actor speaks is an interpretation of the playwright's words, every movement an actor makes is an interpretation of the script, and every design is an interpretation of the playwright's wishes. French director and critic Jacques Copeau was describing the interpretive approach when he stated in his manifesto that the director's job is to faithfully translate the playwright's script into the "poetry of the theatre."

Interpretive directors set out to stage a play as the playwright envisioned it. Some playwrights won't allow anyone but interpretive directors to produce their plays. One such playwright is Edward Albee, who collaborated with director Robert Falls on a 2003 production of his The Goat, or Who Is Sylvia?*, a play about a man whose interspecies relationship threatens to ruin his marriage. This production featured (l to r) Patrick Clear, Michael Stahl-David, and Barbara Robertson.*

Michael Brasilow/The Goodman Theatre

Creative Directors

Creative directors often add concepts, designs, or interpretations atop the playwright's words that were never intended by the playwright. Their plays are sometimes called **concept productions**, because the director's artistic vision, or concept, dominates. In 1937 American director Orson Welles (1915–1985), famous for writing, directing, and starring in the movie *Citizen Kane*, directed one of the most celebrated concept productions. For a production of Shakespeare's *Julius Caesar*, he placed the action in pre–World War II Rome. He made the character of Caesar into the dictator Benito Mussolini and replaced the Shakespearean music with the anthem of Mussolini's fascist regime, thereby making a statement about the politics of the day. English director Peter Brook staged another famous concept production in 1970 when he turned Shakespeare's *A Midsummer Night's Dream* into a circus, with magic tricks, trapeze artists, and actors spinning plates on sticks. Brook and his designer, Sally Jacobs, set the play within a roofless white box with ladders, swings, and catwalks. The result was an athletic, acrobatic performance that did not look like anything Shakespeare originally intended. Today, concept productions are common, with directors

For concept productions, creative directors take the play in directions that the playwright perhaps never envisioned. In this University of Idaho production, co-directors David Lee-Painter and David Eames-Harlan staged Shakespeare's A Midsummer Night's Dream *in a new and colorful direction. The costume design was by Cheri Vasek. The scenic design by Stephanie Miller. It featured Trevor Hill as Bottom and Audrey Bensel as Titania. Also pictured are Katherine Kerrick, Mandie Jensen, Becca Bujko, Kate Belden, Jenna Guguierre, Chrystal Bain, Rachel Bruch, Amy Dexter, Dana Gladish, Heather McQuarrie, and Nicole Serhan.*

Krysta Ficca/Micki Panttaja

staging *Hamlet* in Chicago during the gangland wars of Prohibition and *The Taming of the Shrew* in the Wild West. Creative directors stage concept productions in order to capture the spirit of the play, modernize the play, or simply create a unique evening of theatre.

Some creative directors go so far as to almost discard the playwright's words, using the script as only a loose outline. These directors believe that the script should mutate to fit the needs of an individual director or production. Of course, the main problem for these directors is the small number of plays they can direct, because playwrights own the copyright to their plays and have the right to deny production to any director who does not properly follow the script. Directors who wish to alter a playwright's intention must gain the playwright's permission or wait until the play is in public domain, as are Shakespeare's plays. (For more on copyright and public domain, see Chapter 2.) There have been several famous battles between playwrights and directors over who controls a play. One of the most famous took place in 1984 during a production of Samuel Beckett's *Endgame* at the American Repertory Theatre. (See the Spotlight "Playwright Versus Director.")

Contemporary Trends

Traditionally, theatre artists were divided into *creative artists,* the playwrights who create the scripts, and *interpretive artists,* the directors, actors, and designers who work within the parameters the playwright has set. This dividing line between creative and interpretive artists is now being questioned by many directors as well as playwrights and actors. They are blurring the traditional assignments and creating and staging plays that allow all the members of the ensemble to be creative artists and share in the development of the play. Plays have always been developed; seldom does a playwright labor in total isolation and then suddenly put forth a finished script. Most plays go through an extensive process of readings and workshop productions that help the playwright rewrite. But now many directors and actors are getting involved in the development process much earlier, even at the moment of conception. So instead of the production being an interpretation of the playwright's script, the production is the creation of an ensemble of playwright, designers, actors, and director.

Playwright Caryl Churchill often workshops her plays using a communal method of development that allows actors to help create the script through improvisation and the director to co-determine the direction of the final script. Such was the case with Churchill's play *Cloud Nine,* the story of several generations of a family and how they are governed by class, race, and gender—a play, by the way, that features cross-gender casting. Instead of writing in a secluded study, she spent several weeks working with the director on the idea and setting for the play. Then actors were brought in to improvise as they jointly workshopped the idea. Churchill took what she learned and wrote a tentative script with rudimentary dialogue. This first script was again workshopped with the director and actors to refine the dialogue, and this collaboration resulted in the final production. Another famous example of this new method of directing is Moisés Kaufman's play *The Laramie Project,* a docudrama about the murder of a gay university student. The play was researched by a company of actors who conducted personal interviews with people who lived in the town in which the student was

SPOTLIGHT ON Playwright versus Director

In 1984 JoAnne Akalaitis directed Samuel Beckett's *Endgame* at the American Repertory Theatre. Samuel Beckett is one of the world's most famous absurdist playwrights. *Endgame* is the story of two clown-like characters, Hamm and Clov, one of whom is partially paralyzed and the other acts as his servant. Other characters are Hamm's parents, who live in trash cans. Beckett's stage directions state that the play takes place in a room with two windows and little else. But Akalaitis saw the play differently. She set the action in a New York City subway station after a nuclear holocaust, which changed the meaning of the play. When Beckett heard about the production, he went to court to shut it down. In the end, they settled out of court. The production was allowed to go forward, but the program included a note, written by Beckett, condemning the production. The note says that the American Repertory Theatre's production is a "complete parody" of his work, and that anyone who cares for the play can't help but be "disgusted" by what Akalaitis did to it. The theatre's artistic director responded in a program note that reads in part, "To insist on strict adherence to each parenthesis of the published text not only robs collaborating artists of their interpretive freedom but threatens to turn the theatre into a waxworks."

This exchange defined one of the greatest problems of the relationship between the director and the playwright: Who has the power? Is the play set in stone when the playwright writes it, or can it be adjusted to fit the director's artistic vision? Some directors have attempted to solve the problem by saying that the playwright should be in charge of only the dialogue and the director in charge of the staging. This division of labor doesn't solve the problem because playwrights also write the stage directions that describe the physical aspect of the play, and both are copyrighted. With Hollywood films, screenwriters have lost this battle. Writers for movies are secondary characters whose vision is seldom realized. In the theatre, the battle has just begun. However, unlike screenwriters, playwrights have a powerful advantage because they own the copyright, so they may not be so quickly defeated. Recently some better known directors have been contending that their blocking and production concepts should also be copyrighted and are filing lawsuits to ensure that no one can replicate their staging without permission and payment. Concerning the mess, the playwright and screenwriter Paul Rudnick (*I Hate Hamlet*) said, "From now on I'm only going to have my plays directed by lawyers." Needless to say the battle over creative control and copyrights in the theatre will be hotly debated on the stage and in courts for many years to come.

Richard Feldman

In recent years, playwrights have sometimes threatened legal action to stop directors from altering their work. Examples include a production of Edward Albee's Who's Afraid of Virginia Woolf?, *in which a man in drag was cast as Martha, and a play by an experimental theatre company that incorporated a portion of Arthur Miller's play* The Crucible. *One of the most famous cases of a playwright intervening to stop a production of one of his plays involved JoAnne Akalaitis's 1984 production of Samuel Beckett's* Endgame *(pictured here).*

murdered. Kaufman acted as both director and playwright as he worked with the actors to develop the final production.

Curtain Call

In the end, all directors are judged by process and product. The process is everything that leads up to opening night; the product is opening night and beyond. A good process doesn't always lead to a good product, but occasionally a good product is born of bad process. The acid test for the process is if all the members of the ensemble have clearly seen and added to the production. Did the environment allow meaningful creativity for all the members? The acid test for the product is far more subjective, because more people are involved, including the audience and critics. But, as director Peter Brook says in *The Empty Space*:

> I know of one acid test in the theatre. It is literally an acid test. When the performance is over, what remains? Fun can be forgotten, powerful emotions also disappear and good arguments lose their thread. When emotion and arguments are harnessed to a wish from the audience to see more clearly into itself—then something in the mind burns. The event scorches onto the memory an outline, a taste, a trace, a smell—a picture. It is the play's central image that remains, its silhouette, and if the elements are rightly blended this silhouette will be its meaning, this shape will be the essence of what it has to say.

So the acid test for a production is whether its meaning stays with the audience. The playwright's words will be forgotten or paraphrased, the actors' names will disappear, the designer's colors will fade, and the set will be discarded, but the director knows that the production was successful if the thought remains.

Summary

In order for a production to succeed, dozens of artists, technicians, and other personnel must work together with a singleness of purpose seldom found outside the theatre. The director is the leader and coordinator who takes the playwright's words and frames them into a production. The job requires many skills: The director must know how to work with and inspire actors, designers, and playwrights, and how to coordinate all the elements that make up a production. Yet the director is one of the newest positions in the theatre. For thousands of years playwrights and actors essentially functioned as directors. It wasn't until about 150 years ago, when realism became popular, that the duties of the director were separated into a single job. Two early directors who helped define the position were the Duke of Saxe-Meiningen and Konstantin Stanislavsky.

The director's job can be split in two parts: pre-rehearsal and rehearsal. Prerehearsal is spent evaluating and researching the script, conceiving a production concept, and working with designers. To analyze a play, a director often breaks it into french scenes and beats. Dividing the play into these small units helps the director discover the structure and understand the play moment by moment. Once the director has done careful analysis and research, it is time for meetings with the designers in order to find a production concept, or central metaphor, that unites all the elements of the production. Only after weeks or months of work does the director finally cast the play.

The director has many casting options, including casting to type, casting against type, gender-neutral casting, cross-gender casting, and color-blind casting. During rehearsals the director blocks the play to lead the audience's eyes and achieve focus. The methods the director can use to pull focus include body position, stage area, level, contrast, and triangulation. Directors also use picturization to tell the play's story.

The director's job is so complex that it often requires several assistants, such as an assistant director and a stage manager. Additionally, some productions also need a movement coach, a voice and dialect coach, and a fight director. Musicals need a musical director and a choreographer to work with the musicians and teach the actors the songs and dance numbers (for more on these additional ensemble members, see Chapter 5).

No two directors have the same working methods. But they can be divided into two broad, nonexclusive categories: interpretive directors who are loyal to the playwright's intentions, and creative directors who often impose upon the script their own concept that is independent of the playwright's intentions. Some directors are now challenging traditional ideas by staging plays that allow actors, playwrights, and directors to work on a play from its inception to the opening night.

The Art of Theatre ONLINE 

To access this chapter's interactive theatre workshop activities, along with many other learning tools, log onto your Theatre CourseMate. Access is available at cengagebrain.com.

Key Terms

assistant director / 181
beat / 177
blocking / 181
casting against type / 181
casting director / 180
casting to type / 180
color-blind casting / 181
concept production / 189
creative director / 189
cross-gender casting / 181
didaskalos / 174
director / 171
focus / 181
french scene / 177
gender-neutral casting / 181
interpretive director / 188
Moscow Art Theatre / 175
picturization / 187
production concept / 179
profile / 182
sharing focus / 182
stage area / 183
stealing focus / 183
triangulation / 184
upstaging / 183

Traveler in the Dark, by Marsha Norman. Directed by Gordon Davidson, Mark Taper Forum, Los Angeles, 1985. Set designed by Ming Cho Lee, costumes designed by Susan Denison, and lighting designed by Marilyn Rennagel. This play is about a surgeon who, coping with guilt over the death of his childhood sweetheart, seeks to renew his relationship with his long-estranged father.

Photos on this spread T. Charles Erickson Photography

CHAPTER

The Art of Design

OUTLINE

The house lights dim, the curtain rises, and we see a solitary actor standing in the center of a bare stage. There is almost nothing to support the actor—simple work lights, no costume, no set, nothing but a blankly lit empty space. Could this be theatre? Absolutely. Yet theatre also often uses designers to assist the actors, playwright, and director by setting the stage. When sets, lights, sounds, and costumes are added, the audience is immersed in the world of the play even before the first line is spoken. Theatre is intended to be experienced by our eyes, our ears, our mind, our whole being, so theatre has always had designers in one form or another to help create the experience.

Today, most plays have set, lighting, and costume designers, but some also have sound and makeup designers. All these artists must work together to create the visual effects of a dramatic production—in other words, the play's environment. Environment is integral to any story.

Every plot, conflict, and character would change if they were moved to new surroundings. Imagine the Christmas movie *Miracle on 34th Street* transported to the steamy South or the chilly moral fable *Fargo* set in sunny Hawaii. Their stories, characters, and possibly themes would be transformed. Even the most well-known plays by Shakespeare seem new and different when they are set in unexpected periods and locations, such as when the feud between families in the early Renaissance Italy of *Romeo and Juliet* is transformed into a contemporary gang war in the Leonardo DiCaprio movie version. The plots and most of the dialogue are unchanged, but the shift in environment drastically alters the tone and the characters. Whether the set is complicated or simple, familiar or novel, the designer's duty is to create a virtual environment that will remind the audience who the players are and where they're supposed to be. Design can communicate the spirit and soul of the play to the audience.

From Page to Stage

Design is an act of transformation. In working with a director, a designer transforms words into a world within which actors are engaged in human action. It might be a metaphoric world, an emotional world or an architectural world, but it is a process of bringing design ideas into a place where they can be executed.

Ming Cho Lee,
Theatre designer

There are as many methods of designing a virtual environment as there are designers and productions, so this will be a sweeping look at what might be called a typical design process: taking the play from the page to the stage. "My approach, after reading the script," says Ming Cho Lee, one of the United States' premier set designers, "is to question the director about an overall production scheme, discussing choices: Should it be realistic or abstract? Should it be period or not? Should the material be metal, wood, granite? Then I do a rough sketch for the director to find out if I'm going in the right direction. Then I make a one-half-inch scale model and paint it up. All this takes time." In fact, the process can take so much time that designers must begin their work many months before the actors arrive on the scene.

Doing the Homework

Long before the rehearsals begin, the designers begin work by studying the script. The playwright has created the blueprint for a production; in order for the play to exist, the words on the page must be transformed into action and environment on the stage. The designer's analysis of the script is as detailed and comprehensive as any director's or actor's. A complete understanding of the characters is essential because the characters define the environment and the environment reveals the characters, especially their personal surroundings—their home, office, or room. Characters' tastes, lifestyles, incomes, jobs, educations, and temperaments are reflected in the environment they've created, just as the décor of your dorm room and how you dress reflect your character.

Understanding the characters and script, however, is only the beginning. In order to create an accurate virtual environment, set, lighting, sound, costume, and makeup designers must often do detailed investigations into the location and historical period. They may need to study the architecture, the color schemes, and the styles. They might also study the customs, manners, and cultures. This research helps the designers answer dozens of critical questions, including the

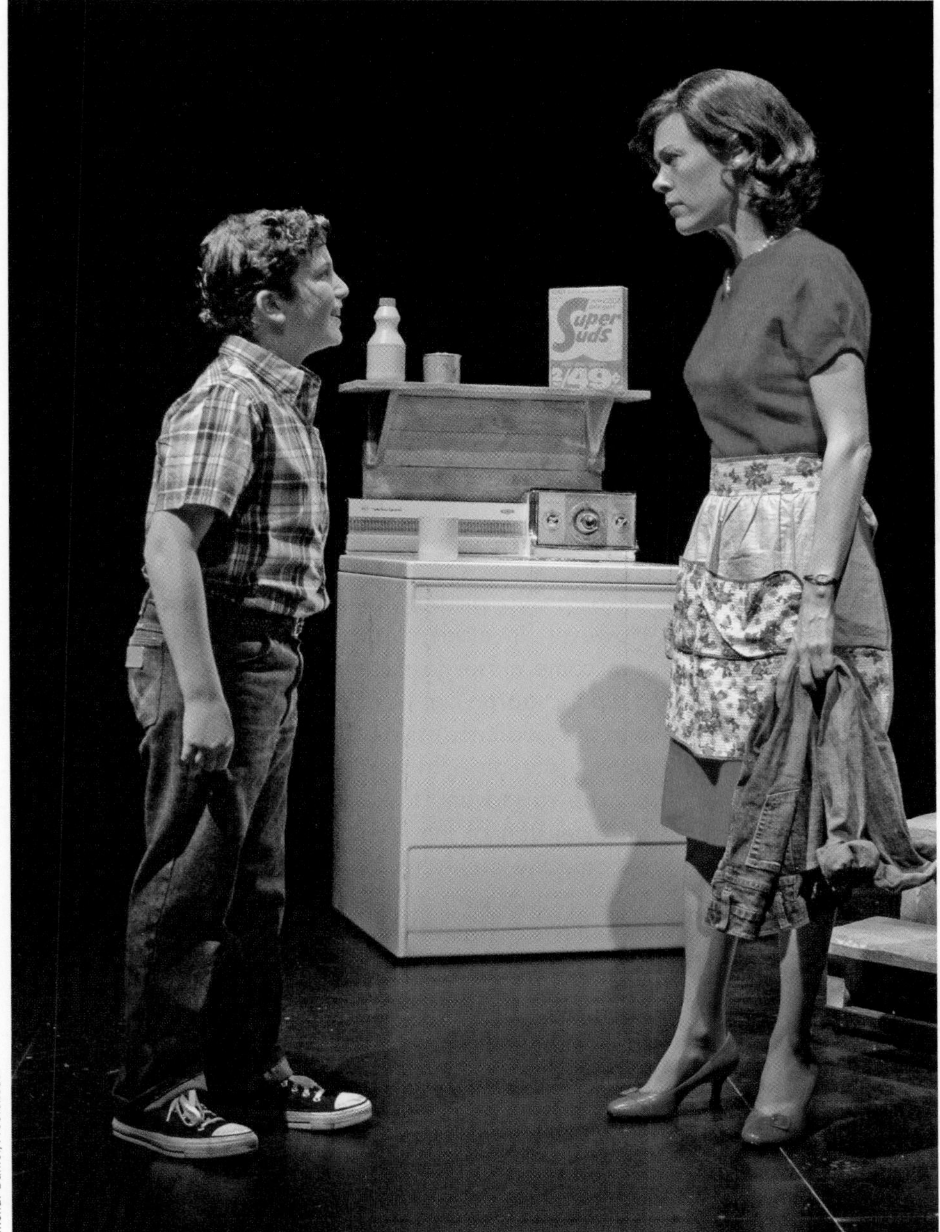

Michal Daniel/Proofsheet

To create an environment that accurately reflects the mood and content of a play, theatre designers research the time and place in which the play's story happens. For example, the historically accurate set and costumes of Caroline, or Change, *about an African American maid and the Jewish family she works for, depict the racial and economic politics of 1963 Louisiana. This 2003 production featured Tonya Pinkins as Caroline and, shown here, Harrison Chad and Veanne Cox. Book and lyrics by Tony Kushner, music by Jeanine Tesori, sets by Riccardo Hernández, costumes by Paul Tazewell, and lighting by Jules Fisher and Peggy Eisenhauer. Directed by George C. Wolfe at the Public Theater, New York.*

following ones:

- How does the play's environment affect and reflect the story and characters?
- How do the story and characters affect and reflect the environment?
- What significant details of the environment will define and individualize the characters?
- How do the characters feel about their environment?
- How does the environment relate to the play's theme?
- Is the personal environment in or out of harmony with the characters?

There are also historical considerations:

- What is the time period of the play?
- What was the religious, social, and political climate of that period?
- What was the religious, social, and political climate when the play was written?

Designers also consider practical questions, such as these:

- What are the mechanical requirements, such as the number of doors needed for exits?
- What are the budgetary limitations?
- What are the deadlines?

SPOTLIGHT ON Theatre Spaces

Environment begins with the theatre itself. Theatre can take place just about anywhere, from stages to street corners. For much of its history, theatre has not been performed in theatre buildings but in what are called **found, or created, spaces**. Typically, these have been parks, churches, and town squares, but they can also be basements, warehouses, gymnasiums, jails, or subway stations. Theatre can take place just about anywhere an audience can gather. Set designer Robert Edmond Jones said, "In its essence, a theatre is only an arrangement of seats so grouped and spaced that the actor—the leader—can reach out and touch and hold each member of his audience. Architects of later days have learned how to add conveniences and comforts to this idea. But that is all. The idea itself never changes." The standard types of theatres today are proscenium arch, thrust, arena, and black box.

The most common type is the **proscenium arch**. The word *proscenium* comes from the ancient Latin word for "stage." The proscenium arch originated in Italy in the 1500s. Proscenium arch theatres are a little more formal than the other types because the audience is separated from the actors. As in a movie theatre, the audience sits safely in the dark, looking through a picture frame at the actors on the other side. In fact, proscenium arch theatres are sometimes called "picture frame" theatres. In some theatres, the separation between actors and audience is made even greater with the addition of an orchestra pit between the audience and stage. However, in modern proscenium arches the actors can come closer to the audience on what is called a **lip** or **apron**, a part of the stage that extends into the audience's side of the picture frame. Some aprons are on a hydraulic or manual elevator and can be raised and lowered; at stage level they are an extension of the stage, and when lowered they become the orchestra pit. Above the stage, a traditional proscenium arch hides an elaborate network of pulleys, riggings, and counterweights called a **fly system** that raises scenic pieces out of the audience's sight. Fly systems can tower 80–100 feet above the stage and are usually manually operated, although some modern proscenium arch theatres have computerized fly systems. At the sides of a proscenium arch stage are the **wings**. Out of the audience's sight, the wings are areas from which actors make their entrances and where set pieces can be stored or moved onto the stage.

A **thrust stage** has a lip (apron) that protrudes so far into the auditorium that the audience must sit on three sides of the stage. This "peninsula" or "runway" type of stage reduces the distance between the actors and audience. Even from the back rows, the distance is small. This allows for a more intimate style of acting. Occasionally called "three-quarters-round," many thrust theatres have passageways or tunnels called **vomitories**, or "voms," that run into and under the audience to allow actors quick access to the stage. Vomitories are just like

- What are the physical limitations of the stage?
- What are the physical dimensions of theatre in which the play will be performed?

Like baseball parks, no two theatres are exactly the same. The size, seating arrangement, and layout can directly affect the design. (For more on types of theatres, see the Spotlight "Theatre Spaces.")

In order to answer all these questions, designers must have well-rounded educations in history, dramatic structure, art, art history, and criticism. Many universities offer an MFA (Master of Fine Arts) degree in set, costume, light, and sound design. Designers must also have a great deal of imagination, because, in the words of Robert Edmond Jones (1887–1954), one of the United States' foremost set designers, they need to "immerse themselves in [the play]" and even "be baptized by it." Only then can they begin their work on the design.

---

the stadium tunnel a football team disappears into at halftime. Historically, it is unclear how the word vomitory came to be used for a theatre space, but the word comes from the Latin verb *vomere*, which means to "spew out"; literally, actors are "spewed out" from the stage down these tunnel-like exits.

The thrust stage is much older than the proscenium arch theatre. Twenty-five hundred years ago, ancient Greek tragedies were performed on a version of the thrust stage. Four hundred years ago, Shakespeare's plays were first performed on a thrust stage.

Arena theatres are far less common than proscenium arch or thrust theatres. Often called "theatres-in-the-round," arenas have the stage in the center, like an island, surrounded on all sides by audience. Arena theatres resemble sports stadiums, boxing arenas, and circus rings. Like thrust theatres, arenas have vomitories to allow actors easy access to the stage as well as a close relationship with the audience. Arena productions may cost the least to stage because elaborate scenery is not possible. Walls, doors, and large furniture pieces would only block the audience's view, so sets are kept simple. Although this keeps expenses low, it limits the number of plays that can be effectively produced. The major challenge for productions on arena stages is the audience's **sight lines**, because there are few places the actors can stand or sit without blocking someone's view. To solve this problem, actors often try to keep their backs to the vomitories so they are open to a majority of audience members. Another solution is to keep moving. Some directors make the actors move, shift, or turn every thirty seconds or so to ensure that no one audience member's view is blocked for too long. Arena stages are probably the oldest type of theatre, for whenever people gather for an outdoor event, whether a tribal ceremony, a sporting event, or a rally, a circle seems to be our natural method of gathering.

Most **black box theatres** seat fewer than a hundred people. The audience sits close to the actors, making these theatres ideal for small, intimate plays. Sometimes called "studio," "flexible," or "experimental" theatres, most black boxes have no permanent seating arrangement. They are bare spaces that allow seats to be arranged differently for every production. The space can be set up as a proscenium arch, a thrust, or an arena, or it may be configured in some experimental, nontraditional actor/audience arrangement. In some black box productions, audience members have sat on stage with the actors or followed the actors from location to location or looked down into a pit where the action was taking place. Black box theatres are often in found spaces, such as converted warehouses or storefronts. They are called "black boxes" because the walls are usually painted black to de-emphasize them, and the space is often square. However, no two black box theatres are exactly alike.

Proscenium arch theatres are sometimes called "picture frame" theatres because the arch resembles the frame of a picture. Today proscenium stages, like this one in Canada's Avon Theatre, are the most common type of stage in North America, but they originated in Italy during the Renaissance.

Courtesy of The Stratford Festival of Canada

Thrust stages, like that of the Festival Theatre in Canada, protrude into the auditorium so that the audience sits on three sides. Like the proscenium arch, thrust theatres have been around for hundreds of years. In fact, William Shakespeare's plays were first performed on a thrust stage.

Courtesy of The Stratford Festival of Canada

Design Team Meetings

Once the designers have researched and studied the play, they are ready for the artistic and production meetings. The director, stage manager, and designers begin by reviewing practical issues: the physical limits of the theatre, safety concerns, budget limitations, and scheduling. Soon they get down to finding, understanding, and communicating the production concept. As you read in Chapter 8, the production concept is the master symbol or allegory that the director, playwright, and designers conceive as the central metaphor. The director and designers use this metaphor to physically express the mood, tone, theme, and philosophy of the script.

It can take many meetings for the director and designers to agree on a production concept. During these meetings they talk about how they see the play, how they feel about each scene, and how they hope to affect the audience. The director may tell personal stories that connect to the play's theme or discuss

In arena theatres, or theatres-in-the-round, the audience surrounds the stage, as in a sports arena. Performing on an arena stage can be a challenge because actors must often shift positions to remain open to the audience. This example is the Fichandler Stage of Arena Stage in Washington, DC.

Scott Suchman/Arena Stage

Black box theatres, such as the National Theatre's Cottesloe in London, are also known as studio, flexible-space, or experimental theatres and they come in all shapes and sizes. They are called black box theatres because their walls are almost always painted black and they often have a boxlike shape.

Royal National Theatre

reasons for staging the play. Some directors use models, sketches, photos, paintings, and even music as well as words to communicate their ideas about the production concept. "Designing is something that you don't approach in a linear way like you approach climbing a ladder, one step at a time," says set designer Ming Cho Lee. "It's actually a constant exploring of ideas. It's about how you connect with a play, how you live the life of the play." During these meetings the director and designers also talk about mood, pace, atmosphere, and colors, as well as character and story. The director also talks about the production's style—perhaps realism or expressionism or some combination of "isms." (For more on style, see the Spotlight "Theatrical Styles.")

Designers in the theatre communicate the production concept—the central metaphor of the play—through lights, sound, sets, and costumes. They make a play's ideas more clear and complete than they would be in real life. Nothing on stage is arbitrary. Everything, from a costume's button to the color of the light to the angle of a door, is chosen to communicate the production concept.

SPOTLIGHT ON Theatrical Styles

All plays have a style. Style is the way in which a work is expressed or performed. Some plays, like most television shows, are lifelike imitations of nature. This is a style known as **realism**. To design realistic sets, lights, makeup, and costumes, designers pay close attention to details that will make everything appear to be a genuine duplication of real life, whatever the period. For example, if a scene is about a 1950s housewife in her kitchen, then the designers would use historically accurate faucets, running water, and a working refrigerator from the postwar era. They would also design natural-looking light that seems to be coming from a source onstage, such as a ceiling fixture or sunlight flowing in through the window and bouncing off the 1950s flowered wallpaper and linoleum floors. The housewife's costume would be genuine to the period, as if it came off a department-store rack, and the dinette set would look as if it came from the time Eisenhower was president. The only difference from real life would be that one wall of the kitchen is missing so that the audience can peek in on the action.

For some plays, **simplified, or suggested, realism** is appropriate. For this style, designers suggest rather than duplicate the look of a period. What the audience sees is not a carbon copy but a suggestion of a 1950s kitchen, whose details they must fill in with their imagination. This style is sometimes called **selective realism** because some design elements appear authentic, but other elements are stylized. For example, our 1950s kitchen might appear real, but the lights may express the mood rather than seem to come from a source on stage. Or our housewife's costume might be authentic, but the set more symbolic.

Once designers step away from realism, they are free to create virtual worlds with their own logic and rules. They can pursue a metaphorical, symbolic, or stylized look. Stylization can take several forms; one of the most common is **expressionism**. With expressionism, the audience sees the story through the mind of one character. Settings may be distorted by the character's conscious or subconscious phobias, prejudices, or psychoses. Instead of photographic reality, the audience sees

Selective realism gets its name from the selected elements of reality designers choose to highlight. With this style, some aspects of a play's environment are presented realistically, whereas others are merely suggested and allowed to take less focus. In this set designed by Jo Mielziner for a 1949 production of Arthur Miller's Death of a Salesman, *the furniture looks quite real but is placed within a skeletal framework of a house.*

Billy Rose Theatre Collection, The New York Public Library for the Performing Arts, Astor, Lenox and Tilden Foundations

The designers' opinions may change the entire look of the play. For example, when Julie Taymor designed the costumes for the Broadway hit *The Lion King: The Musical*, she wanted race to be an important part of the story. "What I love about *The Lion King*," says Taymor, "is that this is a show with a predominantly nonwhite cast that is not about race. On the other hand, it's all about race—and

the character's inner reality. With an expressionistic style, our 1950s kitchen might have slanted walls leaning in on our housewife showing her feelings of claustrophobia and being trapped in her marriage. The TV shows *Scrubs* and *That 70s Show* have used expressionism to illustrate the mindset of a character, such as someone literally drowning in a cup of coffee or the walls closing in on an office worker.

When stylization is taken to an extreme, little or no attempt is made to re-create reality; instead, oversized symbols and fantastic dreamlike or nightmarish images dominate the stage. With **surrealism**, the subconscious of the characters is emphasized in the design—now our 1950s kitchen is located in Hell. With **symbolism**, a certain piece of scenery, a costume, or light may represent the essence of the entire environment: our 1950s kitchen might have huge faucets that torture the housewife with their incessant dripping.

Finally, some sets contain little that looks real. The purpose of these sets is to remind the audience that they're watching a play. Now our 1950s kitchen has only a sink, and no walls. Instead, advertising posters are hung around the stage with smiling 1950s housewives looking down on our character and extolling the marvels of a modern kitchen.

Few designs have only one style. Designers often mix styles to fulfill their aesthetic goals for an environment that fits the production concept and the needs of the play.

Richard Finkelstein Photography

Whereas realism aims for authenticity, expressionism attempts to re-create the world as the characters see and feel it—subjectively, with their emotions and unconscious thoughts made visible. This 2001 production of Elmer Rice's expressionist play The Adding Machine *at the University of Colorado, Denver, featured a set by Richard Finkelstein, lights by Scott Hay, and costumes by Jane Nelson-Rudd.*

Robbie Jack Photography

Inspired by psychoanalysis and the workings of the human mind, surrealist playwrights attempted to break down the barriers between the conscious and the unconscious. In this 2005 production of August Strindberg's A Dream Play, *adapted by Caryl Churchill, we see inside the mind of the main character as he dreams of his past. Directed by Katie Mitchell and designed by Vicki Mortimer, National Theatre, London.*

that should be acknowledged, because there are very powerful traditions . . . and that fact shouldn't be ignored." The producers, on the other hand, did not think the theme of race was particularly important, but Taymor persisted. During a production meeting, she convinced them to agree to the design for African-inspired clothes. The result was a change in the whole production concept.

Filling the Empty Space

Once the designers understand the production concept, they need to make the leap from words to images. They create drawings, renderings, thumbnail sketches, models, and plans of the sets, costumes, makeup, and lights. After each production meeting, the designers combine the play's needs, their research, the style, and the concept, and let them "bake." Designers may contemplate these issues for weeks to allow their training and their creative mind to conceive ideas that will express the production concept. No two designers work the same way. But they all must take into account the demands of the play and the limitations of the theatre while transforming abstract ideas into concrete designs that convey the central metaphor of the play.

The **basic elements of design**—the designer's toolkit, in a sense—are line, dimension, balance, movement, harmony, color, and texture. If the master symbol of the play is the need to get back to nature, the designers might choose earth tones, the colors of growing plants, and natural textures. If the master concept is to glorify humankind's great achievements as represented in our cities, then straight lines and massive forms that reflect the sun might be used. If the master concept is to show a world out of balance, then the designers might use odd-shaped masses that seem to teeter unsteadily or defy the laws of gravity. The designer's choices are limitless because there are infinite possibilities that could meet a play's production needs. To understand more about the design process, let's look at each of the major design areas: sets, lights, sound, costumes, and makeup.

Designing the Set

Twenty-five hundred years ago in ancient Greece, designers painted screens, sewed costumes, and built masks to help create the characters and suggest the play's virtual environment. During the Italian Renaissance, designers constructed elaborate stage settings using two-dimensional flats that were painstakingly painted to appear as if they were three-dimensional throne rooms, landscapes, and dungeons. At other times in theatre's long history, the set design has been simple. For example, for hundreds of years Chinese opera was performed outdoors on bare platforms. Instead of complex designs, settings were indicated with simple symbolic gestures of the actors or with minimal set pieces. If the story required a character to climb a tall mountain, the actor would pantomime it using only a small stepladder; a plain wooden stool could represent a grand golden throne. This worked for the Chinese opera because the audience knew they had to use their imagination to "see" the set. Today, set designs can be simplistic or complicated. The only limitation is the theatre's budget and the designer's talent and imagination.

Designers often have trouble describing exactly how they do their job. The set designer John Lee Beatty says, "One of the fun things about being a designer is that you don't know where the designs come from—they just come out." Simply put, they take the words of the playwright and the ideas of the director and turn them into visual imagery. Set designers have a strong background in interior design, architecture, and art history, as well as theatrical conventions of various periods. But above all, designers must be artists. They draw and draft

> I'm looking for a connection with the world we live in, a passion for seeing that [connection] translated in visual terms. What I'm trying to train [students in] is the ability to translate text or music into meaningful images.
>
> ***Ursula Belden,***
> Theatre designer and professor

their art by hand, although now the use of **computer aided design (CAD)** programs is more common.

Designers who draw their designs by hand often make numerous thumbnail sketches in an attempt to realize the production concept, taking into account the locations, environment, and historical background of the script. This doodling can be done in pencil, pen, or charcoal. Figure 9.1 shows an early drawing by designer Michael Earl for a production of *My Fair Lady*. After this rough sketch, he decided that the set had to be more open, so he eliminated the pillar on the right and showed more of the city's skyline in the background (Figure 9.2).

Once the director approves the sketch, the designer paints a color rendering (Figure 9.3). After that is approved the designer moves on to blueprints. Like architectural drawings for a building, these blueprints include scale drawings of every part of the set. The view from above is called the **floor plan**; the views from front and back are called the **elevations** (see Figure 9.4). These drawings must be rendered exactly to scale and show the placement of every door, window, and platform, as well as furniture, light switches, and baseboards. They also include the wallpaper patterns, shading, and texture. Once the blueprints are complete, the set-construction crew gets to work, using the designer's exact specifications to build the set. The complete process from production meeting to final design often takes months. Figure 9.5 shows the final set for the production of *My Fair Lady*, generated from the sketches shown in Figures 9.1, 9.2, and 9.3.

Sometimes, if the director wants more help visualizing the set before building it, the designer also crafts handmade three-dimensional scale models of the setting. The preliminary model is called the "white model" because it is made of heavy white paper and white foam board (Figure 9.6). After the director and designer study the white model and agree on changes, the designer now makes a second, more detailed color model. The second model includes every aspect of the set in detail (Figure 9.7). Figure 9.8 shows the final set for a production of *All My Sons*, generated from the models shown in Figures 9.6 and 9.7.

Designers who use CAD follow a similar process but use computers instead of paper, paint, and physical models to produce exact blueprints. CAD was originally developed to help engineers and architects draft buildings and bridges but was quickly adapted to theatre sets. Sophisticated modeling programs can also show the design three dimensionally from almost any angle. This allows the designer to let the director walk through a virtual reality set (much like a computer game). Computer modeling has changed the way set designers design because it allows almost unlimited changes and creative experimentation.

Whether set designers work by hand or with a computer, or both, they must turn out exact designs that take into account durability and safety, as well as the length of time available for construction. Budget is also a concern, as are the physical needs of the play and the structural limitations of the theatre. (For more on set design, see the Spotlight "The Life of a Designer: Ming Cho Lee.")

> A good design . . . is one that takes on significance and that resonates at the end of the show. It needs to unfold and take on meaning, and become imbued with emotion and importance; it needs to connect with the piece in a way that keeps surprising, and that keeps allowing the audience to have ideas and revelations as the evening goes on.
>
> ***Adrianne Lobel,***
> Set designer

Designing the Lights

For thousands of years theatre was performed outdoors, so the sun provided the light. Many of these pre-electricity civilizations built their theatres so that the afternoon sunshine would hit the stage. The first indoor theatres were built

Figure 9.1 *Early rough sketch of a set from a University of Wyoming production of Alan Jay Lerner and Frederick Loewe's My Fair Lady, drawn by designer Michael Earl.*

Figure 9.2 *The later rough sketch.*

Figure 9.3 *The final color rendering.*

about five hundred years ago and used chandeliers filled with sputtering candles to illuminate the stage. In 1545 Sebastiano Serlio (1475–1554) published *Architettura*, a book on Italian set design, in which he described how to change the quality of the light by placing reflectors behind the candles and globes of

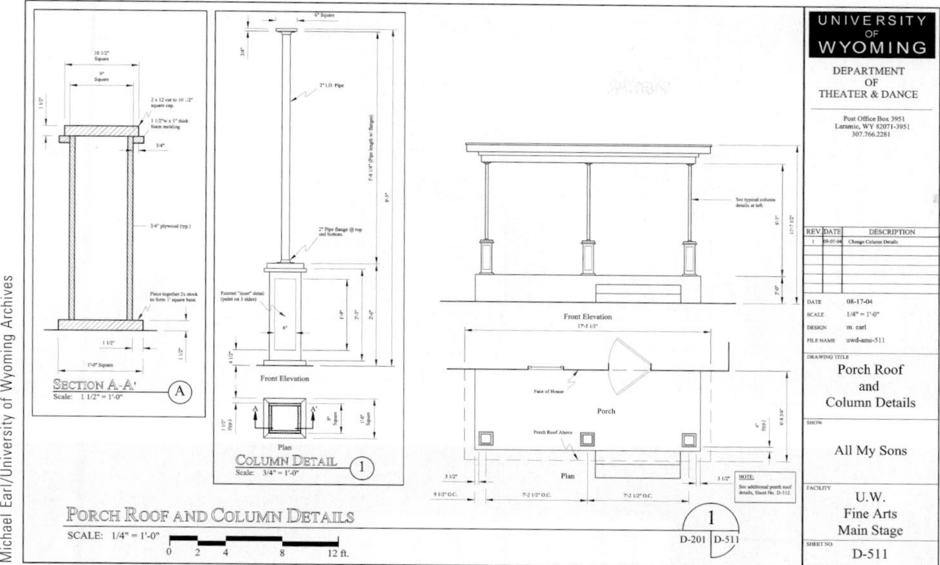

Michael Earl/University of Wyoming Archives

Figure 9.4 *Elevation of a set from a University of Wyoming production of Arthur Miller's* All My Sons, *drawn by designer.*

Michael Earl/University of Wyoming Archives

Figure 9.5 *The final set for* My Fair Lady *at the Struthers Theatre in Warren, Pennsylvania.*

colored water in front. A hundred years later, Nicola Sabbatini (ca. 1574–1654) published the *Manual for Constructing Theatrical Scenes and Machines*, which told how oil lights could be dimmed by lowering tin cylinders over the flames. But these early lighting design techniques were complicated and their effects modest. Because the light in the theatre was so dim, the auditorium and audience had to be lit as well as the stage. The actors resorted to painting their faces with cosmetics so that their expressions could be seen.

By the 1840s gas-lit theatres were common. There were even gas-powered spotlights, in which jets of hydrogen and oxygen were ignited with small bits of

Michael Earl/University of Wyoming Archives

Figure 9.6 *A white model from a production of* All My Sons*, prepared by designer Michael Earl.*

Michael Earl/University of Wyoming Archives

Figure 9.7 *The second model in full color. Both the white and color models must be built exactly to scale so that the director can visualize blocking and anticipate any problems before the set is built. This model and the white model shown in Figure 9.6 are quite small, only about 18 inches wide by 12 inches tall.*

Michael Earl/University of Wyoming Archives

Figure 9.8 *The final set for* All My Sons.

lime; this is the source of the word **limelight** and the phrase "to be in the limelight." Needless to say, all that gas made theatres prone to fire. For example, the Paris Opéra used twenty-eight miles of tubing to carry the highly flammable gas to all its lights. In 1856 the magazine *The Builder* stated that it was the fate of all

SPOTLIGHT ON The Life of a Designer: Ming Cho Lee

Ming Cho Lee has been called the "dean" of American scene design. Born in Shanghai, Lee's parents divorced when he was six and, as was common in China at the time, he lived with his father. "I had weekend visits with my mother, and those were the great moments of my life," he recalled. His mother took him to the theatre, movies, and Chinese opera. She also allowed him to study drawing and watercolor painting. In 1949 he came to the United States and studied art, design, and theatre at Occidental College and UCLA before moving to New York City, where he became the principal designer for the New York Shakespeare Company, the Juilliard Opera Theatre, and the Peabody Arts Theatre in Baltimore.

Lee became known for his minimalist sets that used basic colors and geometric shapes to create "environments" rather than realistic-looking settings. He did not, however, limit himself to minimalism. One of his most famous sets was for Patrick Meyers' play *K2*. Although he made the rocky face of the world's second tallest mountain (Everest is the tallest) from sculpted Styrofoam covered with layers of tissue and paint, the audience could believe that the actors were really hanging hundreds of feet in the air. Lee won the 1983 Tony Award for best set design for *K2*. Other famous shows he has designed include the original production of the rock musical *Hair*, a revival of Arthur Miller's *The Crucible*, Ntozake Shange's *For Colored Girls Who Have Considered Suicide/When the Rainbow Is Enuf*, and Michael Cristofer's *The Shadow Box*.

In 1969 Lee became a professor of design at Yale School of Drama, where he trained many of today's important set designers, including John Lee Beatty, Heidi Landesman, Michael Yeargan, Marjorie Bradley Kellogg, Adrianne Lobel, and Douglas Schmidt. "Teaching," says Lee, "forces a teacher to always go through a process of self-evaluation." And self-evaluation is at the heart of all art.

Lee is a strong supporter of multiculturalism and laments the lack of it in U.S. design today. He believes its absence is "linked to the lack of visibility of designers and production people. A black child can see black actors and say, 'I want to do that.' He or she can read about black directors. But if that child sees a set or a lighting design, there's no sense of who is responsible for it. It's almost as if it came into being completely on its own somehow." Lee feels the only way to combat the problem is for designers of color to become more visible. "We must let young people know, and I mean young Asian, black, Latino, and Native American boys and girls, that this kind of expression is available to them, that they can survive in this field, and they don't have to give up who they are to do so."

AP Photo/Gary He

Theatre designer Ming Cho Lee

Michal Daniel/Proofsheet

This set design by Ming Cho Lee for Eugene O'Neill's Ah! Wilderness *illustrates his characteristically spare use of color and shapes to suggest a more substantial environment. This 2001–2002 production by the Guthrie Theater was directed by Douglas C. Wager.*

> Light is the most important medium on the stage. . . . Without its unifying power, our eyes would be able to perceive what objects were but not what they expressed. . . . What can give us this sublime unity which is capable of uplifting us: . . . Light!
>
> ***Adolphe Appia,***
> Lighting designer

theatres to eventually burn down. In the nineteenth century over ten thousand people died in theatre fires in England alone. That fate changed in 1881 with the advent of electric lights. For the first time in theatre's history, lighting designers could adequately light the stage and allow the audience to sit in the dark. Soon there were master lighting designers, such as Adolphe Appia (1862–1928), who used light, shadows, and color to create complex lighting effects. However, lighting design as an art form continued to be unrecognized until 1970—when the first Tony Award was given for lighting design. Today, theatrical lighting has become a refined art. Designers have a wide range of instruments and effects at their disposal, and new inventions continue to improve the art.

One of the most important advances in lighting design was the invention of computerized lighting, which allows an entire lighting design, including hundreds of exact levels and cues, to be controlled by a computerized light board called a **dimmer**. The first Broadway play to use a computerized light board was the musical *A Chorus Line* in 1975, which was lit by Tony Award–winning lighting designer Tharon Musser. Using computer-controlled dimmers, said Musser, means that a designer can "have consistency and smoothness. You get the same show every night." Today, with a touch of a button, computerized light boards allow the lighting designer to set exact light levels and program fade-ins and fade-outs for hundreds of lights. There are even dimmers that allow audio coordinated light cues to be precisely synchronized with music and sound effects. And when the lighting designer's work is done, an entire lighting design can be stored on a small disk or a keychain flash drive.

Modern, computerized light boards can be found in almost every theatre's light booth. Here, light board operator Danielle Fullerton makes a few adjustments prior to a technical rehearsal. Through the light booth's window she can see the lighting effects on the stage below.

Lou Anne Wright

The latest advances in lighting design are software programs that allow designers to create three-dimensional designs and perform simulated lighting effects on their computers. Before the advent of this technology, their only option was to make simple renderings to demonstrate what the final lighting design would look like. This meant that their design could not be shown to the director until after the lights were actually hung and aimed—just days before a play opened. But today, with the help of these powerful software programs, lighting designers can make photorealistic pictures and real-time lighting computer simulations that allow everyone involved with the production to know exactly what the final results will be, long before the set is built or the costumes stitched.

Before lighting designers sit down with their dimmers or computers, however, they study the script and meet with the director and other designers to discuss the overall look of the production. The most central role of the lighting designer is to evoke mood. Because of this they need more than just knowledge of computer software, lighting instruments, and circuitry. They must also understand art and human emotions. As a result, lighting designers often study painting, optics, and art. The great designer Robert Edmond Jones said, "At rare moments, in the long quiet hours of light-rehearsals, a strange thing happens. We are overcome by a realization of the *livingness* of light. As we gradually bring a scene out of the shadows, sending long rays slanting across a column, touching an outline with color, animating the scene moment by moment until it seems to breathe, our work becomes an incantation. We feel the presence of elemental energies."

Using various instruments and effects, a lighting designer can create almost anything the director or script calls for—from stark earthbound reality to a fantastic sky, as in this dance production designed by Larry Hazlett.

Larry Hazlett/University of Wyoming Archives

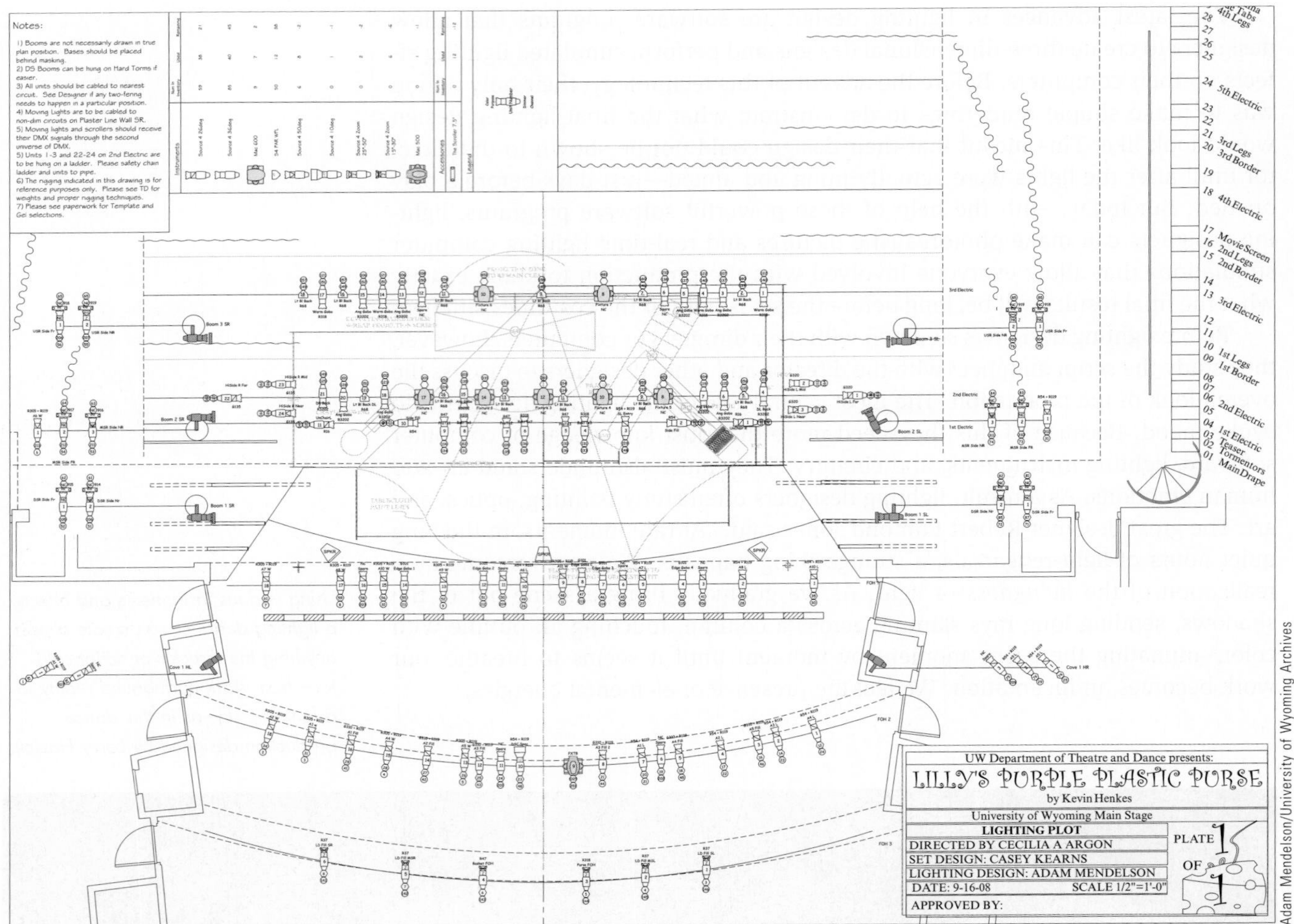

Figure 9.9 *A light plot is a detailed drawing that shows the locations of lighting instruments, wattage, color, and other details necessary to the lighting design. A light plot is a record of the designer's vision and a map that guides the crew in hanging and positioning the lights. The light plot pictured here was created by Adam Mendelson for the children's play* Lilly's Purple Plastic Purse.

Stage lighting can be divided into two categories: motivated and nonmotivated. **Motivated light** comes from an identifiable source such as a candle, a table lamp, or the sun. **Nonmotivated light** reinforces the mood of a scene but doesn't necessarily come from an identifiable or onstage source. Nonmotivated light can be obvious or faint, and the lighting designer can change the light's direction, balance, and color in order to create cool shadows or warm highlights. These shadows and highlights establish a scene's mood, space, and environment. For every light cue the audience is aware of, dozens of other more subtle light changes affect the audience subconsciously.

Once a firm concept is developed, lighting designers draw **lighting plots** (often with the help of computers) that detail the location of each lighting instrument and where its light will be focused (see Figure 9.9). The lighting plot also shows the type of lighting instrument, the circuitry necessary, the wattage, and the colors. Lighting designers employ a multitude of techniques for achieving various effects. They can filter the light through gels to change color. **Gels** were once made of gelatin but today are made of plastic and come in thousands of colors, giving the lighting designer an almost limitless palette. Patterns, such as sunlight coming through the leaves of a tree, can be projected on the stage with metal cutouts, called **gobos**, placed in front of the light. Other more sophisticated devices make it possible to project moving clouds, flickering fire, or twinkling stars. When the lighting plot is finished, the designer gives it to crews and electricians who hang and focus each light. Once each light is circuited to the main lightboard, the lighting designer programs the computer with hundreds of cues, setting the length and intensity of each cue. During technical rehearsals, lighting designers often refine the lights—making sure each light is exactly aimed as they reprogram the computer—so that each fade is to the director's liking. Once the play opens, they leave the running of the lights to the stage manager and electricians.

Designing the Sound

The ancient Greeks used simple implements to imitate wind, rain, and thunder. The Romans went further and built copper-lined thunder tunnels in the floors of their theatres. Stagehands dropped boulders down these tunnels to create the sound of distant thunder or, if the boulders were large enough, an earthquake effect. Some fifteen hundred years later, Shakespeare's plays included the sound effects of trumpet fanfares and cannon fire to thrill the audience and help set the scene. In fact, one of these sound effects was the reason that Shakespeare's theatre burned to the ground in 1613: a spark from one of the cannons lit the roof on fire. In minutes the wooden theatre was engulfed in flames, creating a special effect a little more spectacular than the one Shakespeare intended. Many forms of non-Western theatre also use sound effects. For example, Japanese Kabuki theatre uses special floor resonators to amplify the sounds of the actors' feet as they dance.

> I think of light as music for the eye. I can lead an audience fluidly from one place to another, from one feeling to another. . . . It tells you where to look; it tells you how to feel about what you see.
>
> ***Jennifer Tipton***
> Lighting designer

Today's sound designers can record, mix, filter, reverberate, modulate, amplify, and cue up sound effects exactly when they are needed. They record sounds from real life, and they use sounds from vast sound libraries that contain everything from distant foghorns to birds singing in the morning, and from crickets chirping on a calm night to deadly gunfire. Sound designers in the theatre and in film can also digitally sculpt sounds in order to get the right ring of a doorbell, and they can synthesize sounds for the exact tone needed to convey a particular emotion or meaning. Sound designers may take extraordinary steps to get the perfect sound. The sound of Luke Skywalker's land speeder in *Star Wars* (1977) was made by recording Los Angeles freeway traffic through a vacuum-cleaner tube. The sounds of torpedoes firing in *The Hunt for Red October* (1990) were layered with animal growls, a Ferrari engine, and a screeching screen-door spring.

Theatrical sound designers, like their film counterparts, spend hours trying to synthesize and record the exact sounds needed because the right sound can often express things that words cannot. They also design systems to amplify an actor or singer's voice to make sure they can be heard. Yet their hard work often goes unrecognized—it wasn't until 2008 that Broadway presented Tony Awards for best sound design of a play and of a musical, which went to *The 39 Steps* and *South Pacific*, respectively. Speaking about the lack of recognition, sound designer John Gromada once said, "Often critics credit the directors with the work that we do. . . . I've written to these critics to say, 'I don't care if you like my work or don't like my work. Just mention my name.'"

Sound designers must have a detailed knowledge of acoustics, electronics, digital music editing programs, audio mixing boards and signal processing equipment, microphones, effects processors, and amplifiers. They must also know exactly where to place speakers to get the desired effect. In addition, some sound designers are also composers or musicians: they write and play transition music or underscore scenes with mood music.

> The only time a sound designer is mentioned in a review is when the critic doesn't like what you're doing. "The tinny, loud sound,' they'll write. Or 'the excruciatingly distorted sound." They rarely say anything positive about your sound reinforcement.
>
> ***Scott Lehrer,***
> Sound designer

Designing the Costumes

As long as there has been theatre, there have been costumes. In precolonial African theatre, masks and costumes were an integral part of the performance. Four hundred years before the birth of Christ, the Greeks used costumes in their tragedies to reveal the characters' mood and enhance their performances. In Shakespeare's day, wealthy lords and ladies donated their worn gowns and leggings to the local theatre so that actors might have a variety of outfits to choose from. Costumes can be exaggerated like those in the Japanese Kabuki theatre or understated, as is often the case in modern realistic plays. Whether they are larger than life or subtle, all costumes reflect and establish the character's social and economic status, lifestyle, age, country, occupation, education, and geographical origin. The costumes also reflect the historical period, season, and even the time of day. Further, costumes must fit the needs of the script, the budget of the theatre, the style of the set, the color of lights, and the production concept. Therefore the costume designer must be a visual artist, fashion designer, historian, and psychoanalyst.

Like all other designers, the costume designer is an expert at play analysis, especially character analysis. This is why most costume designers begin with the words the characters say. "I start with the text," says Tony-nominated costume designer Constance Hoffman, "No matter what the nature of the project is, that's where I begin and what I use as a touchstone and a resource for everything that the design becomes." Starting with the text helps the designer determine if a character is going to dress to impress others, to attract a mate, to intimidate, to celebrate, to imitate, to be comfortable, to be in style, to rebel, or for any other purpose. There is no such thing as a "generic" costume; every color, fold, and cut is a reflection of character. As part of their work, costume designers often design accessories such as hats, jewelry, purses, shoes, and even watches because these items reveal character in much the same way that clothing does. For the same reason, they also may design the actors' hairstyles and sometimes even their makeup.

Costume designers use all the standard design elements—line, mass, balance, harmony, composition, movement, texture, and color. Choosing the right colors for a costume not only requires artistic judgment but also an understanding of the psychological effects each color has on an audience, as well as how each color will appear under tinted theatrical lights. Costume designers must also take into account how the costume will fit the body type and shape of the actor cast for the role. In addition, they appreciate the movement of different fabrics—some are flowing and others stiff—and the various effects they can create. Designers must also consider how the costume will work during the performance. If the costume has a large hoop skirt, it must be made to fit through doorways. If there is a fight sequence, then they must build a durable costume that can take wear and tear.

Not all costumes are designed and built from scratch. Sometimes costume designers buy outfits off the rack at local department stores, and other times they will shop for pieces at thrift stores. A theatre can also borrow costumes from patrons or rent them from large costume rental companies. Renting costumes is always a compromise, because what the costume rental companies have in stock is unlikely to fit the production concept. And, although it saves time, renting can be expensive: the rental, insurance, cleaning, and shipping fees add up to a substantial amount. Another option is to "pull" a show, or take the costumes from the theatre's storage vaults. Most college and professional theatre companies have huge costume vaults where they store thousands of costumes of various styles, sizes, and historical periods that were either created for other productions, donated, or purchased. Pulling costumes from a show can save the theatre a great deal of time and money; however, unless the vault contains exactly what the play or director requires, numerous alterations must be made.

Like all other designers, costume designers attend production meetings and use drawings to communicate what the designs will look like. The first costume renderings are tentative sketches, which can go through many variations before the final design is set in stone. Once the designs are agreed upon, the costume designers decide which costumes they will buy, borrow, rent, and build.

In order to build a costume, a designer paints or sketches detailed **costume plates** that the costume construction crew will use to assemble the costumes. These sketches indicate how each costume is shaped, where seams and folds are, how the costume flows, and what fabrics should be used—some designers even attach fabric swatches to the plates. (See Figures 9.10–9.13.)

At smaller theatres the costume designer sometimes doubles as head of the costume-construction crew. But at larger and professional theatres the designer leaves the constructing of the costumes to patternmakers, cutters, tailors, and fitters. Depending on the size and type of show, the building of the costumes can take weeks. Once the costumes are done, a **dress parade** is held. The actors try on their costumes and parade in front of the costume designer and director, who confer on changes needed before opening night.

Lee Hodgson/University of Wyoming Archives

Figure 9.10

University of Wyoming Archives

Figure 9.11

Figures 9.10 shows designer Lee Hodgson's rendering for the University of Wyoming's production of William Shakespeare's Love's Labour's Lost. *Costume renderings give the director and designers a sense of how the costumes will look and move. They are also invaluable guides for the cutters and sitchers who build the costumes. Figure 9.11 shows the finished costumes.*

University of Wyoming Archives

Lee Hodgson/University of Wyoming Archives

Figure 9.12

Figure 9.13

Figure 9.13 shows Lee Hodgson's rendering for the University of Wyoming's production of children's play Lily's Purple Plastic Purse. *Figure 9.12 shows the final costume's appearance Notice how closely the finished costume matches the rendering.*

> As a costume designer, you don't get credit for a great performance, but rarely do you have a great performance with a terrible costume.
>
> ***Susan Hilferty,***
> Costume designer

Designing the Props

One of the rarest designers in the theatre is the prop designer. As discussed in Chapter 5, "prop" is theatre lingo for theatrical property or just property. Properties generally mean **set props**, or anything that sits on the set including sofas, chairs, and beds, and **hand props**, or any objects actors handle while on stage, such as pens, fans, cigars, money, and umbrellas. Prop designers are responsible for envisioning, building, finding, and, if necessary, renting the props. They also find, rent, and design set decorations. **Set decorations** are similar to props except that they are items that are not touched by actors. For example, if an actor touches a picture on the shelf, it is a prop; if they don't touch it, then it is considered set decoration. Generally a prop designer builds props only when they cannot be found. They will often spend their time looking through antique stores, junk shops, and bargain stores trying to find exactly what the play needs. If they can't find it or if the prop is something that doesn't exist in real life, such as the huge man-eating plant in the musical *Little Shop of Horrors*, then the prop designer designs and builds it. Prop designers work much like set designers. They make a series of sketches or use CAD programs to design props. If a theatre doesn't have (or can't afford to hire) a prop designer, oftentimes the set designer must design the props as well.

REUTERS/CORBIS

Makeup design is often the responsibility of the costume designer, but makeup artists are hired for complicated makeup designs, as in the musical Cats. Makeup effects can be achieved by painting the face with color, shadows, and highlights or by using three-dimensional pieces such as beards, wigs, false noses, scars, or, in this case, whiskers.

Preparing Makeup, Wigs, and False Noses

Around the world and over the centuries, actors have used makeup to disguise and to exaggerate their features. Japanese Kabuki theatre is known for its striking, stylized makeup that exaggerates the actors' features. In the West there are two categories of makeup. **Straight makeup** does not change the actors' looks, but makes their faces look more three-dimensional and therefore more visible to the audience because the bright theatrical lights wash out their facial features. Actors also wear makeup so they will look more like the character they are playing and less like themselves. **Character makeup** is an attempt to transform the way actors look—for example, by adding gray hair, wrinkles, and shadows to a youthful actor who must play an old man. The type and the amount of makeup actors need changes with every production. For a realistic play in a small theatre, the actors might wear no makeup. For a realistic play in a large theatre, the actors might wear lots of powder and rouge to add shadows and highlights so that they can be seen from the back row. For a nonrealistic or highly stylized play, they may have to come in many hours before curtain so that an artist can apply layers of special makeup. Actors who are playing a character much older, younger, or different from themselves might also need to wear a beard or a wig. These are often designed by the costume designer and constructed by a specialized wig maker.

If the play requires only straight makeup, the actors often do it themselves. All actor-training programs include classes in how to create and apply a makeup scheme. But more complicated makeup often requires a makeup designer. The musicals *Cats* and *Beauty and the Beast* needed a makeup designer to design exactly how each character should look and to make renderings of the design much like those of costume and set designers. If a special prosthetic piece, such as a scar, a false nose, or a wart, is needed, the makeup designer makes a plaster cast of the actor's face and casts the prosthesis in synthetic rubber. An exact fit allows the prosthesis to be held on with just a dab of nontoxic theatrical glue.

Curtain Call

In the last analysis the designing of stage scenery is not the problem of an architect or a painter or a sculptor or even a musician, but of a poet.

Robert Edmond Jones,
Theatre designer

Once the designs are finished, they are turned over to the technical director (or TD in theatre lingo). The TD turns the designers' drawings, paintings, blueprints, models, and sketches into fully realized sets, lights, and costumes. The TD usually presides over large construction crews who build the set, stitch the costumes, and hang the lights. For a small or simple production these crews may consist of only a few people, but most plays have dozens of crew members and they almost always outnumber the actors. (For more on the ensemble that makes theatre work, see Chapter 5.)

In the end, just days before the play opens, everything comes together with the technical rehearsals. The first tech rehearsals combine sound and lights with the set. These rehearsals are often called so that the crews can ensure they have everything covered. Next come the dress rehearsals when the actors get to rehearse in costumes for the first time. The night before the play opens is the final dress rehearsal. At this point, the only thing missing is the audience—even the curtain call is run to a mostly empty house and the only people sitting in the dark are the designers. (For more on the various types of rehearsals, see Chapter 7.) Although the designers aren't part of the curtain call, their work is onstage for all to applaud.

About the challenges of being a designer, Robert Edmond Jones said:

> The designer is forced to work and think in a hundred different ways—now as an architect, now as a house-painter, now as an electrician, now as a dress-maker, now as a sculptor, now as a jeweler. He must make idols and palaces and necklaces and frescoes and caparisons. As he works, he may be all too well aware of the outward limitations of the play he is to decorate and the actors he is to clothe. But in his mind's eye he must see the high original intention of the dramatist and follow it.

Summary

Designers have been a part of the theatre for thousands of years. Whether plain or complex, their job is to remind the audience of where the characters are supposed to be—in other words, to create the play's environment. To do this, designers must do a lot of homework. They must research and analyze the play's dramatic structure, period, history, location, mood, characters, and theme. They must also take into account the budget and the physical configuration and size of the theatre: proscenium arch, thrust, arena, or black box.

All designers work with a director to create the production concept, which is devised from the master symbol or allegory and becomes the central metaphor for the production. The director and designers must also decide what style the play will reflect: naturalism, realism, selective realism, expressionism, surrealism, or symbolism.

Once they have a production concept, the designers make numerous drawings, renderings, thumbnail sketches, models, and plans of the sets, costumes, and lights. Many, if not most, designers have a strong background in art and history as well as interior design, architecture, and theatre. They must know how to paint, draw, and draft. The process of designing a set can take months as the designers move from thumbnail drawings, rough drawings, and final drawings to models and blueprints. Once the designs are done, the technical director and construction crews turn them into fully realized sets, lights, and costumes. Technological advances have had a great effect on design methods, and therefore on the theatre as a whole. From acoustic modeling of auditoriums and computer-controlled lights to automatic fly systems, the theatre is quickly catching up with the modern world.

The Art of Theatre ONLINE

To access this chapter's interactive theatre workshop activities, along with many other learning tools, log onto your Theatre CourseMate. Access is available at cengagebrain.com.

Key Terms

apron / 198
arena theatre / 199
basic elements of design / 204
black box theatre / 199
character makeup / 217
computer aided design (CAD) / 205
costume plate / 215
dimmer / 210
dress parade / 215
elevations / 205
expressionism / 202
floor plan / 205
fly system / 198
found, or created, space / 198
gel / 212
gobo / 212
hand props / 216
lighting plot / 212
limelight / 208
lip / 198
motivated light / 212
nonmotivated light / 212
proscenium arch / 198
realism / 202
selective realism / 202
set decoration / 216
set props / 216
sight lines / 199
simplified, or suggested, realism / 202
straight makeup / 217
surrealism / 203
symbolism / 203
thrust stage / 198
vomitories / 198
wings / 198

The musical Hair, book and lyrics by James Rado and Gerome Ragni, and music by Galt MacDermot was first staged in 1967. The creators of Hair changed the way audiences viewed the American musical by confronting issues of race, sexual freedom, drug use and America's involvement in foreign wars. This revival opened in New York in 2009

Photos on this spread Sara Krulwich/The New York Times/Redux

CHAPTER 10

A Creative Life

OUTLINE

In his book *The Big Questions,* philosopher Lou Marinoff says, "if you regularly experience hallucinations—that is, if you see and hear things that no one else sees and hears—you might be called "psychotic," and diagnosed with a psychiatric disease. Then again, if you see things that no one else sees and turn them into movies, or hear things that no one else hears and turn them into symphonies, then possibly you are a director or composer." And yet creativity is more than just imagination. It is the adrenaline rush and "aha!" that happens when we find an answer that has not been found before. It is a moment of enlightenment that solves a problem, thereby adding value to our lives. The creative moment may happen in a flash, but it almost always follows years of hard work, research, and thinking. The desire to live a creative life is one of the main reasons people go into the theatre, but creativity is hardly limited to the arts.

Creativity

Mihaly Csikszentmihalyi (pronounced "Chick-sent-me-high-ee"), a leading researcher on creativity, wrote in his book *Creativity*, "Most of us assume that artists—musicians, writers, poets and painters—are strong on the fantasy side, whereas scientists, politicians, and businesspeople are realists. This may be true in the terms of day-to-day routine activities. But when a person begins to work creatively, all bets are off—the artist may be as much a realist as the physicist, and the physicist as imaginative as the artist." Let's clear up some of the many fallacies surrounding creative thinking as we attempt to answer an important question: how can you be more creative, whether as an artist, business person, astronaut, or physician's assistant—in whatever endeavor you pursue?

In order to answer the question, we must first define what creativity is. **Creativity** is discovery. It is the moment someone invents something that is new or transforms something extant, thereby adding value to our culture, society, or lives. It can be a major flash of inspiration that changes the world, or a moment

SPOTLIGHT ON Identify Your Intelligences and Cultivate Your Creativity[1]

One of the keys to discovering our talents and being more creative is to identify the types of intelligences in which we excel. In recent years, the theory of multiple intelligences has become popular among educators because it allows us to account for an expanded range of human potential. Formulated by Howard Gardner, professor at the Harvard Graduate School of Education, the theory states that we all possess different types of intelligence, not just the kind measured with a standard IQ test. It is our unique combination of these intelligences that makes up our talents.

We've all heard stories of geniuses who had trouble with tasks that seem elementary to the rest of us. British playwright, critic, and essayist George Bernard Shaw could write great stories, unforgettable characters, and powerful criticism, but he had trouble spelling. Similarly, American statesman, inventor, and philosopher Benjamin Franklin had trouble with simple math. Because we all possess different degrees of the various kinds of intelligences, we all have areas in which we struggle and ones in which we shine. Often we are unaware of our particular gifts—our talents just seem natural to us. The first step in discovering and cultivating our talents is to find out which types of intelligence are our strengths. In his book *Frames of Mind: The Theory of Multiple Intelligences*, Gardner identifies six forms of intelligence: linguistic, musical, logical-mathematical, spatial, bodily-kinesthetic, and personal.

- **Linguistic intelligence.** This kind of intelligence is the understanding of how language works and the ability to use language to convince others and express ideas. According to Gardner, "In the poet's struggle over the wording of a line or stanza, one sees at work some central aspects of linguistic intelligence." Not only poets but also playwrights, writers, political leaders, actors, and legal experts possess a high level of linguistic intelligence. Its characteristic is a great technical facility with words and language.
- **Musical intelligence.** This is the ability to recognize, remember, and organize tones and musical patterns. The musical mind is concerned with pitch, melody, rhythm, and harmonic elements of sound. We say of these people that they have a "gifted ear." Gardner notes, "Of all the gifts with which individuals may be endowed, none emerges earlier than musical talent." People who have a strong musical intelligence are often also gifted in math. People who possess a high degree of musical intelligence include composers, musicians, singers, music critics, and recording engineers.
- **Logical-mathematical intelligence.** This is the ability to order and unify structures and to perceive patterns and causal relationships. This

[1]Adapted from Howard Gardner, Frames of Mind: The Theory of Multiple Intelligences, 1983. Perseus Books Group.

of insight into just about anything—big or small. For example, David Perkins of Harvard University (co-director of Project Zero, a research project studying cognitive skills among scientists and artists), recalled a story of a friend who stopped to have a picnic while traveling in France. He had all the ingredients needed for a fine lunch: cheese, bread, and wine. But he lacked one key item, a knife with which to slice the cheese. He thought for a moment, took out his credit card, and set out to slice the cheese. Perkins points out that this is a great example of small, everyday creativity. He feels that we should not conceptualize creativity as something that only happens in elitist circles, artistic endeavors, or in ivory towers. Creativity is all around us, and we are all capable of being creative.

Because creative work depends on a certain level of specialized knowledge, some people think that artists must be extremely intelligent people. However, studies have found that an extremely high IQ (intelligence quotient) is not necessarily a great advantage when it comes to being creative. Having an IQ over 120, which is "high-average intelligence" according to the Stanford-Binet Intelligence Scale, doesn't seem to make people more creative. What does matter is the *type* of intelligence an individual has. (For more on this subject, see the Spotlight "Identify Your Intelligences and Cultivate Your Creativity.") As a result, a person of slightly

"Creativity consists of 1 percent inspiration and 99 percent perspiration."

Thomas Edison,
Inventor

ability can be related to material objects but it more often takes an abstract form, as with mathematics. People with a high degree of this type of intelligence look for order in what may appear to be chaos. They can perceive and define the relationship between parts of a whole. Philosophers, scientists, and mathematicians often possess a high level of logical-mathematical intelligence.

- **Spatial intelligence.** This is the ability to sense and retain visual images and to mentally manipulate them. It includes the abilities to transform two-dimensional images into three-dimensional objects and to make mental models, which are the key to understanding many scientific concepts. Sculptors, architects, football coaches, and theatre directors all must have a high degree of this type of intelligence. It is also important to anyone who must read maps or create diagrams.
- **Bodily-kinesthetic intelligence.** At first the idea of body movements being a form of intelligence may seem strange. But our brain monitors our body's activity and allows us to judge the timing, force, and extent of our movements. When certain parts of the brain are injured, motor movements can be impaired even though the muscles are fully capable. This type of intelligence also includes eye-hand coordination and fine motor movements. Athletes, dancers, pianists, and actors need a high level of bodily-kinesthetic intelligence.
- **Personal intelligences.** Intrapersonal intelligence is the ability to understand one's own feelings. This talent can also be turned outward in the form of interpersonal intelligence, or the ability to understand the moods, motivations, and intentions of others. Those who need this ability to "read" other people include political and religious leaders, parents, teachers, therapists, counselors, doctors, nurses, and social workers.

To illustrate these various intelligences, Gardner points out that "Sigmund Freud was the exemplar of intrapersonal intelligence; Albert Einstein represented logical-mathematical intelligence; Pablo Picasso, spatial intelligence; Igor Stravinsky, musical intelligence; T. S. Eliot, linguistic intelligence; Martha Graham, bodily-kinesthetic intelligence; and Mahatma Gandhi, interpersonal intelligence." However, most activities require more than one form of intelligence. Dancers combine bodily-kinesthetic, spatial, and musical intelligences. Journalists use interpersonal and linguistic intelligences. Portrait photographers combine spatial and personal intelligences to fully capture their clientele. Engineers need spatial and logical-mathematical intelligence to create their products and linguistic intelligence to explain them. Our unique combination of intelligences forms the building blocks of our talents, and when we discover our unique talents, we are better able to cultivate our creativity.

> While the intelligent person arrives at the correct answer more or less quickly, the creative individual is more likely to be fluent, to come up with many plausible answers and, perhaps, even with some answers of striking originality.
>
> ***Howard Gardner and Constance Wolf,***
>
> Psychologists, in "The fruits of asynchrony: A psychological examination of creativity"

above-average intelligence can often be just as creative as one with a very high IQ. More important to creativity than raw intelligence are technique and talent.

Creativity and Technique

Imagine a talented actor playing the role of Shakespeare's Hamlet. The audience is enthralled, the performance is winning the hearts of the critics, but is the actor being creative? He may be having an adrenaline rush, but has he come up with unique answers about the role of Hamlet? Is he solving problems, thereby adding value to the role of Hamlet? More than likely, during a performance, the actor is not being creative, but is instead relying on technique. **Techniques** are procedures that have been proven to work repeatedly. They are methods by which a complex task can be accomplished, such as raising a child, fixing a heart valve, or playing a Shakespearean character. Technique is what we learn from being creative. The actual creativity for our Hamlet actor more than likely occurred during the rehearsal process, not during his performance.

Many of us, just like our Shakespearean actor, depend on technique. We learn techniques that are based on other people's creativity; Einstein's equation $E = mc^2$ was originally his creative solution to understanding energy and mass, but today it is part of the standard technique that all students learn in physics class. Only when students master a given subject can they begin to have spontaneous moments of creativity about it. And mastering a subject takes time. In most fields of study, including the theatre, achieving technical expertise can take decades. The French playwright Alexandre Dumas *fils* (1824–1895) ("*fils*" is the French word for son—he was the son of a famous writer of the same name) once said, "Technique is so important that it sometimes happens that technique is mistaken for art."

> It takes at least five years of rigorous training to be spontaneous.
>
> ***Martha Graham,***
>
> Dancer and choreographer

Creativity and Talent

Talent is natural ability. One of the key tests of talent is time. For example, if one hundred people spent ten hours learning to play baseball, all of them would probably understand the game but some would be better players than others. We would say that these players have a talent for playing baseball. A common question is, are we born with talent or can it be developed? The answer is both.

Our environment is one of the chief factors that helps us develop our talents. Even though we are all born with particular talents, environment can dictate whether we develop or deny them. For example, many people who play the piano come from a home where at least one parent played the piano or was interested in music. Drew Barrymore, producer and star of the movie *Charlie's Angels* and a veteran of over eighty other films and TV shows since the age of seven, when she starred in Steven Spielberg's *E.T.*, comes from a family of famous actors going back to her grandfather, John Barrymore. Naturalist Charles Darwin's grandfather was interested in early theories of evolution. Physicist Albert Einstein's father studied math. Our culture, religion, and society, as well as our home environment, can also affect talent. For instance, you may have the talent to be a great dancer, but if you grow up in a cultural environment that forbids dancing, you're less likely to develop that talent.

Different talents develop at different ages. Musical, mathematical, and acting talent can appear at an early age, but talent for playwriting, philosophy, and poetry seldom emerge until people are in their mid or even late twenties.

Robbie Jack/CORBIS

Actors are able to be creative as they explore a character during the rehearsal process. But because they are expected to follow a playwright's direction and dialogue, they are not usually able to be creative during the run of a play. If an actor is not able to be particularly creative during a play, what is it that makes audiences and critics so pleased with her performance? The answer is technique. For example, Nicole Kidman's technique in The Blue Room *won her rave reviews from critics. The play was adapted by David Hare from* La Ronde *by Arthur Schnitzler. The 1998 production also starred Iain Glen and was directed by Sam Mendes at the Donmar Warehouse, London.*

However, even child prodigies can improve upon their natural talent by gaining technique through practice. For example, Austrian composer Wolfgang Amadeus Mozart began studying music at the age of four and wrote his first symphony at the age of eight. But only 12 percent of his compositions were written in the first ten years of his career and few of them are popular today. Yes, Mozart was a child prodigy and he had natural talent, but he needed to develop his technique to produce the works that have made his creativity legendary. In his book *Creativity: Genius and Other Myths*, Robert Weisberg points out that only three major composers produced masterworks before they had at least ten years of musical practice and preparation. Talent is an important part of creativity, but one must develop technique for talent to be fully revealed.

Creative People

Talent and technique are essential to creativity, but creative people also share certain characteristics. Many researchers, including David Perkins of Harvard University, Mihaly Csikszentmihalyi of Claremont Graduate University, John Dacey of Boston College, and Kathleen Lennon of Framingham State College, have attempted to define these common traits. They have found that creative people have a hopeful outlook when facing complex or difficult tasks, are resourceful when unusual circumstances arise, are less afraid of their own impulses, and enjoy being playful. Creativity and play often go hand in hand. (See the Spotlight "Playfulness: The First Quality of Genius.") Researchers have also found that creative people are exceptionally curious, able to concentrate, skilled at finding order and options, and willing to take risks. Many of these characteristics describe theatre people, but they also describe creative people in all walks of life. The more you can indulge these sides of your own personality, the more you can bring creativity into your life.

A Burning Curiosity

Creative people have a deep desire to understand the world and how it works. As a result, they are open to new experiences and are seldom satisfied with the standard authoritative answers offered by governments, corporations, religions, science, or society. In order to search out new answers, creative people must ask questions that others overlook. Our education system is designed to fill us with answers but is less focused on teaching us how to ask questions. As Wendell Johnson said in his book *People in Quandaries*, "Probably the most impressive indictment that can be made of our educational system is that it provides the students with answers, but it is poorly designed to provide them with skill in the asking of questions that are effectively directive of inquiry and evaluation." Or, to repeat an old adage, a fool knows all the answers, but none of the questions. Creative people ask questions—questions to which there may be no answer, at least not yet.

The Power of Concentration

Creativity is seldom as spontaneous as it looks. It typically comes only after months, years, or decades of hard work. For example, Pablo Picasso produced 20,000 works of art in 75 years, Einstein 248 publications in fifty-three years, Darwin 119 publications in fifty-one years, Freud 330 publications in forty-five years, and Shakespeare 37 plays and more than 150 sonnets in twenty-four years. Creative people are often so focused that they make social errors such as forgetting names or appointments. Sir Isaac Newton (1642–1727) the great English scientist, astronomer, and mathematician, would sometimes not arrive to dinner until an hour after he was called. His concentration so was great that he would simply forget to eat. Other times, while entertaining company, Newton would jot down an idea and become so engrossed in what he was doing that he would disappear into his room and forget that visitors were waiting.

Malcolm Gladwell, a regular contributor to *The New Yorker* and best-selling author, has popularized the "10,000-hour rule" in his recent book *Outliers: The Story of Success*. The "10,000-hour rule" specifically suggests that all masters of creativity—from Bill Gates to Mozart to Helen Mirren—spent a minimum of 10,000 hours practicing in their respective fields before they rose to significant and consistent success. If you find yourself well suited to concentrating on particular tasks for long stretches of time, take note: those tasks might reveal important areas of creativity for you.

SPOTLIGHT ON Playfulness: The First Quality of Genius

Playfulness has long been associated with creativity. As Donald Newlove says in his book *Invented Voices*, "Playfulness is the first quality of genius—without it we're earthbound." Not only is playfulness an important part of creativity, but many studies have shown that art can foster creativity in young people and can also improve their ability to succeed in school. A study by the Arts Education Partnership found that students with high levels of arts participation outperform "arts-poor" students by virtually every measure. Shirley Brice Heath of the Carnegie Foundation for the Advancement of Teaching found that disadvantaged youth involved in after-school arts programs do better in school than those who spend their time in after-school sports or community involvement programs. The National Research Center on the Gifted and Talented at the University of Connecticut found that students involved in the arts have greater motivation to learn; instead of just studying to get the right answer, they enjoy learning for the experience itself. Finally, researchers at Harvard University's Project Zero, an educational research group headed by Howard Gardner, found that students whose education includes art often become passionately engaged by subjects that students with less arts education find "boring," such as classical works and Shakespeare.

Theatre is a great way to expose children to the arts because it often includes many different art forms, such as instrumental music, singing, storytelling, dance, and art. Unlike television, children's theatre does not allow children to watch passively; instead they must often join in. The first children's theatre in the United States was founded in 1901. Today, there are hundreds of children's theatre companies across the United States that recognize the connection between children, the arts, and creativity. Many of them have theatre-arts training classes in which children gain greater concentration, coordination, communication skills, and self-confidence, as well as increase their creativity and intelligence. Theatre classes can also enhance children's literacy, develop their storytelling abilities, expand their imaginations, and broaden their cultural and individual identities as it opens their minds to alternative perspectives.

Rob Levine/Courtesy The Children's Theatre Company, Minneapolis

Children's theatre provides kids with a fun opportunity to express their creativity. In this production of Dr. Seuss' The 500 Hats of Bartholomew Cubbins, *kids learned about acting, singing, dancing, and working with older, more experienced actors. This play, based on a book by Dr. Seuss, featured J. P. Fitzgibbons as King Derwin of Didd and Ryan Howell as Bartholomew Cubbins. It was adapted for the stage by Timothy Mason and was directed and choreographed by Matthew Howe.*

The Ability to Find Order

Creative people have the ability to find or create order where others see chaos. Order is created when we make analogies, find similarities, connect ideas that have not been previously connected, uncover new possibilities, and discover or invent structure. Structure can be real, like the composition of an atom, or imagined like the design of a play. Both are important because we not only have the ability to ascertain the world in which we find ourselves, but to recreate it. Structure is essential because, as we mentioned in Chapter 1, when we find or create it, we also discover meaning. Many cultures, governments, societies, and religions have attempted to stifle the never-ending quest for new structures, but the urge is always alive and well as long as a creative individual dares to say, "There must be a better way."

Mental Agility and the Ability to Find Options

Creative people have the ability to let their minds roam as they search for new perspectives and new approaches to problems. They use both convergent and divergent thinking. **Convergent thinking** is measured by IQ and involves well-defined rational problems that have only one correct answer. **Divergent thinking** involves fluency and the ability to generate a multitude of ideas from numerous perspectives. However, creative people do not come up with different questions and answers just for the sake of being different. For example, when a creative person is given a psychological examination such as the Rorschach inkblot test (a clinical personality test that uses splotches of ink on a piece of paper), their answers show originality but are not "weird." ("Weird," in this case, means answers that do not have any stimulus from or basis in the inkblot itself.) For instance, if the inkblot looks vaguely like a monkey, a creative person might answer that it looks like Richard Nixon. In other words, the creative person's answer is rooted in some stimulus from the inkblot: if you think about it, Richard Nixon, from the right angle, did have some simian traits. Creative people have mental mobility and the ability to find options based in reality.

> Most of all, forget those romantic myths that creativity is all about being artsy and gifted and not about hard work. They discourage us because we're waiting for that one full-blown moment of inspiration. And while we're waiting, we may never start working on what we might someday create.
>
> ***R. Keith Sawyer,***
> Psychologist

The Willingness to Take Risks and Accept Failure

It is not enough to have a good idea; creative people test their ideas. They seek criticism and they accept failure. Failure is the difference between what we expect and what we get. For many of us, failure is not an option in our jobs or in our lives. But if failure is not an option, then creativity is not an option, because the vast majority of creative work ends in failure. Thomas Edison conducted 2,004 experiments before he found the right filament for the electric light—that means he had 2,003 failures. Pablo Picasso produced 20,000 works of art but many of them were mediocre. Ludwig van Beethoven's musical sketchbooks contain more than 5,000 pages of music that failed to make it into his symphonies. Even Shakespeare wrote plays that might be considered failures; have you ever seen a production of *Timon of Athens* or *King John*? Hans Bethe, winner of the Nobel Prize in physics, said two things are required for creativity: "one is a brain. And second is the willingness to spend long times in thinking, with a definite possibility that you come out with nothing." Creative people have the ability not only to learn from their failures but also to accept failure as an important part of the creative process. They know that the odds of finding a creative answer to a problem are directly related to the number of attempts.

> Ever tried. Ever failed. No matter. Try again. Fail again. Fail better.
>
> ***Samuel Beckett,***
> Playwright and novelist, in *Nohow On: Company, Ill Seen Ill Said, Worstward Ho*

Enhancing Your Creativity

Too often we think of creativity as happening by chance. Or we assume that creativity is something that happens to only talented people. Certainly, luck is involved with being in the right place at the right time, and talent does make it possible to take advantage of opportunities, but as scientist Louis Pasteur (1822–1895) said, "Chance favors the prepared mind." Or as the lawyer Johnnie Cochran (1937–2005) put it a century later, "Luck is the residue of preparation." In other words, with appropriate techniques and developed talents, we all have the potential to be creative. Let's look at a few basic ways to increase creativity.

Consider Your Environment

Greece in the fifth century BCE, Florence in the fifteenth century, and Paris in the nineteenth century were all centers of creative activity. The mingling of different lifestyles and beliefs and the freedom to express them encouraged people in each of these places to exchange ideas and solve problems in new ways. But there have been many more times in history when the environment limited creativity. Conformist cultures and rigid regimes are not as likely to produce creativity as are those where new voices and ideas can be heard and appreciated. Nor is creativity likely in societies or groups where adherence to tradition limits new ideas. Sir Ken Robinson, an expert on creativity, wrote in his book *Out of Our Minds: Learning to Be Creative,* "Creativity prospers best, under particular conditions, especially where there is a flow of ideas between people who have different sorts of expertise." If you seek out places where creativity is allowed, and spend time with people who have different expertise, you will begin to find that elusive creative environment.

Temper Your Criticism

Creative people are always interested in criticism and feedback, but one roadblock to creativity is allowing yourself to be too critical of your new ideas. People are often more creative when they imagine as many solutions as possible and hold off critical judgment until later. (This process, called *brainstorming*, is discussed in detail later in this chapter.) A recent scientific study placed a group of researchers in a closed conference room with a problem to solve. They were told that they should all analytically judge every suggestion as soon as it was offered. After a day of thinking and judging, they failed to solve the problem. The next day they were given an equally difficult problem to solve, but this time they spent the morning pitching possible solutions without judging them or even considering plausibility. That afternoon, the scientists were asked to critically judge each possible solution. It worked—one of their morning pitches solved the problem. By withholding criticism, they succeeded in increasing creativity.

If you constantly censor your ideas, you will stifle your creativity. The next time you have a problem to solve, write down every solution that comes to mind, without censoring any of them. Soon you'll have a list of possible and improbable solutions. Later, come back to the list and evaluate each solution. Nothing is more detrimental to the creative process than censoring every idea you have the moment it's created; this only causes creative gridlock.

Donald Cooper/Photostage Ltd.

It's possible to be creative in almost any environment, but some environments are more conducive to creativity than others. Throughout history, certain parts of the world exploded as centers of creative thought and activity. Examples include ancient Egypt and Greece, Renaissance Europe, and Harlem's "heyday years" from the 1930s to the 1970s. Sometimes works of art celebrate and explore these creative centers, such as John Van Druten's Cabaret, a play centered around the club scene of pre-World War II Berlin. This 1993 revival starred Alan Cummings as the Emcee. Staged at the Donmar Warehouse, London.

Assess Your Motivation

Experts have found that the reason for wanting to be creative can affect the extent of creativity. If a person's primary motivation is a goal outside the creative act itself, he or she will generally be less creative. For example, Konstantin Stanislavsky (1863–1938), the Russian acting teacher and director, observed that actors' creativity is significantly stifled if they are thinking of the audience rather than concentrating on the artistic task. He said that an actor must be able to develop a "circle of his own attention" where other motivations such as wealth, critical praise, or success are unimportant. Beginning artists who dream of becoming wealthy or a star tend to drop out of art if they are not immediately successful. On the other hand, beginning artists who focus only on the creative process tend to stick with it for years and have more opportunities to be creative—and thus have a great chance of becoming wealthy and a star. The same is true in all fields. If the product is more important than the process, you will generally be less creative.

Adjust Your Schedule

Creativity takes time. People whose lives are totally booked with family and work obligations—dashing from school to soccer practice to piano lessons to a part-time job—seldom have much time to be creative. This is true of many Americans. According to a recent report of the International Labour Organization, the United States has surpassed Japan as the nation whose workers put in the most hours in the advanced industrial world. The average American works eight weeks more per year than the average Western European. All this work can be good for personal wealth, the company, or the country, but it can be dangerous for creativity, especially if it is mindless, follow-the-rules work. Creativity requires time to let the mind wander.

Let Your Mind Wander

If your mind wanders while you are trying to take a final exam, you could be in trouble, but there are times when "zoning out" can be quite helpful. Modern researchers find that on average we do a lot of daydreaming. According to two leading researchers, Jonathan Schooler and Jonathan Smallwood of the University of California, Santa Barbara, our minds wander as much as 30 percent of the time. "People assume mind wandering is a bad thing, but if we couldn't do it during a boring task, life would be horrible," Dr. Smallwood insists. Such mind wandering can help foster imagination and creativity. Psychologist R. Keith Sawyer, in his book *Explaining Creativity: The Science of Human Innovation*, says: "In creativity research, we refer to the three Bs—for the bathtub, the bed and the bus—places where ideas have famously and suddenly emerged. When we take time off from working on a problem, we change what we're doing and our context, and that can activate different areas of our brain." It is heartening to know that allowing our minds to wander in appropriate situations can make us more imaginative, productive, and help to incubate new ideas. (For more, see the Spotlight "Creativity Is More Than Imagination.")

SPOTLIGHT ON Creativity Is More Than Imagination

One of the great modern thinkers on creativity is Sir Ken Robinson, who is internationally recognized as an expert on how to enhance creativity. Not only is he a consultant to many Fortune 500 companies, but Queen Elizabeth II knighted him for his service to the arts.

In his book *Out of Our Minds: Learning to Be Creative,* Sir Ken writes that creativity involves *doing,* not just imagining. We all—more or less—have the ability to imagine. Asked to imagine a blue-eyed dog with three legs, you can picture such a likeness in your mind's eye with relative ease. Our imagination can take us on flights of fancy as we generate mental representations of just about anything. But creativity, says Sir Ken, is more complex than simple imagination, because it involves taking action. Creativity involves doing something like mathematics, writing, music, acting, engineering, building a multimillion-dollar business, or any one of a thousand activities.

Furthermore, Sir Ken says that creativity produces outcomes that are original in some form. For example, creativity may result in something novel on a personal level, or unique to a particular community, or original to humanity as a whole. But uniqueness is not enough. In addition to originality, creativity must also be of *value.* Unlike imagination, creativity advances, changes, or improves an individual, a society, or humanity. Creativity, according to Sir Ken, is "*imaginative processes with outcomes that are original and of value.*"

In order to make something that is both original and of value we must be able to perceive and judge the ideas and beliefs through which we frame our understanding of the world, and then make connections that previously went unconnected. So creativity is not a chance event but a conscious effort. The "aha" moment may happen in a second, but taken as a whole, creativity is a process, not an event.

For more on how to be more creative and teach creativity, read Sir Ken Robinson's books.

Many creative people express their creativity in more than one area. In the arts, filmmaker Kitano Takeshi is also a poet and a painter, playwright Samuel Beckett was also a novelist, actor Juliette Lewis is also a musician, and actor Viggo Mortensen is also a photographer. Renowned playwright Sam Shepard, shown here filming his 1994 movie Silent Tongue, *also acts, directs, and once made his living as a musician. If you'd like to make the most of your creative abilities, consider the tips discussed in this chapter. No matter what you're interested in, there's room in your life for a little creativity.*

Bureau L.A. Collection/CORBIS

Change Your Life

> It hinders the creative work of the mind if the intellect examines too closely the ideas as they pour in.
>
> ***Friedrich Schiller,***
> Playwright, poet, and historian

One of the best ways to enhance creativity is to get regular exercise and plenty of sleep. Pulling all-nighters is not a good way to come up with creative answers. Scientists have shown that people whose lives or jobs make too many demands on their sleep are generally less creative than people who get their full seven or eight hours. After sleeping a full night, according to neuroscientist Candace Pert of the National Institute of Mental Health, the body is capable of releasing more endorphins. Endorphins are chemicals that control the brain's perception of, and response to, pain and stress and can help promote a feeling of well-being. Obviously, a feeling of well-being is more conducive to creativity than the state of feeling stressed out.

One simple way to release endorphins in the brain is through exercise. When you exercise, you put yourself into an "endorphinergic state" that can last for hours or days and can increase creativity.

> The principal goal of education in the schools should be creating men and women who are capable of doing new things, not simply repeating what other generations have done; men and women who are creative, inventive, and discoverers, who can be critical and verify, and not accept, everything they are offered.
>
> ***Jean Piaget,***
> Psychologist

Creativity Is about Problem Solving

Without the ability to solve problems, your creativity will be limited. In order to solve a problem, you must first detect a problem. Mihaly Csikszentmihalyi says, "Many creative individuals have pointed out that in their work the formulation of the problem is more important than its solution and that real advances in science and in art tend to come when new questions are asked or old problems are viewed from a new angle." Once you perceive a problem, you need to look for a creative solution.

Here are steps that artists as well as scientists often use when trying to solve a problem:

- **Specify the problem.** The first step in problem solving is to identify the problem in specific terms. In his book *People in Quandaries*, Wendell Johnson recalls a psychiatrist who was often sent patients who had been diagnosed as seriously maladjusted. He noticed they weren't necessarily more maladjusted than the average patient, but they all had one thing in common: "They were unable to tell him clearly what was the matter." They had not been able to tell their doctors what the problem was, so their doctors had been unable to suggest solutions. Johnson goes on to say, "By far the most important step toward the solution of the laboratory problem lies in stating the problem in such a way as to suggest a fruitful attack on it. Once that is accomplished, any ordinary assistant can usually turn the cranks and read the dials. . . . There cannot be a precise answer to a vague question."
- **Break the problem into manageable components.** Most problems are made up of dozens of smaller problems. We need to unravel the strands of the problem to begin to analyze it. Break the problem into manageable components, and there is a good chance you can solve them one at a time. For example, when actors rehearse a play, they stop, go back, and try it again, over and over, in order to solve one little problem at a time; they don't take on the entire play all at once. Inability to solve a problem is often due to trying to solve too many problems at once.
- **Brainstorm possible solutions.** Once you have identified the problem and broken it into manageable components, you can start *brainstorming*, or coming up with possible solutions. Recall the example from the previous section about the scientists pitching solutions to a problem. Their brainstorming helped stimulate their creativity, which resulted in a number of good ideas for an effective solution. Sometimes brainstorming yields ideas about how to solve a problem by using existing techniques. In these cases, it may seem that brainstorming didn't stimulate any creativity because it did not result in a brand-new technique. However, it did generate a moment of insight into the fact that an appropriate technique to solve the problem already exists.

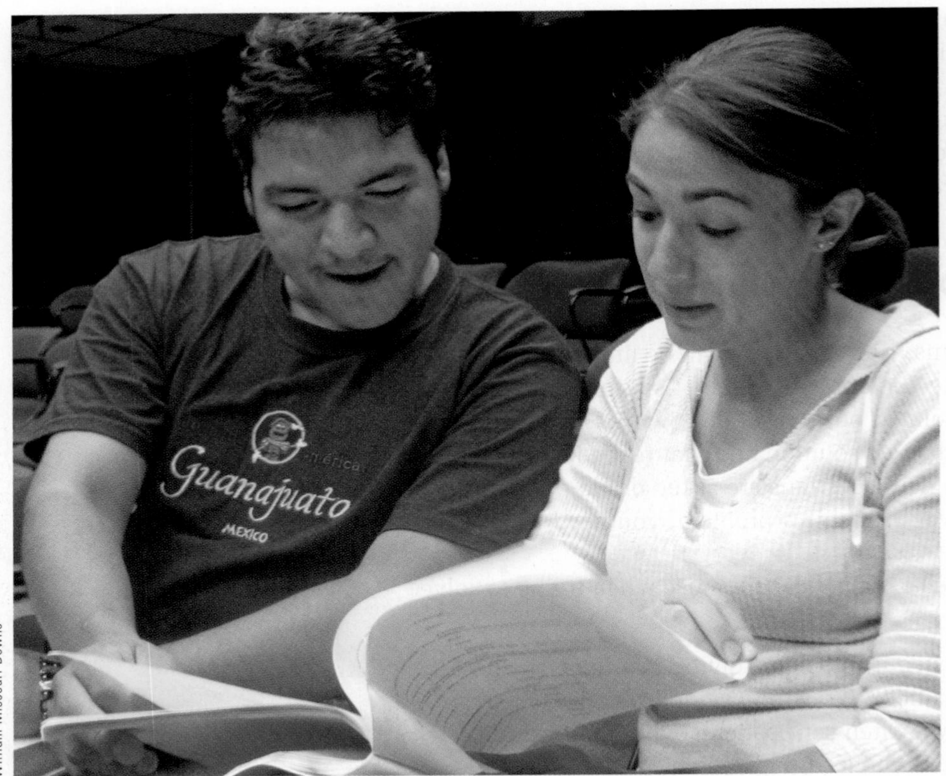

William Missouri Downs

Every production is filled with hundreds of problems that must be solved in order to ensure a smooth performance. Here director Rachel Rosenfeld and playwright Jaime Cruz work to resolve script problems long before rehearsal begins.

- **Test the solution to see if it works.** Here is where you use critical thinking skills to see if the first three steps have in fact provided a solution. Testing the answer is often the longest step, particularly in the sciences, where collecting data can take years. Testing the solution in the theatre also requires data. For example, most new plays are "workshopped," or read in front of an audience numerous times before the official premiere; the playwright evaluates audience reaction to new scenes as the work continues to evolve through development.

At the end of the process, if the most likely solution fails, it's time to start over with step one—did you clearly specify the problem?

If these steps sound similar to the scientific method, they should. In many ways, art and science are closely related. They both rely on experimentation, research, free speech, curiosity, originality, intellectual examination, and creativity. So the next time you attend a jazz concert, watch a ballet, or go to the theatre, think of all the problems the artists had to solve in order to create an evening of entertainment and art. As they express themselves, they realize that art is about more than expressing emotions; it is also about finding those moments of insight that make a live performance communicate ideas and provide a magical experience.

> Creative activity involves a combination of control and freedom, conscious and unconscious thought, and intuition and rational analysis.
>
> ***Sir Ken Robinson,***
> Writer and arts education adviser

Curtain Call

The Intellectual Property Association in Washington, D.C., a trade association for owners of patents, trademarks, and copyrights, estimates creative ideas in the United States to be worth around 360 billion dollars a year. Such a huge resource generates more income than agriculture, automobiles, or aerospace.

In the theatre creativity often depends on the interaction of individuals who must not only work together but also build on each other's creativity. The finished product is not only limited by time and money but also by the egos, techniques, and collaborative creativity of the ensemble. Most people who go into the theatre do not do it for the money but rather the hope of living a creative life. Many factors lead to creativity, but most people who work in creative fields would probably agree that the best way to live a creative life is to just do it. As Anne Bogart writes in her book *A Director Prepares*:

Do not assume that you have to have some prescribed condition to do your best work. Do not wait. Do not wait for enough time or money to accomplish what you think you have in mind. Work with what you have RIGHT NOW. Work with the people around you RIGHT NOW. . . . Do not wait for what you assume is the appropriate stress-free environment in which to generate expression. Do not wait for maturity or insight or wisdom. Do not wait till you are sure that you know what you are doing. Do not wait until you have enough technique. What you do now, what you make of your present circumstances will determine the quality and scope of your future endeavors. And at the same time be patient.

> I'd say one of the most common failures of able people is a lack of nerve. They'll play safe games. . . . In innovations, you have to play a less safe game if it's going to be interesting. It's not predictable that it'll go well.
>
> ***George Stigler,***
> Economist and Nobel Prize winner

Summary

Creativity can be defined as a moment of insight. Closely tied to creativity are technique and talent. Technique is composed of the lessons learned from creativity, and talent can often be developed or denied by our environment. To be more creative, it is important to examine and emulate the traits of creative people. Creative people have a burning curiosity, strong concentration, and a mental agility that allows them to find order where others see only chaos. They also have the ability to accept failure, because more often than not creative solutions fail. IQ is a factor in creativity, but studies have found that an extremely high IQ does not make people more creative. The key is to find the kinds of intelligence in which you excel. Howard Gardner's theory of multiple intelligences identifies linguistic, musical, logical-mathematical, spatial, bodily-kinesthetic, and personal intelligences.

In order to enhance your creativity, you need adequate amounts of exercise and sleep as well as an environment that nourishes creativity and allows time for you to be creative. It is also important to examine the reason you want to be creative; if your motivation is too far removed from the creative act itself, you will probably not be very creative. Another important aspect of being creative is to generate ideas without immediately censoring them. One of the best ways to enhance your creativity is to learn to solve problems. The steps of problem solving include specifically defining the problem, breaking the problem into manageable components, brainstorming possible solutions, and testing to see if the most likely solution works.

The Art of Theatre ONLINE

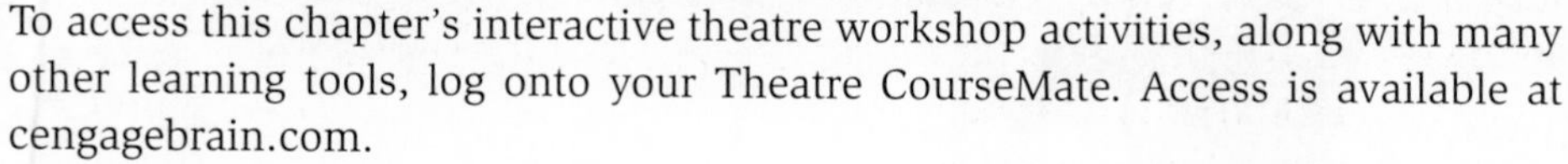

To access this chapter's interactive theatre workshop activities, along with many other learning tools, log onto your Theatre CourseMate. Access is available at cengagebrain.com.

Key Terms

convergent thinking / 228
creativity / 222
divergent thinking / 228
talent / 224
technique / 224

Boesman and Lena, by Athol Fugard. Directed by Noel Raymond, Pillsbury House Theatre, Minneapolis, 2002, featuring (l to r) James A. Williams and Faye M. Price. This play dramatizes the oppression and exploitation of apartheid through the story of a South African couple left homeless and wandering by the razing of their shantytown. Once happy, the couple now takes their misery and anger out on each other while struggling to maintain their dignity in desperate circumstances.

Photos on this spread Michal Daniel/Proofsheet

CHAPTER 11

The Many Types of Theatre

OUTLINE

Today's theatre is diverse. On Tuesday night you might see a play that features realistic situations with actors chatting in everyday language; on Wednesday night, a historical play performed in wigs and spoken in rhymed couplets. On Thursday you might attend a fantastic, nonrealistic performance based on a dream, whereas Friday the bill may feature a wild farce that follows the structure of a joke.

Saturday you might see a dark drama with a theme on the meaninglessness of human existence, but Sunday the fare may be a Romantic comedy that reaffirms life, love, and happy endings. There are dozens of types of theatre, from multimedia performances that combine the live stage with television, to **happenings**, which are unstructured improvised theatrical events; and from **hip hop theatre** influenced by hip-hop music, art, and culture, to **performance art**, a term used to describe performances that mix theatre, visual arts, music, dance, gesture, and ritual (for more on performance art, see Chapter 3).

Performance artist Laurie Anderson (b. 1947) began her career in New York in the 1970s, a time that fostered experimentation, a blending of art forms, and a willingness to perform in informal art spaces. In addition to working as a musician and a visual artist, Anderson collaborates with other artists to create large-scale theatrical works that incorporate storytelling, music, video, and projected imagery and that often transform the ordinary into the strange. Like many other performance artists, she uses her work to explore conceptual and social issues, such as our perception of time, the challenges we face maneuvering through a digital age, and our fascination with crime and justice. Of her audiences, Anderson says, "I like it when we fall into that communal dream."

Lynn Goldsmith/CORBIS

One way to understand theatre is to look at its many variations, which you began to examine in the "Theatrical Styles" Spotlight in Chapter 9. At the most basic level, theatre can be divided into two broad categories: plays with music and plays without. Plays with music are called musicals and will be the subject of Chapter 12. In this chapter we will cover plays without music, which are sometimes called **straight plays** in theatre lingo. "Straight" here has nothing to do with heterosexuality or the level of a play's seriousness—it is a way of stating that a play either lacks music or that any music in it doesn't dominate the production. For example, many of Shakespeare's plays are straight: they have song and dance but are not considered musicals. Within each of these two categories, musicals and straight plays, there are dozens of genres.

As we discussed in Chapter 6, *genre* is a category of music, film, literature, or theatre. Everything within a particular genre has a similar form, style, structure, technique, tone, or subject matter. In the theatre a genre is sometimes called an "ism." These isms include realism, Romanticism, absurdism, as well as some forms that do not actually end in -ism, such as melodrama and epic theatre. Each ism works by a set of conventions covering the play's style, purpose, staging, and scale of production. In order to fully appreciate a performance, it helps to understand the basic concepts of the key isms and a little about how they came into existence.

Comedy and Tragedy

All isms fall under two broad categories: comedy and tragedy. It is often said that comic plays have a happy ending, and tragedies end on a sad note, but there are many more differences. For example, tragedies often end with characters alone or introspective, whereas comedies end with the characters joining together for a party, celebration, or reaffirmation of life. Tragedies often end with the main characters losing power or happiness; within comedies, characters ascend to power or happiness. Despite their different outcomes, comedy and tragedy have one important element in common—they deal with the same conflicts or life's most serious problems, including love, hate, pain, jealousy, revenge, birth, and death. They are the yin and yang of life, and in order to have one, you must have the other. In fact, one of the oldest sayings in the theatre is, "If you want to make the audience cry, first make them laugh."

Comedy

Why we laugh and what we laugh at has been the subject of countless social and psychological studies. As far as scientists are concerned, human beings are the only truly laughing animal, and there's no doubt we have a lot to laugh about. Not only do we laugh when something is humorous or witty, we also use laughter to alleviate surprise, nerves, and embarrassment, as well as to proclaim triumph. There is also the gentle laugh that can accompany inner peace or simple happiness. The philosopher Nietzsche said that mankind had to invent laughter to preserve its sanity, and it's clear from the myriad ways we use laughter how important a tool it is for society.

In the theatre, comedy can be divided into two broad categories: high and low. **High comedy** includes any play that depends on sophisticated humor, wit, political satire, or social commentary. **Low comedy** depends on gags, clowning, puns, and slapstick. The terms "high" and "low" can be deceptive. When one says a play is low comedy it does not necessarily mean that it is less crafted, important, or respectable than high comedy. In fact, comic geniuses have existed in both areas and the line between high and low comedy is often blurred. For example, the comedies of William Shakespeare often contain low puns and gags in combination with intellectual wit (see the Spotlight "Understanding Shakespeare").

There are many types of comedy. Anton Chekhov the great Russian playwright called many of his plays comedies even though they covered such depressing subjects as debt, lost love and missed opportunities. This University of Wyoming production of Chekhov's comedy The Cherry Orchard featured Megan Antles, Katrina Despain and Kenneth Stellingwerf.

William Missouri Downs

One of the most popular forms of low comedy is **farce**. A farcical play traps the characters in a fast-paced situation with wild complications, mistaken identities, and incredible coincidences. The pace of a farce can be so fast that they are sometimes called "door-slamming farces" because the characters are constantly running in and out of doors. One of the most famous farces of all time is *Tartuffe, or the Imposter* (1664), written by the great French playwright Molière (1622–1673). *Tartuffe* tells the story of a wealthy gentleman who, in order to fulfill the spiritual needs of his family, brings home a man named Tartuffe whom he believes is exceptionally pious. Tartuffe professes his desire to save souls but is, in reality, a swindler and a seducer. In the face of mounting evidence, the wealthy gentleman refuses to believe that Tartuffe is a con man. As a result, Tartuffe manages to cheat the family out of its fortune and seduce the wealthy gentleman's wife. Only the sudden entrance of the king of France stops Tartuffe and ensures a happy ending for this comedy. One of the most popular contemporary farces is *Noises Off* by Michael Frayn, which examines the crazy, roller-coaster events that happen during the rehearsal and production of a play. Everything that can go wrong, does. Actors flub their lines and miss entrances, while the scenery collapses and props explode.

There are many types of high comedy, including **Romantic comedy**, which examines the funny side of falling in love. These plays often have sympathetic young lovers kept apart by complicated circumstances, who in the end surmount any obstacles and live happily ever after. Shakespeare's *Much Ado About Nothing* is a perfect example of a Romantic comedy. **Sentimental** and **domestic comedies** take an entertaining look at the problems and complications of common everyday people. Modern plays like *The Dining Room* by A. R. Gurney (b. 1930) and *The Man Who Came to Dinner* by Moss Hart (1904–1961) and George Kaufman (1889–1961) are examples of these comedies. **Comedy of manners** plays are set during the age of aristocrats and kings and poke fun at the bedroom escapades, marital infidelities, and hypocrisies of the upper classes. A classic example of a comedy of manners is William Congreve's (1670–1729) *The Way of the World* (1700), the story of shallow, deceitful aristocrats who plot to prevent two lovers from marrying.

Another form of high comedy is **comedy of ideas**, cerebral, socially relevant plays that force audiences to reassess their culture, community, and values. One of the greatest writers of comedy of ideas was George Bernard Shaw (1856–1950), who wrote plays filled with characters who cannot resist a good argument about society, politics, morals, or religion. One of his most famous comedies of ideas was *Man and Superman* (1903), based on the philosophy of Nietzsche. Shaw felt that the prime function of theatre was to expose society's blemishes and that one of the best ways to do this was through political satire; Shaw wrote comedies that forced the audience to think about their politics and the social order. Needless to say, such comedies were and are often censored in more repressive societies.

Comedy can sometimes be rather gloomy, even sinister, as is the case with **dark comedy**. This type of comedy allows the audience to laugh at the bleaker and more absurd aspects of life. One of the most famous dark comedies is *Little Murders* (1968) by Jules Feiffer (b. 1929), a play that examines how random violence and paranoia affect a dysfunctional urban family. By the end of the play, the family members have become snipers taking potshots at innocent people on the street below.

Marc & Evelyne Bernheim/Woodfin Camp & Associates

Griots are African storytellers who often incorporate theatrical elements such as song, mime, and impersonation into their telling of folk tales, tribal histories, and myths. Here, a traditional storyteller recites tribal legends to young members of Yaou village on the Ivory Coast. The storyteller appears in many theatrical forms, from Greek choruses to contemporary narrators such as the Stage Manager in Thorton Wilder's Our Town.

Donald Cooper/Photostage Ltd.

Once the strict rule of the Puritans ended in England, Restoration theatre rebounded with ribald comedies that exposed the social follies of the upper class. Known as the comedy of manners, the most popular plays of this period were rife with marriages of convenience, sexual confrontations, marital infidelities, and coy lovers. A classic example of the comedy of manners is William Congreve's The Way of the World, *the story of shallow, deceitful aristocrats who plot to prevent two lovers from marrying. Complex and funny, this play is notable for its witty and well-written conversations. This 1992 production featured Tom Hollander, Emma Piper, and Barbara Flynn. Directed by Peter Gill, Lyric Hammersmith, London.*

Tragedy

A tragic play is one that takes a serious look at the meaning of life and human suffering. Tragic plays are based on the idea that virtue can grow out of hardship and wisdom from suffering. These plays ask powerful questions: What is humankind's purpose? Are we at the mercy of fate or can we rise above our destiny? Which set of rules do we follow when moral codes are in conflict? Can we recognize our character flaws before they destroy us? The purpose of these plays is not to make the audience feel depressed but rather to enable them

ArenaPal/Topham/
The Image Works

Sophocles' Oedipus is the quintessential Greek tragic hero. His fatal flaw, or hamartia, is his hubris, or his arrogance, which prevents him from seeing his flaws and acting in a way that spares him terrible suffering. This 1992 production of the Oedipus plays at the Royal Shakespeare Company featured Gerard Murphy as Oedipus (bottom), shown with Tiresias, the blind seer who predicts Oedipus' fate (top). Today, the classical tragic hero is much less common in plays and movies, but aspects of this type of hero can be seen in contemporary characters like Jack Nicholson's Randle Patrick McMurphy in One Flew over the Cuckoo's Nest *(1975).*

to experience an intense, twofold feeling of pity and fear known as **catharsis**. Catharsis can occur when one truly encounters life and confronts its many riddles.

A tragic play often revolves around a **tragic hero**, an extraordinary person of noble birth or a person who has risen to great political or social heights, yet is someone with whom the audience can empathize. The tragic hero is not a victim who suffers an accident or a catastrophe over which he or she has no control. Rather, tragic heroes are characters able to make choices, take action, bring trouble upon themselves, and ultimately take responsibility for their choices. At the beginning of a play, the tragic hero is often successful and happy but makes an error in judgment or has a **character flaw** (sometimes called a tragic or fatal flaw), a personal failing that leads to his or her downfall. The ancient Greeks called this flaw the **hamartia**. A common hamartia is **hubris**—overbearing pride or arrogance. The tragic hero's hamartia leads to **peripeteia**, or a radical reversal of fortune. This reversal is followed by **anagnorisis**, in which the hero goes through a process of self-examination and recognizes his or her flaw and true identity. In the end, the hero suffers the terrible consequence of committing the tragic error. This consequence is often death or a life worse than death. The punishment the hero suffers always seems undeservedly harsh, which leads to the purging of emotions and catharsis as the audience members feel great pity and fear: pity for the hero's misfortune and fear that they also might possess the same tragic flaw.

Tragedy originated with the ancient Greeks but it has remained an important part of theatre for thousands of years. (See the Spotlight "Understanding Greek Tragedy.") For example, Shakespeare's *King Lear*, *Hamlet*, and *Othello* are considered tragedies. Today, some theatre scholars say that tragedies are no longer possible because extraordinary persons of noble birth are few and far between. Therefore modern versions of tragedies are called **tragedies of the common man**, which, just as in ancient Greek tragedies, leave the audience with a feeling of catharsis but, unlike the ancient Greeks, base heroes on common people. Examples of tragedies of the common man are Tennessee Williams's (1911–1983) *The Glass Menagerie* (1945) and Arthur Miller's (1915–2005) *Death of a Salesman* (1949). Just as with the Greek tragedies of 2,400 years ago, these modern tragedies are intended to inspire the members of the audience to examine their lives and purge themselves of flaws they share with the tragic characters.

Realism

The most common type of theatre today is **realism**. Realistic plays have natural-sounding dialogue and characters whose behavior is much like that of everyday modern people. Realistic characters also have specific psychological motivations and come from a particular place, social class, and background; these factors affect who they are, what they believe, and what they do. Realistic plays do not have supernatural moments, dream sequences, or unbelievable endings. They

SPOTLIGHT ON Understanding Greek Tragedy

Tragedy originated in Ancient Greece as a part of a celebration to the god Dionysus, the god of wine and fertility. Four hundred fifty years before the birth of Christ there were many great tragic playwrights, including Aeschylus (ca. 525–456 BCE), Sophocles (ca. 496–406 BCE), and Euripides (ca. 480–406 BCE). Based on the rich tradition of Greek tragedy, the philosopher Aristotle wrote *Poetics*, the first known treatise on dramatic structure (for more on *Poetics*, see Chapters 1 and 4).

Ancient Greek tragedies were extravagant spectacles brimming with song and dance. Performances were divided between the actors who played individual characters and a chorus of singing and dancing men who played group characters, such as crowds of concerned townspeople or supernatural beings. Instead of modern acts and intermissions, ancient Greek tragedies—many of which are still regularly performed today—have a more complicated framework consisting of five elements: a prologue, a parodos, alternating episodes and stasimons, and an exodos. Performances begin with a **prologue**, which is a short speech or scene to set the location and time and provide necessary mythological exposition. Greek plays are often based on myths and occasionally on historical events. The prologue tells the audience which myth or historical event is the basis for the play; however, plays do not always follow the myth exactly. Ancient Greek playwrights could interpret, change the theme, or alter the parable in order to explore political or social issues.

The prologue is followed by the parodos. **Parodos** means "entrance," and it marked the entrance of the **chorus**. The parodos contains many songs and dances as the chorus tells the audience who they are in the play and provides needed background information. The chorus may have included as many as fifty dancing and singing men. The chorus serves many purposes during the course of a performance: they can portray crowds of warriors, citizens, or mythological characters; they can chant the playwright's comments; through choral songs, they can debate the play's moral themes. The parodos is followed by the first episode.

In the first **episode**, the actors play a scene from the story. Ancient actors often wore masks. This was necessary because the theatres in which the plays were performed were often huge, with as many as 17,000 seats. Many believe that these masks helped the actors project the sound to the back row, and they certainly conveyed an emotional state in a larger fashion than can a raised eyebrow or a frown seen from a great distance. The acting style was probably declamatory, meaning that speeches were given in an impassioned yet rhetorical style to describe how each character felt.

Each episode is followed by a **stasimon**, which contains more songs and dances by the chorus as it comments on the action of the play as it proceeds. During the stasimon, the actors exit to prepare for the next episode. The play follows this basic pattern—episode followed by stasimon followed by episode—until the **exodos**, which is a summation by the chorus on the theme and wisdom of the play. The play ends in a processional song as the chorus leaves the stage.

also discard a theatrical convention called a *soliloquy* in which the actor talks to himself alone on stage, and the *aside* in which the actor makes comments directly to the audience (though some modern realistic plays break these rules—see the section "Mixing Isms," later in this chapter). In fact, actors in realistic plays are taught to perform as though there were an invisible wall between them and the spectators. This wall is known as the **fourth wall**, which is a term that comes from the box sets common with realistic plays. A box set has three or more walls that are built more or less true-to-life and a nonexistent fourth wall that allows the audience to "spy" on the characters' private lives. Modern realistic plays typically take place in common spaces like living rooms, front porches, and kitchens. Today, so many realistic plays take place in kitchens that this genre is sometimes referred to as "kitchen-sink realism."

Realistic playwrights are not interested in frivolous entertainment that avoids the troubles of the world; instead, they seek to promote change in the state, the community, the church, and the family as they lead the way to a new social order. As a result, realistic plays often present complex, sometimes disturbing views of modern life. This is why realistic plays are sometimes called **problem plays**, because playwrights feel that before the problems of the world can be solved, society must first understand that those problems exist.

The Origins of Realism

Realism, which began more than one hundred fifty years ago with the invention of photography around 1840, changed the way people looked at the world. Now, a boy in London could see an actual photo of the Civil War battlefield of Bull Run in Virginia, not an artist's depiction. A mother in Michigan who wanted to see the U.S. president's face could study his photograph rather than a drawing. Soon after, "real" was all the rage, especially in the theatre where there were calls for sets to be more "genuine," acting to be more "honest," and dialogue to be modeled after everyday speech.

Contributing to realism was Thomas Edison (1847–1931), whose invention of the incandescent light bulb in 1879 meant that, for the first time in the history of the theatre, every kind of lighting effect—from a stormy night to a warm summer day—could be realistically presented and controlled. English naturalist Charles Darwin (1809–1882) also affected realism when he observed that humans are animals. This theory had an enormous impact on the theatre because in order to portray a realistic character, the playwright and actors had to understand the character's environment and heredity. The Viennese psychologist Sigmund Freud (1856–1939) influenced realism with his revolutionary ideas about how the human mind worked. Theatres soon followed his lead and began presenting characters whose conscious and unconscious motivations were well justified. Additionally, the German philosopher and social scientist Karl Marx (1818–1883) influenced realism by spotlighting human oppression. The theatre began following Marx's lead, telling stories about divorce, euthanasia, women's rights, sexual double standards, venereal disease, religious hypocrisy, unregulated capitalism, blind patriotism, the plight of the poor, and the grim realities of everyday life.

> [I]n real life people don't spend every minute shooting each other, hanging themselves, and making confessions of love. They don't spend all their time saying clever things. They're more occupied with flirting, eating, drinking, and talking stupidities. . . . Let everything on the stage be just as complicated, and at the same time just as simple as it is in life. People eat their dinner, just eat their dinner, and all the time their happiness is being established or their lives are being broken up.
>
> ***Anton Chekhov,***
> Playwright

For some, however, realism was not real enough. Soon directors, actors, and playwrights began calling for an even more extreme form of realism, an accurate "slice of life" look at existence. They named this new genre **naturalism**. Two proponents of naturalism were the Russian playwright Maxim Gorky (1868–1936), whose play *The Lower Depths* (1902) took a stark look at people living in the cellar of a Moscow flophouse, and the French director André Antoine, who staged the play *The Butchers* (1888) with actual sides of maggot-infested beef. Today, most TV dramas today are very realistic, whereas reality-based TV shows are a direct descendent of naturalism.

Realistic Plays

The most famous realistic playwright is Henrik Ibsen (1828–1906), who is often called the father of realism. One of Ibsen's most important realistic plays was *A*

Doll's House (1879), the story of Nora, a pretty housewife who is expected by her banker husband and a patriarchal society to be cheerful, obedient, and mindless. Ibsen's intent is not to condemn Nora but to make a statement about a society that limits women by sheltering them. In the course of the play, the petted and spoiled Nora begins to examine her life. She realizes that men have always dominated her, first her father and now her husband. In the end, she leaves her husband and children and strikes out on her own to redefine her identity. Ibsen went on to write other famous realistic plays including *Ghosts* (1881), which examines incest and the devastating effects of venereal disease; *Hedda Gabler* (1890), a psychological study of a sexually repressed and destructive woman; and *Enemy of the People* (1882), about an idealistic doctor who tries to save a resort city from its polluted waters only to discover that the community is more interested in capitalism than in the safety and health of its citizens.

Today realism incorporates a broad range of plays that sometimes mix realism with other isms (see the section "Mixing Isms," later in this chapter) and includes the work of playwrights like David Henry Hwang, Caryl Churchill, August Wilson, Sam Shepard, and David Mamet. David Henry Hwang (b. 1957), the son of Chinese immigrant parents, often writes about the conflicts of Chinese immigrants who are expected to abandon much of their Chinese identity in order to fit into mainstream U.S. culture. Caryl Churchill (b. 1938) wrote *Cloud Nine* (1979), a provocative study of colonialism and sexual politics. August Wilson (1945–2005) is famous for plays like *Ma Rainey's Black Bottom* (1984), about 1920s blues musicians and their struggle against white recording companies. (For more on David Henry Hwang, Caryl Churchill, and August Wilson, see Chapter 3.) Sam Shepard (b. 1943) is known for plays like *Buried Child* (1978) about a drunken father, a decaying family, and a grandson who demands to be recognized as the heir to the family farm. David Mamet (b. 1947) writes plays like *Glengarry Glen Ross* (1984), which exposes the greed and cynicism of real estate salesmen, and *Oleanna* (1992), which looks at charges of sexual harassment against a male professor by one of his female students.

Naturalism often represented the seedy side of life in order to show the audience life as it is rather than as we would like it to be. Perhaps the best example of naturalism is Maxim Gorky's The Lower Depths, *a study of wretched derelicts in a horrible tenement run by greedy landlords. Konstantin Stanislavsky directed this original 1902 production at the Moscow Art Theatre. It later toured Western Europe and the United States.*

Michal Daniel/Proofsheet

Norwegian playwright Henrik Ibsen wrote many plays about the moral failings of modern society. In Hedda Gabler, *the title character, a bored and destructive young woman, amuses herself by gossiping, engaging in almost-adulterous relationships with her husband's acquaintances, and manipulating the actions and emotions of those around her. Her aristocratic contempt for her husband's bourgeois family and friends leads to tragedy. This 2000 production featured (l to r) Sean Haberle, Christina Rouner, Laila Robins as Hedda, and Stephen Yoakam. Directed by David Esbjornson, Guthrie Theater, Minneapolis.*

Robbie Jack Photography

Modern plays, such as David Mamet's Oleanna, *often explore current social issues.* Oleanna *is about a power struggle between a university professor and a female student who accuses him of sexual harassment. Inspired in part by the 1991 Senate hearings in which law professor Anita Hill brought charges of sexual harassment against Supreme Court nominee Clarence Thomas, the play addresses such timely issues as political correctness and power dynamics in relationships. This 2004 production starred Aaron Eckhart and Julia Stiles. Directed by Lindsay Posner, Garrick Theatre, London.*

Romanticism and Melodrama

Romantic plays take a heartfelt look at life. The Romantic playwrights, like their Romantic poet counterparts, feel that cold realistic logic is not adequate to describe the full range of human experience, and their plays stress instinct, intuition, and emotions. They want to go beyond reason to a transcendent realm of sensation where experience cannot be rationally explained. Romantic plays often have headstrong, sensitive protagonists isolated from society, inspiring emotions (particularly love), and knowing in their unique hearts that they are right to rebel. Needless to say, it's clear why many American musicals are written in the Romantic style (see Chapter 12).

One of the most common types of Romanticism today is called melodrama. The word **melodrama** is a blend of *melody* and *drama* and refers to the background music once played during performances (much like modern movie sound tracks). Melodramas have formulaic plots filled with oversimplified moral dilemmas and support the values of love, marriage, God, and country. Melodrama is popular in our society, existing in television soap operas, made-for-television movies, and popular films such as *The Count of Monte Cristo, Star Wars,* and the *Indiana Jones* franchise.

The Background of Romanticism

Romanticism was a reaction to the Enlightenment (1650–1800), a period of great philosophical, scientific, technological, political, and religious revolutions that changed human thought forever. During the Enlightenment, intellectuals and philosophers began to believe that reason and science might conquer fear, superstition, and prejudice. But cold reason seldom makes for great theatre—theatre is about emotions. Soon poets, novelists, and playwrights began to question the Enlightenment's obsession with logic. These writers, known as **Romantics**, felt a purely empirical, scientific, and mathematical view of the world would lack poetry, faith, passion, and most important of all—romance.

The French philosopher Jean-Jacques Rousseau (1712–1778), who said, "I am not here to think, but to be, feel, live," is sometimes called the father of the

Enormously popular, melodramas dominated nineteenth-century stages. Audiences loved them because they included a sympathetic protagonist who suffered at the hands of an evil antagonist, lots of exciting action, thrilling suspense, and a happy ending that promoted middle-class values. This poster depicts an eventful evening in the life of the long-suffering heroine of Theodore Kremer's For Her Children's Sake *(1902). It's easy to see from this scenario how modern soap operas descended from theatre's melodramas.*

SPOTLIGHT ON Understanding Shakespeare

Almost four hundred years after his death, Shakespeare (1564–1616) is one of the most produced playwrights in the world. More than three hundred movies and television shows have been based on his plays, including the musical *West Side Story* (1961) and the science fiction movie *Forbidden Planet* (1956). During the last few years, a great many of his plays have been turned into movies, including *Titus Andronicus* with Anthony Hopkins and Jessica Lange; *A Midsummer Night's Dream*, starring Calista Flockhart, Michelle Pfeiffer, and Kevin Kline; and a musical adaptation of *Love's Labour's Lost* starring Alicia Silverstone. There was also an MTV-style adaptation of *Romeo and Juliet* starring Leonardo DiCaprio and an adaptation of *The Taming of the Shrew* called *10 Things I Hate About You*, which featured the late Heath Ledger in a leading role.

Perhaps the reason Shakespeare is popular is because he gives the audience what it wants. He often started his plays with an event, a jolting moment to get the audience interested, just as many modern Hollywood screenwriters do. His plays jump from location to location and fill the stage with lots of implied sex, overt violence, and emotional conflict. Shakespeare's plays were written without intermissions or acts (again, just like most modern movies). The acts and intermissions you see in published versions and during performances were added after his death.

Shakespeare's theatre did not use complicated sets. Instead the actors would describe the setting using what is called **verbal scene painting**. This means that the actors let their words paint pictures so that the audience could "dress" the stage in their imaginations. For example, in Shakespeare's *Macbeth* the king paints the scene of a large manor in a picturesque rural landscape when he says, "This castle hath a pleasant seat; the air nimbly and sweetly recommends itself unto our gentle senses."

What these productions lacked in sets, they made up for in costumes, which were often extravagant affairs of gold, lace, silk, and velvet, donated to the theatre by aristocratic patrons. There was no attempt, however, to make the costumes historically accurate. Actors performing Shakespeare's *Julius Caesar* (1598) wore Elizabethan costumes, not togas. Their aim was not to give a history lesson but to entertain. Performances had music and plenty of special effects and realistic swordplay. Actors hid bladders filled with sheep's blood under their costumes so that during fight sequences, when they were "stabbed," real blood would ooze out. The stage was filled with trapdoors so that actors playing ghosts and spirits could mysteriously appear and disappear. Above the stage were cannons filled with blanks that could be fired to create realistic battle sequences.

Shakespeare wrote many of his plays in blank verse and iambic pentameter. **Blank verse** is sim-

Romantic movement. Blaise Pascal (1623–1662), the French physicist, mathematician, and philosopher, expressed the essence of Romanticism when he said, "The heart has its reasons that reason does not know." It is from this age that we get the idea of artists being obsessive, moody, and lovesick.

Romantic Plays

Examples of Romantic dramas include Johann Wolfgang von Goethe's (1749–1832) *Faust* (Part 1, 1808; Part 2, 1832) and Edmond Rostand's (1868–1918) *Cyrano de Bergerac* (1897). William Shakespeare (1564–1616), perhaps the most famous Romantic playwright, did not live during the Romantic Period (1800–1850). Shakespeare's comedies such as *A Midsummer Night's Dream* and tragedies such as *Romeo and Juliet* are considered Romantic in style (for more see the Spotlight "Understanding Shakespeare").

ply poetic lines that do not rhyme, whereas **iambic pentameter** describes the accent and length of each line. Iambic means that the accent goes on the second syllable like this, de-DUM, de- DUM, de-DUM, and "pentameter" means that there are five pairs of syllables per line. The famous Shakespeare line, "Shall I compare thee to a summer's day" is a perfect example of iambic pentameter as it has ten syllables and the stress goes on the second syllable.

We can't know, of course, but it may be that Shakespeare would be shocked to learn that four hundred years after his death he is considered one of the greatest writers of all time. In his own day, he was not as highly esteemed—audiences loved his plays but many of his contemporaries often looked down on him as an uneducated hack writer because he was not a university man. Shakespeare's influence today, however, is far greater than any of his contemporaries. Many words and phrases from Shakespeare's plays and poems have become part of everyday speech. He coined more than 1,700 of our common words by changing nouns into verbs, verbs into adjectives, and by connecting words that had never before been connected. For example, among the words he invented are *assassination, eventful, dwindle, courtship, and lonely*. And he is the source of the phrases "to catch a cold," "fair play," "foregone conclusion," "as luck would have it," "too much of a good thing," "in one fell swoop," "cruel to be kind," "play fast and loose," "good riddance," "vanish into thin air," and "in the twinkling of an eye."

Lou Anne Wright

William Shakespeare (1564–1616)—great playwright or great front man? The world may never know for sure.

The best-known Romantic play today is *Les Misérables*, based on a novel by the French playwright Victor Hugo (1802–1885), who also wrote *The Hunchback of Notre Dame* (1831). *Les Misérables* takes place in 1815 and tells the story of a man named Valjean who was sent to prison for fifteen years—five years for stealing a loaf of bread and ten years for trying to escape. After his release, a kind Bishop offers him food and shelter. Valjean does not return the favor; instead he steals a pair of the Bishop's silver candlesticks. When he is caught, Valjean expects to be sent back to prison, but instead the Bishop gives Valjean the candlesticks as a gift. Humbled by the Bishop's mercy, Valjean spends the rest of the play practicing kindness and understanding. *Les Misérables* has been adapted to the screen more than forty times, including a 1998 movie starring Liam Neeson, Uma Thurman, and Geoffrey Rush. A modern musical version has been performed almost continuously on various stages around the world since 1980.

William Missouri Downs

The modern Chinese opera uses little in the way of sets, but does have spectacular costumes. These performances are filled with dance, song, and stylized makeup and speech. Plots are drawn from traditional stories, legends and Chinese history.

Expressionism

Expressionism started in Germany around 1910 as a reaction to a new kind of painting called Impressionism. Monet, Renoir, Cezanne, and other Impressionist painters were interested in how reality appears to the eye at a particular moment—in other words, a subjective account of an objective perception. With expressionism an artist imposes her own internal state of mind onto the outside world; therefore, **expressionism** is a subjective account of a subjective perception. For example, if a person who is intoxicated says that he sees pink elephants on the wall, he is not describing objective reality, for there are in fact no pink elephants on the wall. Rather, he is revealing his own internal state. Unlike in a realistic play, expressionistic plays show the audience those pink elephants, so how the characters feel is expressed on the set, walls, environment, and even other characters. Expressionists would argue that realism attempts an objective observation of the world using the five senses, but that reality is never objectively observed. In short, expressionist playwrights feel that reality is affected by the way we perceive it.

Expressionist plays often use deliberate distortion—walls slanted inward to make the room feel claustrophobic, wallpaper striped like prison bars, or trees having the form of huge strangling hands. Similarly, some characters may not be portrayed as real people, but as the protagonist perceives them—perhaps as cogs in an industrial machine or mindless puppets acting out a grotesque parody.

The Background of Expressionism

In the early 1900s movies began to take a toll on the live theatre. By 1911, 1,400 legitimate stages in the United States had been converted to movie houses. By 1915, the number of touring theatre companies had dropped from 300 to 100, and soon the number fell to less than ten. One of the reasons movies grew so popular so quickly was that their admission price was cheap. Attending a movie in 1910 cost only about 5 cents, whereas a ticket to a play cost five to ten times more. Theatre practitioners took notice of the trend and began considering how the theatre could save itself from extinction. Many playwrights and directors believed that the biggest problem was realism and naturalism, because stories in these styles could be depicted much more easily with film. For example, depicting a sunset on stage takes a battery of lights, detailed sets, plus a crew of stagehands, and even then it doesn't look completely real. For a movie to show a real sunset, all that's needed is a camera at the right location at sundown.

Soon there were calls for theatres to "re-theatricalize" by doing what the camera could not do. Many theatre artists began to reject naturalism and realism, and a variety of new styles began to emerge. These new perspectives on the human experience led to avant-garde theatrical styles, each with its own systems and theories. The word **avant-garde** can describe any work of art that is experimental, innovative, or unconventional. Symbolism, Dadaism, surrealism, absurdism, and expressionism are some of the avant-garde styles, the isms, that playwrights, directors, and designers created in order to rebel against realism and naturalism and draw audiences back to the live stage.

> The only theatre worth saving, the only theatre worth having, is a theatre motion pictures can not touch. When we succeed in eliminating from it every trace of the photographic attitude of mind, when we succeed in making a production that is the exact antithesis of a motion picture, a production that is everything a motion picture is not and nothing a motion picture is, the old lost magic will return once more.
>
> ***Robert Edmond Jones,***
> Theatre set designer

Expressionist Plays

One of the most famous expressionist plays is *A Dream Play* (1902) by Swedish playwright August Strindberg (1849–1912), a fourteen-act play that follows the disconnected logic of a dream. Another example is Elmer Rice's (1892–1967) *The Adding Machine* (1923), about a man named Mr. Zero, who is fired from his job and replaced by an adding machine. Common expressionist themes include conflicts between truth and illusion, life and art, reality and appearance. The classic *Six Characters in Search of an Author* (1922) by Luigi Pirandello (1867–1936) embodies all of these themes—in this play, six characters take on a life of their own when the playwright fails to complete the play in which they were supposed to appear.

One of the most famous expressionist playwrights is Eugene O'Neill. O'Neill (1888–1953) was the first American playwright to win the Nobel Prize for literature (1936). His expressionist play *The Hairy Ape* (1922) is the story of Yank, a stoker in the engine room of an ocean liner. At the beginning of the play, Yank thinks that his life is important and useful because he is one

In 1922 New York's Provincetown Players staged the original production of Eugene O'Neill's expressionist play The Hairy Ape, *featuring Louis Wolheim as Yank (standing). The Provincetown Players was formed by avant-garde theatre artists who rebelled against the big Broadway productions of light musicals and other flimsy entertainment. The Players' no-star policy reflected their support of socialist causes, and their willingness to experiment supported many different forms of drama outside theatre's mainstream.*

Vandamm Theatre Collection/The New York Public Library, Astor, Lenox, and Tilden Foundations

of the men who make the great ship move. But when the ship owner's daughter visits the engine room, she is shocked by what she sees. To her, the room resembles a steel cage, and the stokers look like Neanderthals. Overwhelmed by the sight, she faints. Because of her reaction—which reveals a subjective account of reality that differs from his own—Yank begins to question his point of view. When he visits New York City, his perception is that identical puppets with simpering, toneless voices inhabit it. When these "puppets" ignore him, Yank lashes out and lands in jail. He decides to seek revenge by destroying the complex social machine controlling his life, but he can find little support. He goes to a zoo, where he finds a gorilla that seems to understand him. When Yank frees the beast, it crushes him and throws him into the cage. In the end, Yank dies bewildered and humiliated, realizing that he had no power over the massive machine that dominated his life.

Epic Theatre

Most plays have a limited scope. In other words, they tell a story using a small number of characters and only show a few critical hours or minutes within their lives. But not all stories fit within such limitations. An *epic* is a story, play, or poem that covers a long period, and includes a large number of sometimes unrelated incidents. Epic plays open the narrow confines of the stage and allow for wider, sweeping plots, with frequent shifts in location and large casts. The great scope of epic drama allows it to be less structured, less focused, and more like real life. Modern epic theatre also often incorporates political themes and staging that allows the audience to actively contemplate the play's message.

The Background of Epic Theatre

Epic theatre has existed for hundreds of years. During the Middle Ages, working class people often produced daylong cycle plays that told the story of the Bible.

Today, epic theatre is most often associated with the work of Bertolt Brecht (1898–1956), the German poet, director, and playwright who challenged traditional ideas about theatre. Brecht saw the grand scope of epic theatre as the perfect way to confront the social and political problems of his day. He took epic theatre to a new level by eliminating the vicarious experience and catharsis that had been standard in the theatre for thousands of years. He rebelled against theatrical illusions such as suspense, rising action, climax, and other plot devices that lull the audience into a trance-like state and emotional catharsis. If you've ever become so involved in a play or a movie that you forget time is passing, then you know what Brecht was rebelling against. Brecht wanted the audience to be aware that the play is only an illusion and to be conscious enough to consider and judge the political, social, and economic implications of the story. He did this by using the alienation effect.

The **alienation effect**, unique to Brecht's idea of epic theatre, happens when a dramatist or director tries to distance or estrange the audience so that they can consciously think about the themes of the play. Brecht alienated the audience by using various techniques: the actors addressed the audience while out of character, he often exposed the lights and removed the proscenium arch and curtains, and the actors performed on bare platforms and simple sets (sometimes adorned with political slogans). In this way, Brecht argued, the audience could intelligently and objectively perceive the moral issues of the play rather than being drawn so deep into the plot they lost themselves and failed to think about what was being said.

R. Finkelstein

The Threepenny Opera, one of Bertolt Brecht's best-known plays, incorporates many elements that foster the alienation effect. Political slogans are projected onto the back wall of the set, characters sometimes deliver their lines with their backs to the audience, and songs serve to keep the audience from getting too attached to the characters. This recent production staged by the University of Cincinnati College-Conservatory of Music further enhances audience alienation by placing larger-than-life images of Brecht around the stage and prominently featuring signs that indicate settings, characters, and even the name of the play. Directed by Worth Gardner. Scenic design by Richard Finkelstein.

Epic Plays

A few of the most popular epic plays are Brecht's *Galileo* (1945), *The Good Person of Setzuan* (1947), and *The Caucasian Chalk Circle* (1948). Perhaps his most famous is *Mother Courage and Her Children* (1941), set during the Thirty Years' War (1618–1648), a series of religious and political wars between the Protestants and Catholics that eventually involved most of Europe. The action of the play is epic: Mother Courage travels with her canteen wagon through Sweden, Poland, and Germany, profiting from the war by selling goods to the soldiers. *Mother Courage* makes a powerful statement about capitalism and war. Brecht's themes were often anti-capitalist, expressing the views that capitalism makes people work against one another and that it encourages selfishness and greed as well as injustice. A contemporary example of epic theatre would be Tony Kushner's sweeping two-part play *Angels in America I: Millennium Approaches* and *II: Perestroika* (see Chapter 3).

Absurdism

Absurdist playwrights believe that human beings face a cold, hostile universe and that most plays fail to reflect the ridiculousness, anxiety, and chaos of the world. These plays feature characters trapped in garbage cans, caught in coffins, or buried to their necks in sand and who spend their time engaged in philosophical arguments, notable small talk, detailed analyses of unimportant things, and action-filled moments that go nowhere. Absurd characters are often filled with anxiety, anguish, and guilt as they suffer and endure for no reason. The sets are often barren, with austere landscapes; some are even placed in environments that appear to be blackened by nuclear war.

It is sometimes useful to view **absurdism** as loosely divided into three broad categories that often overlap: fatalist, hilarious, and existentialist. Fatalistic absurdism suggests we are trapped in an irrational universe where even basic communication is impossible. Hilarious absurdism highlights the insanity of life in a comical way. Existential absurdism holds that human beings are naturally alone, without purpose or mission, in a universe that has no God. The absence of God means that humans have no fixed destiny, but, for the existentialists, this is not a negative, for without a God humans can create their own existences, purpose, and meaning. Existentialists feel that we can escape from the chaos of the world only by making significant decisions, taking action, and accepting complete responsibility, without excuses, for our actions.

The Background of Absurdism

> [Absurdism] is that which is devoid of purpose. . . . Cut off from his religious, metaphysical and transcendental roots, man is lost; all his actions become senseless, absurd, useless.
>
> ***Eugène Ionesco,***
> Absurdist playwright

The atrocities, devastation, and genocide brought on by World War II left millions dead, millions more homeless, and millions refugees. It was a dirty war full of political prisoners, slave labor, and death on such an unparalleled scale that even today the casualties can only be estimated. It was a war in which entire cities were eliminated in a flash, where famine and epidemics raged throughout the world, and millions were murdered in gas chambers. Destruction on such an immense scale forced many to rethink their philosophical justifications. Albert Camus (1913–1960), the French journalist, essayist, philosopher, novelist, and playwright, described the human condition as "absurd." Scottish psychiatrist

Ronald D. Laing said, "Madness is a sane response to an insane world." How could one remain optimistic after the insanity of two massive world wars and the threat of a world-ending third? How could one remain confident in a universe that was unfriendly, irrational, meaningless, and therefore absurd? Many began to believe that the German philosopher Friedrich Nietzsche (1844–1900) was right when he proclaimed, "God is dead." Many playwrights and directors began to think that life was not governed by rational principles but was unjust and meaningless. Absurdism was born in this era of despair and doubt.

Absurdist Plays

Perhaps the most famous of the absurdist playwrights was Samuel Beckett (1906–1989). Beckett could be considered a fatalist, though his work is sometimes hilarious and can ask existential questions as well. His plays include *Endgame* (1957), *Krapp's Last Tape* (1958), and *Happy Days* (1961), but his most famous work is certainly *Waiting for Godot* (1953), about two clown-like tramps who meet each day on a barren plain, a dreamlike vacuum some critics say is the aftermath of a nuclear holocaust, and wait for Godot. They try to break the monotony of waiting by bickering, doing comic routines, and contemplating suicide, but Godot never shows up. The play is about our inability to take control of our existence and the absurdity of wasting our lives hoping to know the unknowable.

One of the best-known hilarious absurdist playwrights is Romanian-born French playwright Eugène Ionesco (1912–1994). His play *The Bald Soprano* (1949)

Samuel Beckett's Happy Days *is an absurdist play about a husband and wife. The wife, played here by Felicity Kendal, spends the duration of the play half-buried in a pile of dirt. As time goes slowly by, she finds occasional happiness in chatting with her husband and engaging in petty rituals such as brushing her hair. In true absurdist fashion, her predicament is never explained. Absurdist playwrights would agree with Scottish psychiatrist Ronald D. Laing (1927–1989), who said, "Madness is a sane response to an insane world." This 2003 production was directed by Peter Hall, Arts Theatre, London.*

Robbie Jack/Corbis

is a parody of the middle class. Mr. and Mrs. Smith and Mr. and Mrs. Martin, polite but empty people, spend a social evening together and engage in silly small talk, full of clichés. Often in a very comical way, his plays convey the seeming uselessness of trying to find meaning in a universe ruled by chance and irrational values. One of his most famous plays is *Rhinoceros* (1959), in which the characters are slowly transformed into horned, thick-skinned mammals; although this vision of humanity is certainly fatalistic, chilling, and insightful, it is also hard not to laugh when we see and hear this transformation from human to beast.

Harold Pinter (b. 1930), winner of the 2005 Nobel Prize for literature, is another influential hilarious absurdist playwright. Pinter writes "comedies of menace," which both frighten and entertain. Pinter is famous for his dialogue, which captures the incoherence, broken language and pauses of modern speech but also has a **Kafkaesque** quality, meaning that it is marked by surreal distortion and impending danger. This term comes from the writings of Franz Kafka (1883–1924), whose books described an unintelligible and hostile world. One of Pinter's most popular plays is *The Dumb Waiter* (1957), about two hired killers, Ben and Gus, employed by an enigmatic organization to murder an unknown victim. The two hit men wait for instructions in a dingy basement that contains a dumbwaiter (a tiny elevator used to convey food from one floor to another). All they know is that instructions will soon arrive; they'll make the hit and drive off, as they always do. Then an envelope with matches is mysteriously pushed under the door. Ben and Gus become nervous. Next the dumbwaiter moves, and someone from above orders "two braised steaks and chips, two sago puddings and two teas without sugar." Fearing that they will be discovered, Ben and Gus attempt to placate whoever is above by sending up bits of food. It doesn't work, for the dumbwaiter comes back down with requests for Greek and Chinese dishes. When Gus goes out for water, Ben gets instructions on the dumbwaiter to kill the next person who enters the room. Moments later, Gus is pushed in. He's stripped of his jacket, tie, and gun. He is the next victim, and the play ends.

A notable existentialist playwright is French philosopher Jean-Paul Sartre (1905–1980). His plays included *The Flies* (1943) and *No Exit* (1944). *No Exit* was first performed in France in May 1944, just before the liberation of Paris and a year before the end of World War II. It is the story of a man and two women who find themselves in Hell, which just happens to be a living room decorated with Victorian furniture. For Sartre, existence is the will to create our future, and the opposite of existence is not having the power to create our future or giving that power away—whether through law, religion, or government. Sartre said, "Man is nothing else but what he proposes, he exists only in so far as he realizes himself, he is therefore nothing else but the sum of his actions, nothing else but what his life is."

Mixing Isms

Plays seldom fall into a single ism. Sometimes playwrights, directors, and designers mix isms to form a unique evening of theatre. For example, a designer might create an expressionistic set for a play staged with realistic acting; a director might call for realistic acting within a play written using Romantic language; or a performance might blend comedy and tragedy to form **tragicomedy**. Mixing isms can be very difficult, because if it is not done well it can unintentionally alienate the audience and irritate the critics. One of the most famous playwrights

SPOTLIGHT ON Understanding Non-Western Theatre

Non-Western theatre such as African ritual theatre, Japanese Kabuki, and Islamic shadow puppetry can be difficult for Westerners to fully comprehend because of unfamiliar theatrical conventions and the haze of translation. Much of non-Western theatre is closely tied to ritual, and incorporates color, dance, song, and movements to exaggerate, stylize, and symbolically represent life.

- **African Theatre: Precolonial African theatre** grew out of ritual and storytelling. It incorporated acting, music, poetry, dance, costumes, and masks to create a theatre that combined ceremony with drama. But, unlike contemporary Western theatre during which the audience sits quietly and watches actors perform, precolonial African theatre seldom separated the audience and the performers. Instead, African ritual theatre encouraged the audience to sing and dance as they formed a circle of participants that fused the two most important institutions of precolonial Africa: religion and community. Because the performers often used masks, the audience could be part of the performance yet look different from the performers.
- **Sanskrit Drama: Sanskrit drama** is named for the ancient Indian language in which its plays are performed. For more than a thousand years, beginning around 200 BCE, professional touring companies performed Sanskrit drama in courts, temples, palaces, or temporary theatres on special occasions. Sanskrit plays, based on Indian myths, combine the natural and the supernatural, the believable and the unbelievable. These productions include comic and serious themes, fables with poetry, heroism, mythological characters, and love stories in which the righteous triumph and virtue is rewarded. The characters in Sanskrit drama are standardized types, and the acting is anything but realistic. Instead of learning how to conjure real emotions, actors of Sanskrit drama study for many years to learn representations of emotions through highly stylized gestures.
- **Peking Opera: Peking opera** is a synthesis of music, dance, acting, and acrobatics.

  Although it is called *opera*, all it has in common with Western-style opera is singing and musical accompaniment. Because they originally performed outdoors, Peking opera actors had to develop a piercing style of singing their lines in order to be heard over boisterous crowds. The orchestra—made up of gongs, cymbals, lutes, rattles, drums, castanets, and a two-string violin—also had to turn up the volume. The sets had to be kept simple so that the stage could be quickly set up and struck. Because there was little scenery, audience members had to use their imaginations. Scenes could be changed rapidly because a song, dance, pantomime, or symbolic movement would indicate the locale. For example, by circling the stage, an actor signified that he was on a long journey; by running across the stage holding a piece of flowing cloth, the actor showed that it was windy; if the story required the character to enter on horseback, the actor pantomimed a stylized gallop while swinging a riding whip.
- **Japanese Theatre:** Like the Japanese tea ceremony, Japanese drama emphasizes mood, serenity, contemplation, and simplified movements. To fully appreciate the Japanese theatre, one must prepare to receive the dreams, poetic vision, and beauty that are derived from simplicity and restraint. There are two types of traditional Japanese theatre: Noh drama and Kabuki.

Japanese **Noh** drama developed during the 1300s from the dance-prayers of Buddhist priests, who danced, sang, and prayed at religious shrines. Noh theatre reached its present form in the 1600s and has remained practically unchanged ever since. Today, the Noh actors' stylized performance techniques have become living traditions handed down from father to son. Every detail of the performance, every movement and vocal intonation, even the costumes and makeup are strictly regulated and cannot be altered.

Noh drama was designed for aristocrats and shoguns; there were few performances for the general public. By the seventeenth century, however, a robust and spectacular version of Noh was created for the masses. It was called **Kabuki**, from the characters for "song" (*ka*), "dance" (*bu*), and "skill" (*ki*). Over the centuries, Kabuki has become a popular form of mass entertainment. Although it borrowed a great deal from Noh, Kabuki is decidedly less restrained. It has a greater variety of characters, contains more battle scenes, and enacts many melodramatic moments. Kabuki actors wear colorfully embroidered, gold-lined kimonos and elaborate makeup and wigs just as in the Noh theatre, but Kabuki adds spectacular scenery, revolving stages, trapdoors, and breathtaking special effects.

Kabuki acting is so highly stylized that the movements are almost puppet-like. In fact, Kabuki borrowed many of its movements from **Bunraku**, the Japanese puppet theatre. In Kabuki, every movement of the body or limbs is exaggerated. At particularly intense or profound moments in the drama, the actors perform what is known as a ***mie* pose**. This is a sudden, striking pose accompanied by several powerful beats of wooden clappers known as the ***Ki***. During a classic *mie* pose, the actors strike a fierce posture, with their eyes crossed, chin sharply turned, and big toe pointed towards the sky, while the *Ki* sounds with several sharp blows or accelerates to a crescendo.

- **Islamic Theatre:** In the ancient Muslim world, theatre was not seen as a viable social entity, so plays were not an important part of Islamic culture. The Koran, Islam's holy book, contains a warning about "graven images," similar to the one in the Bible (Exodus 20:4). This prohibition applies to dolls, statues, portraits, live actors, and puppets so, in some Islamic countries, performers skirted the rules by backlighting two-dimensional figures and casting their shadows on a screen. The audience watched the silhouettes while a narrator told a story. In some ways this theatre might be compared to an archaic television set. **Shadow theatre**, as it is called (and which still exists today), probably originated in China around 100 BCE, but later developed into this unique form of Islamic theatre.

William Missouri Downs

Storytellers got around Islamic laws forbidding "graven images," including acting, by staging shadow plays with puppets. The puppets were generally made from the hides of camels or cows and were brightly painted.A puppeteer manipulated the puppets behind a transparent white curtain; lit from behind with candlelight, the shadows of the puppets were thrown onto the curtain.

Lou Anne Wright

Later Chinese opera stages shared some characteristics with Shakespeare's Globe Theatre. Although there was no historical connection, it is interesting to study their similarities. This stage located in Shanghai was built in 1888 and features a high thrust stage, a decorative roof, and seating galleries for patrons.

Dinodia Photo Library

The Sanskrit play Ramayana (ca. 300 BCE) chronicles the life and adventures of the virtuous king Rama, an incarnation of the god Vishnu. In this modern production, Rama battles the evil, multi-headed king Ravana, who kidnapped Rama's wife, Sita. This ancient story provides Hindus with a code of ideal conduct, much like the Bible does for Christians, and so has long been popular in India—when it was made into a 78-episode TV series in the 1980s, India almost came to a standstill every time it aired.

Michael S. Yamashita/CORBIS

Kabuki theatre began in the early 1600s as a popular form of Noh drama. Kabuki is known for stylized movements, singsong speech, and energetic characters. Over the years, Kabuki has gone in and out of fashion in Japan; it was briefly banned by occupying U.S. forces after World War II, but today it is the most popular form of traditional theatre. It has long influenced Western theatre and film artists, and elements of Kabuki can even be seen in contemporary TV cartoons—when called to action, the Mighty Morphin Power Rangers strike mie poses.

to successfully mix isms is Arthur Miller. His *Death of a Salesman* (1949) combines realism and expressionism. It is about Willy Loman, an unsuccessful traveling salesman. The realistic parts of the play cover the last twenty-four hours of Willy's life and his blind desire to attain the elusive, perhaps nonexistent, American dream. The expressionistic parts of the play show several sequences from Willy's point of view; these express his rosy visions of the past, including the great hope that he has for his two sons.

Tennessee Williams' drama was a skillful mix of genres or isms. *The Glass Menagerie* (1945) tells the story of Tom, his disabled sister Laura, and their controlling mother Amanda, who is desperate to make a match between Laura and a gentleman caller. The style of *The Glass Menagerie* has been called **poetic realism** because the acting is realistic and yet the dialogue has a poetic quality. The play also changes rules depending on where Tom is. When he is in the living room of the house the play is realistic, but when he steps on to the fire escape he breaks the fourth wall and talks directly to the audience. *The Glass Menagerie* is often staged with an expressionistic setting. (For more on mixing styles, see the section on "Cross-Cultural Theatre" in Chapter 3.)

Today, Western playwrights, directors, and designers also draw inspiration from Eastern theatrical traditions. For example, the Broadway production of *The Lion King* by American director and designer Julie Taymor (b. 1952) was heavily influenced by puppetry and masks, drawn from African and Asian traditions. (See the Spotlight "Understanding Non-Western Theatre.")

Curtain Call

Individual playwrights, actors, directors, and designers have their own unique style but often they express themselves with the help of various isms. Each ism is an interpretation of life. For example, naturalism and realism see life through the five senses and Romanticism experiences life from the heart, whereas expressionism projects the characters' emotions onto the canvas of life. In his famous introduction to *The Story of Art*, E. H. Gombrich says, "There is no such thing as art. There are only artists." This is certainly true in the theatre—how each designer, director, actor, or playwright sees life affects the style of the plays they create. Some find truth and reality in slapstick comedy and others in life-affirming melodrama, still others in absurdist tragedies. It could be argued that life is in fact all of these things rolled into one, and it is only the point of view of the individual that highlights one more than another. Whichever ism a theatre artist uses, it is important to know that there are many truths in the theatre and many ways to experience life.

Summary

Today's theatre can be divided into many different genres or "isms." We have not only comedy and tragedy, but the many other forms that help define how a play is staged, acted, and written. The most popular type of theatre today is realism, influenced by the ideas of Charles Darwin, Sigmund Freud, and Karl Marx. Realistic plays feature true-to-life, well-motivated characters and themes that examine problems of society. In an attempt to be more real, realistic plays often use box sets to allow audiences the feeling of spying on the action of the play. Naturalism was an outgrowth (and some said "more real" version) of realism.

In the early part of the twentieth century, the film industry began to take its toll on the theatre. Thousands of theatres were closed or converted into movie theatres. Movies could produce realism and naturalism better than the theatre, so theatre artists decided to "re-theatricalize" the theatre. Their efforts led to many avant-garde isms. One of the most popular is expressionism, which attempts to show life from the point of view of a particular character. Absurdism resulted from of the atrocities of the world wars, and it often helps to classify absurdism into three broad, overlapping categories: fatalist, existentialist, and hilarious. Fatalists show people trapped in an irrational universe where even basic communication is impossible. Existentialists believe that God is dead and that we must now do everything for ourselves. Hilarious absurdist playwrights highlight the insanity of life in a comic way.

The plays of epic theatre have a grand scope: a large cast, a long period of time, and a wide range of sometimes unrelated incidents. One of its greatest proponents was Bertolt Brecht, who also advocated an "alienation effect" to make the audience aware of watching a play. Brecht wanted the audience to confront political, social, or economic injustices.

Playwrights and directors often mix various isms in order to create a unique story. For example, some plays are part realism and part expressionism, whereas others tell realistic stories with lyrical language.

The Art of Theatre ONLINE

To access this chapter's interactive theatre workshop activities, along with many other learning tools, log onto your Theatre CourseMate. Access is available at cengagebrain.com.

Key Terms

absurdism / 254
alienation effect / 253
anagnorisis / 242
avant-garde / 251
blank verse / 248
Bunraku / 258
catharsis / 242
character flaw / 242
chorus / 243
comedy of ideas / 240
comedy of manners / 240
dark comedy / 240
domestic comedy / 240
epic theatre / 252
episode / 243
exodos / 243
expressionism / 250
farce / 240
fourth wall / 243
hamartia / 242
happening / 238
high comedy / 239
hip hop theatre / 238
hubris / 242
iambic pentameter / 249
Kabuki / 258
Kafkaesque / 256
Ki / 258
low comedy / 239
melodrama / 247
mie pose / 258
naturalism / 244
Noh / 257
parodos / 243
Peking opera / 257
performance art / 238
peripeteia / 242
poetic realism / 259
precolonial African theatre / 257
problem plays / 244
prologue / 243
realism / 242
Romantic comedy / 240
Romantics / 247
Sanskrit drama / 257
sentimental comedy / 240
shadow theatre / 258
stasimon / 243
straight plays / 238
tragedies of the common man / 242
tragic hero / 242
tragicomedy / 256
verbal scene painting / 248

The hit musical Hairspray *has music by Marc Shaiman, lyrics by Scott Wittman and Marc Shaiman and a book by Mark O'Donnell and Thomas Meehan; the show is based on the 1988 John Waters film of the same name. This production was staged at the Neil Simon Theater on Broadway.*

Photos on this spread Sara Krulwich/The New York Times/Redux Pictures

CHAPTER 12

The Musical

OUTLINE

No doubt about it, Americans love musicals. From Broadway theatres to high schools, from cruise ships to casinos—musicals are everywhere. Not only are they often big box office hits, but some of the longest running shows in the history of the theatre have been musicals. For example, the musical *Cats* ran on Broadway for nearly eighteen years; hundreds of thousands of people saw the 7,485 performances—and then touring companies took the play to theatres around the country. Broadway shows sell over $1 billion worth of tickets annually, and the majority of those seats are for musicals.

> American musical theatre is our indigenous art form. We can't claim drama, ballet, or opera, but musical theatre is our very own. . . . Musicals are in our blood and in our bones, are part of our collective personality.
>
> ***Molly Smith,***
> Artistic director of the Arena Stage

Why are musicals so popular? Perhaps it's because music—from deafening car stereos, to telephone-hold Muzak, to our favorite tracks that get us through the day—is a constant for most of us. Perhaps the rhythmic repetition of our heart beating inside of us gives music its power. Researchers have shown that music can intensify our emotions, increase our blood pressure, cause our pupils to dilate, and raise our heart rate. It also can calm our breathing and help us relax. The right music can even cause hens to lay extra eggs and help cows to produce more milk. Music can make us dance with joy or trigger depression; it can inspire us to make love or to make war. French emperor Napoleon Bonaparte summed up the power of music when he said, "Give me control over he who shapes the music of a nation; I care not who makes the laws." In this chapter we will examine one of the oldest forms of theatre, the play that combines music and drama, and its popular modern variation, the American musical.

Something for Everyone: What Makes a Musical?

There are two categories of theatre: plays with music and plays without. Plays without music are sometimes called **straight plays**. Plays with music come in all shapes. Let's make a quick survey of the various forms before we look at the elements and the history of musical theatre. **Opera**, such as Giacomo Puccini's (1858–1924) *Madama Butterfly* (1904), is a drama that is set entirely to music; all the lines are sung, usually to grand classical music. **Operetta**, or light opera, such as *The Mikado* (1885) by Gilbert and Sullivan, differs from "grand opera" because it has a frivolous, comic theme, some spoken dialogue, a melodramatic story, and usually a little dancing.

The play called the *musical* is a form you probably saw performed by your high school's drama department. There are a few varieties of musicals. A **musical comedy**, such as *Guys and Dolls* (1950), is characterized by a light-hearted, fast-moving comic story, whose dialogue is interspersed with popular music. A straight **musical**, such as *West Side Story* (1957), has a more serious plot and theme. A **rock musical** uses rock music—the rock and roll of the 1950s (*Grease*, 1972), the psychedelic rock of the 1960s (*Hair*, 1967), or contemporary pop and rock (*Rent*, 1996).

A program of sketches, singing, dancing, and songs pulled from previous sources is called a **revue**, or musical review; a program of unrelated singing, dancing, and comedy numbers is called a **variety show**. Variety shows and revues descend from **vaudeville**, a popular form of stage entertainment from the 1880s to the 1940s. An evening of vaudeville included a dozen or so slapstick comedy routines, song-and-dance numbers, magic acts, and juggling or acrobatic performances. Vaudeville descends from **burlesque**, a form of musical entertainment featuring bawdy songs, dancing women, and sometimes striptease. Burlesque began in the 1840s as a parody of the pretentiousness of opera—and of the upper class who could afford to attend it.

Whether opera, rock musical, or burlesque, no matter what your taste, you are sure to find a type of musical theatre to your liking. Now let's take a closer look at the structure and music of most forms of musicals.

Good Things Come in Threes: The Scripts of Musicals

Musical scripts have three components: book, music, and lyrics. The **music** is the orchestrated melodies, the **lyrics** are the sung words, and the **book** is the

Ethan Miller/Getty Images

Avenue Q represents a new twist on the traditional musical comedy, where irreverence and racy humor take center stage. Featuring puppets manipulated by bunraku-like handlers, this innovative musical tells the story of Princeton, an eager college graduate who comes to New York City with big dreams and little money. He settles into a slightly shady neighborhood populated by a motley host of characters in search of work, love, and a reason to be. A sort of Sesame Street *for adults,* Avenue Q *showcases songs such as "I'm Not Wearing Underwear Today," "Everyone's a Little Bit Racist," and "What Do You Do with a B.A. in English?" Book by Jeff Whitty, lyrics and music by Robert Lopez and Jeff Marx. Directed by Jason Moore, John Golden Theatre, New York, since 2003.*

spoken lines of dialogue as well as the plot. Unlike most straight plays, musicals often need several writers. The **librettist** writes the book, the **composer** writes the music, and the **lyricist** writes the lyrics. For example, Joseph Stein wrote the book for *Fiddler on the Roof* (1964), Jerry Bock wrote the music, and Sheldon Harnick wrote the lyrics. Occasionally, a versatile writer, such as George M. Cohan (*Fifty Miles from Boston*, 1908) and Meredith Willson (*The Music Man*, 1957), can write all three, but the duties for most musicals are shared. And these creative teams don't appreciate it when only one member of the team is credited for the entire work, as often happens. The wife of lyricist Oscar Hammerstein, a famous name in musical theatre, once overheard someone at a party say, "I just love Jerome Kern's 'Ol' Man River'" (from the musical *Show Boat*). She indignantly corrected the guest by pointing out that her husband had written the lyrics and that all Kern wrote was "Dum, dum, dum dum; dum, dum, dum dum."

Musicals with a particularly well-developed story and characters, such as *Fiddler on the Roof*, are sometimes called **book musicals**. *Fosse* (1998) and other **dance musicals** feature the work of a director-choreographer such as Tommy Tune, Michael Bennett, or Bob Fosse. Musicals that feature a particular band's songs are called **jukebox musicals**, like *Mamma Mia!* (2001), which was built around the music of Abba. Musicals that are mostly singing and have less spoken dialogue, such as *Les Misérables* and *Evita*, are known as **operatic musicals**. Operatic musicals are similar to operettas, but their tone is often much darker and more dramatic. For example, Steven Sondheim's operatic musical *Sweeney Todd: The Demon Barber of Fleet Street* features a story of betrayal, seduction, and revenge, subjects that are far too serious for light operettas. (For more on Sondheim and *Sweeney Todd*, see the Spotlight "Steven Sondheim.")

> One difference between poetry and lyrics is that lyrics sort of fade into the background. They fade on the page and live on the stage when set to music.
>
> ***Stephen Sondheim,***
> Musical theatre lyricist and composer

Sara Krulwich/The New York Times /Redux Pictures

Perhaps the most famous of Stephen Sondheim's works is West Side Story. *He was only 26 years old when he wrote the lyrics for this classic retelling of Shakespeare's* Romeo and Juliet. *The revival pictured here, produced at the Palace Theater in New York, starred George Aram, Karen Olivo, and Cody Green.*

> A song without music is a lot like H_2 without the O.
>
> ***Ira Gershwin,***
> Musical theatre lyricist

From Ballads to Showstoppers: The Music of Musicals

A traditional musical begins with an **overture**—a medley of the show's songs played as a preview. The overture lets the audience know that it's time to stop talking because the performance is about to begin; it can also provide time for latecomers to take their seats. At one time, overtures were the standard opening for all musicals. *The King and I*, *My Fair Lady*, and *Gypsy* all had overtures. But in 1975 the musical *A Chorus Line* cut out the overture; one was written but cut before the show opened because the show's creators felt that it might destroy the illusion that the audience was watching a real chorus line audition. Since then the overture has become optional. Musicals like *The Producers*, *Wicked*, *Spamalot*, and *The Color Purple* have traditional overtures. Other musicals, such as *Chicago* and *The Drowsy Chaperone*, have short mini-overtures, whereas *Rent* and *Spring Awakening* dispense with the overture altogether.

During the show, different types of songs are used for different dramatic and theatrical purposes. Leonard Bernstein and Stephen Sondheim use a large variety in *West Side Story*, a retelling of *Romeo and Juliet* set on the streets of New York. "Tonight" is a **ballad**, a love song for Tony and Maria. "Gee, Officer Krupke" is a **comedy number** that provides comic relief. "A Boy Like That," a sung conversation between Maria and her best friend, advances the story line. And "America" is a big production number called a **showstopper** because of the torrent of applause that such numbers often receive, literally stopping the show.

Songs are placed strategically within the story, usually at points where dialogue is not sufficient, so the characters must break into song to fully express what they are feeling. Some songs are followed later by a **reprise**, a repetition of the song, sometimes with new lyrics, sometimes with the same lyrics but with new meaning or subtext in order to make a dramatic point.

SPOTLIGHT ON Stephen Sondheim

One of the most accomplished lyricists and composers of contemporary American musicals is Stephen Sondheim (b. 1930). Sondheim wrote his first musical at the age of fifteen, but his remarkable career officially began when he became a protégé of legendary lyricist and producer Oscar Hammerstein II (1895–1960). Sondheim's Broadway credits begin with the lyrics for *West Side Story*, including the famous "I feel pretty / Oh, so pretty / I feel pretty and witty and bright!" He went on to write the lyrics for the golden-era musical *Gypsy* (1959) and was lyricist and composer for the ever-popular *A Funny Thing Happened on the Way to the Forum* (1962).

Sondheim has also written less traditional musicals like *Company* (1970), *Follies* (1973), *A Little Night Music* (1974), and *Pacific Overtures* (1976). These musicals are known as "concept" musicals because they focus on a particular event rather than a more traditional cause-and-effect story plot. For example, *Company* follows the main character, a single guy named Bobby, through a series of dinners with his somewhat neurotic friends. *Follies* tells the story of a condemned theatre building in which a series of vaudeville-like *Follies* had run many years ago. Because the theatre is due to be demolished to make room for a parking lot, all of the old "follies girls" return to the theatre for a reunion. The story runs in both the present and the past, showing the audience the younger versions of these characters. *Pacific Overtures* (1976), which was staged Kabuki style, portrays the ways in which Japan's culture was affected when the United States forced the isolated islands to open up to international trade in 1853.

One of Sondheim's most famous musicals is *Sweeney Todd: The Demon Barber of Fleet Street* (1979), which combines a conventional plot structure with an operatic score. *Sweeney Todd* explores a subject that is highly unusual for musicals: revenge-based serial murder and cannibalism. The musical is the story of Benjamin Barker, a barber who has led a beautiful life until a corrupt and depraved judge convicts him on trumped-up charges. After serving his time on a prison island, Benjamin returns, assumes the name Sweeney Todd, and sets out on a mission of revenge, slitting the throats of men who come to his shop for a shave, and then giving them to his neighbor, Mrs. Lovett, who turns the bodies into meat pies. Recently Sondheim reimagined his musical as a Hollywood movie starring Johnny Depp (2007). The film version, with more dialogue and less singing, is more of a book musical, whereas the original was an operatic musical. Other popular Sondheim musicals include *Sunday in the Park with George* (1984), loosely based on the life and loves of French neo-Impressionist painter Georges Seurat while he was creating his famous painting *A Sunday on La Grande Jatte; Into the Woods* (1987), which combines classic fairy tales into a story that shows that life seldom ends happily ever after; and *Assassins* (1990), which explores the history of presidential assassins in America, from John Wilkes Booth to John Hinckley, Jr.

Sondheim's work proves that a musical can be about any subject. As Sondheim's mentor, Oscar Hammerstein, once said, "It is nonsense to say what a musical should or should not be. It should be anything it wants to be, and if you don't like it you don't have to go to it. There is only one absolutely indispensable element that a musical must have. It must have music."

Robbie Jack/CORBIS

One of Stephen Sondheim's most famous musicals, Sweeney Todd *is the tale of a murderous barber who wreaks havoc in eighteenth-century London to avenge his unjust imprisonment. Supposedly based on a real case, the story of Sweeney Todd fascinates audiences as much as the mystery of Jack the Ripper. Music and lyrics by Stephen Sondheim, book by Hugh Wheeler. Royal Opera House, Covent Garden, London, 2003.*

Musicals: Then and Now

Although it's often said that the musical is an American invention (and that may be true), music, dance, and song have been a part of the theatre since its beginnings. Traditional African dramas and ritual plays have always incorporated music and dance. Twenty-five hundred years ago, Greek tragedies depended on a chorus of singing and dancing men. Aristophanes may have been creating musical comedy when he combined parody, satire, wit, and music in his plays. Then, for hundreds of years the Roman stage was filled with bawdy song and dance, and during the Middle Ages traveling bands of performers offered popular songs mixed with stories full of slapstick comedy. Elizabethan plays often included folk songs—Shakespeare's *The Tempest* alone includes nine songs. Japanese Kabuki plays depend on dance, music, and song. Musical masques, operas, burlesques, minstrel shows, variety shows, and music hall revues are all ancestors of the modern American musical. Though Americans were not the first to add song and dance to the theatre, they did make a unique form of musical theatre by borrowing from and combining earlier forms. Let's take a closer look at musicals throughout history.

Opera: High Art and Comic Relief

In opera, there is no spoken dialogue. Instead, the actors sing and sometimes chant their speeches and conversations. Opera developed five hundred years ago during the Italian Renaissance. Its creators were attempting to imitate ancient Greek tragedies; many scholars of the time thought the plays of Aeschylus, Sophocles, and Euripides were intended to be sung rather than spoken. In the end, they created a hybrid of music and drama, an art form in which the actors sang all their lines. The word *opera* comes from the Latin for "work";

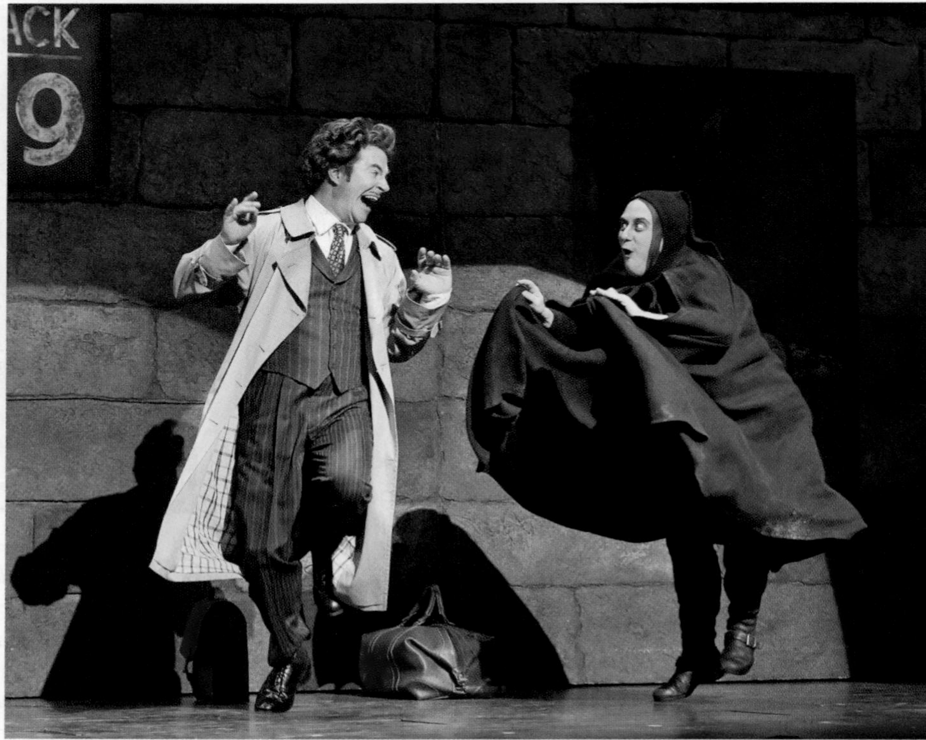

Sara Krulwich/The New York Times/Redux Pictures

Modern American musicals are sometimes based on movies with which the audience is familiar. There have been musical versions of Legally Blonde, The Lion King, The Producers, *and many others. One of the latest is Mel Brooks' musical version of his movie* Young Frankenstein, *pictured here.*

the Italians may have originally called these singing plays "works in music" or "musical works for the stage." The first operas were staged in Italy in the late 1500s, and the first public opera house was built in Venice in 1637. Opera proved to be so popular that by the end of the century Venice alone had eleven opera houses. Opera hit its peak in the nineteenth century. Notable opera composers include Richard Wagner (1813–1883), Giacomo Puccini (1858–1924), Wolfgang Mozart (1756–1791), Gioacchino Rossini (1792–1868), and George Frideric Handel (1685–1759).

Today, traditional opera is not as common as it once was. It's also often considered an elitist form of entertainment enjoyed primarily by the wealthy and well educated. But other forms of opera are still quite popular. **Comic opera**, including operetta, developed out of *intermezzi*, or comic interludes performed during the intermissions of operas. This style of opera became widely popular with the work of Sir William Schwenck Gilbert (1836–1911) and Sir Arthur Seymour Sullivan (1842–1900), including *The Pirates of Penzance* (1879), *The Mikado* (1885), and *H.M.S. Pinafore* (1878). When Gilbert and Sullivan's *H.M.S. Pinafore* was staged in

Michal Daniel/Proofsheet

Gilbert and Sullivan's The Pirates of Penzance *is the story of Frederic, a child mistakenly apprenticed to a band of kindhearted pirates. In his twenty-first year, Frederic has fulfilled his apprenticeship and is eager to return to respectable society. However, the pirates inform him that he was bound until his twenty-first birthday, and since he was born in a leap year on February 29, technically he has celebrated only five birthdays. When Sir Sullivan was working on* Pirates, *he wrote to his mother, "I think [the opera] will be a great success, for it is exquisitely funny, and the music is strikingly tuneful and catching." He was right—*The Pirates of Penzance *was an instant hit and is still performed regularly. This 2004 production featured Dan Callaway as Frederic and was directed by Joe Dowling, Guthrie Theater, Minneapolis.*

the United States in 1879, it was a triumph. Soon, American theatres added song and dance wherever possible in their shows.

Early American Musicals: The Good, the Bad, and the Ugly

The earliest American musicals were **ballad operas**, brought from England and popular during the colonial period. These comic operas mixed popular songs of the day with spoken dialogue. About a hundred years later, around 1840, burlesque was all the rage. It featured songs, skits, and plenty of racy dancing girls in a "leg-show"; later burlesque shows often also included striptease acts. The original purpose of burlesque was to lampoon high society's operatic tradition by turning it into a kind of sexy caricature. Today, burlesque lives on in The Pussycat Dolls, an all-female group of dancers, whose lineup has included Carmen Electra and guest stars Britney Spears and Gwen Stefani. These modern acts no longer satirize high art, but they continue the tradition of striptease's sly humor and sexual innuendo.

By 1890, vaudeville had replaced burlesque as the dominant form of American musical entertainment. It was designed to be more respectable, wholesome, and family oriented. It added acts by ventriloquists, acrobats, jugglers, magicians, male and female impersonators, and monologists (early stand-up comedians) to the toned-down song and dance numbers. Vaudeville shows could also include animal acts; ballroom dancing; demonstrations of scientific discoveries; famous criminals recounting their lurid past; comic skits featuring actors playing Irish, Jewish, Italian, or "blackface" stereotypes; and sing-alongs of "Camptown Races," "Swanee River," "Oh! Susanna," and other popular songs written before the Civil War.

Most vaudeville companies were small and traveled the rails from town to town putting on one-night shows in local theatres. Big-time vaudeville was the *Ziegfeld Follies* (1907–1931), a series of lavish musical reviews on Broadway, featuring Will Rogers, Fanny Brice, and other popular stars. (In many ways, the *Follies* live on in today's Las Vegas stage shows.) Many early movie stars got their start in vaudeville, including W. C. Fields, Al Jolson, Buster Keaton, Fred Astaire, and the comedy team George Burns and Gracie Allen. The vaudeville circuit was also a popular subject of early American movies. On television, the *Ed Sullivan Show*, the *Sonny and Cher Comedy Hour*, and the many other variety shows from the 1950s through the 1970s were descendants of vaudeville. Today, shows like *America's Got Talent* and *American Idol* are descendants of this tradition, recreated within a reality-TV format.

Another popular form of musical theatre in the nineteenth century was the **minstrel show**. Unique to the United States, these shows came to prominence in the 1830s and lasted well into the twentieth century. The shows included comic scenes, dance interludes, and sentimental ballads, all based on white stereotypes of black life in the South. These shows flourished for a couple of reasons. First, black music was very popular, but it was considered improper for whites to go to a theatre to hear black musicians play, so white performers put on black makeup—called *blackface*—and performed what was supposedly black music, such as Thomas Rice's song "Jump Jim Crow" (ca. 1828). (For more on blackface, see the Spotlight "Blackface, Redface, Yellowface" in Chapter 3.) Second, minstrel shows provided Northern white audiences with an idea of what the

Bettmann/CORBIS

In the late nineteenth century, vaudeville was the dominant form of musical entertainment in the United States. Intended as a family-friendly alternative to burlesque, vaudeville often featured family acts such as The Three Keatons (who, incidentally, shared the stage with escape artist Harry Houdini and his wife, Beatrice). The Keatons' shtick included skits that showed their audiences how to "properly" raise a child, but included throwing the youngster though fake walls and scenery. The youngest member of this act grew up to become one of America's greatest silent film stars: Buster Keaton, the great stone face.

lives of the slaves were like, albeit in a highly distorted and romanticized way. These early minstrel shows were nothing but entertainment and they never challenged white audiences to think about the atrocities of slavery.

As the shows became more popular, their structure became standardized. The first part had musical numbers with bits of comic dialogue; the second was full of songs, dance, and standup routines; and the third segment typically featured a one-act play. The skits in the minstrel shows often contained illiterate and foolish exchanges that made fun of blacks. Yet, because the blackface makeup provided a kind of mask, some performers felt free to incorporate social commentary about abolition and women's rights into the skits. This was particularly true of shows in the 1860s, the Civil War years, when some black performers also painted their faces black and formed their own minstrel troupes. In fact, the most famous minstrel performers in the late 1800s and early 1900s were black.

When Hollywood got into the act, the faces under the black makeup were once again white. The first "talkie" movie, *The Jazz Singer* (1927), featured white actor Al Jolson in blackface performing in a minstrel show, and later the famous stars Fred Astaire and Judy Garland portrayed minstrel show performers in blackface. Not until the 1950s and 1960s brought the civil rights movement did minstrel shows fall into total disrepute.

The Black Crook, a melodrama about black magic staged in New York City in 1866, is often called the United States' first modern musical. The story was a Faust-like melodrama about a crook-backed practitioner of black magic (hence the title) who makes a pact with Lucifer that allows him to live one extra year for each soul he delivers to hell. His first victim is the virtuous Rudolphe, who has been imprisoned by an evil count. However, Rudolphe escapes, frees a trapped fairy queen, discovers buried treasure, and saves the day. In the end, the sorcerer fails to deliver any souls and is carted off to Hell himself. By most accounts the play was poorly written and doomed, but just before it opened, the producers had an odd stroke of luck when the nearby New York Academy of Music caught fire, stranding a troupe of Parisian ballet dancers. The enterprising producers of *The Black Crook* hired the dancers and quickly restaged the play, combining the melodrama with music and dance into a production described as an "extravaganza" that included demons and sprites and "bare-armed" women. *The Black Crook* opened September 12, 1866, and was a massive success, running for 475 performances and making over $1 million on an investment of only $25,000—a considerable profit even today. It would be revived on Broadway an unprecedented eight times and have more than 200 performances in London.

The success of *The Black Crook* spawned a host of similar extravaganzas that were, by today's standards, just musical reviews containing unrelated but toe-tapping songs by a number of composers, chorus girls dancing in elaborate production numbers, and plenty of spectacular costumes and magnificent sets without regard for the story or characters. The joke-filled dialogue was only an excuse to get from one song to the next. These early musical plays lacked strong plot and believable characters, but both were deemed unnecessary because entertainment was the primary purpose, not drama.

African American Musicals: Opening New Doors

The success of *The Black Crook* also opened the door for the first full-length musical comedy conceived, written, produced, and performed by African Americans in New York. Composer and producer Bob Cole, along with lyricist Billy Johnson, formed a production company and opened *A Trip to Coontown* at the Third Avenue Theater in 1898. The story of a con man, the musical used minstrel stereotypes and spoofed *A Trip to Chinatown*, a popular musical comedy. But one of its songs challenged the racist policies of the day: a young black man sings about how he and his date were denied entry to a nightclub because of the color of their skin. *A Trip to Coontown* played to both whites and blacks and had two long runs in New York and a successful tour.

That same year, the ragtime musical *The Origin of the Cakewalk* (1898) became the first all-black show to play at a top Broadway theatre. But getting onstage required some ingenuity. The play's black composer, Will Marion Cook, went to the theatre and confidently informed its manager that the white owner had sent the troupe to perform that night. They were such a success that the manager immediately signed them for a long run. Only later did he find out that the theatre owner had known nothing about Cook's players.

By the 1920s there were a host of black musicals and revues including *Runnin' Wild* (1923), *Dixie to Broadway* (1924), and *Blackbirds* (1926). They had black casts and many had black writers, but blacks and whites acting together on stage was still considered improper, at least by whites. Broadway had opened its door a crack for black librettists, lyricists, composers, and actors, but not until 1959 did a straight play by a black playwright make it to Broadway—Lorraine Hansberry's *A Raisin in the Sun*. Of course, blacks were not the only ones discriminated

Shuffle Along (1921) was a wildly popular all-black musical review and a first in many respects: it introduced jazz dancing to Broadway, premiered such notable black entertainers as Paul Robeson and Josephine Baker, and featured the first realistic African American love story at a time when onstage love scenes between blacks were taboo. The show's catchy music included "I'm Just Wild about Harry," which years later became Harry Truman's presidential campaign song. Here, Noble Sissle poses with some of the Shuffle Along *showgirls. Sissle and Eubie Blake, a team made famous on the vaudeville circuit, wrote the music and lyrics. Another famous vaudeville team, Flournoy Miller and Aubrey L. Lyles, wrote the book.*

against. Women also ran up against discrimination. (See the Spotlight "Unsung Heroines of the American Musical.")

The Railroad, the War, and All That Jazz

In 1869 the Union Pacific met the Central Pacific Railway at Promontory Point, Utah, completing the first transcontinental railroad across the United States. By 1900, nearly three hundred touring theatre companies were taking advantage of this new, relatively fast form of travel. All the larger towns along the tracks built a theatre where these companies could play one-night or one-week stands. Most of the plays were melodramas, but there were also plenty of musicals, which were fast becoming America's favorite form of entertainment. Even today, successful musicals usually spawn one or more road companies that travel around the country.

SPOTLIGHT ON Unsung Heroines of the American Musical

Women have always sung, danced, and acted in musicals on the U.S. stage, but for a hundred years, almost all the composers, librettists, and lyricists have been men. According to the Dramatists Guild, in 2008 women wrote only 17 percent of Broadway and Off-Broadway musicals and plays; women of color wrote only 2 percent of that.

The gender disparity goes the other way for audiences; most of the audience members are women:

- The audience for the 2001–2 Broadway season was 63 percent female, according to the League of American Theatres and Producers.
- Of the respondents to the 1997 NEA Survey of Public Participation in the Arts, 26.7 percent of the women and 22.3 percent of the men had attended a musical in the previous twelve months.
- Of the plays produced in professional theatres at the national level in 2001–2002, 17–18 percent had been written by women, and 16 percent had been directed by women, according to *American Theatre Magazine*.

In spite of their lack of recognition and opportunity, some women have been successful writers for musicals. Dorothy Fields (1905–1974) wrote the lyrics for *Sweet Charity* (1966) and the book for *Annie Get Your Gun* (1946) and gave us such great songs as "I Can't Give You Anything but Love" and "The Way You Look Tonight." Betty Comden (1919–2006), with her partner Adolph Green (1915–2002), wrote lyrics for *On the Town* (1944), *Wonderful Town* (1953), *Subways Are for Sleeping* (1961), *Hallelujah, Baby* (1967), and the movie *Singin' in the Rain* (1952). Some of their best-known songs are "The Party's Over," "Make Someone Happy," and "New York, New York."

The Ronald Grant Archive

Although it's true that men have always dominated the creative and business sides of the entertainment scene, women have long played a part in bringing quality shows to the stage and screen. Betty Comden and her partner Adolph Green, the longest-running creative partnership in theatre history, collaborated on many award-winning Broadway shows and Hollywood musicals. One of their most famous films is Singin' in the Rain *(1952), starring Gene Kelly and Debbie Reynolds—this movie routinely makes critics' lists as one of the best films of all time.*

By World War I, the music of George M. Cohan (1878–1942) and Irving Berlin (1888–1989) was dominating Broadway. Their big-ticket musical comedies, such as Cohan's *Hello, Broadway* (1914), were patriotic and sentimental. They had cardboard characters and flimsy stories in which the guy always got the girl, good always triumphed over evil, and life was all ice cream, apple pie, and the American way. The plots never stood in the way of giving audiences an evening of pure entertainment and plenty of catchy tunes such as Cohan's "You're a Grand Old Flag" (1906) and "Yankee Doodle Dandy" (1904) and Berlin's "God Bless America" (1918).

After the war, jazz began influencing the American musical. Brothers George and Ira Gershwin (1898–1937 and 1896–1983) wrote a string of successful musical comedies whose songs are still popular today: *Lady, Be Good!* (1924) with the song "Fascinating Rhythm," *Strike Up the Band* (1930) with "I've Got a Crush on You," and *Girl Crazy* (1930) with "But Not for Me," "Embraceable You," and "I Got Rhythm." Playing in the orchestra for these shows were soon-to-be-famous big band leaders Glenn Miller and Benny Goodman.

These early musicals had simple stories about charming princes, gallant young men, romantic swashbucklers, and wealthy gentlemen, all of whom were looking for love. Happy endings and no mention of the dark side of life were a must; the few plays that ended unhappily always did so for the good of humanity. For example, at the end of Sigmund Romberg's *The Student Prince* (1924), the kind young heir to the throne sacrifices his personal happiness for the good of the kingdom when he sorrowfully pulls himself away from his true love, a beer-hall girl, in order to marry a princess whom he does not love. The characters and stories of these sweetheart musicals may have been simple, but most of the musical comedies we enjoy today follow the same formula.

The *Show Boat* Revolution

In 1927, lyricist-librettist Oscar Hammerstein and composer Jerome Kern (1885–1945) revolutionized musical theatre with *Show Boat*. It combined musical comedy and serious drama to create what we recognize today as the quintessential American musical. The story begins aboard the show boat *Cotton Blossom* in 1880s Mississippi. Gaylord Ravenal, a riverboat gambler, comes aboard and falls for Magnolia, the daughter of the ship's captain, Cap'n Andy. When the star of the *Cotton Blossom*'s show, Julie, is forced out by the local sheriff because she is a mulatto woman married to a white man, Magnolia and Gaylord fill in. Years later, Gaylord and Magnolia are married and have a daughter, Kim. After Gaylord racks up sizable gambling debts and leaves Magnolia, she looks for a singing job to support herself and Kim. She runs into Julie at a club, and the kindhearted Julie lets Magnolia take her own singing job. At a New Year's Eve show, Cap'n Andy comes to the club and is surprised to see Magnolia on stage. When she is almost booed off stage, he brings the crowd around in a magnificent sing-along. He then convinces her to return to the *Cotton Blossom*, where a contrite Gaylord is waiting to be reunited with his family.

Unlike the musicals that came before, *Show Boat* had a consequential story, powerful dialogue, three-dimensional characters, and songs and dances that tied directly into the plot. Instead of a line of pretty dancing girls, the chorus consisted of black dockworkers, and they portrayed real people rather than the black stereotypes common at the time. The theme was more serious and dealt with, among other subjects, racial issues. Moreover, black and white actors performed on stage at the same time, which was still a rare occurrence. Yet old attitudes and customs don't reverse themselves overnight; in the original production the role of Queenie was played in blackface by a white actress named Tess Gardella (1897–1950), who was famous for playing "Aunt Jemima" or "mammy" characters in vaudeville.

In spite of its shortcomings, *Show Boat* was the first production to combine dancing, choruses, toe-tapping melodies, and huge spectacle with a strong

The Ronald Grant Archive

Today we are used to seeing realistic relationships between black and white characters portrayed on stage and screen, but when Hammerstein and Kern's Show Boat *premiered in 1927, such portrayals were a revelation.* Show Boat *was based on a book by novelist and playwright Edna Ferber, who was well known for strong female protagonists and strong secondary characters who managed to rise above racial or other discrimination. Adapting* Show Boat *for the stage is a testament to the courage of Hammerstein, Kern, and producer Florenz Ziegfeld; they took a huge chance staging a story of such depth for audiences accustomed to much lighter fare. This photo from the 1936 film version of* Show Boat *features Paul Robeson (center), who sang one of the musical's signature songs, "Ol' Man River."*

plot and plausible characters. In 1932, following on the heels of *Show Boat*'s tremendous success, Ira Gershwin and George S. Kaufman's musical *Of Thee I Sing*, a biting satire of Washington politics, became the first musical to win the Pulitzer Prize—the highest award given for American drama. Although frothy love stories didn't disappear from Broadway, more musicals featured complex characters: the professional gambler who can't turn down a bet, Sky Masterson, in *Guys and Dolls* (1950); the bombastic but vulnerable king of Siam in *The King and I* (1951); the self-important but charming Professor Higgins in *My Fair Lady* (1956); and the kindhearted con man, Harold Hill, in *The Music Man* (1957). The American musical was becoming a serious art form, and more musicals won the Pulitzer, including *South Pacific* (1950), *Fiorello!* (1960), *How to Succeed in*

Business without Really Trying (1963), *A Chorus Line* (1976), *Sunday in the Park with George* (1985), and *Rent* (1996).

> I know the world is filled with troubles and many injustices. But reality is as beautiful as it is ugly. I think it is just as important to sing about beautiful mornings as it is to talk about slums. I just couldn't write anything without hope in it.
>
> **Oscar Hammerstein,** Lyricist and producer

Thoroughly Modern Musicals

During the 1927–28 season, Broadway had more than seventy theatres with a total of 264 productions, including 46 musicals—a record that has never been broken. The great stock market crash of 1929 drastically reduced their numbers. George and Ira Gershwin's operatic musical *Porgy and Bess* (1935), Marc Blitzstein's (1905–1964) labor parable *The Cradle Will Rock* (1938), and other musicals of the Great Depression took on the tone of the times. After the United States entered World War II at the end of 1941, musicals returned for a while to flimsy plots with a patriotic flair. But in 1943, Richard Rodgers (1902–1979) and Oscar Hammerstein's *Oklahoma!* came to Broadway. Like *Show Boat*, it had well-developed characters, song-and-dance numbers integrated into the story, and some serious plot elements, including a murder. It even incorporated classical ballet. The story of *Oklahoma!* is simple—it is the tale of a cowboy and a farmhand competing for the affections of a farm girl in Oklahoma Territory in 1906. However, it was influential because it incorporated storytelling techniques new to musicals, and the use of dance to develop the plot and the characters.

The 1950s and 1960s produced some of the most beloved Broadway musicals of all time. These "golden age" musicals not only told entertaining and exciting stories, but also featured perennial favorites, such as "There's No Business Like Show Business" (Annie Get Your Gun) *and "Luck Be a Lady"* (Guys and Dolls). *One of the most popular golden age musicals was* The Sound of Music, *which recounted the adventures of the singing von Trapp family, featuring the timeless songs "Do-Re-Mi" and "My Favorite Things," and was made into an Academy Award-winning movie starring Julie Andrews. In the original Broadway production (1959–1963), Mary Martin played the plucky governess, Maria Rainer. Music by Richard Rodgers, lyrics by Oscar Hammerstein II, book by Howard Lindsay, Russel Crouse, and Maria Augusta Trapp. Directed by Vincent J. Donehue. Lunt-Fontanne Theatre, New York.*

At the end of the war, Americans seemed filled with optimism, believing that they had saved the world for democracy and that the American dream of prosperity, order, and happiness was within everyone's grasp. This optimism led to the two decades that many consider the golden age of American musicals. Broadway was filled with great musicals: *Carousel* (1945), *Annie Get Your Gun* (1946), *South Pacific* (1949), *Guys and Dolls* (1950), *The King and I* (1951), *My Fair Lady* (1956), *West Side Story* (1957), *The Sound of Music* (1959), *Fiddler on the Roof* (1964), and *Man of La Mancha* (1965). All provided more than just light entertainment; they combined powerful, often serious stories with musical numbers that advanced the plot. Stephen Sondheim recalls a man walking out on *West Side Story* when it was first produced: "He wanted a musical—meaning a place to relax before he has to go home and face his terrible dysfunctional family. Instead of which he got a lot of ballet dancers in color-coordinated sneakers snapping their fingers and pretending to be tough. His expectation had been defeated." Today, a golden age of musicals exists not in the United States but in India; although "Bollywood" musicals don't have the robust stories of America's golden age musicals, they are just as rich in spectacle and song—and they are as immensely popular as U.S. musicals once were. (See the Spotlight "Hooray for Bollywood!")

Musical theatre in the 1960s and 1970s broke even more expectations and took more risks. *Cabaret* (1966) showed Germany's period of political freedom and cultural experimentation just before the Nazis came to power. *Hair* (1967) introduced rock music, hippies, and nudity to the musical. *The Wiz* (1975) retold the story of the Wizard of Oz from the perspective of an African American schoolteacher and her streetwise companions, who travel through an Oz with an urban flavor in search of happiness. *A Chorus Line* (1975) dealt with homosexuality in a matter-of-fact way. These plays once again challenged the traditions of the American musical and brought a new strain of intellectual complexity to this fun-loving form of theatre.

The Wiz is a good example of the chances musical theatre artists took in the 1970s. A funky take on the well-loved story of The Wizard of Oz, this musical not only draws heavily on African American musical forms such as gospel, jazz, R&B, and disco, it also touches on topics of concern to the black community at the time, such as drug addiction and a focus on following hip trends rather than addressing social ills. This 1975 production featured Stephanie Mills as Dorothy. Music and lyrics by Charlie Smalls. Book by William F. Brown. Directed by Geoffrey Holder at the Majestic Theatre, New York.

SPOTLIGHT ON Hooray for Bollywood!

The term *Bollywood* blends "Hollywood" and "Bombay" and is often used in the West to refer to the cinema of India. Some consider the term pejorative slang, but others take it as a compliment. An average of eight hundred films are made every year in India, and many of them are musicals. That's more than twice the number of films Hollywood produces per year, making India not only the top producer of movies around the world but also the top producer of musicals. Movies are India's sixth largest industry and employ more than 300,000 people.

Indian movie stars such as Madhuri Dixit, Shilpa Shetty, Aishwarya Rai, and Karishma Kapoor are mobbed everywhere they go and, just like Hollywood stars, must hire bodyguards to protect them from admiring fans and overzealous paparazzi. Bollywood directors such as Rakeysh Omprakash Mehra, Raj Kapoor, Gugu Dutt, Mehboob Khan, and Bimal Roy are as famous in India as Alfred Hitchcock and Steven Spielberg are in the United States. Every year the Bollywood version of the Academy Awards is watched by a half a billion people in 110 countries.

Since the first Indian talkie in 1931, song and dance have been an integral part of Indian films; even many nonmusicals include a few songs. Bollywood musicals typically have stock love stories, heroes, heroines, love affairs, song-and-dance sequences, and happy endings. Here's how the Bollywood musical goes: A young man and woman fall in love. After their first meeting, the man sings a love song rhapsodizing about his beloved's beauty. However, some obstacle keeps the lovers apart, and they sing in a split-screen duet about their painful separation. In the end, they are reunited and celebrate their love with a huge song-and-dance number as flamboyant as any 1940s Broadway musical. Although most Bollywood musicals follow this formula, audiences are satisfied as long as the songs are fresh and exciting.

It is not surprising that musicals are so popular in Indian cinema. For thousands of years, song and dance have been an integral part of ritual, religious, and social life in India. Modern Indian theatrical music traces its roots to the Urdu Parsee theatre of the 1930s, which drew its inspiration from classic Indian literature and its staging techniques from nineteenth-century British melodrama. Bollywood movies and musicals have helped to define the national character of this huge country with seventeen major languages, five thousand gods, and six primary religions. Now Bollywood films are becoming popular around the world. Every year 3.5 billion people see a Bollywood movie. That is one billion people a year more than see Hollywood movies. Bollywood musicals have even begun to inspire Hollywood movies (*Moulin Rouge!*, 2001) and Broadway musicals (*Bombay Dreams*, 2005). There are now more than one hundred cinemas in the United States that show Bollywood movies.

Photostage

A tongue-in-cheek homage to the musicals of Indian cinema, Bombay Dreams *tells the typically Bollywood story of a poor Bombay tour guide, Akaash, who becomes a superstar with the help of Priya, an independent filmmaker, and Rani, a glamorous movie star. As Akaash gains money, fame, and the attentions of Rani, he wonders if these things can take the place of his family, friends, and relationship with the girl-next-door Priya. This 2002 production at the Apollo Victoria Theatre in London featured Ayesha Dharker as Rani. Book by Meera Syal, music by A. R. Rahman, and lyrics by Don Black.*

The End or a New Beginning?

During the 1920s an average of forty musicals per year were produced on Broadway. During the depression years of the 1930s the annual average fell to about eighteen. During the war years of the 1940s the average was sixteen. By the 1990s the number had fallen even farther, to only about five musicals per year. In the 1994–95 Broadway season, only two new musicals were produced. Over those decades, musicals also fell out of favor in Hollywood. (See the Spotlight "The American Musical and the Movies.") Even though the brilliant composer-lyricist Stephen Sondheim had been writing such notable musicals as *Company* (1970), *Sweeney Todd* (1979), and *Into the Woods* (1987), many felt that the golden age of the American musical had passed.

The main problem for musical theatre today is the cost. Unlike straight plays, Broadway musicals almost always cost big money. For example, *Phantom of the Opera* had 36 actors, more than 50 crew members, and 30 musicians. It needed 120 wigs, 260 costumes, and a massive set—not to mention the 20,000 AAA batteries it used each year. When it opened on Broadway in 1988, the cost was $375,000 a week. In comparison, the entire Broadway run of *The King and I* (1951–1954) cost $360,000. Even taking inflation into account, production costs have skyrocketed from decade to decade. In 1956 *My Fair Lady* cost $401,000 to produce; in 1975 *A Chorus Line* cost $1,145,000; in 1986 *Phantom of the Opera* cost over $7 million. Today, a Broadway musical can cost $5–$15 million on average to produce. The

The most expensive Broadway play ever produced was Spider-Man: Turn Off the Dark. *With music and lyrics by Bono, this comic book musical cost over 75 million dollars to stage and required over 180 previews before it finally opened.*

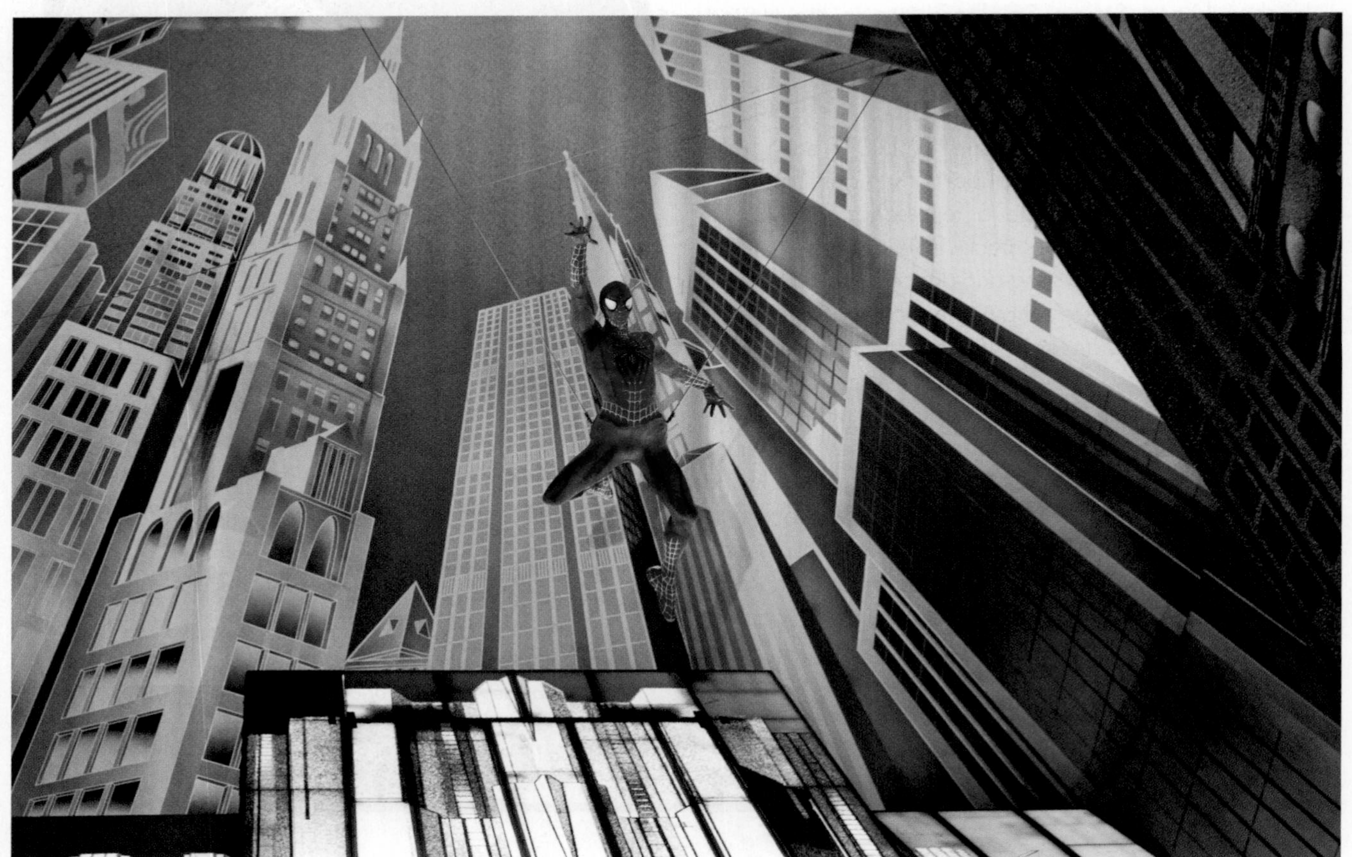

Sara Krulwich/The New York Times/Redux Pictures

most expensive musical ever—perhaps the most expensive play ever—is the spectacle *Spider-Man: Turn Off the Dark*, which originally cost over $75 million to stage.

As production costs have increased, so have ticket prices. When *A Chorus Line* opened on Broadway in 1975, the best seats sold for $15. Fifteen years later, when it closed, the price of a ticket was $50. Today, a ticket to a Broadway musical typically costs $100. (For more on production costs, see the Spotlight "Theatre Can Be Expensive" in Chapter 2.)

Today, only Walt Disney and other huge corporations can afford to foot the bill for huge new musicals. Consequently, some Broadway producers have turned to staging revivals of popular older musicals that have a greater chance of making back their investment. Others are trying to ensure success by basing "new" musicals on well-known Hollywood movies, such as *Big* (1996), *Footloose* (1998), *Thoroughly Modern Millie* (2002), *The Producers* (2001), *Hairspray* (2002), *Legally Blonde* (2007), and *Young Frankenstein* (2008). Expensive musicals such as *Phantom of the Opera* and *Miss Saigon* are still popular, yet there still seems to be room for smaller musicals such as revivals of *The Fantasticks* (1960) and *I Love You, You're Perfect, Now Change* (1996) that have small casts and can be produced on a shoestring. Whenever people say the American musical is on its way out, the art form always seems to stage another comeback. Today, new musicals such as *Urinetown* (2001), *Avenue Q* (2003), *Wicked* (2003), *The 25th Annual Putnam County Spelling Bee* (2005), *Monty Python's Spamalot* (2005), and *Spring Awakening* (2006) are keeping the art form alive and pushing it to new levels. Another method of creating hit musicals is to build stories around popular music the audience already knows, as is the case with *Mamma Mia!* (2001) and *Jersey Boys* (2005).

Sara Krulwich/The New York Times/Redux Pictures

Because big Broadway musicals can be so expensive to produce, smaller musicals such as The 25th Annual Putnam County Spelling Bee *are becoming increasingly popular. This musical takes an affectionate look at the mortifications of middle school via six misfits who compete for a spelling bee trophy. Because* Spelling Bee *has a small cast, a simple set, and cost a mere $3.5 million to produce, it broke even after only eighteen weeks on Broadway. As long as the public clamors for musicals—and they always do—producers will find innovative ways to keep this fun-loving art form alive. This production of* Spelling Bee *premiered in 2005 and was directed by James Lapine at the Circle in the Square Theatre, New York. Book by Rachel Sheinkin, music and lyrics by William Finn.*

Curtain Call

Depending on whom you talk to, the American musical is alive and well or on its deathbed. Musical theatre historian Denny Martin Flinn is one who has sounded the death knell for the musical: "When *A Chorus Line* gave its final Broadway performance fifteen years after it opened, the last great American musical went dark, and the epoch was over." Stephen Sondheim, who gave us such great musicals as *Sunday in the Park with George* and *Sweeney Todd*, recently told critic Frank Rich that only two types of Broadway musicals exist today: "revivals" and "the same kind of musicals over and over again." In his opinion, most musicals today are nothing more than "spectacles" and "stage versions of a movie." "We live in a recycled culture," said Sondheim. "I don't think the theatre will die per se, but it's never going to be what it was. You can't bring it back. It's gone. It's a tourist attraction."

SPOTLIGHT ON The American Musical and the Movies

The musical became popular in Hollywood the moment talkies were invented. The very first talking movie, *The Jazz Singer* (1927), had several musical numbers. Hollywood's golden age of musicals lasted from the 1930s to the early 1960s. From the dance extravaganzas of Busby Berkeley to the water ballets of Esther Williams, musicals were Hollywood's biggest moneymakers. But a decade after what has often been called Hollywood's best musical, Gene Kelly's *Singin' in the Rain* (1952), the musical was no longer a Hollywood mainstay.

By the 1980s, musicals had disappeared from the screen almost completely. Today, a few musicals are still made in Hollywood, but they are seldom *originated* by Hollywood. Rather, they are based on successful stage musicals such as *Chicago, The Phantom of the Opera, Rent*, and *Sweeney Todd*. Or they are quirky independent films, such as *Hedwig and the Angry Inch* (also based on a stage show) or "straight" movies, such as Woody Allen's *Everyone Says I Love You*, that parody or pay homage to old movie musicals. An exception is Baz Luhrmann's *Moulin Rouge!* (2001), starring Nicole Kidman and Ewan McGregor, though even this innovative movie musical uses songs recycled from Elton John, Madonna, Patti LaBelle, and other pop stars. In fact, the movie is considered innovative because it uses contemporary popular music in an attempt to generate in contemporary audiences an excitement similar to what the original Moulin Rouge audience felt in 1899 as they watched well-executed burlesque.

Some have speculated that the demise of the Hollywood musical is due to the demise of American optimism during the Vietnam War; others think the rise of music videos killed off the form; and still others say that movies today are far too realistic for the actors to suddenly break into song. All of those reasons may apply to Hollywood, but musicals are still as popular as ever in the live theatre.

Pictorial Press Ltd/Alamy

Baz Luhrmann's Moulin Rouge *is the tragic tale of Christian, a young British poet, who falls in love with Satine, the star of a lush cabaret show in turn-of-the century Paris.* Moulin Rouge *reflects numerous cultures and genres, including European opera, Greek myths, Bollywood movies, American pop, rock and disco.*

> It is clear that the musical theatre is changing. No one knows where it is going. Perhaps it is going not to one place but to many. That would be healthy, I think, just as the search in itself can be healthy. . . . Thus it was for Shakespeare in Elizabethan times; thus it was for writers of musicals after Rodgers and Hammerstein; and thus it will be again.
>
> ***Tom Jones,***
> Lyricist

However, this kind of pessimism is common each time there is a new turn or major development in musical theatre. There may be good years and bad, but the American musical is far from dead. It is simply in another transition as it evolves to become what culture and business require of it, just as it evolved to allow blacks and whites together on stage with *Show Boat* in 1927. Music and theatre have been traveling hand in hand for thousands of years, and even though the shape of the musical can't be predicted, there will be musicals as long as people like a story told with song.

Summary

Musical scripts are made up of three parts: book, music, and lyrics. The librettist writes the book, the composer writes the music, and the lyricist writes the lyrics. Musicals that feature a well-developed story and characters are called book musicals. Musicals that emphasize dance are called dance musicals, and musicals in which singing dominates are known as operatic musicals.

Music, dance, and song have been a component of theatrical traditions around the world for thousands of years. The modern American musical has evolved from a number of musical traditions, including opera, operettas, musical reviews, variety shows, vaudeville, and burlesque. The distinction of the first modern American musical is often given to *The Black Crook*, a melodrama about black magic staged in New York City in 1866. In 1898 the ragtime musical *The Origin of the Cakewalk* was the first all–African American show to play at a top Broadway theatre.

By World War I, big-ticket, sentimental musical comedies dominated Broadway. They seldom told complex stories or featured well-developed characters. The first big revolution in the American musical came in 1927 when Oscar Hammerstein and Jerome Kern wrote *Show Boat*, which combined aspects of musical comedy and serious drama to create what today we consider the quintessential musical. Sixteen years later, another well-rounded musical advanced the form: Richard Rodgers and Oscar Hammerstein's *Oklahoma!* Like *Show Boat*, *Oklahoma!* featured serious plot points, well-developed characters, and songs and dances used to develop the plot.

The musicals of the 1960s, 1970s, and 1980s brought a new round of innovation by taking on a wide variety of social and political issues. Today, there are musicals to fit every taste: rock and roll musicals, musicals based on movies, and traditional revivals of Broadway classics.

The Art of Theatre ONLINE 

To access this chapter's interactive theatre workshop activities, along with many other learning tools, log onto your Theatre CourseMate. Access is available at cengagebrain.com.

Key Terms

ballad / 266
ballad opera / 270
book / 264
book musical / 265
burlesque / 264
comedy number / 266
comic opera / 269
composer / 265
dance musical / 265
jukebox musical / 265
librettist / 265
lyricist / 265
lyrics / 264
minstrel show / 270
music / 264
musical / 264
musical comedy / 264
opera / 264
operatic musical / 265
operetta / 264
overture / 266
reprise / 266
revue / 264
rock musical / 264
showstopper / 266
straight play / 264
variety show / 264
vaudeville / 264

Glossary

A

absurdism An avant-garde "ism" that was the result of the two world wars. It has three types: fatalist, existentialist, and hilarious.

action The characters' deeds, their responses to circumstances, which in turn affect the course of the story.

Actors' Equity Association The union that represents stage actors; often shortened to "Actors' Equity" or "Equity." See also *Equity waiver*.

aesthetic distance The audience's awareness that art and reality are not the same. Closely tied to *willing suspension of disbelief*.

aesthetics The branch of philosophy that deals with the nature and expression of beauty.

alienation effect The result of techniques to keep the audience aware that what they are witnessing is only a play; used by Bertolt Brecht. Alienation techniques include having the actors address the audience out of character, exposing the lights, removing the proscenium arch and curtains, and having the actors perform on bare platforms or simple sets that are sometimes punctuated with political slogans.

American Federation of Television and Radio Artists (AFTRA) The trade union, affiliated with the AFL-CIO, that represents talk-show hosts as well as announcers, singers, disc jockeys, newscasters, sportscasters, and even stuntpeople.

anagnorisis (an-ag-NOR-i-sis) Element of a Greek tragedy; the tragic hero's self-examination leading to realization of true identity; follows *peripeteia* (radical reversal of fortune).

antagonist (an-TA-guh-nist) The character who stands in the way of the protagonist's goals. See *protagonist*.

apron See *lip*.

arena theatre A type of theatre with the stage in the center, like an island, surrounded on all sides by audience; also called theatre-in-the-round.

artistic director The person in charge of the overall creative vision or goal of the ensemble; often chooses which plays to produce, who will direct, and who will design; is also an ambassador to the community, a fundraiser, and the theatre's chief promoter.

assistant director A person who helps stage scenes and manage the production crew.

assistant stage manager A person who helps the stage manager run the show during performances and assists the director with the rehearsal process.

avant-garde (ah-vahnt-GARD) Any work of art that is experimental, innovative, or unconventional.

B

back story Dialogue about what happened to the characters before the play began and what happens between the scenes and offstage; also called *exposition*.

ballad A love song.

ballad opera Comic opera that mixed popular songs of the day with spoken dialogue; brought from England to the colonies during the colonial period.

basic elements of design Line, dimension, balance, movement, harmony, color, and texture.

beat A section of dialogue about a particular subject or idea; the smallest structural element of a script.

black box theatre A small theatre that generally holds fewer than a hundred people and has moveable seats so that audience groupings can be changed for every production.

blackface Black makeup used by white performers playing African American roles, as in minstrel shows.

blocking The movement of the actors on stage during a production; the technique the director uses to achieve focus and "picturization."

blocking rehearsals A series of rehearsals in which the director and actors work out the *blocking*, or the movement of the actors on stage during the play.

book For a musical, the spoken lines of dialogue and the plot; written by the *librettist*. Compare *lyrics* and *music*.

book musical A musical with a particularly well-developed story and characters, such as *Fiddler on the Roof*.

bourgeois (boorzh-WAH) **theatre** Commercial theatre productions that, like big-budget Hollywood films, pursue maximum profits by reaffirming the audience's values.

bowdlerize (bohd-luh-RISE) To edit out any vulgar, obscene, or otherwise possibly objectionable material before publication. The origin of the word is Thomas and Harriet Bowdler's prudishly sanitized edition of Shakespeare's plays for Victorian-era family consumption.

Bunraku (bun-RAH-koo) Japanese puppet theatre with large wooden puppets with many movable parts, onstage puppeteers dressed in black, and a narrator who chants the script.

burlesque (bur-LESK) A form of musical entertainment that features bawdy songs, dancing women, and sometimes striptease. Begun in the 1840s as a parody of opera and the upper class.

C

call The time the actors arrive at the theatre.

callback list During auditions, a list directors keep of actors they want to call back for subsequent auditions as they narrow the field of candidates.

casting against type Casting an actor who is very different from, or even the opposite of, the type of person who would be expected to play the part.

casting director A person who specializes in finding the right actors for parts; especially common in Hollywood.

casting to type Casting an actor who physically matches the role or who has a deep understanding of the character's emotions and motivations.

catharsis An intense, twofold feeling of pity and fear that is the goal of Greek tragedy.

cattle call An audition to which anyone may come and be given a minute or so to perform for the director; also known as an "open call."

censorship The altering, restricting, or suppressing of information, images, or words circulated within a society.

character flaw An inner flaw that hampers a character's good judgment and leads the character to make unfortunate choices; sometimes called *fatal flaw, tragic flaw,* or *hamartia.*

character makeup Makeup that completely transforms the way actors look, such as shadows, wrinkles, and gray hair to turn a young actor into an elderly character; compare to *straight makeup.*

choreographer The person who creates the dance numbers for a play or musical, or who teaches the dance numbers to the actors.

chorus In ancient Greek plays, an all-male group of singers and dancers who commented on and participated in the action.

climax The point of the greatest dramatic tension in the play; the moment the antagonist is defeated.

closed-shop union A union to which all employees *must* belong and which the employer formally recognizes as their sole collective bargaining agent; also called a "union shop." Compare *open-shop union.*

cold reading Audition in which actors read from a script without any preparation.

color-blind casting Casting actors without regard for their race or ethnic background.

comedy number A song in a musical that provides comic relief.

comedy of ideas A form of high comedy comprising cerebral, socially relevant plays that force audiences to reassess their culture, community, and values.

comedy of manners A form of Restoration comedy that features wit and wordplay and often includes themes of sexual gratification, bedroom escapades, and humankind's primitive nature when it comes to sex.

comic opera A style of opera, including operetta, that developed out of *intermezzi,* or comic interludes performed during the intermissions of operas. Popularized by the work of Gilbert and Sullivan.

commercial theatre The type of theatre that, like the majority of Hollywood screen entertainments, has entertainment and profitability as its reason for existence.

composer For a musical, the person who writes the music.

computer aided design (CAD) Programs used by set designers to create blueprints of set designs.

concept meeting An artistic gathering to interpret the playwright's script; the director and designers brainstorm, research, and experiment with different set, costume, and light possibilities.

concept production A production of a play dominated by the director's artistic vision, or concept.

conflict The key to the movement of a story; the element that qualifies a theatrical work as a "play."

convergent thinking Thinking that is measured by IQ and involves well-defined rational problems that have only one correct answer.

copyright A legal guarantee granted by the government to authors, composers, choreographers, inventors, publishers, and corporations that allows them to control and profit from their creative work and intellectual property.

corporate funding Money contributed to the arts, including the theatre, from companies of all sizes. Compare *government funding* and *patrons.*

costume plates Drawings that indicate how a costume is shaped, where seams and folds are, how the costume flows, and what fabrics are to be used.

costume shop The sewing machines, fabric-cutting tables, fitting rooms, and laundry facilities needed to create and maintain the costumes for a theatrical production.

creative director A director who adds concepts, designs, or interpretations to a playwright's words.

creativity A moment of insight when something new is invented or something that already exists is transformed.

cross-cultural theatre Theatre that joins contrasting ideas—whether staging techniques or myths and rituals—from diverse cultures into a single work in order to find parallels between cultures and promote cultural pluralism.

cross-gender casting Intentionally casting men to play women's roles and women to play men's roles.

cultural theatre The type of theatre that is designed to support the heritage, customs, and point of view of a particular people, religion, class, country, or community.

culture The values, standards, and patterns of behavior of a particular group of people expressed in customs, language, rituals, history, religion, social and political institutions, and art and entertainment.

curtain Usually the start of a show, but can also be the end of a show or an act, signaled by the raising or lowering of the curtain.

cyclorama (often shortened to "cyc" [SYK]) A large, stretched curtain suspended from a U-shaped pipe to make a background that can completely enclose the stage setting. Lights are often projected on the cyc to indicate a location or a mood.

D

dance musical A musical that features the work of a director-choreographer such as Tommy Tune, Michael Bennett, or Bob Fosse.

dark comedy Comedy that is gloomy, even sinister, allowing the audience to laugh at the bleaker and more absurd aspects of life.

dark moment The end of the middle section of a formula play, when the protagonist fails (for internal or external reasons), the quest collapses, and the goal seems unattainable.

dark night The one night of the week when a play is not performed and the theatre is closed; typically Monday night.

denouement (DAY-noo-MAH) The outcome of a play, a short final scene that allows the audience to appreciate that the protagonist, because of the preceding events, has learned some great or humble lesson.

dialogue The spoken text of the play; the words the characters say.

didaskalos (dih-DAH-sko-los) In ancient Greece, a playwright who staged the plays he wrote, instructing the performers and advising the designers and technicians.

dimmer A computerized light board.

director The person who turns a printed script into a stage production, coordinating the work of theatre artists, technicians, and other personnel.

director's note A note in a program in which the director conveys to the audience his or her artistic or personal thoughts about a play.

disturbance An inciting incident that upsets the balance and starts the action of a play by creating an opportunity for conflict between protagonists and antagonists.

divergent thinking Thinking that involves fluency and the ability to generate a multitude of ideas from numerous perspectives.

domestic comedy A type of play characterized by stories about common everyday people, rather than ones of noble birth, whose problems and complications are lighthearted and entertaining.

drama A form of theatre that tells a story about people, their actions, and the conflicts that result.

dramatic criticism A discriminating, often scholarly interpretation and analysis of a play, an artist's body of work, or a type or period of theatre.

Dramatists Guild of America (DGA) The playwrights' union in the United States; an open-shop union.

dramaturg (DRAH-mah-TURG) A literary advisor and expert in theatre history who helps directors, designers, and actors better understand the specifics and sensibilities of a play and who can also help playwrights find their voice (sometimes spelled *dramaturge*).

draper A person who, after studying the costume designer's drawings and renderings, cuts fabric into patterns that realize the design.

dresser A person just offstage who helps actors make quick costume changes.

dress parade A tryout of the completed costumes by the actors for the costume designer and director so that necessary changes can be made before opening night.

dress rehearsals The final rehearsals, when costumes and makeup are added, before the play opens.

E

elevations The views of a set design from front and back.

emotional memory An acting technique pioneered by Konstantin Stanislavsky in which the actor recalls the visual and auditory images, or physical circumstances, of a real-life (or imagined) event in order to relive the emotions accompanying it. Also called sense memory or affective memory.

empathy The ability to understand and identify with another's situation to the extent of experiencing that person's emotions.

enculturation The process by which we learn about our culture.

enlightenment The protagonist's realization of how to defeat the antagonist; often related to the theme of the play.

ensemble The crews of technicians, the assistants, and the artists including actors, directors, speech coaches, playwrights, and designers who use a wide variety of art forms including painting, drawing, writing, and acting as well as set, lighting, and costume design to create a theatre production.

epic theatre Features plays that have a grand scope, large casts, and cover a long period and a wide range of sometimes unrelated incidents.

episode One scene in an ancient Greek play; alternates with *stasimons*.

Equity waiver An exception to Actors' Equity Association wage standards that allows members to work for free in small productions. See *Actors' Equity Association*.

ethnocentrism The practice of using one's own culture as the standard for judging other cultures.

event An unusual incident, a special occasion, or a crisis at the beginning of a play that draws the audience's interest.

exodos (EKS-oh-dos) In ancient Greek theatre, the summation by the chorus on the theme and wisdom of the play.

experimental play A play that pushes the limits of theatre by eliminating the distance between actor and audience, trying out new staging techniques, or even questioning the nature of theatre.

exposition Dialogue about what happened to the characters before the play began and what happens between the scenes and offstage; also called *back story*.

expressionism A style that shows the audience the action of the play through the mind of one character. Instead of seeing photographic reality, the audience sees the character's own emotions and point of view.

F

farce A popular form of low comedy where the characters are trapped in a fast-paced situation with wild complications, mistaken identities, and incredible coincidences; also called "door-slamming farce": the pace of can be so fast because the characters are constantly running in and out of doors.

fatal flaw See *character flaw* or *hamartia*.

fight director A specialist who choreographs stage combat from fistfights to swordplay.

final dress rehearsal The last rehearsal before an audience is invited. See *dress rehearsals*.

flats Originally, the wood-and-muslin units that made up three walls of a room on stage; now, plain wall units as well as doors, windows, and fireplaces.

floor plan The blueprint of a set design that shows the view from above.

fly system The elaborate network of pulleys, riggings, and counterweights that allows scenic pieces to be "flown" up and out of the audience's sight in a traditional proscenium arch theatre.

focus The actor, action, or spot on the stage to which the director draws the audience's attention. See also *sharing focus, stealing focus, triangulation*, and *upstaging*.

found, or **created, space** Spaces where theatre can be performed, such as parks, churches, town squares, basements, warehouses, gymnasiums, jails, subway stations, and street corners.

fourth wall An imaginary wall separating the actors from the audience; an innovation of Realism in the theatre in the mid-1800s.

french scene A structural element of a play that begins with any entrance or exit and continues until the next entrance or exit.

G

gels (JELLS) Sheets of colored plastic attached to the front of lighting instruments.

gender-neutral casting Casting without regard for the character's gender.

general working rehearsals Rehearsals during which the director and actors work on individual scenes and concentrate on understanding the characters' motivation, emotions, and personality.

genre (ZHAHN-ruh) A category of artistic works that share a particular form, style, or subject matter.

ghost light A single bare light bulb mounted on a portable pole left to burn all night in the middle of the stage as a safety precaution.

given circumstances Character-analysis approach that begins with examining characters' life circumstances: their situations, problems, and the limits life has placed on them. Can include general background such as upbringing, religion, and social standing, as well as what happened to the character the moment before entering the scene.

gobos (GOH-bohz) Metal cutouts placed on the front of lighting instruments to project patterns (such as sunlight coming through the leaves of a tree) on the stage.

government funding The money spent each year on the arts by federal, state, and local governments. Compare *corporate funding* and *patrons*.

greenroom A small room for actors waiting for their cues, located just off the stage and out of the audience's earshot.

group dynamics The functioning of people when they come together into groups.

H

hamartia (heh-mar-TEE-eh) In ancient Greek tragedies, a personal weakness (also called a *tragic flaw* or *fatal flaw*) that leads to a tragic hero's downfall. A common hamartia is *hubris*.

hand props Any objects actors handle while on stage, such as pens, fans, cigars, money, and umbrellas.

happenings Unstructured theatrical events on street corners, at bus stops, in lobbies, and virtually anywhere else people gather.

Harlem Renaissance An African American literary, artistic, and musical movement during the 1920s and 1930s centered in the Harlem neighborhood in New York City.

high comedy A style that depends on sophisticated humor, wit, political satire, or social commentary. Compare *low comedy*.

hip hop theatre Productions influenced by hip-hop music, art, and culture.

historical theatre Dramas that use the styles, themes, and staging of plays of a particular historical period.

house A theatre's seating area.

house manager In charge of all the ushers; deals with any seating problems and makes sure the audience finds their seats and that the play begins on time.

hubris (HYOO-bruhs) The term used in classical Greek drama for overbearing pride or arrogance. A type of *hamartia*.

I

iambic pentameter Poetic lines of a play that describe the accent and length of each line; there are ten syllables per line (pentameter) and the stress goes on the second syllable (iambic).

inner conflict Some sort of unfinished business that is so compelling that it handicaps the character until it is confronted.

International Phonetic Alphabet (IPA) A system for transcribing the sounds of speech that is independent of any particular language but applicable to all languages.

interpretive director A director whose goal is to translate a script from page to stage as faithfully as possible.

J

jukebox musical A musical that features a particular band's song.

K

Kabuki (kuh-BOO-kee) A popular, robust, and spectacular version of the Japanese Noh theatre. The name comes from the characters for "song" (*ka*), "dance" (*bu*), and "skill" (*ki*). See also *Noh*.

Kafkaesque Marked by surreal distortion and senseless danger; a term that comes from the way that Czech writer Franz Kafka (1883–1924) depicted the world.

Ki In Kabuki theatre, wooden clappers whose beats accompany a *mie* pose at a particularly intense or profound moment.

L

League of Resident Theatres (LORT) An association of professional theatres that work together to promote the general welfare of the major regional theatres around the United States. Members of LORT also negotiate collective bargaining agreements with actors, directors, choreographers, and designers.

legs The curtains at the sides of a stage in a proscenium arch theatre.

librettist For a musical, the person who writes the *book*, or the spoken lines of dialogue and plot.

Licensing Act of 1737 An English law that gave the Lord Chamberlain the authority to censor plays. The term "legitimate theatre" comes from the time of the Licensing Act.

lighting plot A detailed drawing that shows the location of each lighting instrument on the hanging grid, where its light will be focused, its type, wattage and the circuitry needed, and its color.

limelight In the mid-1800s, a gas-powered spotlight in which a jet of oxygen and hydrogen was ignited with small bits of lime. Now, the word means "the center of attention."

lip Also called an *apron*, the area of a proscenium arch stage that extends into the audience's side of the picture frame.

literary arts Arts created with written language.

literary manager The liaison between playwrights, agents, and the theatre who reads and evaluates new scripts. Also, this person often writes grant applications to help support new play development and stage readings of new plays.

low comedy A style that depends on gags, clowning, puns, and slapstick. Compare *high comedy*.

lyricist For a musical, the person who writes the lyrics.

lyrics For a musical, the sung words; the writer is called a lyricist. See also *book* and *music*.

M

magic *if* A technique pioneered by Konstantin Stanislavsky for developing empathy with a character. It involves searching for the answers to the question "What would I do *if* I were this character in these circumstances?" The magic *if* allows actors to find similarities between themselves and a character and to explore the intimate emotions and thoughts that result.

major dramatic question (MDQ) The hook (or question) that keeps an audience curious or in suspense for the duration of the play; an element in the beginning of a formula play that results from the *disturbance* and the *point of attack*.

medium The method, substance, and technique used to create a work of art.

melodrama Most popular in the late nineteenth century, a type of play that usually features working-class heroes who set out on a great adventure; story lines that praise marriage, God, and country; and florid background music. The word is a blend of "melody" and "drama."

method acting Also known as "the method," this system of realistic acting was distilled by followers of Konstantin Stanislavsky and has been taught primarily since the 1930s in America. See *Stanislavsky system*.

***mie* pose** In Kabuki theatre, a sudden, striking pose (with eyes crossed, chin sharply turned, and the big toe pointed toward the sky) at a particularly intense or profound moment; accompanied by several beats of wooden clappers, the *Ki*.

minstrel show Stage entertainment consisting of songs, dances, and comic scenes performed by white actors in blackface makeup; originated in the nineteenth century.

mission statement A theatre's purpose and key objectives, which can include quality, diversity, and accessibility, as well as the type of theatre to be produced.

Moscow Art Theatre A theatre company founded in the late nineteenth century by a group of Russian producers, actors, directors, and dramatists. Made famous by the plays of Anton Chekhov and the acting techniques of Konstantin Stanislavsky.

motivated light Stage lighting that comes from an identifiable source, such as a candle, a lamp, or the sun.

motivation The conscious or subconscious reason a character takes a particular action.

movement coach A specialist who instructs actors in various styles of movement.

multiculturalism The attempt to achieve a pluralistic society by overcoming all forms of discrimination, including racism, sexism, and homophobia.

music In a musical script, the orchestrated melodies, which are written by the *composer*. See also *book* and *lyrics*.

musical A type of theatre that features song and dance interspersed with spoken text. The genre includes not only modern musicals with popular songs and impressive spectacle (e.g., *Miss Saigon, Phantom of the Opera*) but also the masques, operas, burlesques, minstrel shows, variety shows, and music hall reviews of earlier periods. Compare *straight plays*.

musical comedy A type of musical characterized by a lighthearted, fast-moving comic story, whose dialogue is interspersed with popular music.

musical director A specialist who works with the musicians and teaches the actors the songs for a musical.

N

National Endowment for the Arts (NEA) The federal agency that disburses tax dollars as grants to fund cultural programs.

naturalism A style of theatrical design and acting whose goal is to imitate real life, including its seamy side. Also called "slice of life" theatre.

Noh (NOH) A form of traditional Japanese drama combining poetry, acting, singing, and dancing that was developed during the 1300s. Compare *Kabuki*.

nonmotivated light Stage lighting that reinforces the mood of a scene but doesn't necessarily come from an identifiable or onstage source.

O

off-book rehearsal The rehearsal when the actors must have their lines memorized because they no longer have the script ("book") with them on stage.

open-shop union A union in which membership is optional, such as the Dramatists Guild of America; compare *closed-shop union*.

opera A type of drama introduced at the end of the sixteenth century that is entirely sung.

operatic musical A musical that is mostly singing, with less spoken dialogue and usually a darker, more dramatic tone than an operetta has. Examples are *Les Misérables* and *Evita*.

operetta Like an opera, a drama set to music, but with a frivolous, comic theme, some spoken dialogue, a melodramatic story, and usually a little dancing. Also called "light opera." Popularized by Gilbert and Sullivan.

overture At the beginning of a musical; a medley of the songs played by the orchestra as a preview.

P

paper the house To give away free tickets to the families and friends of cast members in order to make it appear as though the play is popular.

parenthetical A short description such as *(loving)*, *(angry)*, or *(terrified)* to help the actor or the reader interpret a particular line of dialogue.

parodos The entrance of the chorus into the playing area in ancient Greek theatre.

parody The exaggerated imitations that are done for comic effect or political criticism.

patrons Individual contributors to the arts. Compare *corporate funding* and *government funding*.

Peking opera A synthesis of music, dance, acting, and acrobatics first performed in the 1700s in China by strolling players in markets, temples, courtyards, and the streets. Known in China as the "opera of the capital," or *ching-hsi*, it was founded by Qing dynasty Emperor Ch'ien-lung (1736–1795).

performance art An art form from the mid-twentieth century in which one or more performers use some combination of visual arts (including video), theatre, dance, music, and poetry, often to dramatize political ideas. The purpose is less to tell a story than to convey a state of being.

performance report Detailed notes to the actors and crew informing them of any problems that occurred and what needs to be fixed before the next performance.

performing arts Arts, such as theatre, music, opera, and dance, whose medium is an act performed by a person.

peripeteia (pehr-uh-puh-TEE-uh) In ancient Greek tragedies, a radical reversal of fortune experienced by the hero. See also *hamartia* and *anagnorisis*.

pictorial arts Arts, such as drawing and painting, created by applying line and color to two-dimensional surfaces.

picturization Composing pictures with the actors to reinforce an idea in the story; a technique used by directors.

playwright's note A note in a program in which the playwright conveys to the audience his or her artistic or personal thoughts about writing the play.

plot The causal and logical structure that connects events in a play.

plot-structure The playwright's selection of events to create a logical sequence and as a result to distill meaning from the chaos of life.

poetic realism A style of realism that is expressed through lyrical language.

point of attack The point in the beginning of a formula plot where the protagonist must make a major decision that will result in conflict.

political theatre Theatre in which playwrights, directors, and actors express their personal opinions about current issues.

pop culture Short for "popular culture," the fads and fashions that dominate mainstream media, music, and art for a period of time.

precolonial African theatre Indigenous African theatre that grew out of ritual and predates contact with Europeans. A combination of ritual, ceremony, and drama, it incorporates acting, music, storytelling, poetry, and dance; the costumed actors often wear masks. Audience participation is common.

presentational theatre Type of theatre that makes no attempt to offer a realistic illusion on stage. The actors openly acknowledge the audience, often playing to them and sometimes even inviting members to participate.

preview performance Performance of a play open to the public before the official opening night (and before the critics see it).

problem play A play that expresses a social problem so that it can be remedied.

producer or **producing director** In the United States, the person or institution responsible for the business aspects of a production. Producers can be individuals who finance the production with their own money or who control investors' money, or they can be institutions—universities, churches, community organizations, or theatre companies—that control the business side of the production.

production concept The thematic idea, symbol, or allegory that conveys the tone, mood, and theme of a play (e.g., a post-nuclear *Hamlet*).

production meeting One of a series of meetings between a director and designers to discuss how to realize the production concept as well as the play's philosophy, interpretation, theme, physical demands, history, and style.

profile An actor's position at a right angle to the audience; halfway between open and closed.

prologue In ancient Greek theatre, a short introductory speech or scene.

prompt book A copy of the play on which the production's sound and light cues, blocking notes, and other information needed for rehearsal and performance are recorded.

prop check The prop master ensures props are placed where they need to be and that they are in working order.

prop master A person who finds and buys props for productions, or designs and builds them; also in charge of *rehearsal props*.

props Short for *properties*; includes *set props* such as sofas and beds and *hand props*, or small objects actors handle on stage such pens, guns, cigars, money, umbrellas, and eyeglasses.

prop table A backstage table with each prop laid out and clearly labeled; where actors must place their props before leaving the area.

proscenium arch A formal arch that separates the audience from the actors, or a theatre with such an arch. Also called "picture frame" theatre.

protagonist (pro-TAG-uh-nist) In an ancient Greek play, the main actor. Now, the central character who pushes forward the action of a play. See also *antagonist, deuteragonist, tritagonist*.

public domain The legal realm of intellectual property that is not protected by a copyright or patent and belongs to the community at large.

publicity department People who promote a theatre and its upcoming productions.

R

realism A style of theatre that attempts to seem like life, with authentic-looking sets, "honest" acting, and dialogue that sounds like everyday speech. See also *poetic realism, selective realism, simplified* (or *suggested*) *realism*.

realism The cultural movement behind theatrical realism, it began around 1850 and popularized the idea that plays could be a force for social and political change.

rehearsal See *dress rehearsals, final dress rehearsal, general working rehearsals, off-book rehearsal, run-through, special rehearsal, table work*, and *tech rehearsals*.

rehearsal costume A temporary costume used during rehearsal so that the actors get a feel for the actual costume before it is ready.

rehearsal prop A temporary prop used during rehearsal to represent the real property that the actors will not be able to use until a few days before the play opens.

rehearsal report The stage manager's written report for the entire ensemble on how rehearsal went and about any concerns or ideas that affect the set, lights, props, or costume.

repertory A group of plays performed by a theatre company during the course of a season.

representational theatre A style of theatre in which the actors attempt to create the illusion of reality and go about their business as if there were no audience present.

reprise In a musical, the repetition of a song, sometimes with new lyrics, in a later scene. The new meaning or subtext makes a dramatic point.

reviews Published or broadcast opinions of critics about whether a particular play is worth seeing. Compare to *dramatic criticism*.

revue A program of satirical sketches, singing, and dancing about a particular theme; also called a "musical review." Compare to *variety show*.

rigger A person who mounts and operates curtains, sets, and anything else that must move via the fly system above the stage; also called "flyman."

rising action The increasing power, drama, and seriousness of each subsequent conflict, crisis, and complication in a play.

road house A theatre that has no resident company of actors of its own, but instead accepts productions from touring theatre companies.

rock musical A musical that uses rock and roll music, psychedelic rock, or contemporary pop and rock.

Romantic comedy A style of theatre that examines the funny side of falling in love—often with sympathetic young lovers kept apart by complicated circumstances, who in the end surmount any obstacles and live happily ever after.

Romantics Enlightenment-era poets, novelists, and playwrights who questioned the Scientific Revolution's obsession with logic; they felt that science was not adequate to describe the full range of human experience, and stressed instinct, intuition, and feeling in their writings.

royalty payment Payment to playwrights or their estates in exchange for staging a copyrighted play.

running crew Everyone who helps out backstage during a play.

run-through A rehearsal to go through an act or the entire play from beginning to end with as few interruptions as possible.

S

Sanskrit drama One of the earliest forms of theatre in India, performed in Sanskrit by professional touring companies on special occasions in temples, palaces, or temporary theatres.

Screen Actors Guild (SAG) The union that represents film and television actors.

scrim A curtain of open-mesh gauze that can be opaque or translucent depending on whether the light comes from in front or behind it.

selective realism A design style that mixes authentic-looking elements with stylized ones.

sentimental comedy A type of comedy that features middle-class characters finding happiness and true love.

set decoration A prop that is part of the set and is not touched by actors.

set designer The person who interprets a playwright's and director's words into visual imagery for a production; usually has a strong background in interior design, architecture, and art history, as well as theatrical conventions of various periods.

set prop Any prop that sits on the set, such as sofas, chairs, and beds. Compare *hand prop*.

shadow theatre A form of theatre created by lighting two-dimensional figures and casting their shadows on a screen. Probably originated in China around 100 BCE and later became popular in Islamic lands, where people were prohibited from playing characters.

sharing focus A position for two or more actors, each with a shoulder thrown back so that the audience can see them equally. See also *focus*.

showstopper In a musical, a big production number which receives so much applause that it stops the show.

sight lines Audience members' view of areas of the stage.

simplified, or **suggested, realism** A design style that suggests rather than exactly duplicates the look of a period.

sound board operator A person who runs the sound board during various sound cues throughout a production; also ensures that all the speakers, mixer, amplifiers, backstage monitor, and intercom are working prior to curtain.

sound designer A person who synthesizes and records the sounds for a production and designs systems to amplify an actor or singer's voice; has a detailed knowledge of acoustics, electronics, digital music editing programs, audio mixing boards and signal-processing equipment, microphones, effects processors, and amplifiers; and sometimes writes and plays transition music or underscore scenes with mood music.

souvenir program Programs sold at large professional performances that have more pictures and information about the production and cast than the basic program.

spatial arts Arts, such as sculpture and architecture, that are created by manipulating material in space.

special rehearsal A rehearsal for a special element, such as fight scenes, musical numbers, dance numbers, or dialects.

stage area One of the nine sections of the stage labeled according to the actors' point of view, such as downstage right, center stage, or upstage left.

stage directions Notes that indicate the physical movements of the characters.

stage door The back door that actors use to enter and leave the theatre.

stagehand A person who helps shift scenery and generally sets up the play for the next scene.

stage manager The most important assistant to a director; the person who is responsible for running the show during the performance and helping the director during auditions and the rehearsal process by taking notes, recording blocking, and scheduling rehearsals.

standing ovation When the audience stands to applaud a play—this is reserved for only the most extraordinary performances.

Stanislavsky system An individualized, psychological approach to acting pioneered by Konstantin Stanislavsky; also known as *method acting*.

stasimon In ancient Greek plays, a choral interlude between episodes.

stealing focus Taking focus out of turn; also known as *upstaging*. Compare *sharing focus*. See also *focus*.

stereotypes Generalized assumptions about people who are not like us.

stitcher The person who sews fabric patterns together creating the full costumes, and also builds or finds the *rehearsal costumes*.

straight makeup Makeup that does not change actors' looks but makes their faces look more three-dimensional and therefore more visible to the audience; compare to *character makeup*.

straight play In contrast to a *musical*, the category of plays without music.

subject What a work of art is about, what it reflects, and what it attempts to comprehend.

substitution Replacing a character's emotions with unrelated personal emotions; a technique used when the actor has not had the experience or emotional reaction of the character.

subtext The hidden meaning behind a line of dialogue; the real reason a character chooses to speak.

superobjective The driving force that governs a character's actions throughout the play.

surrealism A genre of theatre that emphasizes the subconscious realities of the character, usually through design, and often includes random sets with dreamlike qualities.

symbolism A design style or theatre genre in which a certain piece of scenery, a costume, or light represent the essence of the entire environment.

synthespian Digital actor created by computer animators.

T

table work The first step in the rehearsal process; the actors read through the play while seated around a table. Afterward, the director and actors discuss the characters, motivations, and meaning, and the designers may present their ideas to the cast.

talent Natural ability; it is innate but also can be developed.

talk-back A post-performance discussion where the audience gets a chance to meet and perhaps ask questions of the director, actors, and sometimes the playwright.

teaser The curtain that frames the top of the stage. Compare *legs*.

technical approach Acting from the outside in, concentrating on physical details. Compare to *method acting*.

technical director The person who coordinates, schedules, and engineers all the technical elements of a production.

technique Proven procedure by which a complex task can be accomplished, such as raising a child, fixing a heart valve, auditing books, or acting in a play.

tech rehearsals Rehearsals that include the lights, sound, costumes, more complex props, and final set pieces.

theatre A performing art that is always changing and whose every performance is unique.

theatre of identity Plays by and about a particular culture or ethnic group.

theatre of protest Plays that criticize the policies of the dominant culture and demand justice.

theatre of the people A type of theatre that provides a forum for everyday people to express themselves.

theme A play's central idea; a statement about life or a moral.

thrust stage A theatre with a lip that protrudes so far into the house that the audience must sit on one of the three sides of the stage.

tragedies of the common man Modern versions of tragedies that, just as in ancient Greek tragedies, leave the audience with a feeling of *catharsis* but, unlike the ancient Greeks, base heroes on common people.

tragic flaw An unchangeable trait in a character that brings about his own ruin (e.g., Oedipus's arrogance in ignoring the oracle). Also known as *character flaw* and *fatal flaw*. See also *hamartia*.

tragic hero In ancient Greek tragedies, an extraordinary but empathetic person of noble birth or a person who has risen to prominence and makes a choice (due to bad judgment or to a character flaw) that leads to trouble, but who ultimately takes responsibility for the choice.

triangulation A technique for drawing focus when three actors or groups of actors are on stage; the person or group at the upstage or downstage apex of the triangle takes the focus. See also *focus*.

U

upstaging Taking focus out of turn; also known as *stealing focus*.

V

values The principles, standards, and qualities considered worthwhile or desirable within a given society.

variety show A program of unrelated singing, dancing, and comedy numbers. Compare to *revue*.

vaudeville (VAHD-vill) A popular form of stage entertainment from the 1880s to the 1930s, descended from *burlesque*. Programs included slapstick comedy routines, song-and-dance numbers, magic acts, juggling, and acrobatic performances.

verbal scene painting A technique used by English and Spanish playwrights to set the mood or place of a scene. Because the words paint pictures, the audience "dresses" the stage in their imagination.

vocal coach A specialist who helps actors with speech clarity, volume, accent reduction or acquisition, and preservation of their voices for the long run of a show.

vomitories (often shortened to "voms") Tunnels, like those in sports stadiums, that run into and under the tiers of audience seats to allow actors quick access to the stage.

W

Will Call A booth or stand where audience members pick up the tickets they previously ordered by telephone or over the Internet.

willing suspension of disbelief The audience's acceptance of the quasi-reality of a work of art that enables the playwright, director, and actors to communicate perceptions about reality; the term was coined by English poet Samuel Taylor Coleridge. Closely tied to *aesthetic distance*.

wings Areas out of the audience's sight from which actors make their entrances and in which sets are stored.

writers for hire Writers, such as screen and television writers, who sell their words to production companies rather than retaining a copyright to them.

Writers Guild of America (WGA) The closed-shop union that represents screen and television writers.

Y

Yiddish Broadway The Jewish theatre district on Second Avenue in New York City in the late nineteenth and early twentieth century.

Index

B

D

E

F

G

H

I

J

K

L

M

P

Q

R

S

T

U

V

W

Z